The Bulgarians in the
Seventeenth Century

*In memory of
my father*

LOUIS P. HUPCHICK
(1914–1985)

The Bulgarians in the Seventeenth Century

Slavic Orthodox Society and Culture Under Ottoman Rule

DENNIS P. HUPCHICK

McFarland & Company, Inc., Publishers
Jefferson, North Carolina

The present work is a reprint of the library bound edition of The Bulgarians in the Seventeenth Century: Slavic Orthodox Society and Culture Under Ottoman Rule, *first published in 1993 by McFarland.*

LIBRARY OF CONGRESS CATALOGUING-IN-PUBLICATION DATA

Hupchick, Dennis P.
 The Bulgarians in the seventeenth century : Slavic Orthodox society and culture under Ottoman rule / Dennis P. Hupchick.
  p.   cm.
 Includes bibliographical references and index.

 ISBN 978-0-7864-9350-0
 softcover : acid free paper ∞

 1. Bulgaria — Civilization —17th century.
 2. Bŭlgarska pravoslavna tsŭrkva — History.
 3. Orthodox Eastern Church — Bulgaria — History.
 4. Bulgaria — Church history —17th century.
 I. Title. II. Title: Bulgarians in the 17th century.
 DR82.15.H86 2014
 949.77'015 — dc20   92-50889

BRITISH LIBRARY CATALOGUING DATA ARE AVAILABLE

© 1993 Dennis P. Hupchick. All rights reserved

No part of this book may be reproduced or transmitted in any form or by any means, electronic or mechanical, including photocopying or recording, or by any information storage and retrieval system, without permission in writing from the publisher.

On the cover: Inside Rila Monastery, Bulgaria (iStock/Thinkstock)

Manufactured in the United States of America

McFarland & Company, Inc., Publishers
 Box 611, Jefferson, North Carolina 28640
 www.mcfarlandpub.com

Contents

List of Maps and Tables	vii
Author's Preface	ix
Acknowledgments	xii
Note on Transliteration and Spelling	xiii
Abbreviations	xv
Maps	xix

Introduction   1

One. **The Bulgarians in Seventeenth Century Ottoman Society**

1. The Social Position of the Bulgarians   13
   Demographic Overview   13
   The Rural Situation: Common and Privileged Reaya   18
   The Urban Situation: Artisans and Merchants   37
   Social Institutions and Cultural Life   50

2. Threats to Bulgarian Orthodox Culture Posed by Ottoman Society   57
   Conversions to Islam and Muslim Reaction   57
   Greek Domination of the Orthodox Church Hierarchy   66
   Roman Catholic Missionary Efforts   73

Two. **Seventeenth Century Bulgarian Orthodox Culture: Nature and Forms**

3. Monasticism and the Cultural Role of Mount Athos   87

4. Slavic Education: The Foundation for Cultural Expression   99

5. The Forms of Orthodox Culture 109
   Writing and Literature 109
   Religious Art 127

Three. Seventeenth Century Bulgarian Orthodox Culture: Expression

6. Major Centers of Orthodox Cultural Activity 143
   Rila Monastery 143
   Sofia 152
   Etropole Monastery 165
   Vratsa 174
   Karlovo, Adzhar and Kuklen Monastery 178

Conclusions
   Overview of Extant Evidence 183
   General Summary 190

Appendix I: *Glossary* 201
Appendix II: *Statistical Tables* 207
Appendix III: *Chronology* 225

Notes 233

Bibliography 269

Index 299

List of Maps and Tables

Maps

1. The Ottoman Empire in Europe, 17th Century — xix
2. The Core Bulgarian Lands in the 17th Century — xx
3. Region of the Rhodope (Chepino) Islamic Conversions — xxi
4. Rila Monastery and Surrounding Regions — xxii
5. The Sofia Region — xxiii
6. The Etropole Region — xxiv
7. The Vratsa Region — xxv
8. The Areas of Karlovo, Adzhar and Kuklen Monastery — xxvi
9. Distribution of Known Bulgarian Cultural Sites, 17th Century — xxvii

Tables

1. Population of the Ottoman Balkans by Religion, Early 16th Century — 207
2. Estimated Bulgarian Population During the 17th Century — 207
3. Estimated Bulgarian Population Change, 17th Century — 208
4. Average Estimated Bulgarian Population, 17th Century — 208
5. Estimated Number of Bulgarian Settlements, 17th Century — 209
6. Average Size of Bulgarian Rural Settlements, 17th Century — 210
7. Average Size of Bulgarian Urban Settlements, 17th Century — 211
8. Registered *Has* Settlements in the Bulgarian Lands, 17th Century — 212
9. Registered *Vakıf* Settlements in the Bulgarian Lands, 17th Century — 213
10. Registered *Çiftlik* Settlements, Bulgarian Lands, 17th Century — 214
11. Distribution of Bulgarian Cultural Sites, 17th Century — 214
12. 17th Century Bulgarian Cultural Sites by Region — 215
13. Types of Bulgarian Cultural Sites by Region, 17th Century — 216
14. Bulgarian Educational Activity by Type of Site, 17th Century — 216
15. Literary Evidence for Bulgarian Cultural Sites by Region, 17th Cen. — 217
16. Literary Evidence by Type of Cultural Site, 17th Century — 217
17. Average Number of Citations per Type of Cultural Site, 17th Cen. — 218
18. 17th Century Bulgarian Literary Culture, Manuscript Types — 218
19. Bulgarian Subjects in Bulgarian Literary Culture, 17th Century — 219

20. Contents of 17th Century Bulgarian Manuscript Notations 220
21. Social Position of 17th Century Bulgarian Literary Intelligentsia 221
22. Major Centers of Bulgarian Literary Culture, 17th Century 221
23. Bulgarian Art Cultural Sites, 17th Century 222
24. Social Position of Bulgarian Artists, 17th Century 222
25. Social Position of Total Bulgarian Cultural Intelligentsia, 17th Cen. 223
26. Social Position of Bulgarian Cultural Patrons, 17th Century 223

Author's Preface

The idea for the study that follows originated in a conversation with the late James F. Clarke over sandwiches and drinks in a small, dingy Pittsburgh sandwich shop. At the time, Clarke was aware that he was nearing the end of his teaching career at the University of Pittsburgh, so his mood was one of reminiscing about aspects of Bulgarian history that he had never made any serious efforts to pursue. One of his musings concerned the process by which the Bulgarians had managed to preserve a sense of their own self-identity throughout 500 years of Muslim Turkish and Orthodox Greek cultural domination without being transformed into Turks or Greeks. How had this been accomplished? Surely, some form of national consciousness had existed among them prior to the somewhat feeble beginnings of the modern Bulgarian national revival in the mid eighteenth century. Perhaps the clue to this problem lay in the wall and ceiling murals that the illiterate Bulgarians of the Ottoman Empire saw as they worshiped in their churches, murals that portrayed images of Bulgarian saints identified by Slavic inscriptions. Clarke had remarked on other issues before this and continued on to different topics after, but this particular question remained imbedded in my mind long after the conversation had ended. I resolved seriously to pursue it further. The result of that pursuit is revealed in the following pages.

The issue of Bulgarian survival under Ottoman domination was, and could only be, couched in cultural terms because of the very nature of non-Muslim existence within the context of Islamic rule. The initial problem, therefore, was to define Bulgarian culture. Was it the folk culture of the masses or the religious culture of the Orthodox church, or both? I chose to limit the examination to Orthodox culture for a number of reasons. First, it was widely recognized that the Orthodox church played a seminal role in preserving ethnic traditions among its faithful both because it was never a monolithic entity, like the Roman Catholic church, but rather was composed of various separate ethnic church organizations, such as the Greek, Russian, Bulgarian and Serbian churches, and because it enjoyed a position under the Ottoman Empire that imparted a certain amount of autonomy to its membership. Second, in the writings of the early literary figures of the Bulgarian national revival, such as Paisii Hilendarski (b. *ca*. 1722) and Sofronii Vrachanski (1739-1814), Orthodox religious culture was the bridge used to link fellow Bulgarians to their medieval ancestors. Finally, it was obvious that Orthodox culture was a vital element in approaching the problem and to include further folk culture could not only diffuse the effort but might very well broaden it to a point where it would become unmanageable.

Having defined the focus of the study, the next problem was determining those cultural elements within the corpus of Orthodox cultural expression during the period of Ottoman domination that were particularly Bulgarian. The most reliable and identifiable determinant proved to be the use of a Slavic literary language. Since that language was used by a number of Balkan Orthodox peoples, I chose to examine Slavic sources known to have originated in regions predominantly populated by Bulgarians. This approach was fraught with controversy because of conflicting modern nationalist claims on certain regions of the Balkans (Macedonia, for instance) between Bulgarians, on one hand, and Serbs and Greeks, on the other. It was decided, therefore, to restrict the focus of cultural evidence utilized by the study to the geographical region roughly defined by the borders of present-day Bulgaria, with a few exceptions. The term, "Bulgarian lands," appears frequently throughout the text and its use bears the above connotation. The term might be thought of as representing the "core" Bulgarian lands, where historically Bulgarian ethnicity can be considered unquestionable. In the study, Slavs are referred to as inhabiting the Macedonian lands, the Serbian lands, and so forth, without placing a Bulgarian ethnic connotation on them. Within the context of the issues examined by the study, the ethnicity of the populations in such disputed regions proved of little importance. I realize that many of my Bulgarian and American colleagues may disagree with this approach. To them I can only extend my assurances that the fundamental results of the research expressed in the following study would not be significantly changed by the inclusion of evidence drawn from a wider geographical region.

The choice of the seventeenth century as the period for examination was not made arbitrarily. Scholars working in the field of Bulgarian studies have almost traditionally viewed the seventeenth century as the period representing the nadir of Bulgarian national history. By the beginning of the century the lands inhabited by the Bulgarians had experienced 200 years of Turkish occupation and Muslim rule, which had decimated the native Bulgarian national leadership, the *bolyar* aristocracy, until the final vestiges of that class were either assimilated into the Muslim ruling establishment of the Ottoman Empire, forced into exile, or exterminated during the catastrophic Tŭrnovo Uprising of 1598. A new native class capable of replacing the defunct aristocracy in its leadership role, namely a wealthy Bulgarian middle class, did not attain a commensurate level of influence until the middle of the eighteenth century, when it spawned the Bulgarian national revival and precipitated the first moves toward national independence.

By the dawn of the seventeenth century, not only had the aristocratic patrons of Bulgarian Orthodox cultural life been eliminated but the very fountainhead of that culture, the native Bulgarian Orthodox church, had been decapitated by the

PREFACE

Turkish authorities and placed into the hands of Greek prelates. Thus after two centuries of Ottoman rule the oldest, most productive Slavic Orthodox cultural tradition of the European Middle Ages, which had created the Cyrillic literary language and had produced some of the most renowned works of medieval Christian Slavic literature and art, became the domain of scattered monastic communities and small local parish churches. Precisely because the seventeenth century was considered by numerous Bulgarian scholars as the "Dark Times" (*Mrachnite vremena*) of Bulgarian history, it was the obvious choice for an examination of the process by which the Bulgarians managed to survive as an ethnic entity within a society that threatened to eliminate their self-identity completely over the course of five centuries.

As this study was originally conceived, it was hoped that a close scrutiny of the available sources might reveal the existence of a nascent form of Bulgarian national consciousness among the seventeenth century Bulgarians. After extensive research and numerous conversations with noted Bulgarian specialists, it became obvious that such a hope was futile. What did emerge, however, was a much clearer picture than heretofore realized of the process by which medieval Bulgarian religious culture managed to survive the centuries-long pressures exerted by foreign temporal and spiritual domination. In doing so, it laid the initial basis for the later Bulgarian national revival.

Before closing, a few words about the mechanics of the following study are in order. The overview of Ottoman society contained in the first part of the work is intended to provide the social framework necessary for understanding the cultural examination that follows. It has not been my intention to examine Ottoman society in all of its varied and interesting detail; this has been accomplished in English by Peter F. Sugar in his definitive 1977 work, *Southeastern Europe under Ottoman Rule, 1354-1804.* Since the study will find its primary audience among specialists in Bulgarian, Balkan and Ottoman studies, and among serious students in these fields, the use of certain foreign terms in the text, for which a glossary is provided, has been retained in cases where either they represent the most succinct expression of the idea or they convey a sense of intrinsically Bulgarian expression (*e.g.*, names of persons). Readers should not find any difficulty in this matter. In any case, it is hoped that the following study will serve to stimulate further endeavors to expand our fund of knowledge regarding the historical role played by religious culture in the Ottoman Empire in shaping the development of the Balkan peoples.

Wilkes-Barre, 1992   Dennis P. Hupchick

Acknowledgments

Research grants from the Fulbright Scholars Program, the International Research and Exchanges Board, and the University of Pittsburgh-Sofia University Exchange Program supported a total of over two years spent in Bulgarian libraries and archives. Additional institutional support was provided by the University of Pittsburgh's Center for Russian and East European Studies and Wilkes University.

A number of individuals offered assistance, encouragement and advice (not always followed) over the time that the study was in preparation. The late James F. Clarke provided the initial inspiration and guidance for the early research and part of the first draft. Later drafts were read by S. Béla Várdy, William Chase, John Haskins, Seymour Drescher, and Orysia Karapinka. Robert Donnorummo and Ronald Linden kindly made available the considerable resources of the University of Pittsburgh's Center for Russian and East European Studies when needed. Philip Shashko provided valuable methodological advice, and Marin Pundeff made available his father's study of Bulgarian Paulicians. Others in this country who contributed, knowingly or unknowingly, to the success of the study include, Frederick Chary, Esther Clarke, Suzanne Cooke, Rose Krasnopolar, John Menzies, Peter Sugar, and Roger Whitaker. Notice must be given to Andrew Blasko and Elsa Limbach for their generous and understanding support.

In Bulgaria, colleagues at the Historical Institute of the Academy of Sciences, especially Elena Grozdanova, Georgi Neshev, Snezhka Panova, and Veselin Traikov, and at Sofia University, particularly Petŭr Dinekov, Nikolai Genchev, Tsvetana Georgieva, Andrei Pantev, and Dimitŭr Tsanev, lent useful assistance. So too did three now deceased scholars — Ivan Duichev, Hristo Gandev and Bistra Tsvetkova. Stefanka Nesheva and Minka Petkanova, the librarians at the Historical Institute, were exceptionally helpful. Boris Marinov proofread the Cyrillic notes and bibliography in the final draft. Warm thanks must also be extended to Yaroslav Ivanchenko, Aglika Likova, Tsvetana Micheva, Lyubomir Nikolov, Svetlana Nikolova, Nikolai Popov, and Vladimir Vladov.

Valuable electronic typesetting assistance was provided by Harold Cox at Wilkes University, and the maps were drawn by Howard Ziegler in Pittsburgh.

Special thanks are due Anne-Marie Hupchick, who tolerated all the emotional and physical vagaries of her often preoccupied husband while the study was in progress. Her affection and support proved decisive in bringing the study to a successful conclusion.

DPH

Note on Transliteration and Spelling

The system of transliteration used for Bulgarian terms and names in the text of this work attempts to convey a phonetical rather than a bibliographical context. The system used is as follows:

Cyrillic	Latin	Pronunciation
А а	a	about
Б б	b	book
В в	v	very
Г г	g	good
Д д	d	dart
Е е	e	bet
Ж ж	zh	measure
З з	z	zone
И и	i	machine
Й й	i	yet
К к	k	kept
Л л	l	long
М м	m	man
Н н	n	new
О о	o	open
П п	p	pen
Р р	r	raid
С с	s	send
Т т	t	take
У у	u	food
Ф ф	f	film
Х х	h	Bach
Ц ц	ts	beats
Ч ч	ch	church
Ш ш	sh	sheet
Щ щ	sht	washed
Ъ ъ	ŭ	but
ь ь	yo	yoke
Ю ю	yu	you
Я я	ya	yacht
Ы ы (Russian)	y	yet

Bulgarian and Serbian names in transliteration have been distinguished in the text by the use of š, č, ć, and j for the Serbian, which correspond to the Bulgarian sh,

Transliteration and Spelling xiii

ch and **y**. Turkish terms found in the text follow the modern, Latin form of the Turkish alphabet. A glossary of all foreign terms appearing in the text is contained in Appendix I. Unusual spellings have been avoided as much as possible. An attempt has been made to use traditional Bulgarian names for some towns and villages in cases where the more modern names appear ahistorical within the context of the work, otherwise, contemporary forms are used throughout.

Abbreviations
Used in the Notes and the Bibliography

АрПП	Архив за поселищни проучвания [Archive for Settlement Studies]
Bb	*Byzantinobulgarica*
Бъл стар из Мак	Български старини из Македония [Bulgarian Antiquities in Macedonia]
EB	*Etudes balkaniques*
EH	*Etudes historiques*
ГМ-По	Годишник на музейте в Пловдивски окръг [Annual of the Museums in the Plovdiv Region]
ГНАМ	Годишник на Народната археологическа музей [Annual of the National Archeological Museum]
ГНБП	Годишник на Народната библиотека в Пловдив [Annual of the National Library in Plovdiv]
ГСУбф	Годишник на Софийския университет, богослвски факултет [Annual of Sofia University, Theological Faculty]
ГСУфиф	Годишник на Софийския университет, философско-исторически факултет [Annual of Sofia University, Philosophical-Historical Faculty]
ГСУифф	Годишник на Софийския университет, историческо-философски факултет [Annual of Sofia University, Historical-Philosophical Faculty]
ГСУюф	Годишник на Софийския университет, юридически факултет [Annual of Sofia University, Juridical Faculty]
ИАИ	Известия на Археологическия институт [Journal of the Archeological Institute]
ИБАД	Известия на Българското археологически дружество [Journal of the Bulgarian Archeological Society]
ИБАИ	Известия на Българския археологически институт [Journal of the Bulgarian Archeological Institute]

ABBREVIATIONS

ИДА	*Известия на Държавни архиви* [Journal of the National Archives]
ИЕИМ	*Известия на Етнографския институт и музей* [Journal of the Ethnographical Institute and Museum]
ИИБЛ	*Известия на Институт за българска литература* [Journal of the Institute for Bulgarian Literature]
ИИБЕ	*Известия на Институт за български език* [Journal of the Institute for Bulgarian Language]
ИИДв	*Известия на Историческо дружество* [Journal of the Historical Society]
ИИИ	*Известия на Институт за история* [Journal of the Institute for History]
ИИИИ	*Известия на Институт за изобразително изкуство* [Journal of the Institute for Representational Art]
ИНБКМ	*Известия на Надодната библиотека «Кирил и Методий»* [Journal of the National Library "Cyril and Methodius"]
ИССФУС	*Известия на Семинара по славянска филология при Университет в София* [Journal of the Seminar on Slavic Philology under the University of Sofia]
ИВНД	*Известия на Военноисторическо научно дружество* [Journal of the Military Historical Scientific Society]
ИПр	*Исторически преглед* [Historical Review]
Из истор на старо и въз лит	*Из история на старобългарската и възрожденската литература* [On the History of Old Bulgarian and Revivalist Literature]
Опис I, II	*Опис на ръкописите и старопечатните книги на Народната библиотека в София* [Inventory of the Manuscripts and Old Printed Books in the National Library in Sofia], I, II
Опис III, IV	*Опис на славянските ръкописи в Софийската народна библиотека* [Inventory of the Slavic Manuscripts in the Sofia National Library], III, IV
Опис БАН	*Опис на славянските ръкописи в библиотеката на Българската академия на науките* [Inventory of the Slavic Manuscripts in the Library of the Bulgarian Academy of Sciences]
Опис Пловдив	*Славянски ръкописи и старопечатни книги на Народната библиотека в Пловдив* [Inventory of

	the Manuscripts and Old Printed Books in the National Library in Plovdiv]
Опис Рил ман	Опис на ръкописите на библиотеката на Рилския манастир [Inventory of the Manuscripts in the Library of Rila Monastery]
Опис Св Синод	Опис на ръкописите в библиотеката при Св. Синод на Българската църква в София [Inventory of the Manuscripts in the Library under the Holy Synod of the Bulgarian Church in Sofia]
«Описание»	«Описание на България от 1640 г. на архиепископа Петър Богдан (По случай 300-годишнината)» [Description of Bulgaria from 1640 by Archbishop Pertŭr Bogdan (In Honor of His 300th Anniversary)]
Описание рукописного	Описание рукописного отделения Библиотеки Императорской Академий Наук, I, Рукописи, I [Inventory of the Manuscript Sections of the Libraries of the Imperial Academy of Science, I, Manuscripts, I]
ПСп	Периодическо списание на Българското книжовно дружество [Periodical Bulletin of the Bulgarian Literary Society]
СбНУ	Сборник за Народни умотворения, наука и книжнина [Collection for Folklore, Science and Letters]
СпБАН	Списание на Българската академия на науките [Bulletin of the Bulgarian Academy of Sciences]
«Стари записки,» I, II, etc.	«Стари записки и надписи» [Old Notes and Inscriptions] I, II, etc.
Stojanović I, II, etc.	«Стари записки и натписи» [Old Notes and Inscriptions] I, II, etc.
RESEE	*Revue des études Sud-est européenes*
«Врачанска епархия»	«Църковни старини из Врачанска епархия» [Church Antiquities in the Vratsa Bishopric]

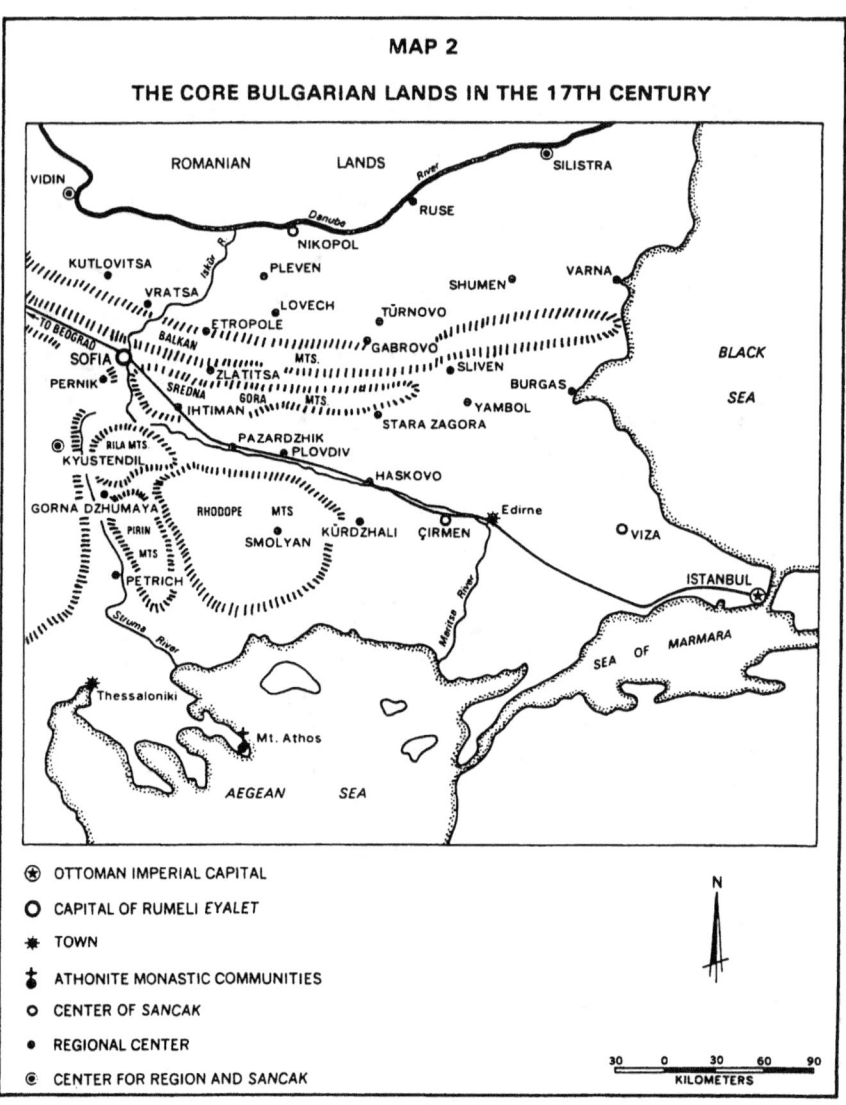

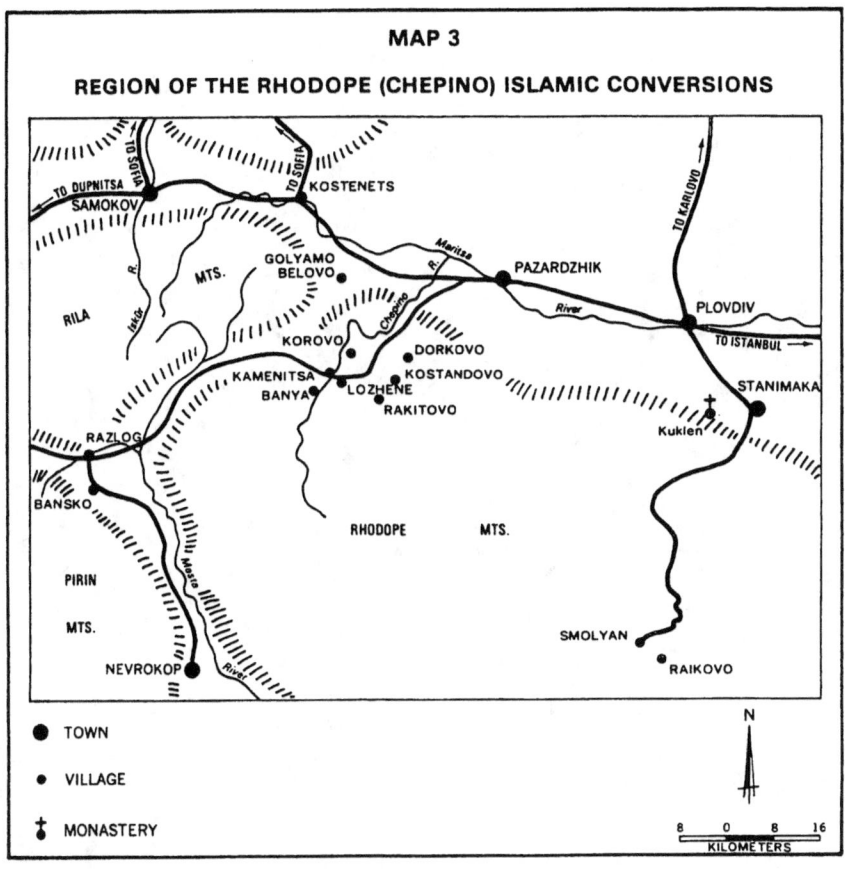

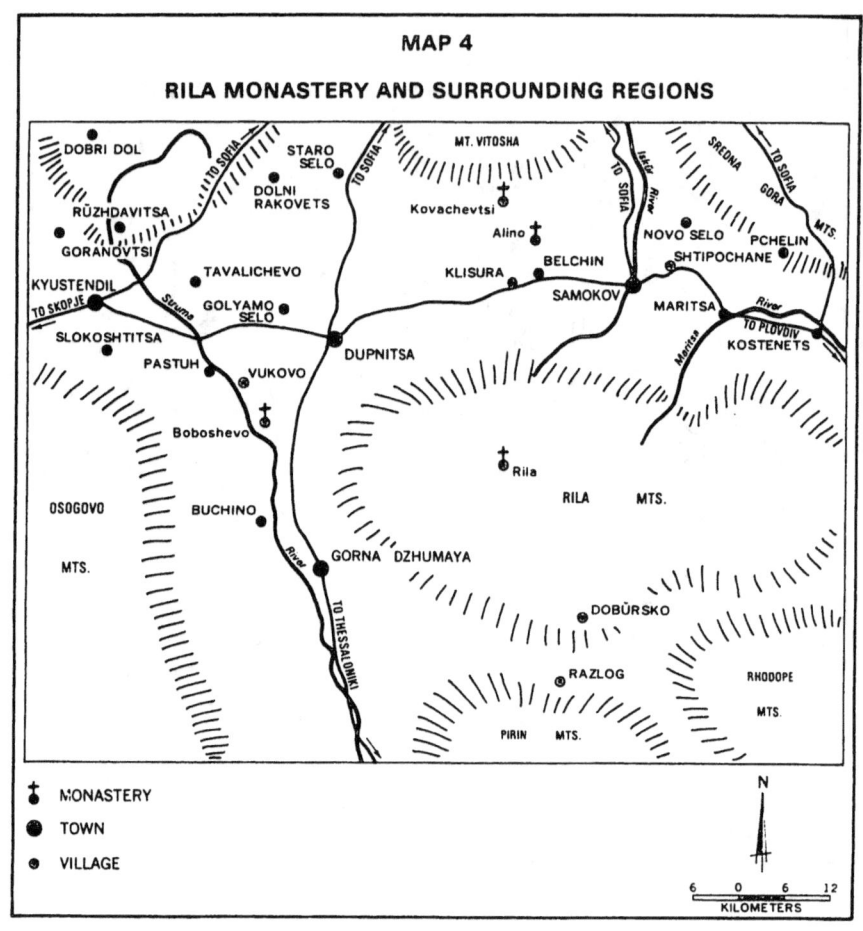

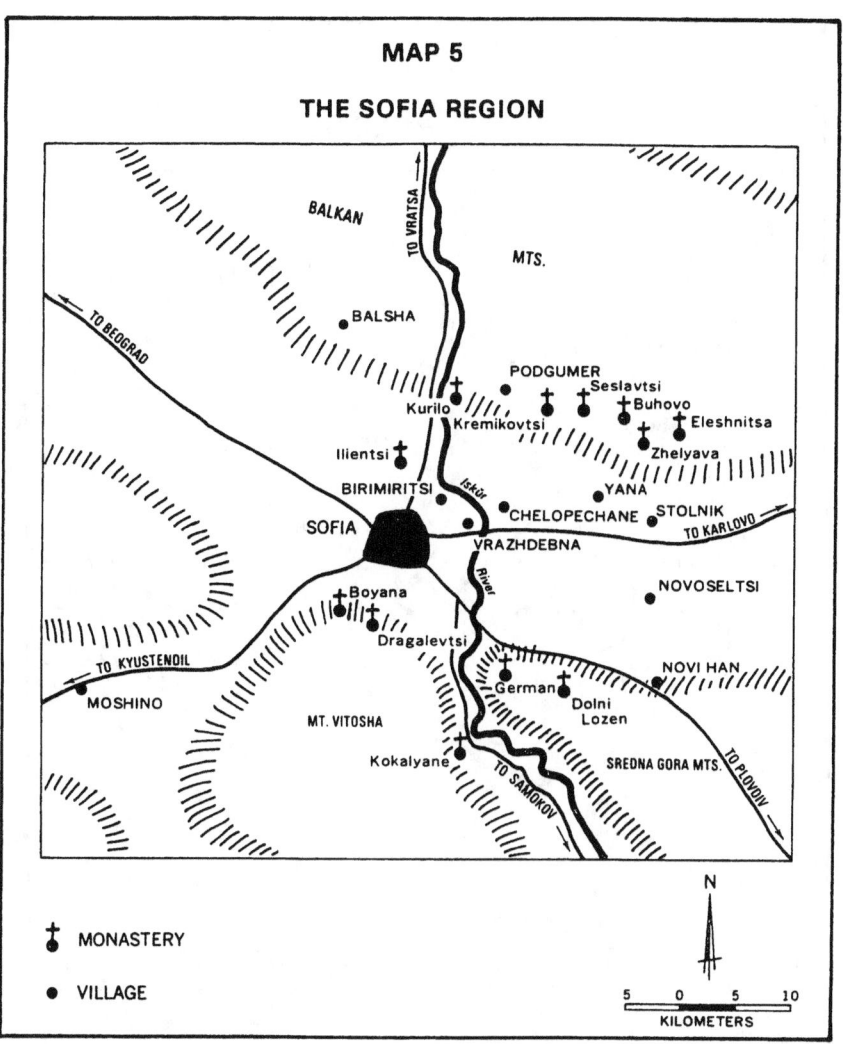

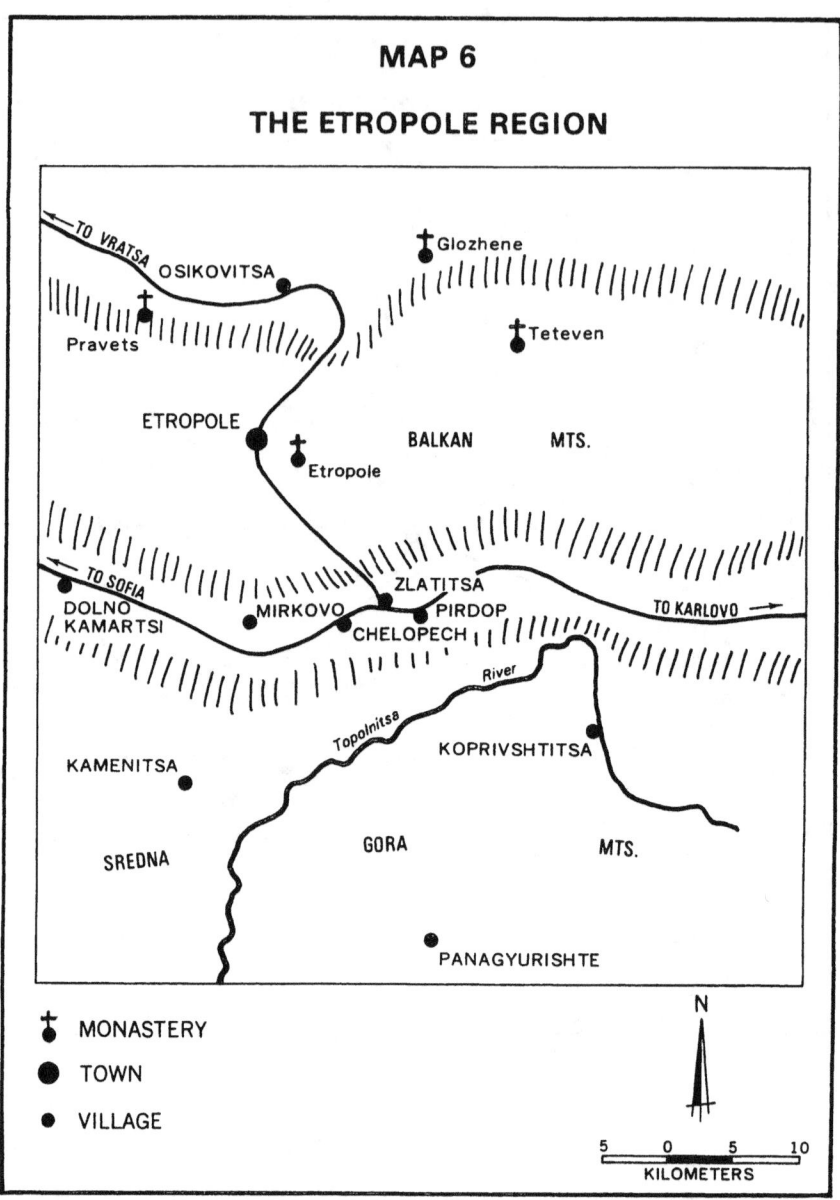

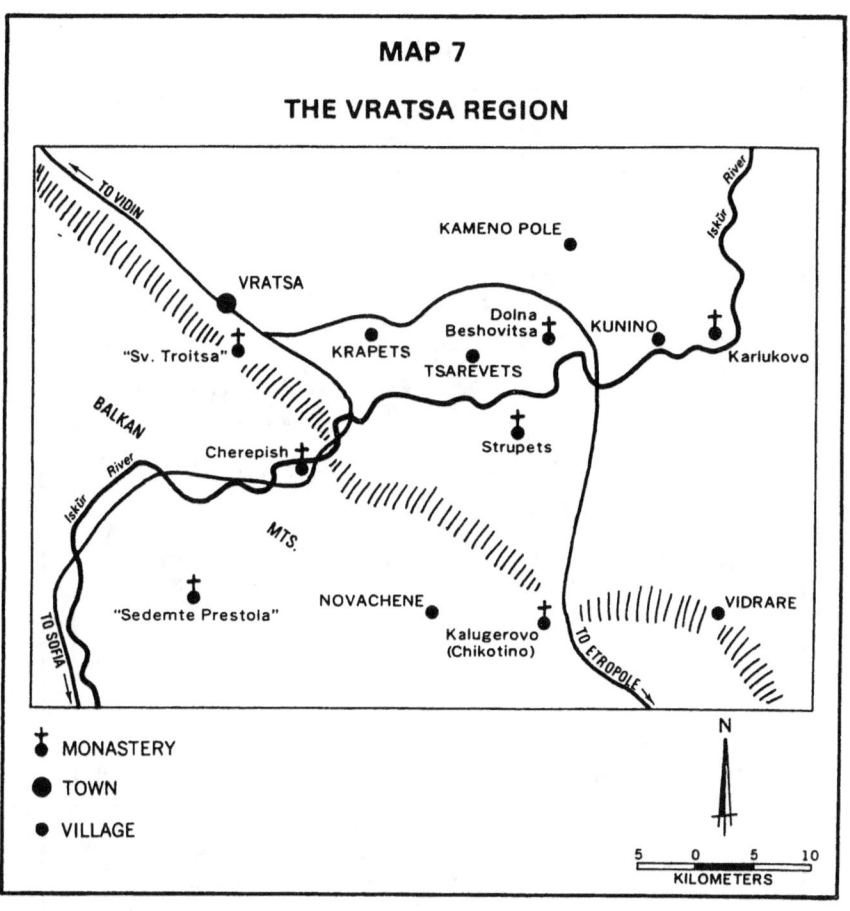

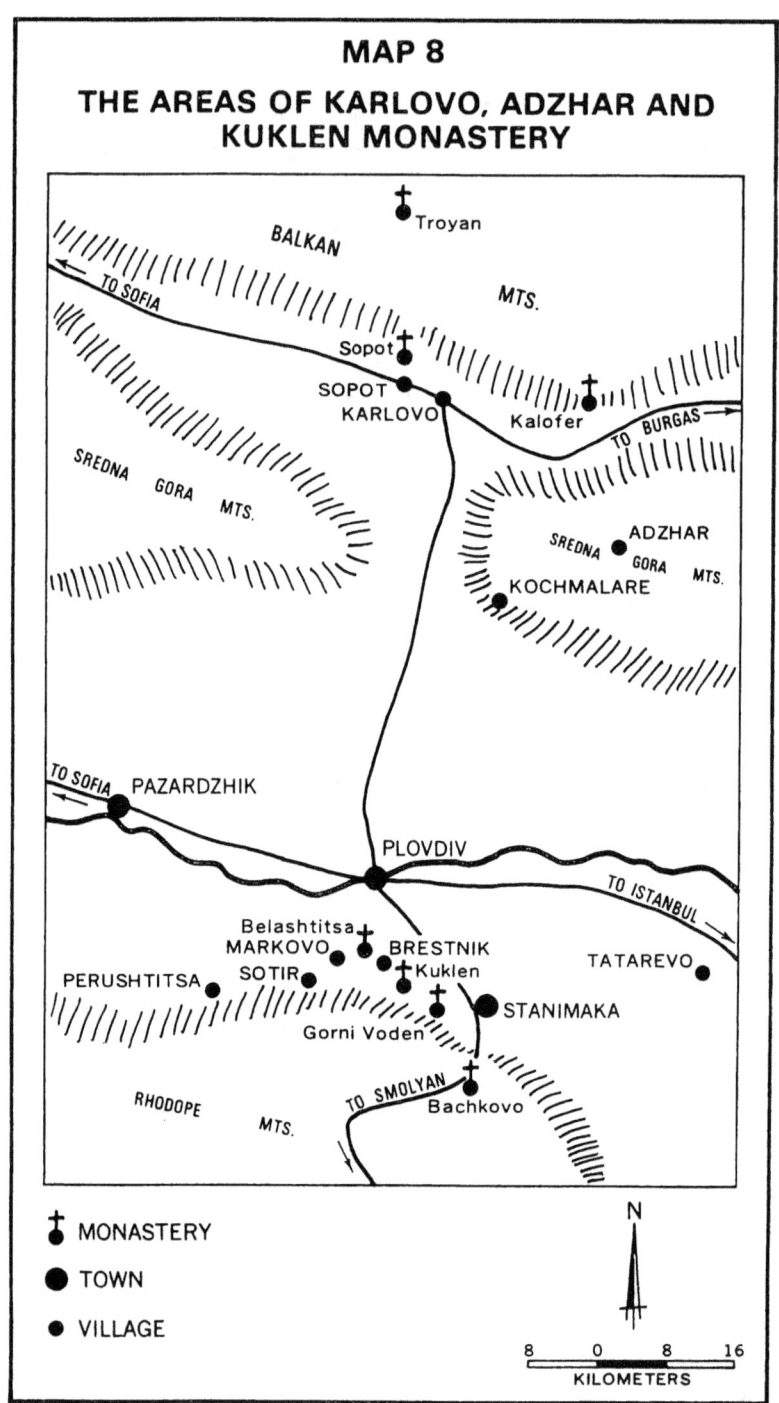

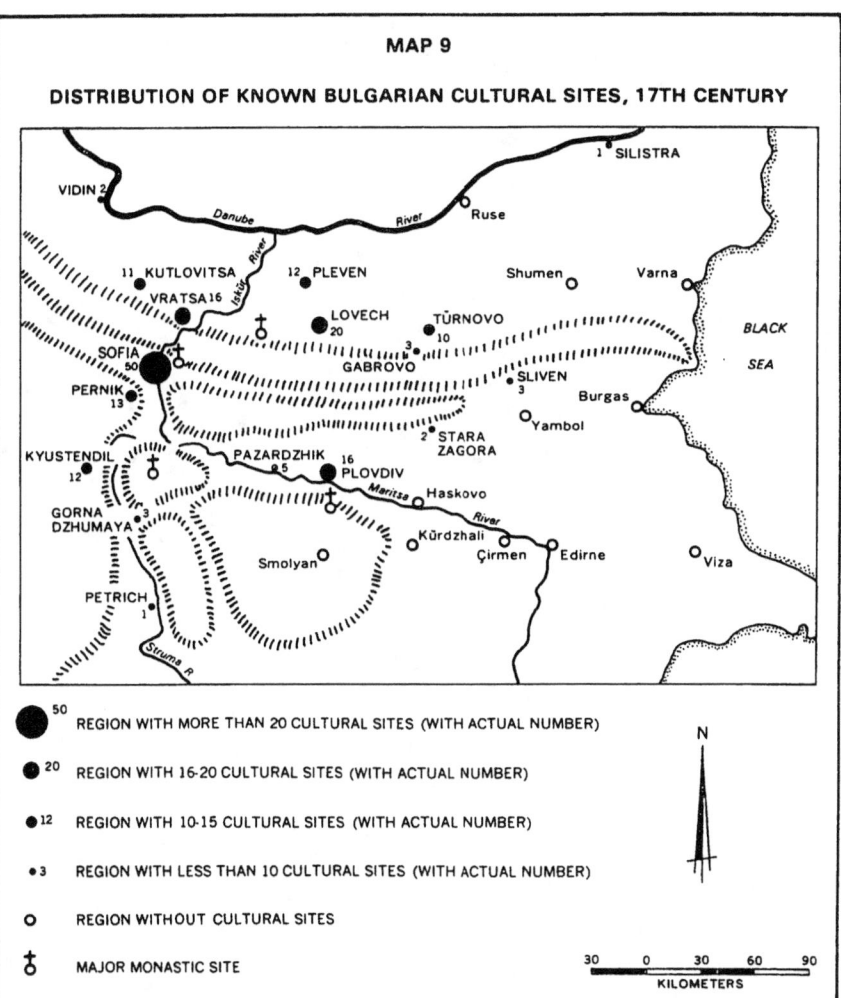

Introduction

Mention of the seventeenth century in European history almost immediately conjures up in the Western mind an image of such crucial developments as the scientific revolution and the rise of powerful, absolutist, imperial nation-states, or the cultural achievements of the Baroque Age and the Dutch School of painting. The image is populated with illustrious thinkers, such as René Descartes (1596-1650), John Locke (1632-1704) and Isaac Newton (1642-1727), and with forceful national political leaders like Louis XIV of France (1643-1715), Oliver Cromwell in England (1599-1658) and Gustavus Adolphus II of Sweden (1611-1632). Set against the backdrop shaped by these movements and men are important works of European culture by such literary giants as William Shakespeare (1564-1616), Jean-Baptiste Molière (1622-1673) and Miguel de Cervantes (1547-1616), along side which rank those by such outstanding artists as Gianlorenzo Bernini (1598-1680), Rembrandt van Rijn (1606-1669), Diego Velásquez (1599-1660) and Christopher Wren (1632-1723), in the fields of the visual arts, and Claudio Monteverdi (1583-1643) and Henry Purcell (1659-1695) in music. These events and individuals form a veritable litany of Western European political and cultural achievement that has had an impact on European society lasting to the present.

There was, however, another part of Europe where the typical image of the seventeenth century did not apply in the slightest, where science remained Aristotelian and superstitious, where Western-type nation-states were not even a glimmer in the imagination of most of the population, and where the literary, visual and musical arts were strictly constrained by religious precepts. Essentially, this part of Europe retained a medieval cultural character that the West had left behind because it did not experience the dynamic forces of change ignited by the Renaissance and the Reformation. It had been given no opportunity to do so, for it was that part of Europe that had been torn from the rest by a dynamic, expanding Ottoman Empire. It was, quite simply, most of the Balkan Peninsula.[1]

Although they were incorporated into a large Muslim state that spanned the two continents of Europe and Asia, and despite the Islamic civilization that was espoused by the Turkish ruling elite and imposed upon them as subjects of the empire, the Christian peoples of the Ottoman Balkans remained European at their most fundamental level. That is to say, they had been Christians inhabiting

Christian states prior to the arrival of the Ottoman forces on the European scene, and they remained Christians after they had fallen to Ottoman military conquest.

Medieval Europe was defined by the level and extent of Christian civilization exhibited by the states that, in one form or another, were the successors of the Christianized Roman Empire on the continent of Europe. Differences certainly existed between the eastern and western halves of Christian Europe based on cultural factors. The West embraced a Latin while the East adhered to a Greek form of Christianity, and though the cultural differences that separated the two were deep and stubborn in their persistence, they shared a common Greco-Roman heritage that had a fundamentally similar Christian faith as the moral basis for its political and social tenets.

Until the Ottoman conquest of the Balkan Christian states of the European East, both halves of Europe experienced a common form of socio-political development, though its actual manifestations were tempered by differing cultural and geographical situations. Both halves of medieval Christian Europe experienced an influx of new, "barbarian" ethnic elements into their native, Greco-Roman populations that was to play a profound role in determining the character of the states formed in each region. In the West, these were mostly Germanic peoples; in the East they were primarily Slavic and Turkic. A system of feudal relationships, again in varying form, arose in both West and East with similar effect on the nature of lord-peasant relationships and of state unity and the central authority of the ruler, although in the East the process of decentralization, though present, was less advanced than in the West because of the debt owed to a living Roman imperial state model, the Byzantine Empire. Both halves of Europe exhibited a fundamental partnership between the Christian church and secular government that served to advance and preserve the interests of the socially elite classes who dominated political and cultural affairs in both institutions.

Such, in brief, was the situation of the Europeans when the Ottoman conquest of the Balkan Peninsula severed the ties of the Eastern Christians who inhabited that region from the common trunk of European evolution. While the West continued on through the Renaissance and the Reformation to attain the level of development that historians tend to call early modern, any further development that the Christians of the Balkans were to experience was achieved within the context of a foreign, Islamic civilization. Yet they persisted in remaining European by resisting, to a great extent, total assimilation into a very un-European Muslim civilization by their continued adherence to the eastern, Orthodox form of Christianity.

Survival within a European context was no easy task for the Balkan Christians conquered by the Ottoman Turks, who imposed on them a society founded upon strictly Muslim precepts. The Ottoman Empire was by nature a militant theocratic Muslim state governed by Islamic sacred law (the *Şeriat*). Under that law, the Christian subjects of the empire were afforded protection, that is, continued existence as Christians, on condition that they acknowledged the domination of Islam and of its temporal representative, the Ottoman sultan. This was effected under the terms of a legal arrangement offered by the *Şeriat* known as *zimma* (protection), which extended tolerance by the Muslim authorities toward indigenous non-Muslim populations incorporated into the state through conquest at the price of their relegation to inferior social status within the state. The *zimmis* (the "protected ones"), as the non-Muslim subjects were classified by this arrangement, were compelled to pay discriminatory taxes, such as the poll-tax (*cizye*), to which Muslim subjects were not liable, and to suffer a number of social and legal restrictions. Such restrictions ranged from regulating the size, height and conspicuousness of non-Muslim religious edifices, so that they would not impinge upon the overt dominance and glory of Muslim civil and religious buildings, to regulating the style, color and type of textiles permissible in clothing, to ensure that the inferior social status of the *zimmis* would be immediately recognizable both to themselves and to any outside observer. *Zimmi* ownership of horses and weapons was, with certain exceptions, forbidden. In Ottoman legal proceedings, *zimmi* defendants and testimony were at a decided disadvantage in cases where they were opposed by Muslims.

The Ottoman sultan secured sovereign control over his vast, heterogeneous empire by a unique form of governmental administration that placed all offices below that of supreme ruler in the hands of his personal slave household, thereby guaranteeing the absolute loyalty and obedience of state officials. For similar reasons, the core of the sultan's military power, the Janissary standing infantry and the elite guard cavalry units, were also recruited from among his personal slaves. Since the *Şeriat* forbade the enslavement of Muslims, the slaves of the sultan were, perforce, non-Muslims in origin.

To fill the ranks of the imperial slave household, the Turks devised an institution known as the *devşirme,* which was a periodically conducted child-levy imposed on the subject Christian population of the Balkans beginning in the fifteenth century. The intervals at which *devşirmes* were conducted varied from between one and seven years. When a child-levy was desired the Ottoman central authorities issued orders to the provincial officials in the Balkans for the collection of eligible young male Christian children from among the *zimmis*. Janissary troops were then despatched to muster youths between the ages of seven and 14 in the towns and villages. Those youths demonstrating physical or intellectual promise were marched off under guard to either Istanbul, the imperial capital, or to Anatolia, where they were converted into fanatically devout Muslims and then trained either to fill posts at all levels in the governmental administration or to enter the ranks of the Janissary infantry units, depending on their individual abilities. Thus the Christian *zimmis* of the Balkans were singled out by the Ottoman authorities as the preferred source for government and military personnel at the cost of relinquishing their very flesh and blood to an alien civilization.

The society imposed on the conquered Balkan Christians by the victorious Muslim Turks was that of a state-wide military compound because the Ottoman Empire was essentially one vast military machine predicated on the confidence that God would grant the Turkish champions of Islam continuous success in expanding the domains of the true-believers at the expense of the non-Muslim "infidels" of the world. Then, as now, the state and the Islamic faith were regarded as one by devout Muslims. The Ottoman capital at Istanbul served as headquarters for the supreme military commander, the sultan, as treasury, and as primary supply depot for the Turkish forces. The provinces of the empire were structured as encampments reflecting the military organization of the Turks.

The highest Ottoman provincial official was, until the mid seventeenth century, the *beylerbey,* who commanded the forces of an *eyalet,* which might be considered analogous to an army corps. For a time following the Turkish conquest of the Balkans all the newly acquired lands of the empire in Europe were designated the *eyalet* of Rumeli, a name derived from the Turkish term for the Byzantine Empire, which had considered itself a Roman state until the Turks put it to death in 1453 and on which point the conquerors agreed. By the seventeenth century the empire had expanded further north into Europe, so such Balkan regions as Bosnia, Herzegovina and small parts of Croatia lay outside Rumeli under newly created *eyalets*. The provincial capital of the Rumeli *beylerbey* was established at Sofia, a town located in the lands of the vanquished Bulgarians, because of its strategic position at the very geographical center of the Balkan Peninsula astride the important Istanbul-Belgrad highway, which represented the primary land route linking West Asia with the European heartlands since classical times and which served the Turks as their most vital military and commercial line of communications in the European half of their empire.

The large region under the authority of the Rumeli *beylerbey* was divided into 26 *sancaks,* a term meaning banner, or standard, in Turkish, which might be thought of as representing military regiments in Western parlance. Each *sancak* was governed by a *sancakbey*. Every *sancak* was further divided into *kazas,* representing the smallest Ottoman administrative unit, that were administered by *beys*. All Ottoman provincial officials, from the *beylerbey* to the local *bey,* possessed both military and administrative authority that, in practice, were virtually indistinguishable from one another. Until the decline of the empire that set in by the seventeenth century, all of these officials-commanders were creatures of the *devşirme.*

The ranks of the free Turkish mobile cavalry (*sipahis*) that comprised the bulk of Ottoman military strength commanded by the provincial authorities were comprised of men supported by a pseudo-feudal form of landholding collectively termed the *sipahilık*. Technically all lands conquered by the advancing Ottoman armies were considered the legal property (*has*) of the sultan. To maintain the numerous cavalry troops under his supreme command with little recourse to the central treasury, which in actuality constituted his personal treasury, the sultan distributed vast tracks of his *has* to the provincial authorities and *sipahis*. The land considered liable for such distribution was classified as *miri* land, as opposed to *mülk*, which was privately owned land, either possessed by the sultan or given by him to others, outside that which could be distributed, and which formed a relatively small part of the lands of the empire.

Unlike the medieval European form of feudal landholding, the Ottoman *sipahilık* system of military fiefs did not grant the *sipahi* recipient the outright ownership of his parcel of land. Instead, he was conferred with the right to collect the taxes due from the peasants living on a particular area of land placed into his trust. The *berat* (warrant) of investiture given the *sipahi* by the central authorities specified the area included in the grant, the amount of taxes due, and the share of those revenues that he might retain to support his military lifestyle. The value of the grant was strictly a factor of financial assessment and not based on the size of the parcel of land involved. Specific value was determined in individual cases by the military grade of the recipient. The common cavalryman received the lowest valued fief, termed a *timar*, which yielded between 2,000 and 19,999 pieces of silver (*akçes*). *Beys* and other high ranking officials-commanders received *zeamets*, valued at between 20,000 and 99,999 *akçes*. Land assessed at 100,000 *akçes* and over was classified as *has* and formed part of the personal properties of the sultan, his family, and his favorites. Some *has* lands were permanently attached to the highest ranking provincial administrative offices.

In return for receiving a *sipahilık* fief, the *sipahi* was required to serve the central government on active duty in military campaigns and to provide his own weapons, armor, horses, and military retinue. Failure to meet these obligations resulted in the *sipahi's* divestment of the fief by the central authorities. The fief technically always remained the property of the sultan.

Zimmi status and the imposition of the *sipahilık* system reduced the European Christian subjects of the Ottoman Empire to a social level somewhat akin to that of sheep in common rural conditions. Although they were left their personal freedom, they were protected and husbanded by their Muslim overlords only so they could be shorn of revenues on a regular basis to maintain the well-being of a society in which they played no other role. In fact, the term used by the Ottoman authorities when referring to them was *reaya*, which meant a flock of sheep with this very connotation.

Until the close of the sixteenth century the Ottoman system of social organization worked smoothly. The *sipahis* were content to wage war and collect taxes from their mostly Christian *reaya*, who, meanwhile, were left relatively unhindered in their local administrative and cultural affairs. So long as they paid their taxes and did nothing to offend or disturb their Muslim overlords, they were left much to their own devices. This situation changed with the end of uninterrupted Ottoman military victories and expansion brought about by the advances made in military technology by the empire's European Christian enemies and the change in international commercial relationships resulting from the European Age of Discovery.

Inability to conquer new territories in Europe meant that the Ottoman central authorities became unable to create new *sipahilık* fiefs, and thus the number of *sipahis* lacking the financial wherewithal to support their military activities customarily drawn from revenues exacted from the land began to outstrip the amount of land available for distribution with calamitous results, both for the effectiveness of the military and for the lowly Christian *reaya*. Frustrated in their hopes of gaining lucrative incomes from the possession of fiefs, growing numbers of Ottoman soldiers, mostly from the ranks of the retainers provided by already enfiefed *sipahis*, turned to banditry to satisfy their war-like lifestyles and financial needs. Simultaneously, the stability of the entire state organization, which depended on the authority exerted by a strong supreme ruler, grew increasingly threatened by a weakening in the office of sultan that commenced with the reign of Selim II the Sot (1566-1574) and continued, with few exceptions, in a progressive decline thereafter. The Janissaries, formerly the elite military formation in all Europe because of their stringent discipline, forced isolation from the affairs and pleasures of civilian society, and utter dependence on the beneficence of the sultan, had gradually evolved into a large prætorian guard able to make or unmake sultans and to break loose from the iron grip of authority that had underlay their military prowess. Many units of Janissaries had been stationed in urban centers throughout the provinces, where they eventually took up crafts, married, and raised families, growing more concerned about their economic affairs than their military duties. As central authority weakened, landless bandit Ottoman soldiers, joined by the now sedentary Janissary troops, caused anarchy in the regions of the Balkans lying outside the capital, plundering and perpetrating any number of depredations on the helpless and hapless subject populations of the empire.

With the European opening of direct sea trade routes to the spice and other luxury commerce of the Far East, the lucrative role of middleman in East-West trade formerly enjoyed by the Turks began to diminish. Western colonial efforts in the newly discovered Americas resulted in the rapid influx of American gold and silver into the European economies, which spread into the Ottoman Levant with crushingly inflationary results. Ottoman silver currency suffered a rapid and continuing devaluation that, by the seventeenth century, was making the fixed incomes of the *sipahis* and Janissaries increasingly worthless and governmental expenses, given the changed military situation that precluded the acquisition of expanded revenues through war plunder, just as increasingly exorbitant. The entire financial situation was exacerbated by a rash of counterfeit coinage that undercut an already increasingly devaluated currency as the vehicle for exchange within the empire.

Declining military fortunes and growing inflation led to the undermining of the traditional *sipahilık* system and, thus, to the entire structure of the state. Those *sipahis* who already controlled fiefs began to take advantage of the declining system and rising anarchy to throw off their military obligations as far as possible and to transform their holdings into private, inheritable, income-producing properties. Important officials and favorites of the sultan bent every effort to expand their *mülk* possessions at the expense of the central authority for similar reasons and goals. The burden of paying the returns to the ever more corrupt ruling elite was, of course, placed almost exclusively on the shoulders of the *zimmi* Christian *reaya*, whose material and financial situation worsened in direct relation to the rising pressures inherent under such conditions.

Perhaps no other Christian European people was so completely submerged into Ottoman lower class society than were the Bulgarians by virtue of their location at the very geographical heart of the Ottoman Empire in Europe, in close proximity to the Turkish capital and through which all overland military, administrative, and commercial communications linking that city with its European possessions passed. The Turks gave such a priority to ensuring completely the security of the Bulgarian lands of their empire that they settled large numbers of semi-nomadic Anatolian Turkish colonists in the Bulgarians' midst, in an effort to numerically strengthen the Muslim demographic base in these strategically important regions of their empire. The *yürüks,* as these tribes of transplanted Muslim colonists were collectively termed, were settled in the southern and eastern regions of the Bulgarian lands, regions that had suffered great demographic and material devastation caused by the constant military operations surrounding the Catalan and civil wars of Byzantium and the internecine conflicts among the various Bulgarian and Serbian feudal states during the fourteenth century. The Turkish colonists were officially charged with performing irregular services in conjunction with regular Ottoman military forces during campaigns in Europe.

While other *zimmi* Christian populations, such as the Greeks and the Serbs, managed to maintain tenuous, if often sporadic, contact with the European world outside the Balkans, the Bulgarians remained virtually isolated from Europe following their conquest by the Turks in the late fourteenth century. They possessed no influential merchant class in the Ottoman capital that could win trading concessions from the conquerors and permit them to participate in commercial relations with outside European powers as did the Greeks. Nor did they lie close to the frontiers separating the Ottoman Empire from its European enemies as did the Serbs, who could maintain contact with the West across the Danube River and by way of Dalmatia or the Croatian military border. The fate of the Bulgarian subjects of the Ottoman Empire was to be sealed tightly within the confines of an alien civilization.

A commonly accepted truism in the field of Southeast European studies is that the Orthodox church played a leading role in preserving the national identities of the Balkan Christians subjugated by the Ottoman Empire that permitted them to rejoin the general European community, albeit in a somewhat retarded condition, following their throwing off of Turkish rule in the nineteenth and twentieth centuries. As in all truisms, there exists both some truth and some fiction in such a statement.

Following the Ottoman conquest of Constantinople in 1453, Sultan Mehmed II the Conqueror (1444-1446, 1451-1481), the victorious Turkish ruler, faced the fundamental problem of devising a legal means of governing a vast, Muslim-led empire that contained a religiously heterogeneous non-Muslim subject population. The *Şeriat* was applicable only to Muslims and possessed no validity among the *zimmi* populations. The *Şeriat*, however, did recognize so-called "peoples of the book," *zimmis* who were monotheistic in belief and who possessed a corpus of religious writings, particularly the Christians, whose faith included the Bible, and the Jews, who possessed the Torah. Both of the religious writings of these faiths had been incorporated in some fashion into the Muslim sacred book, the Koran. Using this fact as his justification, Mehmed's solution to the problem was to divide his subject population into *millets* (nations) based on religious affiliation.

All of the empire's *zimmis* who possessed a sacred "book" were divided among three *millets,* representing the Orthodox Christians, the Armenian Christians (which eventually included any Roman Catholic subjects), and the Jews. Each was made responsible for representing its membership before the Ottoman Porte and for its own internal administration. The non-Muslim *millets* were granted the rights to tax, judge, and order the lives of their respective membership insofar as those rights did not conflict with the *Şeriat* and the sensibilities of the Muslim ruling establishment. The administrative responsibilities of the *millets* were placed into the hands of their highest religious authorities, either prelate or council, which were ultimately held accountable by the Turkish authorities for the proper functioning of the *millets*. In effect, each *millet*, personified by its ecclesiastical administrators, became an integral part of the empire's administrative system and functioned as a veritable department of the Ottoman government. For the majority of the Balkan Christian subjects in the Ottoman Empire, the Patriarch of Constantinople served as the ultimate legitimate representative before the Turkish authorities, and was recognized by the Muslim ruling establishment as responsible for administering the internal affairs of all the subject Orthodox community, in which function he was granted considerable autonomy. Because the Orthodox *millet* essentially operated as an autonomous branch of the Ottoman imperial administrative system, the empire's Orthodox subjects were free to enjoy a measure of self-government and to pursue religious cultural activity.

It is at this point that the truism concerning the advantages of the Orthodox *millet* for all Balkan Christians begins to break down because not all Orthodox Christians shared equally in the benefits bestowed by the *millet*.

When in 1454 Mehmed invested as Patriarch of Constantinople the Greek Bishop Gennadios Scholarios (1454-1457, 1464) and proclaimed him head of the Orthodox *millet* by virtue of an imperial *ferman* (edict), he did so under the mistaken assumption that the office of Constantinopolitan patriarch actually represented the specific interests of all Orthodox subjects in his empire. Unfortunately, what Mehmed and his successors failed to consider when relying on the *millet* system to provide an efficient means for governing their Christian subjects was that not all of the Orthodox *zimmis* were Greeks. Orthodox Bulgarians and Serbs had both possessed their own native church organizations that had been decapitated by the Ottoman conquerors and handed over to the administration of the Greek Patriarchate of Constantinople prior to 1453. With the establishment of the Orthodox *millet* they were forced to stand by while Greek appointees of the Patriarchate filled all posts in the high ecclesiastical hierarchy that now served as their highest official representative to the Muslim masters. Greek interests and culture came to pervade the Orthodox *millet* to the increased exclusion of those of their Slavic charges. A sense of Greek superiority arose within the church hierarchy, while a growing resentment of this situation among the Slavic faithful led to their acquiring a rising sense of ethnic self-awareness and a reactionary animosity toward Greek superiority within the Orthodox *millet*.

For the Orthodox Bulgarians the organization of the *millet* meant that not only were they relegated to the lowest rungs of the Ottoman social ladder but they were also reduced to veritable nonentities in the only powerful institution that could formally represent them before the Muslim authorities. If the Bulgarians were to survive as a distinct group of European Christians under the pressures of Muslim temporal and Greek spiritual domination, then they had to take advantage of any and all opportunities offered by the Ottoman social system to fortify their native Slavic Orthodox cultural traditions. Their ultimate success in surviving was far more attributable to their own efforts at the grass-roots level than to those of the Greek-controlled Orthodox *millet*.

The truism regarding the Orthodox church and *millet* fails to address the reality that only the national interests of the Greeks were ultimately served by any concrete benefits that the church and *millet* bestowed. Little effort has been made by scholars to dig beyond the generalization to uncover the role that the Orthodox faith actually played in preserving ethnic self-identity among those Balkan Orthodox Christians subject to the Ottoman Empire who were not Greek, and to link that role with the social processes that ultimately permitted these non-Greek Christian *zimmis* to survive centuries of foreign domination and eventually to rejoin the community of European peoples.

The study that follows is an initial attempt to rectify this situation.

One.

The Bulgarians in Seventeenth Century Ottoman Society

1. The Social Position of the Bulgarians

Every culture is intricately defined by the society in which it functions. Seventeenth century Bulgarian society can only be understood within the context of the Ottoman social system, which was imposed fairly uniformly throughout the empire. Because of the close proximity of the Bulgarian lands to the capital of the empire at Istanbul and the fact that all important overland lines of communications linking the capital and the Asian lands of the empire to the military and commercial frontiers in Europe ran through them, the unique Ottoman socio-economic system was perhaps nowhere more thoroughly enforced than in those regions of the state inhabited by the Bulgarians. (See Map 1.)

Demographic Overview

The rising Ottoman state of the fourteenth and fifteenth centuries was a predominantly European power. Except for its Anatolian homelands, the territories encompassed by the empire lay in Southeastern Europe. European Christian subject peoples (*i.e.*, Bulgarians, Serbs, Greeks, Albanians, and some Croats and Vlahs) constituted the majority in the total Ottoman population. As late as the second decade of the sixteenth century, at a time when the Turks had begun making significant territorial gains in the Islamic Middle East and North Africa, the European portion of the empire still comprised over two-fifths of the total population (e.g., five out of a total of 12 million people). Christian subjects in the European possessions of the Turks, who numbered more than four million, accounted for over four-fifths of the empire's Balkan population and more than a third of all Ottoman subjects.

The nearly two million Christians who inhabited the core Bulgarian lands possessed the single largest share in the European Ottoman demographic picture of 1520. They were scattered over a territory that encompassed eight of the empire's 29 Rumeli *sancaks* (*i.e.*, those of Paşa, Sofia, Kyustendil, Vidin, Nikopol, Silistra, Viza and Çirmen), in each of which Christian Bulgarians comprised the significant element of the population, and in which they accounted for nearly three-quarters of the aggregate total population. (See Table 1.)

By the close of the sixteenth century the demographic picture of the Ottoman Empire had changed significantly. The far-flung military conquests of Süleyman

I the Magnificent (1520-1566) in Central Europe, North Africa and Iran (Persia) nearly doubled the size of the population to almost 22 million people. The majority of the newly incorporated subjects was Muslim, and the share of the total population enjoyed by the Balkan Christians dwindled by almost 50 percent to less than a fifth. Within the changed demographic picture, the Christian Bulgarians inhabiting the core Bulgarian lands represented a mere eight percent of the Ottoman population and were still declining in numbers as the seventeenth century opened.

A major demographic study by the noted Bulgarian scholar, Elena Grozdanova, based on Ottoman tax registers for the Bulgarian lands dating to the seventeenth century, has helped provide a clearer picture of Bulgarian demography during the period than before possible.[1] Until the appearance of this work most all demographic references to the seventeenth century Bulgarians were matters of conjecture, grounded in the highly subjective and, as the new study demonstrated, usually inaccurate literary descriptions written by Turkish and European travelers in the Bulgarian lands.

According to the newly published Ottoman tax registers, in the second decade of the seventeenth century taxable Christian households (*hane*) in the Bulgarian *sancaks* numbered nearly 126,000, or close to 630,000 persons. It is estimated that the number of Bulgarian Christians who had been granted some sort of tax privileges in return for specified services to the state, and therefore not included on the tax rolls for common *cizye*, may have numbered as many as an additional 59.5 percent of the actually registered population. If such were indeed the case, then the Christian population of the Bulgarian lands at the time could have comprised as many as a million persons (nearly 201,000 *hane*). By the 1680s Christian Bulgarians, both common and privileged, had declined in number by almost 25 percent, to approximately 760,000 persons (close to 152,000 *hane*). (See Tables 2 and 3.)

The possible reasons for the decline of the Christian population in the Bulgarian lands were many. One of the significant factors certainly was a high death rate among the general population caused by epidemics, famine and its attendant starvation, and natural disasters, such as floods and earthquakes. References to such calamities often appeared in seventeenth century manuscript marginalia. Evidence exists for seven periods of plague epidemics during the century in locations scattered throughout the Bulgarian lands, but most especially in urban centers. Since the Bulgarians were primarily a rural population, however, plague probably played a less than significant role in the general decline of the Bulgarian population, acting more as a retardant to growth than as an outright exterminator.[2]

The generally low levels of sanitary and medical conditions common throughout the Bulgarian lands during the period certainly were detrimental to the healthy existence of the general population. The average death rate ran high, and was unusually high among children aged 14 and less, especially between the ages of four and seven. Naturally, such conditions had a negative effect on the average life-span of the typical Bulgarian. Males could expect to live to the average age of 47 years; women tended to live five to eight years less, with a particularly high rate of death occurring among them during the prime child-bearing years between the ages of 20 and 40. As in the case of plague epidemics, however, the death rate tended to bring about stagnation in population growth and not absolute decline.[3]

A more significant role in Bulgarian population decline during the seventeenth century was probably played by the emigration of segments within the population, either from one region of the Bulgarian lands to another (and, therefore, disappearing from the tax rolls in their region of origin and not thereafter appearing in the tax rolls in their region of destination for an indefinite subsequent period of time) or to regions outside the Bulgarian lands, even to outside the empire itself. The causes for such population movements were varied. There were, of course, the aforementioned natural disasters and epidemics, though their cumulative effects were, on the whole, restricted to relatively brief, specific periods of time and population segments, and their overall effects tended to cause limited and short-ranged internal migrations rather than mass exoduses.

More important factors in causing population decline in the Ottoman Bulgarian lands during the seventeenth century were migrations and deaths resulting from the effects of warfare, both directly, as a result of military operations, and indirectly, in consequence of such operations. During the opening decade of the century and throughout most of the two last decades, the Ottoman Empire was engaged in desperate conflict with the Habsburg Empire and its allies along the Danubian frontier. At various times, especially during the Long War in the early years of the century (1593-1606), the fighting actually reached portions of the Bulgarian lands, primarily in the western and northwestern regions. As was common in times of intense military conflict, the population in places directly affected by the fighting suffered. People were killed. Villages, and in some instances towns, were destroyed. Crops were ruined. Rape and pillage were commonplace. Such conditions of instability caused population movements in the locales most directly afflicted. While some inhabitants fled to less threatened regions of the Bulgarian lands to escape the dangers of war, others took the opportunity to shake off Ottoman domination completely by fleeing the empire in the train of retreating Habsburg forces, who during the campaigns of the seventeenth century were consistently unable to make permanent their military advances south of the Danube.

Some Bulgarians played active participatory roles in the military operations of the seventeenth century. The most common form of their direct activity was to take advantage of the unsettled conditions that prevailed in the war-threatened regions of the Bulgarian lands by forming bands of *haiduts* (bandits) and preying upon the Turkish lines of communications in the rear of the forces facing the Habsburgs. While *haidut* activity was endemic in the Bulgarian lands throughout the entire period of Ottoman domination, their numbers tended to increase during periods of active military operations, and the Danubian warfare during the early and late seventeenth century was no exception. The raiding operations of these bandits were of marginal military value but they certainly helped contribute to the suffering of the local population in the western and northwestern Bulgarian regions affected by the campaigns. Many *haiduts* were killed in the course of their activities and many joined the Habsburg retreats from the Bulgarian lands.

Authentic anti-Ottoman military activity on the part of local Bulgarians during the seventeenth century was demonstrated in two bloody uprisings in the decade of the 1680s. Both the Tŭrnovo (1686) and the Chiprovtsi (1688) uprisings were planned to coincide with expected Russian and Habsburg military operations south of the Danube, which they depended upon for their ultimate success. Each failed when the expected succor failed to materialize. Both entailed a great loss of life among the rebel ranks after the Ottoman authorities mobilized the forces necessary to crush them. Each resulted in the mass migration of local Bulgarians to regions outside the borders of the Ottoman Empire.

Reprisals and repression followed in the wake of the actual military operations and the uprisings. For the Bulgarians of the empire these probably accounted for the bulk of the negative demographic effects resulting from warfare during the seventeenth century. In those regions where *haidut* and rebel activity had been most intense, the entire Christian Bulgarian population was held accountable. The regions of Tŭrnovo, Gabrovo, Lovech, Sofia, Vidin and Kutlovitsa were ravaged in varying degree by reprisals for anti-Ottoman activity. Many Bulgarians were put to death and habitations and other buildings destroyed. The increased repression caused numerous Bulgarians to migrate out of the empire at their earliest opportunity.

Added to the adverse demographic effects of direct warfare and reprisals were similar subsidiary effects caused by Ottoman efforts to mobilize and muster the reinforcements necessary to meet the military challenge posed by Habsburg forces on the Danube. In 1689 the Crimean Tatars under *han* Selim Giray were summoned by the Ottoman Porte to reinforce the Turkish forces facing the Habsburgs in the central Balkans. Their trek across the Bulgarian lands left a swath of death and devastation in its wake, which was particularly intense in the regions of Lovech, Pleven and Kyustendil. Naturally, death and migration took a further toll on the number of Bulgarians residing within the borders of the Turkish empire as a consequence.

Of equal or more significance to the effects of warfare on the demographic decline of the Christian Bulgarian population of the Ottoman Empire during the seventeenth century was the process of islamization among the non-Muslim subjects inhabiting the Bulgarian lands. This topic will be examined in greater detail later in our study. At this point, suffice it to say that the process was continuous over the course of the century. Thus the anti-Christian reprisals for rebel and *haidut* activities and the advent of the Tatar reinforcements both were accompanied by conversions of Orthodox Bulgarians to Islam, with a stake in preserving the empire as it stood. As will be discussed later in this study, numerous Christian Bulgarians in the Rhodope and Danubian regions of the Bulgarian lands were assimilated into the Muslim ranks during the seventeenth century, most of whom forsook their native language, culture, mores and traditions for those of the Turks and thus ceased to exist as Bulgarians, both statistically and culturally.

Bearing in mind the above conditions, the average number of Christian Bulgarians inhabiting the Bulgarian lands during the seventeenth century probably approached 890,000 (over 176,000 *hane*). (See Table 4.)

While the Ottoman authorities officially divided their possessions into administrative units (*eyalets, sancaks* and *kazas*) and taxation districts (*vilayets*), the Bulgarians themselves conceived of the Bulgarian lands as being composed of geographic regions, each centered on and named for an urban or village center that served as the primary focus of local economic and cultural activity. Some regional centers (*e.g.*, Sofia, Kyustendil, Vidin, Nikopol and Silistra) served as Ottoman *sancak* centers, others (*e.g.*, Vratsa, Lovech, Tŭrnovo and Plovdiv) were ecclesiastical seats, and still others primarily were of local significance. In all, the Bulgarian lands examined by our study were comprised of some 28 regions, 25 of which have been well documented in extant seventeenth century Ottoman tax registers. (See Map 2.)

The Bulgarian population of the 25 documented regions for the century inhabited over 3,300 settlements, nearly all of which were rural. (See Table 5.) Not surprisingly, the heaviest regional concentrations of Bulgarian villages were in the mountainous western Bulgarian lands around Sofia (the most densely settled region), Pernik, Kyustendil, Gorna Dzhumaya, Vidin and Kutlovitsa. The rugged, broken terrain in those regions rendered a measure of isolation and, thus, protection from encroachments by Turkish authorities or colonists, who demonstrated a marked proclivity for either urban centers or for more flat, open countryside in their habitation patterns. On the other hand, the geography of the western lands mitigated against populous village settlements since habitable space was limited by the restricted availability of cultivatable land. Although the average size of a seventeenth century Bulgarian village was approximately 164 persons (*i.e.*, 32.8 *hane*), those located in the western lands consistently fell below the average. The largest villages tended to be located in the eastern Bulgarian lands, which geographically were far more open and less mountainous, and which, though blessed with abundant land for cultivation and thus able to support larger numbers of inhabitants, were also more attractive to Turkish colonists and easier to control for the Ottoman authorities, since the regions offered few naturally concealed sanctuaries. (See Table 6.) The largest known 17th century Bulgarian village was that of Kotel (545 *hane,* or 2,725 inhabitants, in 1648), situated in the Kotel Pass through the Balkan Mountains in the Burgas region. Yakoruda (493 *hane,* 2,465 persons) in the Sofia region and Elena (265 *hane,* 1,325 persons) in the Tŭrnovo region were also among the most populous village settlements in the Bulgarian lands during the century.[4]

The 35 urban centers situated in the Bulgarian lands of the seventeenth century accounted for only one percent of all settlements, and the Bulgarian element in their populations represented only two and a half percent of the average Christian Bulgarian population. (See Table 7.) Even if the Muslim and non-Bulgarian Christian urban-dwellers were to be added to their figures, the total urban population of the Bulgarian lands would equal approximately four percent of the total population of those regions. When one considers that a century earlier urban-dwellers in England comprised 20 percent of the total English population, the disparity between western European and Balkan societies receives graphic confirmation. If Russian society during the seventeenth century is considered, then the disparity disappears. During that period in Russia, only three percent of the total population was urban.[5]

Generally, the towns with the largest numbers of Bulgarian inhabitants were located, once again, in the eastern regions of the Bulgarian lands, although the two largest, Silistra and Nikopol, were more accurately Danubian commercial centers than eastern towns. The latter were primarily ports on the Black Sea. In nearly all cases, however, Bulgarians represented a minority element in urban populations, which included significant numbers of Turkish, Greek, Armenian and Jewish inhabitants and, often, small enclaves from Dubrovnik and other commercial colonists.

The Rural Situation: Common and Privileged Reaya

Ottoman society primarily depended on the revenues extracted from land to support the military-administrative establishment that served as the guarantor of the empire's continued strength and viability. This meant that the onus of providing livelihoods for the Turkish administrators and warriors controlling the *sancaks* encompassing the Bulgarian lands rested on the shoulders of the vast majority of Bulgarians, who were peasants residing on the land. They bore the ultimate responsibility for ensuring the well-being of their foreign sovereigns.

Because of this particular relationship between rulers and ruled, the subject peasantry was denoted by the term, *reaya,* literally meaning "the flock at pasture." Like a good shepherd, the Ottoman state was bound to keep a close watch on its charges and to make certain that they prospered so that they could be beneficially fleeced.

Under the *sipahilık* system of the empire, the resident peasants enjoyed direct use of the land encompassed by the various fiefs. The legal terms and limitations of their land usage, spelling out the actual relationship between them and the fief-holder, were defined in a document, the *tapu* (lease or deed), drawn up by the Ottoman holder of the fief and granted to his resident peasants. The *tapu* enjoined obligations on both parties to the arrangement. Ideally, since actual ownership of the land played no part in the matter (the sultan legally was the owner of all lands within the empire), the responsibilities defined by the document were to ensure the continuous financial productivity of the land involved. The fief-holder was obliged to facilitate the uninterrupted cultivation and habitation of the land to guarantee a stable basis of income from the fief. The peasants assumed the obligation to regularly sow and cultivate their parcels of land and to make timely payment of taxes.

Other than the small *çift* granted each fief-holder as his personal income-producing plot, the land included in the fiefs was divided into numerous autonomous plots (*bashtinas*) in the hands of the peasants. The *tapu* provided the right to hold and work those plots. Thus the Bulgarian peasants submerged in the Ottoman rural social system were not left landless. Neither were they enserfed. The price of retaining use of the land and of their personal freedom was submission to levies and restrictions imposed by the Ottoman authorities.

Assorted threats were used by the authorities to ensure that the peasants paid their taxes and met their various agricultural and service obligations. Withdrawal of the *tapu* and doubled tithes and taxes owed the fief-holder were among the more commonly imposed punishments for a peasant's neglect in land cultivation or arbitrary land abandonment. So long as the central authorities in Istanbul maintained a strict supervision of the *sipahilık*, there were relatively few recourses to grave legal action against the peasants in such matters. After all, it was in the interests of the central authorities and of the entire society that the peasantry not be ruined by excessive duties. The tax base that supported the military-administrative system of the empire had to be preserved at a stable level of profitability.[6]

Most all the land in the Bulgarian lands was *miri* and, therefore, divided into *sipahilık* fiefs. Because of this situation, the Bulgarian peasants had certain obligations to both the central Ottoman fisc and to the holders of fiefs.

By the late sixteenth century the most important fiscal obligation owed by the non-Muslim peasantry to the Ottoman state was the annual *cizye* (poll-tax), paid by all males over the age of 12 and capable of work. It represented one of the oldest discriminatory burdens placed on *zimmis* in an Islamic society; it was a graphic reflection of their inferior social status. The *cizye* was one of the most lucrative sources of income for the central Ottoman treasury. Because this tax was restricted to the all-important non-Muslim income-producing sector of Ottoman society, the *cizye* cadastres provided the authorities with the demographic information necessary for maintaining control of their subject peoples, much as would a regular census, which the authorities did not take until long after the period of our study. Registration of a peasant in the *cizye* cadastres entailed legal obligations to the land, to *corvées,* and to certain restrictive social measures.

Another annual state tax for which the Bulgarian peasants were liable was the *haraç* (land-use tax), which was levied on all rural subjects of the empire irrespective of religious affiliation. Originally, the *haraç* had been restricted to non-Muslims in a fashion similar to the *cizye* but under the Ottomans its imposition had grown general and applied to all agricultural sectors of society. In times of emergency, the central authorities could also call upon all subjects for extraordinary taxes (*avaris*), which were supposed to be temporary but, by the seventeenth century, often continued in force after the immediate emergency had passed, becoming customarily collected periodic levies. Added to the general assortment of taxes were the usual dues and fees for such civil services as court costs, legal documents, and the like.

Other obligations owed by the *zimmi* peasantry to the state were in the form of *corvées* and various labor service demands. Such service demands usually had a military purpose. Bulgarian peasants were frequently called upon to furnish transport for military supplies or to undertake construction projects, which might include building or repairing fortifications and bridges. Peasants could be asked to perform courier service or to work on road maintenance. In keeping with the trend within Ottoman society toward a monetary rather than a labor orientation in social relationships, by the seventeenth century many of the labor obligations owed by the general *zimmi* population had been commuted to an annual cash payment (*çift resmi* — "yoke tax") by the villagers to reimburse the state for the elimination of those duties. Certain groups of peasants continued to provide the Ottoman authorities with various specialized labor services even after such duties had been commuted for the general peasant population, in return for which they received certain tax privileges. Herein lay the fundamental basis for differentiating the Bulgarian peasantry between common and privileged *reaya.*[7]

The Ottoman central government wielded supreme authority over *miri* land but local fief-holders were given broad mastership over the peasants inhabiting their benefices. It was through the holder of the fief that the peasants received the *tapu* granting them legal right to work the land. That right carried with it certain obligations to the fief-holder. Until the late sixteenth century the holder of a fief normally took little direct interest in working his personal çift plot, his being more concerned with military matters and the possibilities for easily acquired wealth through campaign loot. Since he often found the pleasures and diversions available in urban centers more congenial than life in the countryside when not on campaign, the peasants were commonly spared labor obligations. If the fief-holder desired, the peasants living under his *tapu* could legally be asked to reap hay on his çift but they were not obliged to transport what they reaped. If labor services on the çift were demanded, they were limited to a total of three days during any given year for an individual villager. Villagers might also be asked to construct a granary for the fief-holder but they were not required to build any other structure on his çift.[8]

Tithes in kind and cash payments were the preferred forms of peasant obligations to the fief-holder. Payments in kind ensured that the holder of the fief possessed the basic necessities in food and craft goods. The single most important tithe in kind was that levied on crops. The peasants were required to transport their tithes in kind to the granary of the fief-holder or to the nearest market if so ordered, so long as the distance to the market was no more than a day's travel.

Payments in kind took another form if the fief-holder paid a visit to villages on his fief. Villagers were then required to furnish free of charge basic forms of support (food, shelter, fodder) to the holder of the fief, his retinue, and their animals for the duration of their stay. Fortunately, Ottoman law placed a limitation on the number of persons who could accompany the fief-holder on such occasions, limited the duration of a visitation in any one village to three days, forbade numerous visits to any particular village during a single year, and required that the fief-holder pay for anything he received beyond the minimum gratis support.[9]

The three days labor service and many of the payments in kind were eventually commuted to cash payments by the seventeenth century, adding to the traditional monetary burden already owed the fief-holder. Those traditional cash payments included tithes required of the *zimmi* population, technically owed the central authorities but from which the fief-holder drew a large, if not complete, share as his basic income from the fief, and taxes levied on most of the components of agrarian life, such as livestock, mills, forges, and milking facilities.

Until the late seventeenth century taxes and labor services, whether owed the central fisc or the fief-holder, were not levied on the individual but on the household (*hane*). There were two types of households differentiated by the Ottoman authorities, that which was liable for the *cizye* and that which was responsible for *avaris*. The *cizye* household was the basic unit; an *avaris hane* comprised three to 12 *cizye* households. The actual number of individuals who constituted a taxable household has been a subject of much debate among scholars, since the Ottoman authorities did not define a household by the number of persons living together but by a living unit falling under the general authority of a single head. Thus a *hane* could range from a single person living alone to a relatively large extended or multiple family dwelling under a common roof.[10]

The rationale of using the household rather than the individual as the fundamental basis for taxation in the Ottoman Empire was ingenious, but probably expedient. It made payment a collective responsibility, and by so doing sought to ensure that the members of the household would remain working on the land, thus guaranteeing a stable source of tax revenue and special services. Since the rates of taxation and labor obligations on the *hane* were fixed, any decrease in the size of the household through flight or migration meant increased financial and physical burdens for the remaining members. The Ottoman authorities, however, must not be credited with demonstrating any great spark of originality in designing this system. They owed much to the traditions established by their Selcük, Abbasid and Umayyad predecessors.

A talent for creating a workable imperial structure under the pressure of expediency caused by rapid successes during the early years of conquest in the Balkans seems to have been a trademark of the Ottoman Turks. The territories comprising many Ottoman provincial *sancaks* were most often those formerly encompassed by similar administrative units of the conquered Christian states. This was particularly true of the *sancaks* controlling the Bulgarian lands. The nature of the *sipahilık* system of military fiefs owed more to the similar *pronoia* system current in Byzantium and the medieval Balkan successor states than to the feudal arrangement common in the West. In the Bulgarian lands many of the Ottoman fiefs were merely those of the old Bulgarian kingdom under a transformed management. Essentially, the victorious Turks recognized the advantageous utility of retaining, with slight modification to fit Islamic precepts, workable structures and institutions of the conquered states and societies. By taking the stance that what worked in the past should work in the present, the Ottoman approach to state building minimized the effort needed to effect the incorporation of the conquered Christian territories into an Islamic state and somewhat eased the disruptive conditions that accompanied that transition.

The social importance of the family unit among the conquered Balkan subjects of the Ottoman Empire was institutionalized in the *hane*. *Hane* could be either common, or subject to *cizye* and listed as such in the cadastres, or privileged, that is, released from certain tax obligations, particularly the *cizye*. These privileged households were grouped into corporate categories based on the nature of the services for which they were favored. There were 26 categories of corporate service groups in the Bulgarian lands of the seventeenth century. They were divided into two basic functional groups: those with military assistance functions, and those whose purposes were mainly commercial or productive. Many were completely freed of *cizye* obligations, while others might only enjoy such "free" status from extraordinary taxation or from the *devşirme*.[11]

Among the military category of Bulgarian privileged corporate service groups in the seventeenth century, the most numerous and important were the *voynuks*, who supplied the Ottoman military forces with horses, and the *dervencis*, who were charged with defending and maintaining mountain passes and roads considered of military importance by the authorities. Other groups included *martoloses* (local militiamen), *akıncıs* (irregular cavalrymen), *müsellems* (landholding light cavalrymen), and *yamaks* (auxiliary Janissaries). Bulgarians serving in the ranks of *yürük* formations were also part of the privileged military category.

Voynuks constituted the single largest military service group in the Bulgarian lands. In the sixteenth century nearly 8,000 households (or almost 40,000 Bulgarians) were listed as *voynuk* in Ottoman administrative registers. By the early years of the eighteenth century their number had declined to 6,500 (approximately 32,500 persons). They could be found spread throughout most regions of the Bulgarian lands but they tended to be concentrated in the valleys of the Balkan, Sredna Gora and Rhodope mountains in the western lands, especially in the regions of Sofia, Kyustendil, Pernik, Lovech, and Kutlovitsa, as well as on the Danubian Plain around Nikopol and in the Yambol region of the eastern lands. The greatest individual concentration of *voynuks* lay in the Sofia region, where in the mid seventeenth century nearly 2,000 *voynuk hane* (close to 10,000 people) were located.[12]

In return for freedom from *cizye*, obligations to *sipahilık* fief-holders, and *corvée* duties, and for the privilege to wear bright, variegated colored clothing, the *voynuk* households were required to breed horses for the Ottoman military and the imperial stables. They also had to drive their stock to their destinations at specified times during the year or upon demand at times of active military campaigning. *Voynuks* might also be required to accompany the military forces while on campaign as drivers for the horse herd, although active *voynuk* service declined during the seventeenth century. When active service was required of them, some remained at home performing the actual task of breeding while others rotated in the term of service. Bulgarian *voynuks* enjoyed a high reputation in their calling and were customarily used to staff the sultan's personal stables at Istanbul.[13]

The *dervencis* were concentrated in the more mountainous regions of the Bulgarian lands because of the very nature of their service as guardians of passes and mountain roads. They inhabited villages in the regions of Kutlovitsa, Gabrovo, Tŭrnovo, Shumen, Varna, Pazardzhik, Yambol, Sliven, Burgas, and Kŭrdzhali, with the highest concentration found in areas of the Balkan Mountains. Interestingly, *dervenci* villages tended to be among the largest in the Bulgarian lands. Nearly 18 percent of *dervenci* villages were comprised of between 100 and 150 households, almost four times the average size of Bulgarian settlements during the seventeenth century. The largest known village at that time, Kotel (545 households in 1648), in the region of Sliven, was a *dervenci* village. It may be suggested that among the reasons for the unusually large average size of *dervenci* villages was the *dervencis'* right to bear arms. That, and the usual mountainous locale of their settlements, would have made their villages seem natural refuges for those Bulgarians who sought to flee the increasingly anarchistic conditions that came to characterize much of the seventeenth century in the Bulgarian lands.[14]

Aside from their right to possess weapons, *dervencis* enjoyed tax and labor service privileges similar to those of the *voynuks*. The right to bear arms was also extended to the *martolos* militia and to all groups who actively participated in Ottoman irregular military formations.

The second category of privileged *reaya* constituted those who acquired membership in rural corporate service groups that received tax privileges from the Ottoman authorities in return for producing materials and goods needed by the imperial economy or court, primarily ores and foodstuffs. Included in this commercial type of service classification were metal ore miners and processors (*madancıs*), sheep and other livestock dealers and breeders (*celeps*), salt producers (*tuzcıs*), raisers of falcons (*sokolars*), and rice producers (*çeltukçıs*).

The *madancı* population in the Bulgarian lands tended to be concentrated in the hilly terrain of the western lands, especially in the regions of Sofia, Pernik, Kyustendil, Vratsa, Kutlovitsa, and Etropole. The towns of Samokov and Etropole were leading iron ore processing centers for the mining activities undertaken in their respective surrounding countrysides. In the Kutlovitsa region, Chiprovtsi and other nearby villages constituted the heart of the gold and silver mining industry in the Bulgarian lands. In return for performing the backbreaking work of extracting and processing the ores needed by the Ottoman military machine, the *madancıs* received the standard tax relief granted the military service corporations. The physical presence of the Turkish authorities was sparse in the mining regions of the Bulgarian lands, permitting the *madancıs* a greater than usual sphere of local autonomy, even in the urban centers involved in the ore industry.[15]

It appears that the Bulgarians themselves were never very active in the field of ore mining. Most of the miners who inhabited the western Bulgarian lands were the descendants of predominantly Serbian colonists, who had settled in the western lands during the fourteenth century or had later been invited in by fifteenth century Ottoman authorities, in bids to develop those regions' mining industries. Saxons had also been brought into the northwest Bulgarian lands prior to the Ottoman conquest, settling in the Kutlovitsa region in the Chiprovtsi villages. By the seventeenth century both the Serb and Saxon colonists were well advanced along the road toward assimilation into the general Bulgarian population. While the common Orthodox faith shared by Bulgarians and Serbs expedited the assimilatory process of the latter into the former, the Bulgaro-Saxon descendants of the original German colonists retained their Roman Catholic religious culture despite ethnic intermingling with the surrounding Bulgarians, thus preventing their complete assimilation. The Bulgaro-Saxons of Chiprovtsi were the leading supporters of the seventeenth century Catholic missionary effort in the Bulgarian lands, and that effort was thus significantly aided by the privileged *reaya* status enjoyed by the Chiprovtsi miners and metalworkers.

Another important and numerous rural commercial corporation was that of the *celeps*. Originally, the term *celep* was used to denote an agent of the Ottoman authorities, usually residing in the provinces, who was charged with obtaining a determined amount of food for the capital at prices fixed lower than common market prices. The food usually involved was livestock of various kinds or cereals, with the former the most common. If the dealer was also expected to raise the livestock himself, he was termed a *celepkeşan*. By the seventeenth century this distinction had largely disappeared, and all individuals involved in livestock-breeding for Ottoman domestic imperial markets and for foreign commercial markets in the Bulgarian lands were termed *celeps*. When the *celep* system was initiated in the sixteenth century, participation in this food-gathering activity was forced upon individuals by the central authorities, and the position of *celep* was unpopular, given the nature of the charge. By the seventeenth century *celeps* resembled the other corporate service groups in that their work had become a family profession.[16]

The role played by the *celeps* in supplying the Ottoman authorities and commerce with livestock was not minor. In the late sixteenth century *celeps* from the Bulgarian lands were supplying the capital with an annual 440,000 head of sheep.[17] The yearly drive of *celep* sheep took place in the spring, in time for the opening of the military campaigning season. Besides Istanbul, Bulgarian *celeps* drove flocks and herds to markets scattered throughout the Bulgarian lands, and dealt as far afield as Thessaloniki and Transylvania. The wool sheared from *celep* sheep reached markets in Bosnia, Serbia, Budapest and Vienna. As did the *voynuks*, the *celeps* rotated their terms of service among themselves. While some remained in the countryside breeding and tending new flocks, others undertook the task of driving the ready sheep to the markets. The very nature of their service as dealers in a marketable commodity, and the ever present possibilities for embezzlement in market transactions conducted in behalf of the central authorities, resulted in the *celeps* evolving into the wealthiest group among the rural Bulgarians in the seventeenth century.

Aside from the two primary categories of privileged rural Bulgarians, there were others who enjoyed more limited tax and service benefits that raised them above the level of the common *reaya*. They were listed in Ottoman *cizye* cadastres as "free" *hane;* not totally free from state taxation but from *avaris* payments or from giving children to the *devşirme*.[18]

"Free" status could be acquired either by performing services for the authorities, similar to the primary groups of privileged *reaya*, or through residence on particular types of land. For instance, a prime example of the former method was that of the "reserve" *voynuks*, who paid common *cizye* but, because they constituted a reserve pool for those *voynuks* on the active registers, were exempt from paying *avaris*. In the second half of the seventeenth century there were almost 3,000 "reserve" *voynuk* households (nearly 15,000 persons) in the regions of Kyustendil and Yambol alone.[19] Since a number of "free" *hane* that also bear titles of the primary privileged service corporations are listed in *cizye* cadastres from the seventeenth century, it can be assumed that most of the primary groups had "reserve" households that enjoyed "free" status similar to the "reserve" *voynuks*.

While most of the territory encompassing the Bulgarian lands was classified as *miri*, and thus liable for division into *sipahilık* military fiefs, some of it fell under the category of *mülk*, or privately owned land. There were various types of *mülk* that could affect the status of those Bulgarians who lived on them. For instance, *has* lands, owned by the sultan, members of his family, or by powerful, high ranking government officials, bestowed "free" status on the peasants who inhabited them as a benefit for working what essentially were capitalistic estates. Although they represented only a small proportion of the Bulgarian lands, nearly all the Vidin region and a significant part of the Kutlovitsa region were *has* by the latter years of the seventeenth century.[20] (See Table 8.)

Residence on *vakıf* lands might also carry with it a limited "free" status.

A *vakıf* was property owned outright, the income from which served as an inalienable endowment for a religious establishment. A number of the large Muslim mosque complexes in Istanbul received financial support from Bulgarian *vakıfs*. Many Bulgarian monasteries, like that of Rila, among others, managed to survive Islamic domination by means of the *vakıf* status granted their land holdings by the Porte, thus ensuring them of an income under Islamic law. Like *has* land, the *vakıf* was primarily a capitalistic enterprise. Both sought to attract and retain laborers by granting tax breaks.[21]

Although the *vakıf* appeared idealistically philanthropic on the surface, the reality fell far short of the ideal, as is usually the case when large sums of money are involved. It originated in the fifteenth century with *mülk*-holders who began to resent the fact that the sultan still retained ultimate authority over holding rights on their supposedly private properties. In the legal donative document that set aside part or all of the revenues from their properties for the purposes of an endowment for specified religious or charitable institutions, the benefactors usually assigned the administration of the endowment to themselves and to their families in perpetuity. The donation also regulated the manner in which the monies would be used. Usually, a large part of the revenues was set aside for the use of the *vakıf's* administrators, thus guaranteeing an inalienable income for the donor and his heirs.

Because *vakıfs*, as major pillars of support for Muslim institutions, enjoyed extensive immunity under Islamic law, the central authorities frequently permitted them the right to collect certain important state taxes, especially the *cizye*. In the donative document for the *vakıf* the amount of *cizye* was specified under the right granted the *vakıf* to collect it for the endowment from all non-Muslim *reaya* living on the land involved. The amount could not be more or less than the amount current for common *cizye* at the time the donation was made. When *cizye* taxes rose over time, the peasants on the *vakıf* lands were assessed a *cizye* "augmentation" tax to increase *cizye* revenues for the *vakıf*. Apparently, this "augmentation" was set at amounts smaller than the difference between the original level of *vakıf cizye* and the level paid by the common *reaya*.[22] Since the *vakıf* administrators operated their charge with profit in mind, the customary *çift* plot was viewed as an important source of revenue. Unlike developments on most of the *miri* fiefs that tended to transform labor *corvées* for working such plots into cash payments, on the rural *vakıfs* no similar transformation occurred. Thus peasants on *vakıfs*, though enjoying minor tax privileges, tended to be bound closer to the land than were even the common *reaya*.

In the seventeenth century, a quarter of all the Bulgarian lands was *vakıf*, upon which close to 30 percent of the registered *cizye* population lived. *Vakıfs* were heavily concentrated in the northeastern Bulgarian lands and in the central and eastern sections of the Rhodope Mountains. The fact that these were precisely the regions of the Bulgarian lands where the most conversions of Orthodox Bulgarians to Islam occurred during the century speaks for a link between that process and the *vakıf* institution.[23] (See Table 9.)

Both *has*, in the hands of those outside the immediate family of the sultan, and *vakıf* lands could change hands through sale and purchase without the state gaining any financial benefit whatsoever. By their very nature as proprietary benefices in private hands, be they secular or religious, they deprived the central government of substantial sources of revenues.

An outcrop of the clan organization of society that was to play a singularly important role in the mundane and cultural lives of the Bulgarians subject to the Ottoman Empire, no matter whether common or privileged in status, was the village commune. Its origins rooted in the medieval Bulgarian past, the village commune was a closed collective organization composed of every inhabitant of a particular village and administered by the village clan elders. All of the lands attached to the village and worked by the villagers fell under its regulatory authority, including those, such as pastures, forests, and clearings, that were held in common. Dealings with neighboring village communes and outsiders were also its responsibilities. As was the case with the family unit social structure, the conquering Ottoman authorities quickly recognized the utilitarian benefit for the state of this existing form of local corporate self-government. The village commune was made the main instrument by which dealings at all levels and on all matters could be effected between the Bulgarian subject population and the ruling Turkish civil and Greek ecclesiastical authorities. Its official institutionalization within Ottoman society freed the Turks from intimate involvement in the most mundane of local affairs, while it granted the rural Bulgarians an extensive amount of local autonomous self-rule.[24]

In structure the commune was an alliance of the families who comprised the population of the village. Typically, a commune averaged 15 to 40 families, who chose the communal officials from among their elders. The communal officials held the highest level of authority on the village level since it was they who decided the day-to-day affairs of the entire community and represented the village as a whole in dealings with other villages, the local fief-holder, any foreigners who might have business in the locale, and with the Ottoman central and Greek ecclesiastical authorities. As a reflection of their important social status in their communities, Bulgarian communal elders often used medieval Slavic official titles, such as *kmet* (mayor), *knez* ("headman" or elder), or *ban* ("leader"). Elders might also use the equivalent Turkish title, *kocabaşı*.[25]

Because the offices of the commune were of such primary importance for the village community, the elders chosen to fill them usually came from the ranks of the most important families in the village and were often the wealthiest and best educated persons in the community. Furthermore, since traditional usage and values lay at the very heart of communal government, it was not uncommon for the village priest to be numbered among the important elders of the commune.

The geographical limits within which the village commune exercised its authority were generally delineated by natural boundary markers, such as streams, hills, rocks, ridges, and ditches, which usually had been in place prior to the Turkish conquest and which the Ottoman central authorities officially recognized and legally registered in documents that resembled the *tapu* in structure, except that they were granted to the village commune as an entity rather than to the individual peasants living in the village. This, and the conferral of collective responsibility on the commune for all relations with the state and *millet*, especially with regard to tax collection, were the fundamental steps taken by the central authorities to ensure the continued integrity of the commune, thereby guaranteeing, as far as possible, a stable fiscal base in the Bulgarian countryside.[26]

Further strengthening by the Ottoman authorities of the village commune as the most important rural social institution in the Bulgarian lands came with their legalization of traditional communal methods of land holding and usage. Village common lands, such as forests, orchards, and pastures, were protected by Ottoman law, as were those plots that were traditionally held and worked by individuals comprising the commune.[27]

Three categories of land were administered by the commune. The largest share of village cultivated lands was that held by *tapu*. These were held and worked by individual families, and they were transferrable within the family by succession. Such a family holding was known as a *bashtina*. The commune enforced a system of obligatory use on all *bashtinas* that determined the sort of crop grown from among a limited number of choices. The mode of crop rotation was regulated; customary law pronounced that a field could not be left fallow for longer than two years, and this tradition was reinforced by its absorption into Ottoman law. While left fallow, *bashtina* lands could be used as communal common pasturage, and while put to such use, they could be opened to peasants from other villages for a fee that did not have to be totally shared with the local *sipahi* fief-holder, although this opening required written permission from the local Ottoman authorities. Finally, to maintain the territorial integrity of the village commune, the Ottoman authorities granted it certain rights over *bashtina* land should it for some reason fall vacant. It could be shared out among members of the commune, but if, by circumstance, vacant *bashtina* land should be in danger of falling into the hands of a person from another village, the local fief-holder had the right to take possession instead.[28]

Lands held in common by the village were the second category of land regulated by the village commune. Pastures, forests, and orchards were among the most commonly found forms of this type. *Bashtina* lands left fallow also came under this category, although such a situation was usually temporary. Every inhabitant of the village who held a *bashtina* and paid the requisite local land tax (*dime*) had the right of equal usage on the common lands, but such usage never involved cultivation. A pasturage tax for use of common lands was assessed on those who did not pay the *dime*. The Ottoman agrarian law of 1609 made it illegal for the commune to buy, sell, or cultivate village common lands. It also removed fief-holders from having any claim on village common lands, including tax claims.[29]

The third category of land that fell under communal regulation was that which was individually owned (*mülk*). The number of Bulgarian peasants who were given outright title to their plots was limited, so this category constituted the least amount of land dealt with by the commune. In many cases *mülk* land was non-existent. On that which did exist, communal rights were strictly regulated by the central authorities and restrained in practice. *Mülk* lands among the Bulgarians seem to have been most prevalent in the western lands, particularly in the Sofia region, where during the seventeenth century they appear to have frequently changed hands. The tendency was for *mülk* to remain within the boundaries of the same village commune in transferal transactions, reflecting the Ottoman authorities' desire to maintain communal integrity. Should *mülk* lands fall vacant, the commune retained the right of preemption, and could divide the vacant plots among its members upon permission of the authorities.[30]

Beyond its primary functions of tax collection and the regulation of land holding and usage, the village commune was responsible for governing all other mundane affairs that effected the lives of its membership. Its judicial responsibilities included serving as the official representative of the village as a whole before the local Ottoman *kadı* (judge) in matters that fell under the general purvey of the state; in cases lying outside the jurisdiction of the *kadı* court, such as those involving internal disputes or relations with neighboring villages, the commune held full responsibility. Decisions on building or renovating structures of economic or cultural importance for the village, such as storage facilities, churches, or monasteries, were made by the commune, which also arranged for raising the necessary funding, organized the work, and supervised the project through completion. The commune also held itself accountable for preserving the traditional customs, mores, and spiritual values of its membership. In the final analysis, the village commune served as the defender of its members' physical and spiritual well-being against threat or encroachment by outside forces.

The collective nature of the village commune meant that, if a village were classified by the authorities as *voynuk, dervenci, celep,* or any other privileged category, then, for all intents and purposes, the members of that village's commune were considered to participate in the service group's activities without exception. In reality, members of the privileged households in such villages continued to farm the village lands in traditional fashion, and the communes functioned in the same manner as did those among the common *reaya*. In any case, the villagers had few interests beyond those of their commune. While such a situation tended to reinforce a sense of worldly isolation on Bulgarian villages, it also tended to alleviate animosities between Muslim and non-Muslim peasants, who often lived together in mixed villages.

The usual absolute religious distinctions between Muslim and non-Muslim found in Ottoman law were absent from laws dealing with the village communes, in which no such distinctions were drawn. At the village level, communal obligations were fixed by the authorities without regard to religious affiliation. The commune was considered the corporate economic, political and legal representative of all its members, whether the villagers were of homogeneous or

30 *The Social Position of the Bulgarians*

of mixed religion. In those villages possessing a mixed Christian and Muslim population, the villagers were united at the basic level as agriculturalists. Religious differences only resulted in a certain differentiation in work functions, village living quarters, and cultural activity. Otherwise, regardless of faith, the villagers usually shared common experiences, traditions, songs, and often languages. Through the village commune, members of both faiths found a unifying sense of common interests.

The importance of the fact that the entire purpose of the organization of rural society by the Ottoman authorities was to ensure a stable source of revenues in support of the political and military institutions of the empire cannot be over estimated. Ottoman power depended on a strong central authority able to command a powerful, obedient military-administrative force. The strength of both was dependent upon a steady supply of income obtained through minimum direct effort and involvement on their part so that they could devote their time and energies to their appointed tasks. The economic, political and military decline of the Ottoman Empire that commenced in the second half of the sixteenth century unleashed forces that had a destabilizing effect on Bulgarian rural society during the seventeenth. These forces intensified as the century progressed.

At the root of much of the rural problems that came to characterize the seventeenth century lay the ever increasing rate of monetary inflation that afflicted the empire. The opening of the Western Hemisphere by the powers of Western Europe had as one of its results an increase of gold and silver currency that eventually found its way into the Levantine markets of the Ottoman Empire. The inflationary effects of that flood of foreign silver into the empire were intensified by the fact that, by the late sixteenth century, the Turks had begun devaluating the silver *akçe,* the fundamental monetary unit in the Ottoman economy, in response to the decline in trade revenues resulting from the shift in European-Asian trade from overland to sea routes. At the same time, the empire ceased to enjoy uninterrupted successes in the military realm. The nearly constant wars fought by the Turks during the seventeenth century consumed an enormous amount of money, and, as their frontiers began to contract in the face of growing military defeat, shortfalls in revenues were directly correlated to lands lost.

Within a decade of 1584 the *akçe* dropped 50 percent in value. By 1587 the *groş* (or *piastre*), which had officially represented the sum of 40 *akçes,* had fallen to 50 *akçes.* During the seventeenth century the spiraling decline in monetary values accelerated. By 1640 the *groş* represented the equivalent of 125 *akçes.*[31] The inflationary conditions led the Ottoman authorities to attempt reducing the amount of currency in circulation and to further reduce the silver content of their coins. This led to economic confusion since the nominal face value of the currency quickly lost any corresponding relationship with the actual value of silver found in the coin itself. Prices and interest rates soared, and speculation became rampant.[32]

The repercussions within the Ottoman ruling establishment of the inflation were felt strongly by both the central authorities and the *sipahılık* fief-holders. In an effort to increase state revenues, the Porte was forced to resort to farming out tax collection. The rights to collect state taxes in a given area of the empire were opened to the highest bidders, who promised to deliver a determined, specified amount of revenues to the government from their tax farm (*iltizam*). As the taxfarmers (*mültezims*) were also seeking to make extensive profits from their *iltizams*, taxes throughout the empire experienced an increase once the system was instituted.

The example set by the central government in buying substitutes for important administrative functions, which the taxfarming system actually represented, filtered down to all administrative levels in the empire. Soon *kadıs* were leasing their courts to substitutes, and bribery within the governing system became rife. All positions within the state administration became means for increasing the individual official's personal wealth. Administrative positions were sold by the state, or their authority was delegated to the bidder who could provide the authorities with the most cash.[33]

Farming out state taxes and selling government posts did not solve the financial problems of the Porte. Continuing needs for more revenues as inflation persisted and grew led the central authorities to begin confiscating *mülk* and *miri* lands, often under the most specious of excuses. *Sipahılık* lands were amassed in the name of the sultan, of which a large percentage was first rented out to moneyed dignitaries and palace favorites, who then sublet their rentals to tenants. The result was that the former *sipahılık* lands involved in these types of transactions not only passed out of direct government control but their transformation into simple sources of revenue had an adverse effect on the military strength of the empire. Sometimes *sipahis* were directly dispossessed of the land by the authorities. At other times, vacant *sipahılık* land was simply converted into *has* and then rented out.

The effect of the government's interference in the military landholding system was utterly negative. The amount of land directly supporting the military class declined. By the second half of the seventeenth century there was not a single military fief in the region of Vidin.[34] The new non-military fief-holders viewed their holdings purely as sources of personal enrichment, free of any military obligation to the state. They bent every rule and took advantage of every proffered opportunity to convert their leases into personal, hereditary *mülk* property. The *sipahi* fief-holders in the countryside began to follow the lead of the newcomers and increasingly lost interest in fulfilling their military duties. A competition for land developed between the rich, non-military landholders and

32 The Social Position of the Bulgarians

the *sipahi* military fief-holders. Each attempted to invest revenues into purchasing new leases on land or into other profit-generating enterprises, such as provincial government offices, with the ultimate goal of casting off completely control of their properties by the central government and transforming them into legally owned sources of personal wealth as capitalistic, market-oriented estates (*çiftliks*). The competition tended to concentrate landholding in fewer hands as the seventeenth century progressed, and resulted in the ruination of the lessor *sipahi* fief-holders.

Renting state lands was but one path toward the formation of privately owned great landed estates. Another was the opportunity offered to rich or influential individuals through buying up land not officially registered in the tax cadastres, or lands long left unworked, by cash payment to the central authorities. Slaves would be brought in to settle these new estates. They would be joined by *reaya* who had fled their original homes for one reason or another, and who were usually not listed on current tax registers. Since Ottoman tax records were often highly confused and commonly out of date, it was easy for peasants to slip through the numerous loopholes. For the same reason, the purchase of state lands through bribery and the forcing of *reaya* to sell their land and enter estate service was not a difficult procedure. Most owners of such new estates came from the ranks of the *sipahi* military class.[35]

A third means available to rich and influential palace figures for establishing a capitalistic *çiftlik* estate was through transforming their *mülk* holdings into *vakıfs*, with themselves and their heirs named as the inalienable administrators. Over the course of the seventeenth century *vakıfs* began to develop into plantation-like estates, free of government interference because of their intimate linkage with the Muslim religious establishment of the state. Slave labor could be used without questions from local authorities. The autonomy enjoyed by *vakıfs* tended to attract fugitive *reaya*, but once they settled on *vakıf* land they found themselves tightly bound to the estate.

Much has been written concerning the detrimental effects of the rising *çiftlik* estates upon the military, economic and social systems of the empire. Undoubtedly, it was an important factor in the abject decline of Ottoman fortunes following the sixteenth century. With regard to conditions in the Bulgarian lands during the seventeenth century, too much should not be made of the *çiftlik* development. Fully developed *çiftliks*, in which all the land was devoted to cash crop farming and the peasants who worked on them were tied rigidly to the soil through labor duties and heavy tithes, were not commonly found in the seventeenth century Bulgarian lands, and only a small fraction of the Bulgarian *reaya* were located on them. The few that had taken shape during the period lay in the regions of Burgas, Plovdiv, Ruse, Varna, Shumen and Tŭrnovo, areas that also experienced strong pressures for assimilating Christian Bulgarians into the

Muslim population.[36] Perhaps the heavy lot of non-Muslim laborers on the *çiftliks* exerted one of the pressures. (See Table 10.)

As the *sipahılık* military landholding system unraveled, the central authorities were forced to rely more on an expanded professional military force. This meant increasing the numbers of Janissaries and standing cavalry units as the mainstays of Ottoman military strength. It also meant that the government was pressured further to obtain the additional revenues to pay the professional troops' salaries. The resultant shift from feudal to professional military forces caused profound changes in the political and social character of the empire. Members of the old *sipahi* aristocracy filled the offices of command in the rising professional forces, an act that guaranteed them political authority and economic prosperity, since their salaries could be invested in capitalistic exploitation of their land. By the mid seventeenth century the Ottoman *eyalets* and *sancaks* had ceased to function as component parts of the *sipahılık* military system. The office of *beylerbey,* the former commander-in-chief of the *sipahis* under his provincial authority, was replaced by that of the *vali,* a high ranking military-administrative office that entailed much fiscal authority and was usually granted to honored men of *vezir* rank. To pay for the troops under his command, the *vali* had the authority to collect taxes in the regions under his control.[37]

The heart of the old standing military forces had been the Janissary slave infantry recruited through the *devşirme*. When their numbers were rigidly controlled and draconian discipline maintained, they had proved the scourge of Europe. Now that the Porte could no longer depend on the *sipahılık* system to provide the massive military support needed to uphold the military, drastic expansion of the Janissaries became a necessity. With the rural population becoming ever more important as a source of revenues in the existing inflationary conditions, the *devşirme* was no longer a viable means of recruitment. The last child-levy of any consequence took place in the Bulgarian lands in 1685.[38]

Sons of Janissaries and native-born Muslims were illegally entered into the ranks of the technically slave army. As their numbers grew, so did their unruliness. The units were dispersed throughout the provinces, taking up residence in all the major urban areas, where they showed more interest in joining the Turkish artisan class than in their military duties. They did, however, relish their official roles as personal guards of local provincial officials, tax collectors, and policemen, since these functions held out the possibilities for monetary gain. The provincial Janissaries also actively participated in the land speculation that was fast leading to the rise of privately owned landed estates. The result was a rapid decline in their military value and dependability. As the growing disruption of the traditional institutions of the empire became more apparent, the Janissaries tended to become a law unto themselves.

34 The Social Position of the Bulgarians

The number of Janissaries stationed in the Bulgarian lands nearly doubled during the seventeenth century. In 1609 there were 37,627 registered troopers stationed in the Bulgarian *sancaks*. By 1687 their numbers had increased to 70,394 men.[39]

Both the Janissaries and the *sipahis* technically were required to live on fixed incomes. The former were paid a salary by the central authorities; the latter possessed revenue-producing fiefs with specified levels of income related to their standing in the military organization. The highly inflationary conditions that prevailed throughout the seventeenth century made a mockery of the salaries and tithes from which they both drew their livelihoods. Conditions forced them to seek augmentation of their fixed incomes by any method available to them. In the Bulgarian lands, the persons who ultimately footed the bill for the mad rush for cash that permeated all levels of the Ottoman ruling establishment were the Bulgarian *reaya*.

The first, and most obvious, impact of the inflationary economy on the Bulgarian peasantry was the continuous rise in state taxes. In the mid sixteenth century the fundamental tax paid by the Christian Bulgarians, the *cizye*, stood at between 40 and 60 *akçes* per household. At the opening of the seventeenth century the *cizye* stood at 140 *akçes*, and by the close of the century, by which time the *hane* had been replaced by the individual male as the basic tax unit for the central authorities, it accounted for between 300 and 325 *akçes* for the average total household.[40] Annual *avaris* taxes were about 250 *akçes* per household, the "yoke tax" paid for commutation of labor services due the authorities stood at 22 *akçes*, and the tax paid the fief-holder in lieu of labor on his *çift* plot was three *akçes* at the opening of the seventeenth century. By century's close, all had spiralled upward.[41]

The Bulgarian *reaya* during the seventeenth century were faced with an increasingly ruinous level of taxation. For instance, the average annual productive value of a Bulgarian household *bashtina* at the close of the sixteenth century was 449 *akçes*, based on the current bulk price obtainable for various agricultural products. The average annual taxes constituted 141 *akçes*, or 31.4 percent of the average value of the family lands. Later in the seventeenth century taxes reached 82.7 percent of the average value. In some cases, taxes even exceeded the total value of the household's *bashtina*.[42]

The tax burden on the Bulgarian peasantry during the seventeenth century reached such proportions that the village communes were often forced to borrow money at interest from the newly arising wealthy landed aristocracy to meet their annual tax assessments. For instance, in 1618 the village of Zhitŭne, in the Sofia region, borrowed 50,000 *akçes* from a certain Mustafa *bey* at 1,000 *akçes* interest to make a final *cizye* payment. The village of Marotin, in the Ruse region, was forced to borrow 85,000 *akçes* in 1656 for a similar reason.[43] Such loans might entail high rates of interest, and usually required that the commune use land as collateral. In consequence of this situation, seventeenth century Bulgarian peasants tended to be heavily indebted to and dependent upon the Turkish estate-owners, who frequently repossessed village lands in default of loan repayments. The plight of near continuous debt was one of the primary reasons for a growing number of Bulgarians fleeing the land during the seventeenth century.

Added to the rising state tax oppression of the *reaya* were other burdensome afflictions. Prices for most purchased necessities rose; taxes on livestock increased. As the rural *sipahilık* system unwound, the newly emerging Turkish estate-owners and the remaining fief-holders made growing illegal requisitions of grain, livestock and cash from villages located on their properties, despite the limitations placed on such demands in the issued *tapus*. In the days of Ottoman greatness, such illegal actions were usually dealt with swiftly and severely. Under the conditions that prevailed in decline, which weakened the authority of the central government in provincial affairs, the landholders were able to break the agrarian laws with impunity.

Compounding the problems for the *reaya* caused by the degeneration of traditional rural social relationships was the growing anarchy that became prevalent in the Bulgarian countryside during the seventeenth century. With the end of uninterrupted Ottoman military expansion in the late sixteenth century, the inability of the Porte to create new *sipahilık* fiefs from conquered territories, and the confiscation of existing *sipahilık* fiefs, the number of landless *sipahis* began to outstrip the amount of land available for distribution among them with calamitous results. Frustrated in their hopes of gaining lucrative incomes from the possession of military fiefs, growing numbers of Ottoman soldiers turned to extortion, and even to outright banditry, to satisfy their monetary desires. They were often joined by men holding provincial posts of authority and by Janissaries in making armed periodic rounds of the Bulgarian countryside, extorting cash, crops and maintenance from the local peasantry through the threat of violence. The Janissary units garrisoned in Bulgarian towns were leading exponents of rural terrorism, using their authority as police to intimidate and exploit the Bulgarian inhabitants of the countryside. Because of the weakness of the Porte, both institutionally and in the quality of the persons who occupied the position of sultan, bandits, landless *sipahis,* Janissaries, rapacious local officials and estate owners caused anarchy in regions of the Bulgarian lands, with plunderings and depredations perpetrated on the helpless Bulgarian population.

As monetary and labor demands rose, and as assorted acts of violence became commonplace, life in the Bulgarian countryside during the seventeenth century became increasingly uncertain and difficult for the Bulgarian peasant. One never knew when some new, violent event would erupt, or how much cash would be needed to satisfy the ever increasing inflationary rates of taxation, or the extent of free labor *corvée* that the local estate-owner might decree. Uncertain, too, was the possibility of satisfying exorbitant loan payments and, thus, being able to retain possession of the family *bashtina*. Given such conditions, there can be little wonder that many rural Bulgarians fled their land to escape the disorders and heavy lot that were mundane realities in the countryside. By the end of the century, these rural refugees were turning to the towns located in the Bulgarian lands for relief from their rural woes.[44]

The Urban Situation: Artisans and Merchants

The small urban segment of the seventeenth century Bulgarian population resided in the 35 towns located throughout the Bulgarian lands. (See Table 7.) Nearly all of these urban centers existed prior to the Ottoman conquest of the second medieval Bulgarian state, when they had served primarily as centers for the handicrafts and mining industries. Some, especially those located on the Black Sea coast and along the Danube, conducted certain important commercial activities. Unlike urban centers in the West during the Middle Ages, medieval Bulgarian towns apparently lacked any development to speak of regarding artisan guilds. Bulgarian craftsmen either served the needs of the Bulgarian government, church and feudal aristocracy or produced for the local urban and rural markets. Long distance commerce was usually in the hands of foreign merchants, who often took up residence in the towns. The royal government ruled urban communities directly through its feudal aristocracy, the *bolyars*. Resident artisans and merchants were granted certain liberties in the direction of self-government and, in turn, the towns served as the principal centers of an official medieval Bulgarian culture that was supported by the ruling class through the Orthodox church.[45]

Under Ottoman rule, the function of the urban centers as local artisan and commercial centers did not change fundamentally. What did change was the ethnic composition of the urban population. During the troubled times that accompanied the Ottoman conquest of Bulgaria, part of the Bulgarian urban population was displaced to make room for Turkish officials, garrisons, artisans and agents. The conquerors brought the remaining Bulgarian residents thoroughly into the Ottoman urban social organization. Gradually, over the course of the fifteenth and sixteenth centuries, the Turkish element in the urban population of the Bulgarian lands steadily increased as further administrative service personnel, Janissary troops, artisan colonists and local *sipahi* fief-holders settled into the towns.

By the seventeenth century towns in the Bulgarian lands, especially the larger ones, such as Sofia, Plovdiv, Varna, Nikopol, Ruse, Tŭrnovo and Vidin, had acquired a distinctly oriental physical and social character. The Turks forbade their Christian Bulgarian subjects to possess large houses or buildings performing social functions. In the countryside, such restrictions ensured that Bulgarian villages remained primitive and without plan or civic buildings. The traditional pre-Ottoman stone structures in the villages were left in neglect, and it soon became common for the typical village house to be a thatched hut, with people and livestock sharing a common living space. In urban centers, where the presence of the foreign authorities was constant and direct, the Bulgarian residents were forced to accept the oriental material standards of urban development espoused by their Muslim overlords. Most Bulgarian towns came to be characterized by minarets and mosques defining their skylines. Many large, well-built Orthodox churches in the towns were transformed into Islamic religious buildings over time, and the centers of the towns were renovated with new, Islamic structures, such as mosques and their attendant satellite buildings, baths, fountains and caravanserais. While the structures devoted to the administrative, cultural and private well-being of the Muslim authorities and residents were usually large and constructed of stone, those of the subject Christian Bulgarians were small and poorly built.[46]

The populations of the towns in the Bulgarian lands during the seventeenth century were either evenly divided between Christians and Muslims or divided slightly in favor of the Muslim element.[47] In all cases, however, Muslims occupied the upper rungs and Christians the lower on the Ottoman urban social ladder. This social positioning was aptly demonstrated in the spatial organization of the urban centers in the Bulgarian lands, which was typical of all towns in the Ottoman Empire. The town center was reserved for administrative, defensive and commercial activities. It was chiefly inhabited by Muslims, who wielded civil and religious authority, and by foreign merchants, in whose hands most long distance commerce was concentrated. Lying in a ring around the center were the residential quarters (*mahalles*), where the general urban population lived in low dwellings that faced the meandering and narrow streets and that were frequently separated from each other by large gardens, which tended to make the towns appear larger than their actual populations would warrant. Muslim quarters were most often found in the oldest and most prominent sections of the town and close to the center, while those of the Christians, the place of their location often termed the *varosh* by the Muslim authorities and inhabitants, were commonly located farther from the center. The homes of Christian town-dwellers tended to be of lower quality than those of the Muslims, having few, if any, windows and structurally oriented toward inner courtyards rather than toward the streets. The residential area was further surrounded by an outlying belt of land that served as the cemetery region for the inhabitants. Even here, Christian social inferiority was emphasized in that Christian graves were usually relegated to the furthest outskirts of this belt.[48]

In the *varosh* of most towns in the Bulgarian lands, the Christian urban population was not exclusively Bulgarian, although Bulgarians usually formed the ethnic majority. In addition to Bulgarians, urban Christians included Orthodox Greeks, Armenians and Albanians, as well as Catholic Croatian merchants from the Adriatic coastal commercial city of Dubrovnik. Because the Ottoman authorities made little or no ethnic distinction among their Christian subjects, except in the case of Armenians, it is difficult to determine with any great accuracy the number of urban Bulgarians during the seventeenth century. It has been estimated that as much as 50 percent of the Christian populations of Sofia, Plovdiv, Tŭrnovo and the towns on the Black Sea coast was Greek and not Bulgarian. Taking this factor into account, it can be estimated that, on average, each town in the Bulgarian lands contained less than 600 Bulgarians during the seventeenth century. The largest urban Bulgarian populations were found in the Danubian port towns of Silistra (over 3,000), Nikopol and Svishtov (both over 2,000). The towns with the least Bulgarians in their populations appear to have been Berkovitsa, Burgas and Provadiya (all with less than 100), which were overwhelmingly Muslim in population. (See Table 7.)

Many of the urban Christians, along with a large percentage of the urban Muslims, were involved in either artisan crafts or in local or long distance commerce. They inhabited crowded urban *mahalles* that usually were centered upon individual streets in the *varosh,* and which were often surrounded by walls whose gates on the main streets were closed and locked at night.

Mahalles tended to segregate the urban population in terms of religion and profession. Most were named after some known building lying within their confines, or after some local town notable who resided in the quarter. In the *varosh mahalles* possessing an exclusively Christian population, they often acquired the names of churches located within their limits (or of the saints to whom the churches might be dedicated) or of noted priests (*pops*) who had lived there. Thus for many urban Bulgarians, their *mahalle* represented their church parish. Other *mahalles* could be named after the profession or trade pursued by the majority of their inhabitants. Such named *mahalles* tended to be less oriented toward the religious affiliation of their inhabitants and so often were of mixed Christian and Muslim composition.[49]

Of the 29 *mahalles* of Sofia in the seventeenth century, eight were Christian in their population, 17 were mixed with a Muslim predominance, and four were mixed with a Christian predominance. In Tŭrnovo at near mid century, nine of the 11 Christian *mahalles* were name after priests, parish churches or Orthodox prelate titles. The remaining two were named after the belt-making and blacksmithing professions. The *mahalles* of Plovdiv were all mixed Christian-Muslim and were named for the trades or professions of their inhabitants.[50]

The ratio in number among Christian, Muslim and mixed religion *mahalles* in any given town did not necessarily remain fixed over time. The town of Nikopol is a case in point. In 1649 the Christians of the town inhabited 12 *mahalles,* but by 1660, when the Turkish traveler, Evliya Celebi, visited, he noted the existence of only half that number of Christian quarters, while Muslim quarters numbered 11. At the end of the century, in 1693, the Christians inhabited nine *mahalles,* some of which were of mixed religious character.[51] As urban populations grew in the towns of the Bulgarian lands near the end of the seventeenth century, new *mahalles* might be formed.

In average size, the Christian *mahalles* resembled that of the rural settlements. Depending on location and time during the seventeenth century, Bulgarian *mahalles* contained between 20 and 43 *cizye*-registered *hane* (or approximately 100 to 215 persons). The resemblance did not end with size. The *mahalle* served as the basic Ottoman vehicle for tax collection in urban centers. The elders of each *mahalle* functioned like elders in the village communes and usually bore similar titles, such as *knez*. Thus the *mahalle* served the same self-regulatory purpose for the urban Bulgarians as did the commune for the rural population.[52]

An important element of the urban population was comprised of artisans, who owned their own shops and whose lives were closely bound to the workings of the Ottoman guild (*esnaf*) system. Unlike the Western guild system, Ottoman guilds were controlled, regulated and regimented absolutely by the central authorities through local urban officials, most especially through the local town *kadı* and his court. All independent activity on the part of Ottoman artisan guilds was severely monitored and restricted. The state set all prices, authorized all sources of supply and material, decided product quotas, and determined the types of products that could be legally manufactured and sold. Since most urban *esnafs* were oriented toward servicing regional or governmental needs and depended on limited geographical regions as sources for their raw materials, the Ottoman guild system was constructed so as to eliminate competition to ensure social and economic harmony, and thus to maintain a stable source of materials and tax revenues for the central government.[53]

The *esnaf* system was largely anti-profit by nature and was subject to the Muslim principle of *hisba*, which protected the interests of the population against profiteering, fraud and speculation under the *Şeriat*. The application of this principle was an obligation of the Islamic state that the Turks originally took very seriously. All types of speculation in the area of the crafts industries were punished as criminal offenses. Religious official set the "just" price for craft goods and determined the "just" profit allowed the artisans concerned. Usually, the "just" profit averaged between ten and 15 percent, depending on the type of product involved.[54]

Each *esnaf* organized the artisans engaged in a particular craft into a social "brotherhood" of sorts, which was the original meaning of the Arabic word, *esnaf*. It collectively represented all its members and their professional interests to the central authorities, and it regulated all economic relations among themselves, including setting the established number of permissible shops and awarding the rights to open new ones as time or circumstance might permit. The Ottoman authorities granted each *esnaf* judicial powers over its membership and complete autonomy with regard to its operational affairs. An *esnaf* was administered by a general council, or assembly (*lonca*), which consisted of all its full members and which usually met once every year. Its most important function was to regulate the manufacturing operations of the membership and to administer the *esnaf's* charter, chronicles, codices and regulations. The *lonca* also elected the permanent council of the *esnaf*, which executed the policies of the general assembly throughout the year. The permanent council, composed of from two to seven individuals, oversaw the legal functions and rights of the *esnaf* to ensure the continued autonomy of the organization. It also functioned as the *esnaf's* internal disciplinary board, a court of arbitration for disputes among the membership, and as the official representative of the *esnaf* before the Ottoman authorities.

Both the *lonca* and the permanent council were headed by the *ustabaşı* (or *kethüda*), the "first master," who was an elected official chosen from among the master craftsmen. He was the actual head of the guild. His term of office was usually one year but it could be extended if mandated by the *lonca*. All financial matters for the *esnaf* rested in his hands, but he was also involved in every matter and decision that affected the *esnaf*, from the smallest to the most important. He was assisted by a *yiğitbaşı*, also elected by the assembly as the second ranking *esnaf* official, and by a *çavuş*, the servant or attendant of the *esnaf's* trustees. The *yiğitbaşı* served as the deputy of the *ustabaşı*. The job of the *çavuş* was to collect membership and other dues, run the guild's club, and to oversee apprentices and journeymen. The *çavuş* was chosen from among the youngest of the masters for various short periods of time, ranging from one to six months.[55]

The treasury of the *esnaf*, which was controlled by the permanent council, received its funds from a number of sources, ranging from membership dues and fines, through taxes paid the guild for various types of transactions, to gifts and donations made by the membership on specific occasions. The monies in guild treasuries would often be put to use as a primitive form of workmen's compensation for injured or disabled members, as funding for public festivals sponsored by the *esnafs*, usually on religious holidays, or as principal for interest-bearing loans to the membership.

The membership of *esnafs* could be either ethnically homogeneous or mixed. Often, the ethnic composition of an *esnaf* depended on the type of craft it represented. For example, the fur and leather craft industries, including the tanning and farrier trades, were commonly concentrated in the hands of Turks, while metal-smithing and most textile-related industries, including tailoring, weaving, carpet-making and lace-making, were chiefly in the hands of Bulgarians. Such endeavors as money-changing, tinsmithing and glass-making were usually conducted by Jews and Armenians. Although no differentiation based on religious grounds officially existed among guild members, by the late seventeenth century many of the craft *esnafs* in the Bulgarian lands were, for all intents and purposes, Christian. In those here membership was mixed Christian and Muslim, the latter displayed extraordinarily great tolerance of the religious and cultural manifestations of their Bulgarian "brothers," even when those manifestations entailed a considerable outlay of *esnaf* funds, such as on certain Orthodox holidays. In mixed guilds, the *ustabaşı* was usually a Muslim and the *yiğitbaşı* a Christian. For most urban Bulgarians, the guilds played an important role in controlling and smoothing their contacts with the numerous non-Bulgarians, especially Muslim Turks, who coexisted with them in the towns of the Bulgarian lands.[56]

During the seventeenth century Bulgarian artisans played prominent roles in the metal-working, textile and leather-working craft industries. In the metal-working field, crafts associated with iron and silver products were especially significant. Samokov, a town located in the Sofia region, was a leading center for the iron-working industry in the Bulgarian lands. Iron foundries and smithies were spread throughout the area surrounding the town, a fact noted by Evliya Celebi in 1661, and Samokov itself served as the chief ore processing center. Each year Samokov provided the Ottoman Empire with close to 8,000 wagon loads of iron for use in the harbor of Thessaloniki. Other leading iron-working centers in the Bulgarian lands included Etropole, the second largest producer after Samokov, Dupnitsa, Sofia and Pazardzhik, with the areas around Kyustendil, Nevrokop and Melnik also active. Besides processing and dressing iron, the metal-working crafts associated with the industry included the production of such finished products as nails, horseshoes, agricultural tools, crowbars, hatchets, bridles and bits, and numerous other metal items, including weapons. In 1612 there was an ironsmithing market street (*çarşi*) in Sofia. By the late seventeenth century Vidin sported a farrier *esnaf* and Ruse one for ironsmiths.[57]

Chiprovtsi and its surrounding locale constituted the most important silver- and gold-working center in the sixteenth and seventeenth centuries, although the veins began to play out in the local mines near the middle of the latter. The craftsmen of Chiprovtsi were known as *Saski,* a term loosely derived from the word, Saxon, referring to the fact that Saxon miners had been brought into the area during the thirteenth and fourteenth centuries, but not used in an ethnic context by the seventeenth. *Saski* was then used to denote the professional metallurgists or miners of the area. In 1640 there were 12 silver furnaces and numerous metal foundries in Chiprovtsi, and one of the town's *mahalles* was named after the silversmithing profession. The towns of Berkovitsa, in the Kutlovitsa region, and Kyustendil also participated in the silver-working industries.[58]

Bulgarian craftsmen were particularly active in the textile industries. Sofia numbered among its Bulgarian, or mostly Bulgarian, *esnafs* those for goat hair carpet-makers, which also maintained its own *çarşi*, and textile dyers. Sofia was particularly famous for its dressmaking and hooded cloak-making artisans. Bulgarians were active in the town's felt-making *esnaf*, which also had a *mahalle* named after their craft. In the seventeenth century the town had a *çarşi* for *aba*, a course woolen homespun cloth much used in cloaks and other types of clothing. In mid century the inhabitants of Sliven were mainly involved in *aba*-making, as well as carpet-weaving and cloak-making. Cloth-making crafts were also important for the artisans of Tŭrnovo and Pleven.[59]

The food and drink industries, featuring the production of breads, cheeses, wines, dairy and meat products, all were heavily populated by Bulgarian artisans. In the seventeenth century, Sofia possessed a noted fresh water fish market supplied by catches from the Iskŭr River and numerous mountain streams in the surrounding region.

Although Muslims tended to dominate the leather and hide crafts in the Bulgarian lands, some Christian Bulgarians participated in these activities. The town of Silistra was strongly identified with the fur crafts. Bulgarians were well represented in the Sofia saddle-makers *esnaf* during the seventeenth century. The artisans involved in the animal hide crafts in the Bulgarian towns of Sofia, Plovdiv, Tŭrnovo, Silistra, Nikopol, Vidin, and Ruse were extremely active in supplying products to merchants plying international commerce. The common trade term for raw hides in international trading markets of the seventeenth century was "Bulgarian" hides.[60]

Placing certain of the urban artisans' crafted products on the international commercial trading markets was the job of the merchants (*tüccars*), many of whom were residents of the towns in the Bulgarian lands. They constituted the smallest element in the urban population. Although less numerous than the urban artisans and certainly far less so than the rural *reaya*, both of whose economic lives were thoroughly regulated by the Ottoman central authorities, merchants residing in Ottoman urban centers enjoyed a certain amount of economic freedom that permitted them to conduct true capitalistic operations. Craftsmen, who sold the products of their own labor, and tradesmen, who sold goods at second hand, were not considered members of the merchant class. To be entitled to the rank of *tüccar* one had to be intensively involved in international or interregional trading activity.

As were the artisans, merchants were organized into *esnafs* according to the type of goods they traded. What distinguished them from the artisan guild members was the fact that they were not subject to the precepts of *hisba*, and thus not regulated in terms of pricing and profits. Merchants were free to accumulate capital, to increase their capital, and to engage in all sorts of trading activity. They fit neatly into the concept of putting money to work that served as a fundamental premise of traditional Islamic society. Since Islamic society was one based on a strong commercial community, the merchant class was traditionally granted social privileges. In return, the Islamic state used the merchant class as a source of steady revenues through customs duties and loan funds, when needed. The urban merchant class also served the state as a mediator between government and governed in tax matters, as a pool for agents and ambassadors, and as a supply source for goods unavailable within the boundaries of the state.

Through their international trading activity, merchants, while supplying the authorities and wealthy with luxury goods, also served an essential purpose in maintaining the very economic foundations of urban society. It was they who provided the larger towns with essential food products and with the raw materials needed by many of the urban craft industries. Conversely, they were the chief agents in distributing the finished craft products to distant markets. Yet despite their crucial role in urban economic life, merchants were often despised by the artisans of the towns, who considered them morally corrupted by their wealth and privilege, but who probably secretly envied them their economic and social position. There were known cases where artisans were actually expelled from their *esnafs* by the rest of the membership under the castigation of having become a "merchant" by growing richer than was acceptable, that is, for making more money than was needed to live.[61]

Merchants played little or no active part in the local markets that existed in all of the seventeenth century Bulgarian towns. Usually held on a weekly or monthly basis, market bazaars saw to the free exchange of materials and goods between the town and its surrounding locale. In the larger towns the presence of actual retail shops permitted local trading and selling to go on continuously when bazaars were not taking place. This was the domain of the craftsmen-shopkeepers. Some of the merchandise sold by the local urban artisans, however, was purchased from merchants who imported items to locales where they were not normally produced. A few merchant families maintained retail shops in their urban home bases that sold products they had purchased from afar. It primarily was in such interregional transactions, and in long distance activity, that the role of the urban merchants took an active turn.

If nothing else, the Ottoman Empire provided a unified market for interregional trade in the Balkan Peninsula. Merchants from the towns in the Bulgarian lands took great advantage of this situation during the seventeenth century. Thanks to their efforts, hooded cloaks crafted by Bulgarian artisans were sold on the markets in Belgrad and Sarajevo; carpets from Pleven were traded in Skopje and Kastoria; Sofia leather goods were marketed in such places as Istanbul and Kastoria. Such interregional trade was highly centralized under state trading monopolies to ensure a steady supply for the Ottoman capital, the military and the sultan's court. For example, Istanbul received grains from the southern regions of the Bulgarian lands, as well as from elsewhere. Goods bound for the court at Istanbul would often first pass through such Bulgarian towns as Vidin, Nikopol and Svishtov on their way south. During times of military need, such as in 1673 and 1674, hundreds of horses were purchased by the Ottoman military from the regions of Nikopol, Pleven, Tŭrnovo and Svishtov in the Bulgarian lands, and in the period of warfare with the Western powers, Poland and Russia (1683-1699) food supplies were purchased for the army from all regions lying along the military routes and ordered transported to designated depots. In all such transactions, urban merchants played a leading role.[62]

While ethnic Bulgarians, many of whom were not actually urban merchants at all but rather were members of the *celep* and *voynuk* privileged *reaya*, were highly active in the sphere of interregional trade, they played a more limited role in the international commercial life of the urban centers in the Bulgarian lands. Ottoman international commerce was mostly concentrated in the hands of either Croatian merchants from Dubrovnik, Greeks, or Jews from Thessaloniki and Istanbul. Together they serviced the important international markets of the Mediterranean and the Levant.

Unfortunately for the Ottoman Empire, the Turks' role in international maritime commerce suffered throughout the seventeenth century. The new sea trade routes to the Far East and the Western Hemisphere forged by England, Spain and Holland in the sixteenth century, and the struggles among various Italian commercial powers for influence and predominance in the Levant during the seventeenth century, reduced the Ottomans to playing a secondary role on the international trading stage, although they were not as yet reduced to the level of utter dependency on the Westerners as they would be in later centuries. The ships of the Italian republics, France, and even of England (under French flags) serviced the Levant ports of the empire, one of the two single most important markets for Western European commerce, the other being the Baltic Basin, which was serviced by the ships of the Hanseatic League. In the Levant, the Westerners dealt extensively through the empire's Jewish merchants. In the Balkans, the Italian traders mostly went into partnership with the Croatian merchants of Dubrovnik, who enjoyed exclusive trading rights granted by the Ottoman authorities within the region.

Because of their thriving commercial skills, the industrious Catholics of Dubrovnik had managed to retain their independence from Ottoman domination through the will of the Porte, which realized the commercial potential offered by using a free, but allied, Balkan merchant class as the middleman in Ottoman international trade relations with the West. In the final decade of the sixteenth century the Ottoman authorities briefly closed the waters of the empire to all foreign ships to ensure that the steady flow of commerce to Istanbul from the West would be concentrated in the hands of merchants who were either subjects or autonomous allies. This move especially benefited the Dubrovnik merchants and the empire's Greeks and Jews. The merchants from Dubrovnik were granted the exclusive right, as the only acceptable foreign traders, to set up shop in urban centers within the borders of the empire. In the seventeenth century there were Dubrovnik merchant companies operating on the ground in such towns in the Bulgarian lands as Sofia, Ruse, Silistra and Shumen. Though their numbers were small, their economic impact was large, for through their hands thousands of items crafted in the Bulgarian lands made their way to Italian and other Western markets.[63]

While Dubrovnik and Jewish merchants controlled most of the Ottoman sea trade with the West, Greek merchants were able to play a part as well. In actuality, the Greeks managed to broaden their role in Ottoman commercial relationships with the West during the second half of the sixteenth century by acquiring the overland trade routes that led to the heart of Europe by way of Transylvania from a declining Saxon merchant class, which was comprised of Germans residing in the major Transylvanian cities. In the seventeenth century the terms "Greek" and "Turk" were used synonymously by the Transylvanians when referring to their trading partners from the Ottoman Empire. By that time, the "Greek" merchants who visited the cities of Transylvania were actually an ethnically mixed lot. Many of these "Greeks" were really Bulgarians. In fact, 12 percent of the "Greek" merchants listed in Sibiu customs registers during the seventeenth century were ethnic Bulgarians.[64]

Transylvania proved to be the great stronghold for Bulgarian merchants during the seventeenth century. Since they were effectively barred from any significant activity in the sea-oriented international market because of the entrenched positions of the Dubrovnik and Jewish merchants, Bulgarian merchants concentrated on the Transylvanian markets opened to them through their association with the Greek overland merchants formed in the late sixteenth century. During the seventeenth century Bulgarian merchant colonies formed in Transylvanian urban centers, especially in Sibiu. They specialized in trading livestock, agricultural produce and hats. By the end of the seventeenth century over 1,300 Bulgarian merchants had traded in Transylvania.[65]

IN THE SEVENTEENTH CENTURY

Most of the Bulgarian merchants who traded on the Transylvanian markets during the seventeenth century were small traders with relatively limited capital. They hailed from such towns as Sofia, Nikopol, Tŭrnovo, Svishtov, Chiprovtsi and Melnik. A few of the larger Bulgarian merchants traveled through Transylvania and continued on as far as Hungary and Poland to conduct their livestock trading. While the few larger Bulgarian merchants might be partners or clients of Dubrovnik or Jewish merchants, the majority of the small merchants operated on their own. All had learned the ropes by serving as agents, assistants and servants of the Dubrovnik and Jewish merchants during the sixteenth century. In no case were Dubrovnik and Jewish merchants directly involved in the Bulgarian trading activity conducted in Transylvania during the seventeenth century.[66]

Both the Dubrovnik and Jewish merchants had a highly developed and tightly structured trade company organization, which required a sophisticated system of credit. The Bulgarian merchants who traded in Transylvania had one as well, though less permanently structured than their sea-oriented counterparts. Partnerships among the Bulgarian merchants tended to be infrequent, unsystematic, and usually limited to one transaction. Most of the Bulgarians trading in Transylvania preferred to do so as independent agents. Since no complex system of credit was involved in the Transylvanian trade, commercial relations were forced to retain a small merchant character. All evidence would indicate that, even if the Bulgarian merchants might have desired to commence actively competing for a share of the sea trade enjoyed by the Dubrovnik and Jewish merchants, they lacked the capital and traditions that would have been necessary. It therefore comes as no surprise that when the Catholic-inspired but ill-fated Chiprovtsi Uprising of 1688 caused the Ottoman authorities to lose trust in the merchants from Dubrovnik, Greeks, and not Bulgarians, received the lion's share of the new trading opportunities opened to merchants from within the borders of the empire.[67]

To portray the Bulgarian population of urban centers in the Bulgarian lands during the seventeenth century as one predominantly composed of numerous artisans and a few merchants would be in error. A significant portion of urban inhabitants engaged in what can be termed rural, that is agricultural, pursuits on land lying on the outskirts of town. These town-dwellers cultivated vineyards, operated grain mills, maintained beehives, and tended fields and meadows as hired day laborers in the immediate vicinity of their urban residences. Taxes on mills, cultivated land, and vineyards formed significant portions of state revenues.[68] If the town of Nikopol in 1693 can be used as a typical example, since it was one of the urban centers with a large Bulgarian population during the century, 11.3 percent of the non-Muslim residents were engaged in some form of agricultural work, mostly as vineyard-keepers and farmhands. Other hired laborers, including construction-workers, constituted 8.6 percent. Only 5.4 percent of the urban non-Muslims of Nikopol were connected with the merchant class, and 27.9 percent were artisans. Another 1.2 percent were priests and teachers. The rest of the non-Muslim population, 45.6 percent, was listed in the tax cadastres for the town as without profession. Not listed also were those non-Muslims who had been granted tax privileges for certain state services, such as those who worked within the fortress of the town, those who crafted certain types of weapons for the military, or those who had joined the *martoloses* of the region.[69]

No matter their professions, Bulgarians did not constitute a particularly affluent element in the urban populations of the seventeenth century in comparison with the wealthy Ottoman dignitaries and absentee landlords. Nor did they equal the economic standing of a great many Muslim artisans, of the resident Greek high Orthodox clergy, or of the wealthier foreign merchants. Bulgarians were mostly part of the small and lower-middle property-owning classes of the towns, possessing properties ranging in value from between 2,000 to 10,000 *akçes*. The upper-middle and upper property-owning classes, with properties valued in excess of 10,000 *akçes*, were almost exclusively comprised of non-Bulgarians.[70]

There did exist, however, some wealthy Bulgarian artisan guilds, such as the Sofia goldsmiths, broadcloth-makers, cap-makers, and *boza*-vendors (who sold millet drink), and a few individual master craftsmen within each of the *esnafs* who were economically better situated than the majority of the Bulgarian guild membership, and who furnished the Bulgarian guilds with their administrative leadership. There also existed a smattering of relatively well-to-do merchant families who were involved in the Transylvanian trade market. In the main, however, seventeenth century urban Bulgarians were either poor or only moderately wealthy members of Ottoman urban society.

Towns in the Bulgarian lands were an integral part of the Ottoman system of landholding that characterized all regions of the empire. They, either alone or in conjunction with neighboring rural areas, constituted *has* or *zeamet* lands. Large towns, such as Sofia and Plovdiv, were originally *has* holdings of the sultan, as were such mining towns as Etropole and Chiprovtsi. Sofia was later (*c.a.*, 1520) transformed into the *has* of the Rumeli *beylerbey*. Some towns were divided into more than one holding, with each holder receiving a share of the total urban revenues proportionate to his rank and the specified size of his holding.

Because of their intimate relationship with *has* lands, *vakıfs* became strongly fused with the urban economy as many holders of urban *has* properties followed the trend taking place in the countryside toward guaranteeing for themselves and their posterity the inalienable revenues associated with administering such lucrative endowments. The incomes derived from the urban *has* and *vakıf* properties were rarely invested directly into the productive sectors of urban society. Instead, they were used by their owners as sources for high-yield interest-bearing loans to merchants, artisans, local peasants and members of the ruling establishment. On the whole, the system tended to concentrate urban wealth in the hands of the Muslim administrative, military and religious authorities.

Urban revenues were derived from the common *cizye,* market and custom duties, *avaris,* tithes on land, vineyards, beehives, gardens and meadows, judicial fines, and yields from neighboring fields, to enumerate the most common sources. Revenues were also extracted from specialized urban industries, such as from metal-working, in which case, taxes were levied on forges, mines and furnaces. Compounding the ordinary taxes for which the urban inhabitants were liable were special state levies of considerable size (*mukataas*) that were collected through taxfarmers, which yielded the Porte significant amounts of revenue. For instance, in 1688 the *mukataa* alone gathered for the central treasury over four million *akçes* from Vidin and its surroundings and over 3.6 million *akçes* from the towns and surroundings of Plovdiv and Pazardzhik.[71]

On average, it has been estimated that the tax burden per non-Muslim urban household was approximately double that of the village household.[72] This, however, did not mean that the financial plight of the urban Bulgarians was necessarily twice that of their rural counterparts. The economic opportunities offered by the towns in the fields of the craft industries, trading, wage-laboring, and the like, provided the townsmen with more access to more currency than was possible in the countryside. It is most likely that, despite the rapidly rising rate of inflation experienced by the Ottoman Empire throughout the seventeenth century, the economic condition of the urban Bulgarians deteriorated far less drastically than did that of the Bulgarians in the villages. Moreover, the status of urban centers as mostly important *has* holdings and primary governmental administrative seats precluded the deleterious developments in the nature of landholding that were wreaking anarchy on the countryside.

The comparatively stable economic and social conditions that prevailed in the urban centers of the Bulgarian lands attracted an ever growing number of rural Bulgarians throughout the seventeenth century. A good part of the migrants to the towns comprised village artisans, who took advantage of an Ottoman law that permitted registered rural craftsmen to leave their land upon payment of a determined annual fee. They could then take up residence in a town, set up shop, and, if successful, live there until such a time as they were registered in the town's artisan records.[73]

The influx of rural Bulgarians into the towns of the seventeenth century, however, was not restricted to village artisans alone. The numbers of peasants who fled the countryside for the town far outstripped those of the village artisans. Their flight was facilitated by the system of landholding itself. Since the Ottoman authorities were primarily concerned with guaranteeing revenue income and not land ownership, peasants were not bound to the land they worked. The purchase and sale of land among peasants was widespread, so long as the revenues owed the state and the fief-holder did not diminish as a result of the dealings. The land involved was encumbered by certain tax obligations no matter the owner. Outright land abandonment was punishable under Ottoman law but cases of such punishment were rare during the seventeenth century, even though there was a growing rate of just such abandonment. Peasants who wished legally to set up farming near a town or to find wage-work in a town needed only to pay a similar annual fee for leaving the land as did the artisans or to find a buyer for their land and its tax encumbrances. Thus the Ottoman legal system proved powerless to prevent large scale migration from the countryside into the urban centers.[74]

Near the end of the century the migrants from the villages began to include significant numbers of *celeps* and *voynuks,* whose dealings in livestock commodities had begun to bring them substantial monetary returns. They took up residence in the towns and began to actively enter the merchant class, thus laying the foundation for their later development into an important element in a native Bulgarian middle class. That development, however, matured after the close of the seventeenth century.

Social Institutions and Cultural Life

The *zimmi* status of the seventeenth century Bulgarians determined their social position within the Ottoman Empire, and the consequences of that status defined their abilities to express their cultural self-identity.

Given the theocratic nature of the Ottoman state, the cultural self-identity of its Bulgarian subjects could only be made manifest through the vehicle of their Orthodox faith. This was so despite a strong family-oriented fundamental social organization that was essentially conservative in function with regard to language, customs and mores. Although important in their own right, language and customs alone were unable to preserve the Bulgarians from cultural pressures that threatened to expunge them as a separate people among the heterogeneous ethnic population of the Ottoman Balkans, as the numerous examples of Bulgarians who were assimilated into Muslim Turkish culture found in extant Ottoman documents dating to the seventeenth century testify. Only by linking language and customs to the Orthodox religion could the Bulgarians continue to exist within the Ottoman Empire as a separate entity.

The importance of religion in Ottoman society was given institutional form in the *millet* system used by the Turkish authorities to administer their subjects.

IN THE SEVENTEENTH CENTURY

As Orthodox Christians, the Bulgarians were placed within the Orthodox *millet* controlled and administered by the Greek Patriarchate of Constantinople and its subordinate hierarchy. Although the *millet* guaranteed the Orthodox Christians a large measure of cultural autonomy, since it essentially functioned as an independent and self-contained administrative department of the Ottoman government, the benefits derived from that situation were not distributed evenly among the various ethnic groups that comprised the *millet*. In the Bulgarian lands, Greeks controlled nearly all of the important posts in the church hierarchy above those of parish priest and local monk. The Orthodox metropolitanates and eparchies located in the Bulgarian lands, seats of archbishops and bishops, tended to exist as enclaves of Greek language and culture, strengthened and perpetuated by a system of Greek education. Essentially, the leadership of the church in the Bulgarian lands was Greek while its flock was primarily Bulgarian. It was thus within the context of the Orthodox *millet,* in which all Orthodox Christian subjects of the empire were officially categorized and over which Greeks and Greek culture ruled, that the language and customs of the Bulgarians played their most significant role in preserving a sense of Bulgarian self-identity.

Stripped of a wealthy native aristocracy by the effects of the Ottoman conquest and lacking representation within the ranks of the controlling Orthodox church hierarchy itself, the Bulgarians were forced to depend upon the beneficence of the lowest, least wealthy, and often hard-pressed elements of Ottoman society in the Bulgarian lands of the seventeenth century for support of their Orthodox culture in its Slavic form. Fortunately for the Bulgarians, Ottoman society unintentionally provided them with social institutions that permitted a measure of continuing support for religious cultural activity on a local level. The circumstances brought about by the Ottoman conquest thus had a profound impact on the relationship of the common Bulgarian to the Orthodox church and its cultural expression. Whereas prior to the Ottoman conquest the Orthodox religion in the Bulgarian lands had been completely dominated by the native aristocracy and may have been viewed by some commoners as a tool in exploiting them for the benefit and glorification of the *bolyars,* under the *millet* system of Ottoman rule that same faith came to represent all of the leaderless subject Bulgarians, and offered them a powerful vehicle for both preserving their native Slavic traditions and for expressing a sense of ethnic self-identity.[75]

Because of the situation of the Bulgarians within the Orthodox *millet,* the foci of Bulgarian cultural life were the parish churches in the villages and local monasteries.

In the countryside, the village commune played a crucial role in supporting Bulgarian Orthodox cultural life. The functions granted it by the Ottoman authorities made the commune the basic social institution available to all rural

Bulgarians, whether common or privileged in status, for preserving their autonomous self-government and basic self-esteem, functions that the village did not possess prior to the Ottoman conquest but were first granted it by the foreign conquerors. Being fundamentally conservative by nature, the village commune operated in a fashion that tended to preserve the unique material and spiritual culture of its membership, as well as its ethnic traditions and customs, by organizing and sponsoring village festivals, usually religious in nature, besides regulating all aspects of village life along traditional local precepts. One of the most important village festivals was that of the local patron saint. This *sŭbor* (fair) was a time for members of the commune to develop and cement social contacts among themselves and to express their common solidarity through their Orthodox faith.[76]

The intimate link between the commune and the Orthodox religion in Bulgarian villages was aptly demonstrated by the fact that the village priest was often numbered among the communal elders and that the village parish church, with its walled courtyard, usually served as the local civic center where communal meetings and village festivities were conducted, and where a school would be founded if it could be afforded. During times of local disturbances, which proved to be unfortunately frequent during the seventeenth century, villagers almost instinctively sought safety within the walls of the church. In times of agricultural abundance, they gathered in the church to express their thanks and to dispense charity. In short, the village church was the center of rural Bulgarian civic and social life.

In villages left without a church since the Ottoman conquest, Orthodox religious services were forced to be conducted in private homes. It became one of the primary social functions of the village commune to seek and obtain the permission of the local Ottoman authorities to rebuild or renovate the village church, which was no easy task since the orthodox Muslim Hanafid school of law forbade the erection of new Christian church structures. The procedure of gaining the permission of the Turkish authorities for new work on a church meant collecting money to pay the necessary bribes to the Muslim officials, meeting all the right Ottoman functionaries, and successfully arguing the case for the need of a church before ever beginning the actual business of organizing the raising of funds and supervising the actual construction work, which, as often as not, was carried out entirely by the villagers themselves, although master artists might be called upon to assist. Church building and renovation thus took on an aspect that was far more than merely religious devotion. They became matters of expressing local Christian village pride in overcoming the social and cultural obstacles posed by Muslim domination. The portraits or inscriptions commemorating local village elders who acted as patrons commonly found in many Bulgarian churches built or renovated during the seventeenth century served not only to demonstrate the devotion of the patrons but also to proclaim a measure of local civic pride on the part of those patrons and their desire to publicly display their successful local authority.[77]

In urban centers and large villages of mixed religious population, the Christian *mahalle* organization and its governing elders played a role similar to the village commune in supporting the local parish church, and for similar reasons. The parish church served here as civic center as well, and this civic importance was often demonstrated by the fact that many *mahalles* acquired the names of the local parish church or of a noted priest who had served as a *mahalle* elder at one time or another. In both villages and towns civic, social and spiritual life were intimately bound together at the grass-roots level, forming a cultural whole that conferred on the Bulgarians the only measure of self-identity that they could possibly possess under the circumstances of Ottoman rule.

The sources of hard, monetary support for the religious cultural life that formed such an important element in that identity were found among the various social niches open to Bulgarians who formed the membership of village communes or urban *mahalles*. In the rural regions members of the privileged corporate service groups, especially of the *celeps, madancıs, voynuks* and *dervencis,* served as the primary staples of cultural patronage since, in general, their various tax privileges provided them with the greater financial wherewithal from among the general population. During the seventeenth century *celep* villages were particularly active in cultural life, sponsoring the building and decoration of new churches in such villages as, for example, Dobŭrsko and Vukovo in the western Bulgarian lands, and in paying for the production of individual works of literature and art that were needed in every church. This is quite understandable since the *celeps'* involvement in the lucrative business of livestock commodity trading placed them in a most advantageous position for serving as cultural patrons. So too were the *madancıs* of the Samokov, Etropole and Kyustendil regions, where much lively seventeenth century Bulgarian Orthodox cultural activity was sponsored directly by thriving local mining and metal-processing populations. The important cultural center at Etropole Monastery and the erection of Alino Monastery, in the Samokov region, are but two of the many examples testifying to the extensive cultural patronage of Bulgarian miners and metal-workers during the period.

In urban centers Bulgarian artisans and their *esnaf* organizations played the leading role in patronage of Orthodox cultural activity. All-Christian and mixed Christian-Muslim *esnafs* expended large sums from their guild treasuries on public celebrations in honor of their various patron saints. Bulgarian guilds were quite active in patronizing urban parish churches, such as that of "St. Petka" in Sofia, which was built and decorated in the early seventeenth century through financial support provided by the saddle-makers *esnaf,* and which has ever since borne the name of the guild along side that of the patron saint. Monasteries lying nearby larger urban centers often received patronage from town guilds, as did, for instance, those of Kurilo and Kokalyane outside Sofia. (See Table 26.)

The Bulgarian lower clergy who staffed the local parish churches did not constitute a social category separate from that of their parishioners. Bulgarian Orthodox parish priests worked the fields or engaged in crafts just as did all the members of their parishes. In Ottoman tax cadastres parish priests were registered as liable for paying the *cizye* and *haraç*. They did, therefore, tend to spring from the more well-to-do families of the Bulgarian *reaya,* since, over top of the usual tax obligations levied on all *zimmi* subjects, acquiring the position of parish pastor usually involved an additional sum of money paid to the local bishopric and thereafter the pastor was responsible for paying an ecclesiastical tax that was higher than that levied on the common parishioner. As a consequence, the parish priest lay under a heavier overall financial burden than the rest of the parish community. This apparently was an important factor in limiting the number of parish priests relative to that of the number of available parishes. In the seventeenth century not every Bulgarian village had a resident pastor.[78]

It was during the seventeenth century that Bulgarian parish priests began to play a part in social functions outside of the strictly religious sphere. Their growing participation in village communal and urban *mahalle* leadership commonly made them spokesmen for the local Bulgarian population to the Ottoman authorities and gave them a voice in all mundane local affairs. Their participation as patrons for Orthodox cultural activity was as much an expression of pride in their new civic functions as it was of their religious devotion.[79] (See Table 26.)

If the local parish church represented the most basic expression of the existing link between seventeenth century Bulgarian society and cultural self-identity, then the monastery constituted the veritable fortress of that linkage, serving as the primary fountainhead for education, art and literary activity, as the conduit for contact with the Orthodox world outside the borders of the Ottoman Empire, and as a social and civic center on a scale broader than the local village or *mahalle*.

Monasteries represented the traditional backbone of the Orthodox religion and, by the same token, they also had played more than a strictly religious role in the lives of the Bulgarians by catering to their economic, political and cultural aspirations. As had been the case in general for the Orthodox church, in pre-Ottoman times monasteries had represented both the glory of the Christian faith and the interests of the upper classes in Bulgarian society. As such, they had become large landowners patronized by Bulgarian tsars and aristocrats alike. With the elimination of these classes by the Ottoman conquest, the monasteries of the Bulgarian lands were transformed, almost by default, into representatives of the common Bulgarian social classes.

IN THE SEVENTEENTH CENTURY

Nearly all of the medieval monasteries in the Bulgarian lands had been damaged, destroyed or abandoned during the course of the Ottoman conquest in the late fourteenth century and during the unsettled times that ensued for almost a century thereafter. By the late fifteenth and gradually over the course of the sixteenth centuries monasteries began to reappear in more secluded regions of the Bulgarian lands off the beaten paths trod by the Turkish armies, administration and colonists. Some of the larger and more famous establishments that were resurrected, like Rila Monastery in the wilds of the Rila Mountains, were able to retain their old pre-Ottoman lands and privileges by the confirmation of *vakıf* status bestowed through official *fermans* (edicts) issued by Ottoman sultans and renewable on a periodic basis. As *vakıfs*, such monasteries were able to receive income as administrators of the *vakıf*, and were responsible for making the annual payment of the endowment revenues to the designated Muslim religious establishments, wherever they might be located. Most, however, did not enjoy such widespread religious renown as did Rila, so the lands attached to them after their founding were classified as *miri* and thus subject to the authority of local *sipahis*, with whom the monasteries were forced to share administrative control, and to the attendant tax obligations placed on all such land.

In return for acknowledging the authority of the Muslim Ottoman state implied by the various landholding relationships, Bulgarian monasteries were granted the right to make use of their share of the income derived from the lands they held outright or in common with the local Turkish fief-holder. A number of the more fortunate smaller monasteries that happened to enjoy the patronage of influential persons or officials, whether Bulgarian, Greek or Turkish, were eventually able to secure certain financial concessions from the Ottoman authorities through the intercession of their patrons and to have certain of their lands declared *vakıfs*, which carried the most favorable status in the Ottoman system of landholding by freeing those monasteries from both the *cizye* and *avaris*.[80]

For the most part, the monasteries that arose after the Ottoman conquest were eventually set up with inviolable land leases, which were worked either by the monks themselves or in conjunction with local villagers. On their lands, monasteries engaged in farming, vegetable gardening, viticulture, dairying, beekeeping, and orchard cultivation. A large part of the average monastic economy was involved with livestock-breeding and the production of leather craft goods. While most of the economy of the monasteries was internally oriented, monasteries often played important roles in the local economy and markets. For instance, monastery food products, especially breads, cheeses, wines and *rakiya* (plum or grape brandy), were sold on local markets in villages and towns. Monasteries often owned and operated water mills for grinding local harvests of wheat and rye. Lumbering and operating lumberyards were common monastic economic activities. On all such endeavors, monasteries were responsible for paying the requisite taxes to the Ottoman authorities.[81]

The reason for the resurrection of Bulgarian monasteries lay in the simple belief held by the Bulgarian population that their Orthodox faith would somehow be incomplete without them. So it developed that the local Bulgarian parish organizations of the villages and towns played the leading active role in recreating these traditional strongholds of the Orthodox faith. Village communes and urban *mahalles* and *esnafs* took on duties as patrons of monasteries throughout the Bulgarian lands, contributing to them their time and money to ensure their continued survival and material well-being. They filled the monastery churches with rich religious vessels, books and icons, and made monasteries beneficiaries of donations and bequests. In return, the monasteries developed into centers of intensive religious and social life. They were schools and cultural centers in the fields of church literature and art. At the same time they served as locations for local festivals, meetings and gatherings of all kinds, market places and bazaars. They often maintained direct contact with their lay patrons by establishing satellite houses (*metohs*) in the midst of village and town communities and by the work of their itinerant, travelling monks (*taxidiots*), who moved throughout the Bulgarian lands on errands, usually involving alms-collecting.

Out of the developments on the levels of the local parish and the monastery brought about by the conditions imposed on the Bulgarians through their complete incorporation into Ottoman society, a new sort of relationship, relative to pre-Ottoman times, arose between the church and the laity in the Bulgarian lands. The church grew more democratic and more closely involved in local social and civic activities than it had been in the past, causing the growth of strong cultural and social ties to form between religion and society. This new course of socio-cultural linkage forged between the Orthodox church and the mass of Bulgarian society led to a strong sense of ethnic self-identity. This process emerged in its mature form during the seventeenth century.[82]

2. Threats to Bulgarian Orthodox Culture Posed by Ottoman Society

The existence of the Bulgarians as a Christian subject population of a powerful Muslim state negatively affected their overall social status. This situation placed serious limitations on their abilities to support Orthodox culture. Moreover, Ottoman society also posed certain cultural menaces for the Orthodox Bulgarians that not only limited their cultural expression but also threatened to extinguish it in large degree, if not entirely. The three foreign cultural threats faced by Bulgarian Orthodox culture during the seventeenth century were rooted in Islam, Greek Orthodoxy and Roman Catholicism.

Conversions to Islam and Muslim Reaction

The most dangerous potential threat to Bulgarian Orthodox culture during the seventeenth century was that posed by the Ottoman Muslim ruling class. The Bulgarians' position as *zimmi* subjects within a Muslim-dominated society was affected by the military and political decline of the empire that set in during the final decades of the sixteenth century and that continued thereafter. The Ottoman economy staggered under heavy inflation, the repercussions of which were felt in the soaring costs of supporting the military and administrative establishments of the state. The Porte was forced to place constantly increasing monetary demands upon its subject populations. The rising tax burden served to erode the potential economic base for the support of Orthodox cultural activity among the Bulgarians, thereby limiting its extent.

The political ailments of the empire were reflected in its social fabric by the dissolution that began to emerge in the system of military fiefs and in the ranks of the Janissary standing military forces. The inability of the empire to expand, and thus create new sources of land, wealth, and slaves that, after all, were the mainstays of both institutions, as well as the harm done to both by the economic crisis that resulted, since both the *sipahis* and the Janissaries depended on fixed incomes, led to a rise in provincial brigandage and summary violence. The economically strapped feudal and salaried troops turned to assorted depredations to gain increased sources of cash while, at the same time, venting their frustrations concerning the unfavorable turn of events experienced by the empire as a whole.

The defenseless Christian subjects of the empire were made the scapegoats for their Muslim lords' political and economic woes. Discontent with the worsening situation of the empire spread from the military ranks to the halls of government.

A few notations found in extant Bulgarian manuscripts dating from the seventeenth century mentioned widespread acts of violence perpetrated by various Ottoman authorities on the Christian Bulgarian population. One of the most thorough of such accounts was a rather extensive chronicle note penned in a sixteenth century work during 1690 by a certain Petŭr, a priest from the village of Mirkovo. In his note Petŭr described the campaigns of Sultan Mehmed IV (1648-1687) in Poland (1672-1676) and Transylvania (1684-1687). At the same time, he decried the destruction of Christian properties located in the western and northern Bulgarian lands that had accompanied those military efforts, as well as the cruel suppression by the Turks of the 1688 Bulgarian Chiprovtsi uprising. Earlier, in 1657, a Bulgarian Roman Catholic bishop, Filip Stanislavov (1612-1674), noted in a letter that the Turks were making a "slaughterhouse" of the Bulgarian lands. There was such desolation of Bulgarian churches during the latter half of the century that a number of foreign travelers' accounts, written by men who passed through the Bulgarian lands during that period, noted the great lack of church buildings among the Bulgarians, the poverty of those that did exist, and the desert-like aspect of large expanses of the Bulgarian countryside.[1]

Acts of violent Muslim reaction against the Bulgarians and the evidence of their Christian culture were not limited strictly to materialistic ends but were also directed against the persons of the Bulgarians themselves. Ottoman law weighted justice in favor of Muslim individuals, especially when questions of mixed religious affiliations were involved. In cases brought before the Turkish *kadı* that pitted Christians against Muslims, even if both sides were of the same family, rulings virtually always were handed down in favor of the Muslim parties. Moreover, only Muslim descendents were permitted to inherit the patrimony of a deceased Muslim, even if the deceased had once been a Christian.[2]

The high Greek clergy who filled the Orthodox church organization in the Bulgarian lands were enmeshed in the grip of heavy indebtedness to their creditors from within the Ottoman ruling class but experienced little direct brutality from the authorities because of the role they played in the political administration of the empire. The lower, Bulgarian clergy, however, were left vulnerable to all sorts of brutalizing acts by their Turkish and, as we shall see, Greek overlords. Hardest hit by the violence that characterized Muslim relations with the Christian Bulgarians during the second half of the seventeenth century were the local village priests. They were in closer contact with local Ottoman civil authorities than were Bulgarian monks, who enjoyed a measure of isolation in so far as the Ottoman authorities were concerned. Incidents such as Ottoman troops chaining clergymen to the doors of their churches and forcing them to pay large ransoms for their release were not unknown.

In 1663 Petŭr Bogdan Bakshich (1601-1674), the noted Bulgarian Roman Catholic bishop, related how one evening while he was at Chiprovtsi Monastery a group of Turkish soldiers arrived and forced him to serve them drinks at table throughout the night. He was also required to furnish fodder for their horses. Bogdan noted that the Turks would often arrive at a church or monastery and demand the finest of the available food, drink, and whatever else that caught their fancy. Meanwhile, they would verbally, and oftentimes physically, abuse the unfortunate priest or monk who had become their unwilling host. No pay was ever offered for the goods and services extracted by these uninvited Muslim guests.[3]

As difficult as were the personal abuse and violence suffered by the Bulgarian lower clergy, who, after all, were the primary purveyors of the Bulgarians' Slavic form of Orthodox culture, a more total threat to that culture was the pressure often exerted on the Bulgarian subjects by the Muslim authorities to forsake the Orthodox church completely for that of the Prophet. Admittedly, much of the pressure for conversion to Islam was inherent in the Ottoman socio-political system itself. The fact that Muslim subjects of the Porte were free of most onerous restrictions, duties, and taxes levied on the "infidel" subjects made voluntary conversion to Islam seem an attractive alternative to many Christian Bulgarians. In effect, conversion meant joining the dominant element in Ottoman society and, because of the decay of the *devşirme,* provided the only opportunity for social advancement. Throughout the entire period of Ottoman rule in the Bulgarian lands a large number of Christian Bulgarians weighed the cultural advantages of preserving their Orthodox faith and, hence, their sense of separate self-identity, against the social and economic advantages entailed by embracing Islam and its culture, and thus, for all intents and purposes, becoming "Turks," and opted for the latter. Once such a step was taken, it was irrevocable. Having accepted the Islamic faith, anyone who then later reverted to his former beliefs was liable for summary execution, as had been Nikolai Novi Sofiiski in the sixteenth century and a number of lesser known Bulgarians during the seventeenth.[4]

The decision to abandon Orthodox Christianity for Islam was eased somewhat for the Bulgarians by the existence of syncretic Muslim religious orders (*derviş* sects) that took root in the Bulgarian lands following their conquest. Those sects, while officially *sunni* (orthodox) in their Muslim faith, formed part of the *sufi* (mystical) branch of Islam, and they often incorporated into their governing ideologies certain elements of Christian or Zoroastrian popular belief, such as the veneration of saints and holy shrines, the Christian concept of confession, and even, in some cases, the Christian idea of the sacrament of holy communion.

Two syncretic Muslim sects grew particularly well established in the eastern Bulgarian lands over the course of the fifteenth and sixteenth centuries. One was the Bedreddin order, which had been founded during the early fifteenth century by *şeyh* Bedreddin, the son of a Muslim *kadı* and a Christian mother. A scholar who had become a Muslim mystic, Bedreddin was a leading spokesman for religious toleration within the Ottoman Empire, the merging of Islam, Christianity and Judaism into a single faith, and the social betterment of rural free peasants and nomads at the expense of the Ottoman feudal classes. The eastern Bulgarian lands became the primary arena of Bedreddin's activities, from which in 1416 he led a popular revolt against Sultan Mehmed I (1413-1421), with many local Christian Bulgarians among his followers. The revolt was crushed by forces loyal to the sultan and Bedreddin met a tragic death. His followers, however, continued to adhere to the sort of religious philosophy that he had espoused and grew into a *derviş* order of some note in their Dobrudzhan strongholds.

The other, and more influential, syncretic *derviş* order in the Bulgarian lands was that of the Bektaşi. The order was founded in the thirteenth century by the semi-mythical figure, *haci* Bektaş Veli, whose ancestry was traced back through caliph Ali to Abu Bekir, the most revered successor of Mohammed among *sunni* Muslims. Such a distinguished lineage gave the order a measure of respectability in high Ottoman legal circles that no other *sufi* sect could match. By the early sixteenth century the Bektaşi were officially recognized as *sunni* by the authorities and quickly became attached to the corps of Janissaries as its spiritual representatives.

The Bektaşi were the most syncretic of all the *sufi* sects. It was they who adopted pseudo-Christian rituals, such as communion and confession (with its absolution of sin), and they went so far as to make the sign of the cross as a gesture of respect. Prohibitions on the consumption of alcohol and pork were relaxed among the order's members, and women were permitted a larger measure of personal freedom than was usual among Muslims. It can be argued that the Bektaşi were actually only quasi or dubious Muslims at best.[5]

Both of these sects shared certain traits in common regarding their origins and their propagation in the Bulgarian lands. Undoubtedly, these syncretic religious orders arose in response to the growing number of non-Muslims, mostly Christians, incorporated into the dominant Islamic faith of the empire. The new converts brought with them their old Christian cultural baggage. Thus the *derviş* orders were an attempt to ameliorate the cultural shock for the converts while, simultaneously, creating areas of possible compromise within the strict precepts of Islam that would facilitate future Muslim expansion within the Christian world.

As wandering members of the *derviş* orders took over formerly Christian churches, and even saints, claiming them as their own Muslim property, the sects grew closer to the common Christian population of the Bulgarian lands.[6]

IN THE SEVENTEENTH CENTURY

Primarily rural in their field of operations, the Muslim sects blended folk Islam, which recognized Muslim "saints," or holy men, and held certain locales as sacred in the eyes of God for one reason or another, with the similar folk Christianity that represented the dominant form of religious belief among the illiterate subject populations of the Bulgarian countryside. In many instances, especially with the Bektaşi, no discernible differences in local religious custom or superstition existed between the *derviş* Muslims and the poor Christian villagers. The flexibility, eclecticism and pragmatism exhibited by the Muslim sects in their systems of belief were virtually boundless, and a place was often found for the most un-Islamic of rituals and practices. There can be little wonder, then, that the wandering *dervişes* scored numerous victories in winning converts for their particular form of Muslim faith from among the rural Bulgarian population.

Working hand-in-hand with the *derviş* orders in providing an avenue for the conversion of Christian Bulgarians to Islam were the Ottoman military formations stationed within the Bulgarian lands. A direct correlation existed between the location of most of such units and the areas of most intensive *derviş* activity. Both were found primarily in the eastern and southeastern Bulgarian regions.

The most obvious military institution involved in the conversion process was the corps of Janissaries, which was traditionally recruited through the *devşirme*. Yet by the seventeenth century the *devşirme* had, for the most part, fallen into decline and was thus a factor of relatively little consequence in the overall scheme of the Muslim conversion process in the Bulgarian lands during the period.

Much the same can be said for the *sipahi* feudal cavalry forces of the empire. Many local Christian *bolyars* had joined the Ottoman ranks in the early years of the period of conquest in the Balkans, fighting along side their mounted Muslim counterparts. Those Christian *sipahis* gradually melted into the Muslim element of the military as they found that membership in the dominant faith made their lives simpler and less taxing (in every sense of the word). Still, in the second quarter of the fifteenth century nearly a third of all Ottoman *sipahi* forces in Europe was Christian. By the end of that century, however, all members of the landed cavalry in Europe were Muslims.[7]

Military formations organized as auxiliaries to the Janissary standing infantry and *sipahi* landed cavalry traditionally played an important role in absorbing Christian Bulgarians into the Muslim ranks and continued to do so during the seventeenth century. Irregular Ottoman units stationed in the Bulgarian lands, such as the *yayas* (free peasant infantry), *müsellems* (free peasant light cavalry) and *akıncıs* (strike cavalry), though in the past often regarded by scholars as exclusively Turkish in ethnic composition, were, by the seventeenth century, of mixed ethnic character, with a significant number of Christians filling their ranks. Most of those Christian Ottoman warriors saw enlistment in the military as a sure way to escape the lot of non-Muslim peasant life. Over time, the Christian members of these units were converted to Islam and melted into the general Muslim population of the Bulgarian lands.

The *yürük* colonists transplanted to the Bulgarian lands from Anatolia by the Ottoman authorities in the fifteenth century played a similar role in assimilating Orthodox Bulgarians into Islamic Turkish culture. Organized under military unit formations (*ocaks*), which originally had been exclusively composed of semi-nomadic Turks, these tribesmen originally performed irregular services in conjunction with Ottoman regular forces during their campaigns in Europe. Losses in battle during the sixteenth century necessitated an influx of new recruits to bolster those units' depleted ranks. At mid century they may have numbered as many as 25,500 effectives. By that time, it is highly likely that the strengths of the originally Turkish *yürük* units were being augmented by enslaved military captives from the armies of the Turk's Christian enemies and by local Bulgarian recruits. Those Christians enlisted into the *yürük ocaks* swiftly underwent conversion to Islam and assimilation into Turkish culture. By the early seventeenth century only a fragment of the Christian inductees retained their faith in any of these military units. By century's end, there were none.[8]

Pressure on the Bulgarians to convert to Islam apparently was, at times, also exerted as part of an active policy pursued by the Ottoman administrative authorities.[9] The regime of Selim I (1512-1520), whose sombre character earned him the sobriquet of "the Grim," was strongly fundamentalist in the expression of Islamic belief and imposed strict enforcement of Hanafite precepts on the Bulgarian subject population. Individual cases of anti-Christian actions were not unknown, such as the martyrdom of Georgi Novi Sofiiski in Sofia (1515). The period of Selim's reign resulted in the total elimination of the native Bulgarian *bolyar* class. Thousands of Bulgarians accepted Islam and its culture and were thus lost to the native Slavic culture of their homeland, as by the close of the sixteenth century both the Ottoman authorities and the subject peoples had come to equate Islam with the concept of all that was meant by the word, "Turk."[10]

The wars of the empire with its European Christian enemies that commenced during the mid seventeenth century fanned the flames of Muslim fanaticism, which found a ready outlet for the authorities' anger over the unpleasantly sterile fruits of combat in terrorizing the subject Christian population nearest at hand — the Bulgarians. Bulgarians converted to Islam in such large numbers during the second half of the century, and the conversions were so extensive, including the populations of entire regions, that nationalist Bulgarian scholarship has attributed the events to a concerted policy of forced mass conversion conducted by the Ottoman civil and military authorities, apparently despite the potential loss to the central treasury of tax revenue and obligatory services that such a step entailed.

IN THE SEVENTEENTH CENTURY

According to this view, since all of the major military routes in the empire's European possessions passed through the Bulgarian lands, the Porte felt that only by such means could the vital military lines of communications linking the European theater fronts to the supremely important base of the empire's capital be made secure.[11]

Nowhere in the Bulgarian lands were mass conversions more far-reaching and dramatic during the seventeenth century than those that occurred during the third quarter of the century in the regions of the Rhodope Mountains. The Rhodope converts, commonly termed *pomaks*, have received particular attention in a number of scholarly studies dealing with the Ottoman period in Bulgarian history.[12] The scholarly popularity of the Rhodope conversions can be explained by the fact that a relatively large number of primary sources purportedly dating to the period of the conversions survived the ravages that accompanied the process.

Three sources in particular expressly dealt with the origins and commencement of the conversions in the Chepino region of the northwestern Rhodopes. The principal source was a lengthy chronicle note written in Bulgarian on the final page of a Slavonic religious text in approximately 1666. The author of the note was a Bulgarian priest, Metodii Draginov, from the village of Korovo in the region of Chepino. In a literary style quite uncommon for notes of that nature and time, Draginov graphically described the events surrounding the forced conversions among the Bulgarian inhabitants of the region.[13] The remaining two sources were shorter in length. One was a note (1670) made in a manuscript once housed in the Pazardzhik monastery of "St. Petŭr." The other, incorrectly dated 1620, was a page from a chronicle written in the village of Golyamo Belovo. Both corroborated Draginov's account and even expanded upon it in minor instances.[14] All told, these three notes provided the most comprehensive story of forced mass conversions in the Bulgarian lands during the entire period of Ottoman rule. It went as the following.

Sultan Mehmed IV despatched his grand *vezir*, Ahmed Köprülü (1661-1676), at the head of a massive land and sea expedition against the Venetian city of Candia on the island of Crete. Part of the land forces that were to participate in the campaign were mustered in the Bulgarian lands near Plovdiv and placed under the command of the Rumeli *beylerbey*, Pehlivan Mehmed *paşa*. Mehmed marched his contingents southward through the Rhodopes to affect a junction with other forces assembling in the Morea. During his march south Mehmed accomplished the conversion of the Chepino Bulgarians. (See Map 3.)

As a pretext for the conversions Mehmed declared the Bulgarians of Chepino rebels against the state. Archbishop Gavril, the Greek metropolitan of Plovdiv, had informed him that the Bulgarians in that region refused to pay the required ecclesiastical taxes due the Plovdiv metropolitanate and were, therefore, rebels.

Armed with such an excuse, Mehmed, upon entering the Chepino village of Kostandovo, threw the village notables and priest into chains and would have had them executed had not one of his *imams* (prayer leaders), Hasan *hoca,* suggested that the Christians pay for their lives by converting to Islam. The prisoners readily accepted this proffered pardon. Mehmed then had declared throughout the Chepino region that, upon his return from the campaign against Candia, he intended to slaughter all the Christians of Chepino. At the same time, Mehmed let it be known that he offered to spare all those Christians who would forsake their Orthodox beliefs for those of Islam. Added incentive for conversion was given by Mehmed's emphasis in his proclamation on the tax benefits to be gained by such action. Hasan and four other assistant *imams,* supported by a detachment of Janissaries, then set about converting the inhabitants of the seven Chepino villages, as well as those of other mountain villages in nearby regions, while Mehmed marched off in the direction of Thessaloniki.

Between the months of May and August Hasan and his companions successfully fulfilled their task. Their work was aided by a local famine that raged in the region during those months. All who accepted the Islamic faith were given grain from the government warehouse in the town of Pazardzhik. Those who refused conversion had their homes destroyed and were forced as refugees into the mountains, where they founded new settlements. To fan the flames of conversion further, the new converts were granted the right to pillage the properties of the Orthodox church in the region. By August over 200 churches and as many as 33 monasteries were destroyed.[15]

Meanwhile, on his way to Thessaloniki, Mehmed marched his troops through the southwestern Bulgarian region of Razlog, where they committed any number of atrocities against the Christian population. A large proportion of the inhabitants fled or were evicted by the Ottoman soldiers, and many Bulgarians, fearing the widespread destruction and violence involved in the nearby Chepino developments, gave up their faith for that of Islam.

The case for the forced conversion of the Chepino Bulgarians would seem indisputable, given the documentation. Unfortunately, none of the three sources used in reconstructing the Chepino affair are extant in the original. All were first published by Bulgarian scholars during the final third of the nineteenth century, which was a period of intense nationalistic fervor among the Bulgarians. Draginov's note appeared in printed form in 1870, eight years prior to the liberation of the country and in the midst of intense anti-Greek and anti-Turkish national sentiments over the question of the Bulgarian Exarchate. The published note contained elements of both. The Pazardzhik note appeared in 1894 and the Belovo chronicle extract followed in 1898. Both restated, in abbreviated form, the tale of Draginov, and both used exactly the same descriptive details and names as those found in Draginov's note. The Belovo chronicle extract, the final source of the three to be published, almost identically followed the style and presentation of the Pazardzhik note in all divergences from Draginov.

Because the circumstances surrounding the "discovery" of the three sources for the Chepino forced conversions remain a mystery, and because the time in which they were "discovered" was so explosively nationalistic, their veracity may be seriously questioned. That mass conversions even occurred during the seventeenth century, therefore, may be questionable. Setting these disputed sources aside, however, the heightened anti-Christian Muslim reaction that found vent in widespread ravages of Bulgarian Orthodox properties and acts of violence against the Christian Bulgarian population, especially in regions affected by the warfare of the second half of the seventeenth century, has been well-documented in extant verifiable sources, such as the note of Petŭr of Mirkovo and those that referred to the devastation that accompanied Ottoman military operations against the Habsburg forces during the final two decades of the seventeenth century.[16]

While much of the violence and destruction was conducted by Ottoman civil and military personnel, a good deal was also carried out by neophyte Bulgarian converts eager to prove their newfound religious devotion to the Muslim authorities. For example, the region of the Rhodopes in the vicinity of Smolyan was ravaged by a small contingent of Turkish troops assisted by a horde of Bulgarian Muslim converts. A number of Orthodox churches, schools, and works of literature were destroyed and most of the region's religious valuables were plundered. The local Orthodox bishop, Visarion, escaped capture by the Muslims and fled into the highlands at the head of a large band of Bulgarians who were determined to fight for their faith. Only Visarion's mountain stronghold of Raikovo was able to withstand the wave of Muslim depredations for a period of a year. In July 1670 Visarion and ten of his bodyguards were captured by an armed troop of Turks after a brief struggle. The captives were taken to nearby Smolyan, where Visarion was tortured and ultimately put to death for refusing to set an example for his followers by renouncing Orthodoxy. His bodyguards were released in the vain hope that, by spreading the tale of Visarion's fate, the rebel Bulgarians' spirits would be broken completely. Eventually, with the aid of the Greek Patriarchate, the Raikovo Bulgarians successfully managed to survive the Muslim threat. Most all of the other villages in the central and northern Rhodopes succumbed, however, and passed out of Bulgarian hands into those of the Muslims.[17]

During 1689 Habsburg forces advanced south of the Danube deep into Ottoman territory as far as Niš in the Serbian and Skopje in the Macedonian lands. The Porte called upon every available ally for assistance in meeting this serious Habsburg threat. One of the allies who responded in that same year to the sultan's call was the *han* of the Crimean Tatars, Selim Giray. He entered the Bulgarian lands from the northeast with an army of 30,000 Tatar cavalry. They passed westward over the Bulgarian Danubian Plain, and by November 1689 they reached the regions of Sofia, Kyustendil and Kumanovo in the western lands. The passing of Giray's Tatar horde left in its wake a belt of widespread destruction of Christian Bulgarian villages and a large number of converts to Islam.[18]

Exactly how many Orthodox Bulgarians were converted to Islam during the seventeenth century is unknown. It is known, however, that the Christian population of the Bulgarian lands declined by over 240,000 persons during that time, and, given the evidence for the intensive forces favoring conversion to Islam that operated widely in those lands, it can be assumed that a substantial portion of the demographic decline of Bulgarian Christians was caused by that phenomenon, whether accepted voluntarily or by force. Those who converted became, for all intents and purposes, Turks.[19]

Greek Domination of the Orthodox Church Hierarchy

An inherent weakness of governing the Orthodox subject population of the empire through the vehicle of the *millet* system first revealed itself within the Bulgarian lands during the seventeenth century. Greek control of the ecclesiastical hierarchy that regulated the spiritual, and often many aspects of the secular lives of an ethnically heterogeneous Orthodox population resulted in the imposition of Greek, hence foreign, religious cultural forms on the non-Greek members of the general Orthodox community of the empire. To be sure, in the period prior to the rise of modern nationalist conceptions, religion more often than ethnicity defined a given people's sense of self-identity. Yet it would be mistaken to discount totally the significance of ethnic identity among the Orthodox Christians of the Ottoman Empire during the pre-modern period. The Bulgarians, whose past political and religious greatness to some extent was preserved in their Slavic form of Orthodox culture, demonstrated their awareness of the difference between Greek and Slavic cultural forms of their common religion, and the danger to their native form of religious culture posed by Greek control of the church in the Bulgarian lands.

One of the consequences of the Turkish conquest of Tŭrnovo in 1393 was the abolition of the Bulgarian Patriarchate of Tŭrnovo (1394) and its reduction to the status of a common metropolitanate under the direct authority of the Constantinopolitan Greek Patriarch. The oldest organized Bulgarian Orthodox church, the Archbishopric-Patriarchate of Ohrid, suffered a less drastic fate. Although Ohrid technically retained its autocephalous status after the Ottoman conquest of the region, and the title, "Bulgarian," remained attached to that seat until 1767, when it was abolished as an autonomous ecclesiastical entity, nearly all of its incumbents and their subordinate prelates were Greeks installed by the Patriarch of Constantinople. The Bulgarian title was, for the most part, empty.[20]

At the time of the reorganization of the Orthodox church in Bulgaria following the Ottoman conquest, Bulgarian clergy occupying the metropolitan seats in the Bulgarian lands were expelled, just as had been Patriarch Evtimii (1375-1393) from Tŭrnovo. In their stead were installed Greek prelates, who were the appointees of the Patriarch of Constantinople. A similar situation developed in the clerical offices at the metropolitan seats. Greek teachers, artists, monsignors and priests filled most of the lower clerical positions at the metropolitanates and episcopates in the Bulgarian lands.

Under the ecclesiastical reorganization, the Orthodox Bulgarians were divided among three separate autocephalous churches. Those Bulgarians inhabiting the Macedonian lands fell under the authority of Ohrid, which until around 1530 also controlled the metropolitanates of Vidin and Sofia. The latter two seats were then taken over by the Patriarchate of Constantinople. When the Serbian Patriarchate of Peć (Ipek) was reestablished in 1557 it received authority over the Kyustendil metropolitanate. All other metropolitanates in the Bulgarian lands were governed directly by the Greek Patriarchate.

The privileged position of the Greek church within the Ottoman administration as chief representative of the Orthodox *millet* ensured that the takeover of the Bulgarian ecclesiastical hierarchy by Greek clergy was sanctioned by the Ottoman authorities. Over the period separating the fifteenth and seventeenth centuries, the Greek metropolitanates in the Bulgarian lands became centers of Greek colonization. By the seventeenth century the towns of Sofia, Plovdiv and Tŭrnovo were teeming, to a greater or lesser extent, with Greek merchants, artisans, subordinate clergy and hellenized Kutsovlahs, who settled in some of the nearby villages (*e.g.*, Stanimaka, near Plovdiv, and Arbanasi, near Tŭrnovo).[21] With the support of the high Greek clergy and colonists, the Orthodox administrative centers in the Bulgarian lands were transformed into Greek cultural centers.

Although the Greek expropriation of the high ecclesiastical offices meant that native Bulgarian clergy were reduced to filling positions lower in the church hierarchy, such as parish priests and friars, Slavic Orthodox cultural activity by the Bulgarians during the seventeenth century was not actively suppressed by the Greek religious authorities to the extent that it was to be during the following two centuries. In church administrative centers the Slavic liturgy was not totally expunged; divine services were celebrated in Slavic if the majority of the attending congregation was Bulgarian. Bulgarian *literati* often worked unhindered at the metropolitan centers (as did, for example, Daniil Etropolski at Tŭrnovo for a time), sometimes at the express wishes and under the personal patronage of Greek prelates. Bulgarian craftsmen and artists were employed in building and decorating churches whose functions were reserved basically for Greek worshipers, such as those in Bachkovo Monastery (1603, 1643) and the church of "The Nativity" in the village of Arbanasi (1632-1681), the decorations in both of which later served as models for Bulgarian revivalist artists.[22]

Despite the few positive aspects in the position of the Bulgarians within the Orthodox church of the empire, negative factors outweighed any benefits derived by the Orthodox Bulgarian population during the seventeenth century. Bulgarians were effectively barred from obtaining any kind of economic support for Slavic Orthodox culture from church treasuries. Bulgarian Slavic cultural activity could usually find patronage only from the lower, parish-level clerics and Bulgarian monastery treasuries. Since such resources were limited, funds for conducting Slavic cultural activity required augmentation by donations from those in the lay population who could afford to spare such monies, such as, for instance, merchant and artisan guildsmen, and members of corporate service groups enjoying fiscal privileges recognized by the Ottoman authorities. Unfortunately, Bulgarian society as a whole suffered under a dual fiscal oppression imposed by both the Ottoman civil and Greek ecclesiastical authorities. Much of the money that should have been available for the support of Slavic cultural activity was drained away by state and church taxes, and was thus placed into the hands of those without thought for the Bulgarians' native cultural well-being.

The monetary crisis of the seventeenth century had repercussions in the Orthodox church's relationship with the Ottoman Porte and with its own internal administration. Following the establishment of the Orthodox *millet* in 1454, it became customary for each newly appointed patriarch to pay a sum of money *(peşkeş)* to the sultan in return for the *berat* that legitimized the prelate's installation. In the late fifteenth century the value of this officially extorted gift to the sultan stood at a thousand *ducats*. By the reign of Grand Vezir Ahmed Köprülü the value had increased to 20,000 *thalers*.[23] To obtain the patriarchal throne a candidate was required to possess either his own personal wealth or a stable source of credit, which usually came from among the Ottoman aristocracy, so that he could pay the fee due the sultan for the *berat* of investiture. In addition, gifts for all the high dignitaries of the Porte were required before a candidate's name was considered for elevation to the highest office in Eastern Christendom.

During the troubled financial times of the seventeenth century the patriarchal throne represented a lucrative source of income for the Ottoman imperial treasury. Patriarchs were appointed and then removed in rapid succession on the slightest of pretexts so that the customary extortion money could be collected as frequently as possible. The internal struggle among potential candidates for the patriarchal throne, which came to characterize the seventeenth century in the

Greek church, resulted in the rise of only the wealthiest Greek clerics to ecclesiastical leadership. By the close of the century the Phanariots, so called because they were scions of wealthy Greek merchant families residing in the Phanar (Lighthouse) district of Istanbul, were firmly entrenched in a monopolistic position as holders of the highest Orthodox ecclesiastical offices, both in Istanbul and in the Ottoman provinces.[24]

Sadly, the expenses incurred in the acquisition of the patriarchal throne were passed along to the subordinate metropolitanates with interest. It became customary for all provincial prelates to pay a similar *peşkeş* to the Patriarch before being affirmed in their offices. The amount of the payment varied according to the assessed value of the seat, but it usually fell between 800 and 50,000 *akçes*. The Porte collaborated with the Patriarch in this matter by stipulating the amount of *peşkeş* due the Patriarch in the mandatory imperial *berats* of investiture given new metropolitans. In addition, every newly installed provincial prelate was required to pay to the Patriarchate an ecclesiastical tax, the *emvatikon*, which could amount to as much as 1,000 *ducats*. Naturally, this situation, which mirrored that of the Patriarch's *vis-à-vis* the Porte, resulted in the Patriarch frequently changing his provincial prelates to collect the investiture fees as often as possible.[25]

As was the case in the capital, the provincial church seats were thrown open to the highest bidders. Quite frequently, men who were totally incompetent to fill administrative offices, or even unable to demonstrate a basic level of literacy, were elevated to high church offices. Also akin to the situation in Istanbul, the struggles for high provincial church offices quite often involved the incursion of huge debts by the contenders, and those debts were usually made incumbent upon the metropolitanate as a whole to repay once the new prelate was appointed.[26]

In the domino effect of Orthodox fiscal responsibility during the seventeenth century, the ultimate bearer of the burden of payment was the local Orthodox parishioner. Not only were the local Orthodox populations responsible for supplying the money to repay the loans of their prelates, they also bore the costs of all the extraordinary payments due the Porte by the church for replacement *berats* of investiture upon the death of the sultan who had issued the originals, as well as of the taxes levied on the church by the state. Fixed ecclesiastical taxes, due both the Patriarch and the local metropolitan, were ultimately raised through collections and imposts on the general Orthodox population. The lower clergy were held responsible for the payment of all the various monies due the church. If the demands for payment were not met, those unfortunate men were forced to answer to the metropolitan at the price of having their church or monastery valuables pawned. Since an individual metropolitan's debts were transferred to his successor in the event that he was replaced or died prior to satisfying his creditors, the financial plight of the lower clergy, local religious establishments and parishioners quite often grew heavy. The more notable the metropolitanate at the time that its leadership changed hands, the more irretrievable became its financial position and the heavier became the poverty of its churches, monasteries, lower clergy and parishioners.[27]

The metropolitan was granted the right by the Ottoman authorities to collect ecclesiastical taxes and fees "conforming to the ancient usage."[28] Ecclesiastical income was derived from contributions made by monasteries *(manastir resmi)*, duties charged by priests for the performance of certain rituals (*e.g.*, baptisms and marriages), special monetary donations on days of religious festivals, devotional tributes imposed at holy shrines, donations made at pilgrimage sites, taxes levied on certain divine services, and from the sale of small religious trinkets. Upon ordination, priests were required to make a monetary payment to the metropolitanate, and upon the elevation of a new metropolitan, the newly invested prelate was granted a cash gift *(philotimon)* from all the parishes and monasteries placed under his authority.[29]

Normally, the monies owed the metropolitanate were dispatched to the city where the seat was located by representatives from the various districts within the metropolitan's jurisdiction. If the metropolitan was in desperate need of funds, however, or a new metropolitan, upon elevation, desired that his *philotimon* and the Patriarch's *emvatikon* be promptly paid, he would conduct a personal tour of the districts falling under his authority, or else order a personal representative to do so. Such tours were apt demonstrations of the position enjoyed by the Greek Orthodox church as a pseudo-official branch of the Ottoman state administration.

In 1640 Petŭr Bogdan described one such tour of the Bulgarian countryside as conducted by a typical Greek metropolitan.[30] He related that the prelate was accompanied by a detachment of Janissaries who acted, in essence, as the church's henchmen. The poverty-stricken peasants were beaten mercilessly if they proved unable to pay the money demanded of them. In effect, the legitimate ecclesiastical taxes were virtually extorted from the parishioners under the threat of violence. Since church taxes constantly increased, only the limitations found in Ottoman *berats* placed on amounts that could be legally demanded prevented totally unbridled extortion on the part of the Greek metropolitans.

Because of such ecclesiastical fiscal oppression, coupled with the exactions made by the Turkish authorities in state taxes, there can be little wonder that a number of Bulgarian monasteries, especially large establishments such as Rila Monastery, dispatched alms gathering delegations to Orthodox lands lying outside the empire, to Russia, for instance, and to the Romanian Principalities. The universal demand for money was such that the Patriarchate itself sent deputies to Muscovy and to the Romanian lands in efforts to solicit donations in behalf of the Bulgarian metropolitanates and monasteries.[31] By the close of the seventeenth century, however, no solution to the constant problem of Orthodox indebtedness and the unremitting impoverishment of the Orthodox faithful in the Bulgarian lands had been found.[32]

It was Greek fiscal, rather than cultural, oppression that during the seventeenth century sparked the first signs of discernible anti-Greek sentiment among the Bulgarians. In the opening years of the century Pohomie, a Bulgarian monk at a Wallachian monastery, decried the Greeks as "accursed," "sly," "deceitful" and "merciless," and warned his fellow Bulgarian monks against mixing in any manner with the Greeks in the monasteries of Mount Athos. Some time later, in 1650, a Bulgarian Athonite monk characterized the Greeks as "sly and cunning" relatives of the Bulgarians and Serbians. The Greeks, in turn, developed an anti-Slavic mentality, and by mid century took to referring to the Bulgarians as "non-people."[33]

As church taxes and fees mounted, the Orthodox Bulgarians had recourse to directing complaints to the Ottoman civil authorities against the Greek prelates' fiscal exactions. Early in 1605 the Bulgarian population in the regions of Sofia, Breznik and Pirot complained to the Turkish military authorities in Sofia about the harassment they had experienced during the collection of patriarchal taxes, and that the taxes in question were inflated far in excess of previous rates of taxation. The complaint was forwarded to Istanbul and in May of that year Sultan Ahmed I (1603-1617) replied. Ahmed made it clear to the Sofia *kadı* that, while he supported the Patriarch in his right to regulate and collect ecclesiastical taxes, he could not agree to the torture of Bulgarian peasants during the collection process. He requested that the *kadı* furnish him with a list of the Turkish Janissary offenders so that he could see to their punishment. Again, in 1624 Bulgarian miners and charcoal-burners from the district of Samokov complained to their local Ottoman administrative council about representatives of the Sofia metropolitanate who had arrived in the region accompanied by numerous Janissaries and *sipahis* for the purpose of collecting the ecclesiastical marriage taxes. An exorbitant amount of money had been demanded of the population, and the locals were then forced to provide food and drink to the entire retinue of tax gatherers free of charge. It was also reported that a number of cruelties were perpetrated during the course of the collection. The Samokov Bulgarians requested that the sultan, Murad IV (1623-1640), remove the unjust tax rate by decree, and that he also grant them protection against reprisals by the metropolitanate and the Ottoman forces involved in the affair. Murad responded in a letter to the Sofia *kadı,* ordering that the Janissaries and *sipahis* not interfere in the work of the Samokov miners or offer them further torment. In both of these cases, the actual actions taken by the Turkish authorities beyond the sultans' letters of admonishment are unknown. Most likely, the local authorities, with their vested interests in the loans granted the Sofia metropolitanate, did little beyond forwarding the sultans' admonishments to the troops. Almost no attempt was made to modify the exorbitant fiscal demands made upon the local Orthodox population. As no further seventeenth century Bulgarian complaints concerning ecclesiastical taxation are extant, it would seem that the Bulgarians came to realize the futility of such action when the local civil authorities were in league with the perpetrators of the crimes.[34]

That the Greek prelates used Ottoman troops in collecting church taxes and fees, in the full knowledge that their use ensured that barbarities would accompany the collection process, graphically demonstrated the low opinion of the Orthodox leadership for the Slavic Bulgarians.

Some Bulgarian monasteries were hellenized in the seventeenth century but the process was far less widespread during the period than has been commonly believed. In the region of Plovdiv, a center of Greek population and culture, the villages and monasteries possessed substantial numbers of Bulgarian inhabitants, who at times expressed their Slavic cultural affinities. The village of Gorni Voden, south of Plovdiv in the Rhodope foothills, was a Greek village forming part of the properties of Bachkovo Monastery, which was also predominantly Greek at that time. Yet in the courtyard of Gorni Voden Monastery a fountain erected in 1696 by *maistor* Nikola, a Bulgarian, bore a Slavic inscription proclaiming for all to read the names of its Bulgarian donors and that of the artist. One of the patrons, *pop* Ananiya, worked in nearby Kuklen Monastery, which during the period of the late seventeenth century was the largest Slavic cultural center in the southcentral Bulgarian lands.[35]

In the western Bulgarian lands, where the Greek presence was primarily in the major urban centers, Greek influence in the rural districts was slight. The western monastic centers, such as Rila Monastery, were relatively free of Greek predominance. The situation was reflected in the literary and artistic monuments created in those monastic communities. Only a few traces of the Greek presence were left on the walls of some monastery churches in the guise of inscriptions in the Greek language.

Hellenization in regions of the Bulgarian lands that later, during the eighteenth and nineteenth centuries, would prove strongholds of Greek population and culture (especially Tŭrnovo and Plovdiv) was incomplete at the close of the seventeenth century. Traces of that process in those regions, however, were already becoming obvious by mid century. Petŭr Bogdan expressed surprise that the former Bulgarian capital of Tŭrnovo was being transformed into a Greek city. He noted, however, that the Bulgarian language was still spoken in the region. In 1681 Tŭrnovo had a church, "St. Georgi," served by two priests who conducted Orthodox services in Slavic. A similar situation existed in Plovdiv. In both regions, Greek culture formed an ancillary layer over top the Bulgarians' Slavic culture. Popular support for Slavic religious culture could still be found in towns with Christian populations possessing 50 percent or more Bulgarian inhabitants.[36]

At no time during the seventeenth century did the Greeks exhibit overt, intentional xenophobic actions with regard to the Bulgarians' continued adherence to Slavic forms of Orthodoxy. Instead, the century represented a period in which was rooted the groundwork for future oppression of Slavic Orthodox culture among the Bulgarian faithful by the Greek church hierarchy. The future religio-national oppression that characterized Greek relations with the Bulgarians during the two following centuries grew out of the financial corruption that permeated the upper hierarchy of the church and the brutal means used in carrying out the church's fiscal policies. It was intensified by the deterioration in the Ottoman Empire's financial situation and the early rise of Greek national consciousness during the eighteenth century. For seventeenth century Bulgarians, the high Greek clergy did not represent a threat in being but, rather, a prelude to the worst that was to arrive later.

Roman Catholic Missionary Efforts

Winning the adherence of the Christian Bulgarians to papal authority had long been a recurring goal of the Vatican. As far back as the mid ninth century the conversion of the pagan Bulgarians to Christianity provided the extraordinary Pope Nicholas I (858-867) with an opportunity to expand the power of the Papacy into the heartlands of the European East at the expense of the Orthodox Patriarchate of Constantinople and the Byzantine Empire. Unfortunately for Nicholas, his ambitious policy was foiled by the equally extraordinary Patriarch Photios (858-867, 877-886) and the military might of Byzantium. Prince Boris I (852-889, 893) of Bulgaria opted for Orthodoxy and the Byzantine East. Once again in the early thirteenth century, papal hopes of bringing the European East under Roman spiritual and cultural suzerainty were revived when Tsar Kaloyan (1197-1207), leader of a newly resurrected Bulgarian state, placed his crown and the Bulgarian church into the hands of Pope Innocent III (1198-1216) in the face of the power vacuum created by the collapse of the Byzantine Empire in 1204 under the blows of the French and Venetian warriors of the Fourth Crusade. The expedient nature of the union was demonstrated when Ivan Asen II (1218-1241) renounced the religious union with the Western church in the wake of his great military victory at Klokotnitsa (1230) over the Despotate of Epiros, which secured Bulgaria's position of preeminence in Southeastern Europe and made her a leading contender for the legacy of the fallen Byzantine state, along with Epiros and the Byzantine successor state of Nicæa. The subsequent proclamation of an autonomous Bulgarian Orthodox Patriarchate sealed the defeat of papal dreams of expansion in the Orthodox East.

Although the larger policy of the Vatican toward Bulgaria came to naught, the brief union of the Bulgarians with Roman Catholicism sowed seeds that were later exploited by the Papacy and the Western great powers (*e.g.*, primarily Habsburg Austria and Venice) in their struggles against the Ottoman invasion of Europe. Under the Second Bulgarian Empire Roman Catholics entered the Bulgarian lands in significant number. They came in the guise of traveling merchant colonists sent out by the city-republic of Dubrovnik and of ore-mining colonists from Saxony, who settled in certain regions of the western and northwestern Bulgarian lands at the invitation of Bulgarian rulers. By the late fifteenth century, after the fall of Bulgaria to the Turks, colonies of Dubrovnik merchants were securely established in all major commercial centers in the Bulgarian lands under the auspices of the Ottoman authorities. Both the Saxon and Dubrovnik colonists constituted small, compact centers of Roman Catholicism, possessing their own churches for worship and a limited number of clergy to serve their spiritual needs.

Following the Council of Trent (1545-1563) the Roman Catholic church once again began to take an interest in the Christian brethren inhabiting the Bulgarian lands. The sixteenth century was a period in which the Western European powers, particularly Habsburg Austria, were confronted with a direct threat posed by Ottoman military might along the northern frontier of the Balkan Peninsula. Under Sultan Süleyman I Ottoman armies advanced to the very gates of Vienna (1529), and, although repulsed, the Muslim forces occupying Hungary posed a continued threat to the Habsburg Empire. In their protracted struggle against the Ottoman menace the Catholic Habsburgs found a willing ally in the Papacy. The existence of Christian subject populations within the borders of the Muslim enemy state offered the possibility of fomenting internal disorders that might weaken Ottoman military efforts. The raising of Christian rebellions within the Ottoman Empire was embraced as sound military strategy by the Habsburgs and their allies. Such a policy not only possessed military advantages but political ones as well, for if the Habsburgs were successful in directing uprisings within the Ottoman Empire, the subject Christians might be oriented away from Russia, an emerging power with nascent, yet growing, ambitions in the Balkans and whose Slavic ethnic character and Orthodox culture potentially made her the natural ally of the Ottoman Christians.

For the Papacy, Catholic infiltration into the Orthodox Balkans not only would assist the West's anti-Muslim war effort but also would serve to open the road toward winning the peninsula for the Holy See for the first time since the Council of Florence in the fifteenth century (1439).[37]

Lacking a military force of its own, the Vatican channeled its efforts in the Bulgarian lands into disseminating pro-Catholic missionary propaganda through its Dubrovnik agents and, most especially, through direct missionary activity. During the final decade of the sixteenth century Franciscan monks were dispatched to the Bulgarian lands from Bosnia and Croatia, where they had been successfully combating dualistic Christian heresies since the thirteenth century. Chiprovtsi, a leading Bulgarian mining and metalworking center located in the northwestern lands in the Danubian foothills of the Balkan Mountains, became the natural headquarters for these Catholic missionary efforts since it served as the center for the largest single, compact colony of Catholics in the Bulgarian lands. The majority of the inhabitants in the region of Chiprovtsi were Bulgarized descendants of fourteenth century Saxon iron ore miners. Despite three centuries of settlement in a region originally inhabited by Orthodox Christians, as well as extensive interbreeding with the local Slavic Bulgarian population, the Bulgaro-Saxons of Chiprovtsi steadfastly held to the Roman Catholic faith of their forefathers. As expert iron and gold miners they enjoyed a privileged position within Ottoman society that was conducive to preserving among them a spirit of personal independence and social autonomy. The Ottoman authorities were represented in Chiprovtsi by only a single *bey* and his limited retinue. The surrounding region primarily lay under the control of local Bulgaro-Saxon clan patriarchs from such families as the Marinovs, Parchevs, Peiyachevs and Markanovs. Not a single Muslim mosque broke the skyline of Chiprovtsi.[38]

The Franciscan mission despatched by the Vatican arrived in Chiprovtsi in 1595. It was led by a Bosnian from Tuzla, Petr Salinat, who in 1601 was elevated to the office of Catholic primate in the Bulgarian lands by Pope Clement VIII (1592-1605). Salinat was nominally designated Archbishop of Sofia but his seat actually was located in Chiprovtsi because Sofia at that time boasted only a small colony of Catholic merchants from Dubrovnik while Chiprovtsi possessed a well established and numerous Catholic population. His mission was to consolidate and expand the Catholic archdiocese in the Bulgarian lands through the establishment of a permanent Catholic missionary organization. Of particular interest to Salinat was the propagation of Catholicism among the heretical *pavlikyani* (Paulician) population in the Bulgarian regions of the Ottoman Empire, which was a familiar course of action similar to that followed earlier by the Franciscan missionaries in Bosnia.

Upon Salinat's death in 1623 a native Bulgarian from one of the Chiprovtsi Bulgaro-Saxon families, Iliya Marinov, was nominated as his successor and raised to the office of archbishop in 1624. Marinov had been chosen personally by Salinat for study in Rome, where during 1603-1604 he attended Clementine College and read law. He was a model monk and earned the respect of the Vatican, and for this he was rewarded with elevation to the Bulgarian primacy. Marinov's term of office (1624-1641) was notable for the establishment of Catholic education in the region of Chiprovtsi and for the extension of Salinat's proselytizing efforts among the Bulgarian *pavlikyani*.[39] From the year of Marinov's elevation to the archbishopric until the catastrophe of the Chiprovtsi Uprising

(1688), the Catholic missionary movement in the Bulgarian lands was administered by native Bulgarian Catholics.

No other aspect of seventeenth century Bulgarian history has received as much scholarly attention as the Catholic missionary movement and the modern concept of nationalism that it espoused.[40] Much has been made of the rise of a specifically Bulgarian form of national consciousness among the Bulgarian Catholics, which antedated by nearly a century the initial appearance of such thought among the Orthodox Bulgarians expressed in the *Slaveno-Bulgarian History* written by the Athonite monk, Paisii Hilendarski, in 1762. Petŭr Bogdan, a native of Chiprovtsi, defined in 1640 the borders of the Bulgarian nation in a report made to the Sacred Congregation in Rome. He also set out to write an ecclesiastical history of Bulgaria, of which only a few chapters and scattered fragments have survived.[41]

Petŭr Parchevich (1617-1674), another native of Chiprovtsi and bishop of the Catholic See of Martsianopol, near the Bulgarian town of Preslav but with its actual seat located in Moldavia, was an active Bulgarian patriot in the modern sense of the term. As did most of the upper Bulgarian Catholic clergy, Parchevich received his higher education in Rome. His term of office was spent in constant travel throughout his bishopric while engaged in religious and political missionary activities. His intense political involvement earned him the temporary ire of the Vatican, as a result of which he was removed from his office as bishop. Parchevich was, however, later rehabilitated and elevated to the rank of cardinal. From 1646 until his death in 1674 he indefatigably toured the courts of Western Europe as a Vatican plenipotentiary in an effort to organize a united political and military front for the liberation of his native lands and people. Parchevich went so far as to suggest a rapprochement between the Vatican and Muscovite Russia to gain Russian support for a war of Bulgarian liberation. Despite all of his tireless efforts, however, Parchevich's plans for a Western crusade that would result in the establishment of an independent Bulgarian state under Habsburg protection failed.[42]

The actual significance for Bulgarian history of Bulgarian Catholic nationalist ideals has often been exaggerated. Some scholars have discovered in the seventeenth century Catholics the nucleus of a future intelligentsia that would play a leading role in the later national struggle of the Bulgarians. Others credit the Catholics with restoring the Bulgarians to the European family of nations by breaking the political isolation that had characterized the relations of the Bulgarians with the European world since the late fourteenth century. It has also been claimed that the Catholic Bulgarians served as a bridge over which Western European culture entered the heartlands of the Balkans.[43]

Such contentions contain kernels of truth but need qualification. Indeed, led by men such as Parchevich, the Bulgarian Catholics did form a nationalistic intelligentsia. The native Catholic leadership had received the benefits of a

Western education in Rome and Lorretto in an environment fed by high political and intellectual culture. Yet such an environment was totally inoperative within the confines of the Ottoman Empire among the subject populations. Also true was the fact that Bulgarian Catholic emissaries, such as Parchevich, argued the political case for their fellow Bulgarians before the major courts of Europe. They were conversant in the history of Bulgaria as it was available to them at the time, and they stressed the existence of a Bulgarian kingdom and their own national identity as Bulgarians. Likewise, after having received their Italian training, the Bulgarian Catholics, upon their return to the mission in the Bulgarian lands, brought with them Western, and especially Italian, cultural concepts in the fields of literature and education. The early Catholic mission schools used Latin texts, and most of the missionary hierarchy wrote their mundane correspondence in Latin or Italian.[44]

Unfortunately for seventeenth century Bulgarian cultural life, the progressive Western concepts espoused by the Bulgarian Catholics had little lasting impact on the mass of the Bulgarian population. Instead of being received as the harbinger of modern national ideology, with its concomitant political and cultural benefits, Catholic missionary activity was met by emphatic resistance, and often outright hostility, on the part of the general Orthodox Bulgarian population. The effects of the Great Schism of 1054 that had rent the medieval Christian church into two antagonistic branches, the Orthodox and Roman Catholic, were still operative in the Bulgarian lands nearly 600 years after the event. The Orthodox Bulgarians viewed the Catholic missionaries with animosity; they regarded them as creatures of papal religio-political ambitions in the European East and as the bearers of a foreign, antagonistical culture. As such, the Catholics posed a threat to the Bulgarians' traditional worldview and only form of self-identity — their Orthodoxy. Since the Catholics lacked the military power to impose their faith upon the Orthodox majority from without, they were a threat that the Orthodox Bulgarians were able to easily overcome.

The only successes scored by the Catholic missionaries working in the Bulgarian field during the seventeenth century were achieved among the heretical *pavlikyani* element of the population. These people were the descendants of Paulician and Bogomil Christian heretics who had settled or arisen in medieval Bulgaria between the eighth and eleventh centuries.

The Paulicians originated in Armenia and were first transferred to the regions of the Balkans that later constituted the Bulgarian lands by the Byzantines during the eighth century in an attempt to weaken their heretical dualistic threat to Orthodox Christianity posed in their homeland. Their numbers were augmented by new colonists during the following century. Once in Bulgaria, the Paulicians pursued an active policy of missionary activity, ironically serving as early harbingers of Christianity to the general Bulgarian population during the period of the conversion to Orthodoxy of Prince Boris I.

Following the conversion of Boris, the work of the Bulgarian disciples of Cyril and Methodius in creating a native Slavic form of Orthodox rite weakened Paulician influence in Bulgaria since the new form of liturgy proved far more acceptable to the Bulgarian masses than did the foreign Greek rite employed by the heretics. Still, the Paulician population in Bulgaria continued to grow during the tenth century because of further population transfers ordered by the Byzantine Empire. The heretics formed a rather large settlement pattern that stretched from the region of Plovdiv, in southcentral Bulgaria, across the Balkan Mountains to the banks of the Danube in the Nikopol region. Intensified anti-heretical persecutions sponsored by both the Bulgarian and Byzantine states resulted in the development of a lasting animosity between the Orthodox and Paulician elements in Bulgarian society. The *pavlikyani* thus believed that they had little stake in a society that regarded them with hostility.[45]

Intermingled with the seventeenth century Paulician population were the descendants of the native Bulgarian Bogomil heretics, who had originally arisen in Bulgaria during the ninth and tenth centuries. The Bogomils were blood relatives of the Paulicians in that both held dualistic systems of belief that evolved out of early Middle Eastern Manichæism. The Bogomils, however, were much more radical in their views and far more contemplative than were the worldly Paulicians. The Bogomils also adhered to some Slavic cultural traditions left over from Orthodoxy that were considered acceptable within the bounds of their heretical beliefs.[46]

By the seventeenth century there existed virtually no discernible distinction between the descendants of these two forms of Christian dualism. It has been estimated that some 1,000 of the 7,000 persons who bore the name *pavlikyani* during the century were the descendants of medieval Bogomils who actively maintained their traditional beliefs in some corrupted form or another.[47]

For the most part, the *pavlikyani* were extremely poor and ignorant villagers, who existed on bad terms with their Orthodox Christian neighbors. The Orthodox Bulgarians viewed them as social outcasts and held their heretical beliefs in utter disdain. In truth, *pavlikyani* spiritual concepts, as espoused in the seventeenth century, were a confused jumble of religious doctrine and fantastic legend. They conceived of themselves as both Romans and Catholics. Doctrinally, they rejected the Christian symbol of the cross, baptism by water, church edifices and the ecclesiastical hierarchy. Fire, instead of water, was considered the cleansing agent in their baptismal rites, although the actual medium used in such services was a flower, which was believed to symbolize the fire of John the Baptist. The *pavlikyani* clergy consisted only of parish priests, who conducted their religious rituals in outdoor open spaces near large trees hung with offerings of mutton and beef. Stone tables under the trees served as altars. Services were conducted amidst a great deal of merrymaking, which included eating the hung offerings in a form of banquet and the consumption of large quantities of alcohol. No clerical office was recognized above that of priest other than that of the Roman Pope, who was viewed as a legendary, almost mythical figure. Sundays and common Orthodox religious holidays were also celebrated by the *pavlikyani*. Their children were all given Christian names at birth. As a people, they were described as being tenacious and conservative.[48]

The *pavlikyani* possessed sacred Cyrillic writings but few of them could read, and fewer still were able to understand what they read or heard read to them. Their sacred books were two to three centuries old by the seventeenth century. Most had been written in Bosnia during the reign of Prince Tvrtko I (1353-1391). Since literacy was rare among them, the *pavlikyani* commonly took to wearing miniature books, or sections of books, in scroll form, as amulets around their necks to ward off physical and spiritual dangers.[49]

Unable to make any inroads among the Orthodox Bulgarian population, the Catholic missionaries turned their entire attention toward the *pavlikyani*. The fact that these Bulgarian heretics possessed a vague affinity for Catholicism and were persecuted by the Orthodox masses facilitated Catholic missionary efforts. Usually, the *pavlikyani* readily gave themselves into the hands of the missionaries, but the process was not entirely without difficulty. Tact on the part of the Catholics was often required. The heretics were rather disinterested in profound theological argument, finding it difficult to grasp philosophical concepts. *Pavlikyani* Catholics continued to adhere to their old heretical beliefs and to comport themselves in a rowdy manner when attending divine services. Furthermore, they barely submitted to any form of Catholic religious education.

In such a situation, the Catholic missionary leadership recognized education as the most important factor in successfully converting the unruly *pavlikyani*. On 18 August 1641 Archbishop Petŭr Bogdan summoned a missionary council in Chiprovtsi for the purpose of discussing the problems in properly converting the heretics and of providing them with a meaningful education. Up to that time Catholic education was conducted with the use of Latin texts printed, for the most part, in Italy for the Bulgaro-Saxon and Dubrovnik colonists. Iliya Marinov had been instrumental in founding the first Catholic school in the Bulgarian lands at Chiprovtsi. His system was heavily influenced by the form of education that he received in Italy. Marinov's work was supervised and expanded upon by Ivan Lilov, the most active educator among the Catholic missionaries, who worked at the Chiprovtsi school for 32 years (1635-1667).[50] The failure of Latin education among the *pavlikyani* pointed out the need for creating a form of education that would play the role of vanguard in missionary activity.

In three days of discussion the Chiprovtsi Council recognized the proselytizing function of education in the case of the *pavlikyani*. Clergy working among them were forbidden to encourage the old heretical customs. The missionary clergymen were required to have a working knowledge of the Cyrillic alphabet, to actively care for educational efforts, and to maintain correct Catholic ritual among their flocks. The council also charged that *pavlikyani* youths demonstrating religious or intellectual aptitude be chosen for study in Lorretto. Schools were to be established among the heretics that would use Slavic books developed centuries earlier for educating the *pavlikyani's* heretical, dualistic relatives in Bosnia. Such texts were obtainable directly from Bosnia but were commonly printed in Rome and Dubrovnik.[51]

In 1649 Lilov sent a request to the Vatican for an order of 20 Slavic grammars, 100 Cyrillic alphabet lists, and mathematics primers for use in the Bulgarian Catholic schools.[52] All of the books dispatched by Rome were written in the Dalmatian dialect of Croatian spoken in Dubrovnik, and this was the language consistently used by the Bulgarian Catholics when writing or teaching Slavic. They called the language "Illyrian," after its Dalmatian origin. The early Franciscan missionaries had brought their Illyrian language with them when they entered the Bulgarian lands. It was also used as the Slavic language of instruction in the Roman colleges open for students sent from the Balkans. Illyrian became the standard literary language of the Catholic missionary schools among the *pavlikyani* and in the native schools of Chiprovtsi.

One literary work of note that emerged from the Catholic missionary interest in Slavic education was produced by a Bulgarian Catholic primarily for use in the *pavlikyani* schools, but also for general mundane religious rituals. In 1651 the Catholic bishop of Nikopol (a seat created in 1648), Filip Stanislavov, a native of the village of Oreshte in the region of Nikopol, published in Rome a Slavic prayer book specifically addressing a *pavlikyani* readership. Known by the title of *Abagar,* because it contained the apocryphal epistles of Prince Abgar to Christ, Stanislavov's compilation included plagiarized versions of apocryphal tales that dated to the ninth and tenth centuries and that were associated with the Bogomil heresy by the Orthodox church organizations in Bulgaria and Byzantium.[53] The legendary letters of Abgar appeared in a number of Slavic books printed in Venice and Dubrovnik during the sixteenth century, and direct copies of the letters and tales found in those works appeared in Stanislavov's *Abagar.* Although apocryphal tales did not constitute the entire contents, for there also were included standard Catholic prayers, their prominent inclusion in the book reflected Stanislavov's awareness that his book had no chance of making an impact on its intended readership without the inclusion of certain elements that spoke directly to the *pavlikyani* on their traditional level of culture. Its approval for printing and circulation by the Vatican demonstrated the willingness of the Catholics to forego their usual aversion toward encouraging heretical concepts so as to score a concrete success for the missionary effort.[54]

Abagar was the only book produced by Stanislavov and the only Catholic Slavic work created expressly for Bulgarian consumption. Shortly after its publication Stanislavov was elevated to the seat of the Nikopol bishopric. Thereafter he devoted all of his efforts toward the duties of his newly acquired office.

As a literary figure Stanislavov was an amateur. His book was a hodgepodge of assorted tales, prayers and myths, and was totally unoriginal. Yet in spite of its shortcomings, *Abagar* holds a place of some interest in the history of Bulgarian literature. It was long considered the first book printed in the New Bulgarian literary language. This contention has been greatly qualified by modern scholarship. It is now held that the language of *Abagar* was actually a mixture of three languages — Croatian (Illyrian), Resava Serbian and New Bulgarian. *Abagar* was far from being a monument of New Bulgarian literature, and, in fact, can only lay claim to the distinction of being the first book printed that contained New Bulgarian linguistic elements. It was probable that Stanislavov acquired some familiarity with Orthodox *damaskin* literature, from which he adapted certain literary elements and the collection-style format of religious and pseudo-religious tracts.

Abagar was successfully received by its intended *pavlikyani* audience. Its content of both canonical and apocryphal prayers designed to meet all religious occasions was put to use in services at the Catholic missions, and this common usage of the book ensured that *Abagar* enjoyed widespread popularity. In fact, the book became so popular that it was known even in high Orthodox circles. It is doubtful, however, that *Abagar* made any significant impact on seventeenth century Bulgarian Orthodox literature.

There was an interesting side effect to the Catholic effort among the *pavlikyani*. The intense interest of the Catholic missionaries in the heretics provoked a reaction within Orthodox church circles. Efforts were made from the Orthodox side to work in the *pavlikyani* field so as to combat the spread of Catholicism, and a growing conflict began to arise between the two branches of Christendom in the Bulgarian lands over the right to claim the former Christian outcasts as their own. In the struggle for the souls of the heretics the Catholics clearly held the advantage. The missionaries were originally from outside the borders of the Ottoman Empire and were, thus, free of the onus connected with taxes levelled on the common Ottoman subject. Those *pavlikyani* who were sent to Italy for study and training were also exempt from those taxes when they returned to the missionary field in the Bulgarian lands. Catholic educational and literary efforts helped elevate the cultural and intellectual levels of the generally repressed and ignorant heretical population, something that positively differentiated the Catholics from the hated Orthodox in the minds of the *pavlikyani*.[55]

The Orthodox opposition began with Vardim, the Greek bishop of Trŭn in the western Bulgarian lands. Priests and monks were ordered to preach among the *pavlikyani*, stressing the common traditions and history of the Orthodox and heretical populations, especially their shared links to the Byzantine Orthodox past. Because the past for most *pavlikyani* was one in which persecution and hatred of their views was the usual Orthodox treatment, it is hardly surprising that the new Orthodox efforts at reconciliation met with little success.

Realizing that a conflict over the *pavlikyani* existed between the Catholics and the Orthodox, the local Muslim authorities sought to turn the rift to their advantage and began efforts to convert the heretics to Islam through the same techniques used throughout the Bulgarian lands for converting Orthodox Christians, which have been discussed above.

In the tripartite religious effort for *pavlikyani* loyalty, the Catholic missionaries scored a clear victory. The least successful were the Orthodox, who remained the traditional enemies of the heretics. That portion of the *pavlikyani* that opted for Islam cut itself completely off from the general Bulgarian population and, instead, was merged into the Turkish population in the Bulgarian lands.[56]

Any possible opportunity for Catholic infiltration into the Orthodox cultural world in the Bulgarian lands that may have been opened by *Abagar* through its language was terminated by the political activities of the Bulgarian Catholics. While activists, such as Parchevich, canvassed the courts of Europe seeking support for a war of Bulgarian liberation, others, such as Georgi Peyachevich (1655-1725), engaged in tireless efforts to organize an armed rebellion against Ottoman rule in the Bulgarian lands. War broke out between the Turks and the Habsburgs in 1682. In response, especially following the repulse of the Turks before the gates of Vienna in 1683 and the subsequent Habsburg conquest of Hungary in 1687, the Chiprovtsi Bulgarian Catholics intensified their efforts to spark a rebellion. The nationalistic fervor generated by the Catholic rebel conspirators raised emotions in and around Chiprovtsi to such a high pitch that some Orthodox Bulgarian inhabitants of the region set aside their religious differences with the Catholics and joined in the preparations. Simultaneously, Bulgarian *haidut* bands were instigated by Habsburg agents operating out of the Danubian Principalities to commence raiding operations on Ottoman targets in the northwestern lands, which were those regions in closest proximity to the steadily southward-moving battle front.[57]

By September 1688 the advancing Habsburg forces had captured Belgrad, and advanced units had penetrated south of the Danube as far as Niš and Pirot. Elements of some units reached Dragoman, only a day's march west of Sofia. In contact with the Habsburg military headquarters and knowing that the Habsburg liberators were so close at hand, the Catholic rebels, led by Georgi Peyachevich, proclaimed their long awaited rebellion. The course of events following the outbreak of rebel activity was disastrous for the Catholic missionary cause in the Ottoman Empire.

Threatened by the uprising at Chiprovtsi in the rear of the main military front against the Austrians, Ottoman troops under the command of Eygen *paşa* quickly arrived in the region during early October and defeated the rebels, who in underestimation of Ottoman military capabilities had attempted to stand and offer battle near Kutlovitsa. The rebel fugitives from the battle fled to Chiprovtsi, where a number of them were trapped in the nearby Chiprovtsi Monastery and butchered by the pursuing Ottoman troops.[58] In angry retribution for the uprising, the victorious Turks devastated the surrounding region. Sections of Chiprovtsi were burnt to the ground and the majority of the town's inhabitants were either killed or enslaved. Similar treatment was meted out to the Catholic villages in the countryside. It has been estimated that no more than a third of the region's population escaped the wrath of the frenzied Ottoman soldiers. Of the survivors of the massacre, the majority later (in 1689) fled north across the Danube to the Banat. In some cases, the fugitives from Chiprovtsi traveled as far north as Transylvania.[59]

The brutal denouement of the Chiprovtsi Uprising spelt the end of concerted Catholic missionary activity in the Bulgarian lands. With the disappearance of the missionaries, the nationalistic ideals they espoused soon faded into vague memory. Throughout the Ottoman Empire Catholics were held suspect by the Ottoman authorities and their formerly lucrative trading privileges were revoked, thus opening broader social and economic horizons to the nascent Bulgarian merchant class.

All told, by the close of the seventeenth century the legacy of the Bulgarian Catholics for the majority of the Bulgarians of the Ottoman Empire was rather slight. Without their spiritual supervisors the *pavlikyani* soon regressed to their former heretical ways. The Western-style system of education established by the Catholic missionaries languished and died. For the Orthodox Bulgarians, the Chiprovtsi affair put an end to a cultural threat that had long before been reduced to impotence by Orthodox rejection.

Two.

Seventeenth Century Bulgarian Orthodox Culture:

Nature and Forms

3. Monasticism and the Cultural Role of Mount Athos

Monasticism and the development of a Slavic form of Orthodox Christianity under the first medieval Bulgarian state were virtually synonymous. Following the conversion of Prince Boris I to Orthodoxy in 865, the Christian church establishment created in Bulgaria was Greek and remained closely allied with the Byzantine Empire. During the period of conversion the initial impact of the situation primarily fell upon the Bulgarian ruling class, which centered itself on the royal court at Pliska-Aboba. The liturgy and culture of the newly adopted religion remained foreign to the majority of the population existing outside the orbit of the court. Tsar Simeon I (893-927), the successor to Boris, realized the political and cultural ambiguity of governing a state whose spiritual hierarchy owed allegiance to a powerful, and potentially dangerous, foreign power lying just across the southern border of his domains. Given the close alliance of state and religion that characterized medieval political relationships as the accepted order of worldly existence, Simeon understood that an official state religion that did not function within the native cultural parameters espoused by the majority of his subjects but, rather, propagated the culture of a neighboring great power would inevitably lead to the loss of Bulgaria's independent existence through ultimate *de facto* incorporation into the Byzantine Empire. With the appearance of the fugitive disciples of the brothers from Thessaloniki, Cyril and Methodius, who brought official Byzantine Orthodox Christianity to the Slavs of Eastern Europe, at his borders following their expulsion from Moravia, Simeon lost little time in capitalizing on the opportunity to create a non-Greek church hierarchy for Bulgaria. The disciples were given a royal welcome and their efforts in creating a Slavic Orthodox liturgy were heartily fostered.

The royal palace in Preslav, Simeon's new, Christian capital, rapidly evolved into a center of Slavic learning and arts. There and in Ohrid, the leading urban and administrative center in western Bulgaria at the time, the disciples were encouraged to develop and expand their work in the fields of Slavic education, literature, and fine arts through the generous patronage of the royal court. The fruit of Simeon's wise decision to embrace the cause of Slavic religious culture blossomed in the eventual displacement of the Greek clergy in the Bulgarian Orthodox hierarchy by native Bulgarians, laying the basis for the continued independence of Bulgaria from Byzantine cultural and, therefore, political hegemony.

The new Slavic liturgy devised by the disciples of Cyril and Methodius would have long remained the exclusive preserve of the royal palaces had it not been for the rapid development of monastic communities throughout the Bulgarian kingdom. From the very inception of Christianity as the state religion of Bulgaria, monasteries played the leading role in developing the Slavic form of Orthodox culture that served as the basis for Bulgarian self-identity and as the cement for unifying the country by propagating the Christian faith among the general population. As with all the other trappings of Orthodoxy, the Bulgarian monastic movement leaned heavily on the Byzantine example. The major point of differentiation lay in the fact that the Greek language was displaced by Slavic.

The earliest Christian monasteries located in those regions of the Balkans that would eventually comprise medieval Bulgaria were probably founded prior to the arrival of the Slavs in the seventh century. That Christianity possessed a foothold among the inhabitants of the infant medieval Bulgarian state can be deduced from the fact that the early ninth century Bulgarian *hans,* Omurtag (814-831) and Malamir (831-836), were strongly anti-Christian. The spread of Christianity among the Bulgarian Bulgar and Slavic populations of the state had been reinforced by the settlement in the country of numerous Byzantine prisoners captured during the wars of *han* Krum (802-814) against Orthodox Byzantium and the colonization of Paulician Christians by the Byzantine Empire in certain regions eventually incorporated into the growing Bulgarian state. Prince Prisiyan (836-852) discontinued the anti-Christian policies of his predecessors, thus easing the way toward the conversion of his successor, Boris. There is tenuous evidence for the existence of a "Bulgarian" monastery in the vicinity of Edirne during the reign of Prisiyan (*ca.* 842-843), meaning that the resident monks were primarily drawn from regions within the frontiers of the Bulgarian state, but details concerning when it was founded and the number of residents are lacking.[1]

The first monasteries in Christian Bulgaria appeared during the late ninth and early tenth centuries in the vicinities of Pliska-Aboba, Preslav and Ohrid thanks to royal and aristocratic patronage. They functioned as virtual satellites of the Bulgarian court and were primarily staffed by members of Bulgarian *bolyar* families, both male and female (but not, of course, in cohabitation). In 889 Boris abdicated the Bulgarian throne and retired to a monastery that he had founded near his capital at Pliska under the adopted Christian name of Mihail, where he died a pious and revered monk in 906. Boris' monastery of Patleina, located high in the mountains only a few kilometers from the capital, was the first Bulgarian educational and literary center following the conversion. It was in this monastery that the disciples of Cyril and Methodius were initially housed. When Boris' son, Simeon, who had originally been chosen by Boris to become the first native Bulgarian archbishop-patriarch and had thus been sent to a monastery in

Constantinople for training, moved the capital of the state to Preslav after he was installed as the successor to Boris in 893, the monasteries in the vicinity of Pliska continued to be active in the religious and cultural fields, augmented in their work by the new monastic establishments founded near Preslav by the former royal monk.

A second period of monastic development, one which made a more lasting impact on the general Bulgarian population, occurred several decades after the first (*ca.* 950-1150). This second period of monasticism witnessed the spread of monastic communities throughout the country. Again, the *bolyar* families led in providing the predominant element in the monastic population, although a growing number of common folk joined their ranks out of a desire to escape the increasingly burdensome lot of supporting a rising feudal-like socio-political system. A prime example of religious escapism among the common Bulgarian population of the time was Ivan Rilski, who founded Rila Monastery, the most renowned Bulgarian monastic establishment, sometime in the early tenth century, and who became the most popularly beloved of all Bulgarian saints. The fame of Rilski was so widespread that hundreds of Bulgarians forsook their worldly affairs to follow his example. The monasteries of this second period played a crucial role in preserving the Slavic form of Orthodoxy among the Bulgarians during the 167 years (1018-1185) of Byzantine domination that followed the crushing defeat of the First Bulgarian Empire by the Byzantine emperor, Basil II Bulgaroktonos (the "Bulgar-Slayer") (976-1025).

A third period of monastic activity occurred in 1350-1393 in the vicinity of Tŭrnovo, the capital of a reestablished medieval Bulgarian state. The residents of the Tŭrnovo monasteries actively participated in the mainstream of Orthodox cultural life, including that flourishing in declining Byzantium and in Russia. No known leaders in Bulgarian cultural life of that time were members of the laity, a fact that underlines the position of cultural dominance enjoyed by monastic communities. Bulgarian monks, especially Teodor Teodosii Tŭrnovski and Evtimii Tŭrnovski, stood in the forefront of Orthodox theological, philological and pedagogical thought, maintaining intimate relations with all of the leading Orthodox cultural centers, particularly Mount Athos and Constantinople.

All three periods of monastic movement were characterized by the leading role monasteries played in developing and disseminating Slavic Orthodox culture.[2] The monasteries of Bulgaria served as veritable citadels of Orthodox education, literature and art. Schools were founded in the monasteries to train native Bulgarians for the clergy. These schools also taught the fine arts of religious writing and painting. In the Bulgarian monastic scriptoria great original ecclesiastical works were produced by the first Slavic writers: men such as Chernorizets Hrabŭr, Konstantin Kostenechki Filosof, and perhaps the greatest of late medieval Bulgarian religious writers, Evtimii Tŭrnovski. The monks working in the medieval Bulgarian monasteries were also active in producing religious paintings of great expertise, most especially icons and monumental church murals. Furthermore, as in Byzantium, all of the higher offices in the Bulgarian Orthodox hierarchy were filled by men who, by taking up the monastic way of life, demonstrated their renunciation of worldly pursuits for a life dedicated to God and the church. After the Ottoman conquest of Bulgaria, the monasteries in the subjugated Bulgarian lands continued to function as Orthodox cultural centers both because of their long-standing tradition of cultural leadership and because, for the most part, they stood outside the attention of the newly imposed civil and ecclesiastic authorities (*i.e.,* the Turks and the Greeks).

The growth of monasticism and its role in Bulgarian Orthodox life were heavily influenced by the example of Byzantine Orthodoxy. No Byzantine model was more influential in Bulgaria than was the renowned monastic community on the Chalcedonian peninsula of Athos. Such a development was no coincidence. An important element in the Byzantine legacy of Orthodoxy adopted by the Bulgarians was that of the monastery as a fortress of Orthodox culture. From humble beginnings in the deserts of Egypt and Palestine, through medieval religious conflicts that rent the fabric of the Orthodox world, Byzantine monasticism rose to the pinnacle of power in the Orthodox church. The seats of all high church prelates became its preserve. Old hellenistic forms of education and art were overthrown and replaced by new forms infused with the aesthetic ideals of the monks who, in the mid ninth century, emerged victorious from the internal Byzantine religious struggle against Iconoclasm.[3] Thereafter, Orthodox education, literature and art in Byzantium found their principles and progenitors within the walls of the numerous monasteries spread throughout the empire, but most especially within those on Mount Athos.

Athos, the "Holy Mountain," was the foremost stronghold of the monastic movement in Byzantium. As early as the final days of Iconoclasm men sought worldly isolation on the slopes of the rugged mountain that formed the tip of the Athos Peninsula. By the mid tenth century large monasteries, patronized by wealthy members of the Byzantine ruling class, had replaced the original individual hovels of the first anchorites. The new establishments swiftly assumed a leading role in Byzantine theological and cultural life. The entire peninsula became relegated to the monastic life-style and achieved a reputation for spirituality that was unrivaled in the Orthodox world. Athonite monastic communities were considered models for all other such establishments, and the prestige accompanying their position of primacy in that regard conferred upon them great influence.[4] Thus the monasteries that arose in Bulgaria during the medieval period, heavily influenced by Byzantine Orthodoxy despite the anti-Greek nature of the Bulgarian Orthodox church, were, for the most part, patterned on the Athonite model, and close ties were maintained between them and those of Athos. As the Orthodox faith radiated outward from Bulgaria to the rest of the Slav-inhabited regions of the Balkans and to Kievan Russia, some of the monasteries of Athos acquired distinctive ethnic characters, as Bulgarians, Serbs and, eventually, Russians joined the original Greek inhabitants on the peninsula and established new communities of their own.

Significant as the influence of Mount Athos had been on Bulgarian monasticism and the Orthodox world in general during the medieval period, its role increased following the fall of the Balkans to the Ottoman Turks. Athos itself surrendered to the conquerors when Thessaloniki was captured in 1430. The timely submission of the Athonite monks spared them the ravages of the conquest that swept through other regions of the Balkans. As a consequence, the Athonite monasteries preserved the internal autonomy that they had enjoyed under the Byzantine state in return for a payment of annual tribute to the Ottoman Porte. The leniency of the Turks in this case might in part be explained by the fact that Athos possessed no intrinsic strategic military or commercial importance since it was isolated from the primary invasion and trade routes in the Balkans. Additionally, the religious prestige enjoyed by the peninsula may have played a role in the Ottoman decision not to subject Athos to the usual pillage and destruction that was commonly associated with the advance of Turkish military forces into enemy territory. The entire Athonite peninsula was, therefore, declared *vakıf,* and an annual tax *(maktu)* was levied on the Athonite communities in common.[5]

Vakıf status, with its concomitant autonomy that held the Athonite communities subject only to the Patriarchate in Istanbul, was a favorable development for Orthodox cultural life on Mount Athos and, through it, for the rest of the Balkan Orthodox world subject to Ottoman authority. Under the new conditions the Athonite monasteries' former Byzantine and Balkan royal patronage was replaced by the benefaction of other Orthodox notables, most especially by *hospodars* of the Romanian Principalities and by Russian tsars. Thus Orthodox cultural life managed to continue unbroken on the Holy Mountain following the Ottoman conquest. The monasteries served as repositories of literature, art and documents of historic import dating from the pre-Ottoman period, while they continued to develop the Orthodox traditions of literature, art and education unhindered in any great degree by their foreign, non-Christian overlords. With Athos as a focal center, the cultural developments occurring there radiated outward to the stricken Orthodox lands of the Ottoman Empire.

Close and direct contacts between the Bulgarians and Athos during the Ottoman period began almost immediately after the fall of the Bulgarian state, as refugees, primarily *literati* from Tŭrnovo, fled to Athos for safety and the opportunity to continue working in freedom. Once conditions within the conquered Bulgarian lands stabilized to some extent, Athos became a popular destination for religious pilgrimages made by pious Orthodox Bulgarians. Because of the widespread poverty common in the Bulgarian lands and the difficulty inherent in long distance travel, the traditional pilgrimage to Jerusalem and the Holy Lands became impractical for all but the few wealthy individuals who remained. Athos evolved into an acceptable and accessible substitute for Bulgarian Orthodox pilgrims. Its indisputable prestige, the pantheon of Orthodox saints who once dwelt there, and its reputed treasures of literature, art and precious metals all exerted their attractions on the Bulgarian faithful.

Upon entering the sacred precincts of the peninsula, pilgrims were dazzled by the overt practice of Orthodox liturgical rituals that had been sadly impaired in their homelands since the imposition of the Muslim Ottoman social system. The sight of the rich, monumental churches, fortifications and towers, fountains, hospitals, murals and icons, richly illuminated liturgical manuscripts and old royal charters granted the monasteries by former Balkan rulers all must have been awe-inspiring for the visitors. Naturally enough, they, in turn, demonstrated their piety and appreciation by making donations in cash and in kind to the treasuries of their hosts on the Holy Mountain.

A continuous flow of Bulgarian pilgrims to Athos during the period following the Ottoman conquest assisted in cementing permanent ties between the population of the Bulgarian lands and the Athonite monasteries. Upon returning to their homelands the pilgrims often spread the news of the spirituality, wealth and overt cultural activity that they had witnessed on Athos. They oftentimes carried home with them material mementos of the flourishing cultural life conducted in Athonite monasteries.[6]

The cultural activity of Athos was fomented by the privileged position of the Holy Mountain within the Ottoman system. The close interaction of varied ethnic traditions within the monastic world of Athos both fed cultural development and, at least originally, fostered ethnic toleration. Bulgarians, Russians, Greeks, Serbians, Wallachians, Moldavians and others lived together on the Holy Mountain in either segregated, ethnically homogeneous monastic communities or intermixed under a common roof. The monasteries and the ethnic groups comprising the population of the peninsula were governed since the tenth century by an assembly of representatives from all the major monasteries, which met on a permanent basis in the centrally located town of Karyes. The *Protos,* or head spokesman of the assembly, was selected by the Greek Patriarch from a list of names approved by the Karyes Assembly. He acted as chief government administrator and head of state for the entire Athonite monastic community, and was assisted by a small group of advisors who served as the Holy Mountain's central administrative bureau.[7]

Until the seventeenth century monks from all parts of the Orthodox world coexisted on the Holy Mountain in relative peace and harmony under the unifying umbrella of Orthodoxy and the Karyes Assembly. Until the seventeenth century and the first stirrings of ethnic awareness among the Greeks, Bulgarians, Serbians and other Balkan peoples, the pilgrims and monks made no great distinction among Bulgarian, Serb, or Russian. The ties of the Bulgarians in the conquered lands to the Athonite monasteries were unclouded by such notions. This unity in Orthodoxy was aptly demonstrated by a treaty of mutual assistance that was struck during 1466 between the Russian Athonite monastery of "St. Panteleimon" and Rila Monastery in the Bulgarian lands.[8]

Unfortunately, the shameful circumstances surrounding the offices of Patriarch and metropolitan in the Orthodox church apparently were not spared the Karyes Assembly and the office of *Protos*. Greeks dominated the central administration of the Holy Mountain. As we have noted earlier in our discussion of general Bulgarian and Greek relations, the earliest recorded evidence of anti-Greek sentiment among the Bulgarians following the fall of the medieval Bulgarian state was expressed by Bulgarian Athonite monks during the seventeenth century. By the mid eighteenth century the rift between Bulgarians and Greeks had grown into mutual national animosity.

Such developments, however, lay mostly in the future. The pre-nationalistic unity of the Orthodox world that pervaded Athos into the seventeenth century, as well as the religio-political autonomy enjoyed by the Athonite community of monasteries, conspired to attract the most culturally illuminated and active men from all regions of that world. In the unfettered environment of Athos those men adopted and diffused new cultural ideas and created new methods and techniques of cultural expression that were firmly grounded in the unbroken Orthodox cultural traditions alive on Athos.

The cultural life thriving on Mount Athos filtered back into the Orthodox lands lying under Ottoman sway by means of two primary channels. One consisted of the pilgrims who came to Athos either as visitors or students. The other was through the work of Athonite monks sent to conduct monastic business in the lands of the Orthodox faithful. In the case of the former channel, a number of pilgrims, usually members of the clergy, would proceed to conduct active work in one or more field of Orthodox culture upon their return to their native lands. In that work they would draw upon their experience and knowledge of Athonite methods. The latter road of dissemination, however — Athonite monks traveling and working in the world outside the Holy Mountain — was by far the most effective means through which Athonite influences affected the cultural lives of the Orthodox Bulgarians.

The monasteries of Athos possessed numerous tracts of land and satellite establishments *(metohs)* throughout the Balkans and other regions of the Orthodox world. These properties enjoyed the *vakıf* status granted the Athonite parent communities by the Ottoman authorities, and, for the most part, they represented possessions granted to the Athonite monasteries during the period prior to the Ottoman conquest by Byzantine and Balkan rulers. Itinerant monks *(taxidiots)* constantly traveled between the far-flung Athonite *metohs* and their parent establishments on such errands as alms-collecting and property administration. The *metohs* themselves represented Athos outside the Holy Mountain, and the monks who took up residence in them entered the mainstream of Athonite Orthodox cultural life. Through the *metohs* the latest trends in traditional Orthodox education, literature and art were disseminated to local Balkan monasteries, villages and towns.

The majority of the Athonite monastic population in the period of the sixteenth to eighteenth centuries was ethnically Slavic. It has been argued that this Slavic majority was primarily composed of Bulgarians.[9] Whether this was in fact the case can be debated. It is certain that Bulgarians were quite numerous in the monasteries on the Holy Mountain. Two establishments in particular — Zograf and Hilendar — were strong bastions of Bulgarian monasticism during the seventeenth century. Both served as repositories for medieval Bulgarian literature and art long after the disappearance of the medieval Bulgarian state. Both also possessed *metohs* located throughout the Bulgarian lands, and both played leading roles in seventeenth century Bulgarian Orthodox culture.

Zograf Monastery, "St. Georgi," was traditionally believed to have been founded in the early tenth century (*ca.* 919) by Moisei, Aron and Ioan, three Bulgarian brothers from Ohrid. It is probable, however, that Zograf actually began as a detached, outside cell *(skete)* of a now vanished Athonite monastery, and that it evolved into a fully independent community sometime around the year 1280.[10] The name of the monastery, which means, "The Painter," was also bound to the tradition of the three brothers. According to the legend, after the brothers had constructed the monastery church they were at a loss as to whom their creation should be dedicated. One night they sought God's assistance in solving their dilemma through prayer. That same night the brothers were informed by God in a common dream that the monastery was to be dedicated to Saint George. The following morning, upon entering the church, the brothers witnessed a miracle. An icon of Saint George was being painted on the iconostasis by an invisible hand without human intervention of any kind. Ever afterward, the monastery was commonly known by the title of Zograf.

As an establishment attributed to Bulgarians from Ohrid, tsars of the Second Bulgarian Empire patronized Zograf. Kaloyan purportedly granted the monastery its earliest royal charter, bestowing upon Zograf lands and *metohs* in the regions of Sofia, Ohrid, Nikopol and elsewhere in his state. The son of Tsar Ivan Asen II, Koloman I Asen (1241-1246), presented Zograf with another charter granting it properties in Sofia. In 1342 Tsar Ivan Aleksandŭr (1331-1371) granted yet another charter to the monastery that included a gift of land in the lower Struma River region of Macedonia.[11]

Although Zograf was commonly recognized as a Bulgarian monastery, Bulgarians were not its sole benefactors. The Serbian tsar, Stefan Dušan (1331-1355), also provided Zograf with a charter.[12] Following the collapse of the Bulgarian state under the blows of the Ottomans, the princes of the Danubian Principalities replaced native Bulgarian rulers as the principle patrons of Zograf during the period of the fifteenth through eighteenth centuries. It has been suggested that the Romanian princes were the logical successors of the Bulgarian tsars because of the close political and cultural interrelationships that had developed between the two regions while the Second Bulgarian Empire was in existence. With the fall of Tŭrnovo, Bulgarian *literati* and artists fled to the nearby Romanian lands, lying just across the Danube to the north, in numbers large enough to have deeply affected Romanian Orthodox culture during the fifteenth through seventeenth centuries. With Romanian financial assistance, Zograf was able to expand its lands and buildings during that same period in which Bulgarian Orthodox culture was playing a leading role in the cultural lives of the Romanian Christians.[13]

The nationality of the Zograf monks remained consistently Slavic and Bulgarian, although in deference to the ruling clique in the Karyes Assembly religious services at the monastery were held alternately in Slavic and Greek.[14] Slavic was also the language of Orthodox cultural activity conducted at the monastery. Monks from all regions of the Bulgarian lands traveled to Zograf to study the finer points of Slavic Orthodox literature and art. A large Slavic school was founded at Zograf during the fifteenth century by refugees from Tŭrnovo. It was the first of its kind founded during the Ottoman period in the Balkans, and it became the model upon which later schools throughout the Bulgarian lands were patterned.[15]

In the scriptorium of the monastery Bulgarian monks busily copied the medieval Bulgarian manuscripts housed in the library and church, thus preserving those works for posterity. Numerous visitors, some of whom were students at the school, penned notes in the margins of these manuscripts, testifying to the readership that these works enjoyed. Many of the readers were visitors to Zograf from the Bulgarian lands during the course of the seventeenth century. Interesting and historically important was the fact that many of the materials read by these men later became prime sources for Paisii Hilendarski when he set about compiling his history that would initiate the Bulgarian national revival in 1762.[16]

Periodic conflagrations, renovations and thefts over the course of time stripped Zograf of most pre-eighteenth century works of religious art. The famous miracle-painted icon of Saint George survived; so too did a thirteenth century mural of the Virgin in the monastery chancel.[17] Despite the paucity of extant works of art, Zograf certainly constituted a major center of fine arts education during the sixteenth and seventeenth centuries. At some approximate time during the late sixteenth or early seventeenth centuries the church at Zograf was decorated with new murals and icons. One of the artists involved in that work was a Bulgarian resident at Zograf, Pimen Zografski from Sofia, a master artist of great renown. Pimen soon thereafter returned to his native Bulgarian land to work and to teach.

Literary endeavors flourished at Zograf during the seventeenth century. Unfortunately, in 1654 a Russian monk, Arsenii Suhanov, traveled throughout Athos collecting hundreds of Slavic manuscripts from the various monasteries, Zograf among them, and then transported his acquisitions back to Moscow. Suhanov's wholesale rape of Athonite Slavic works of literature has made it difficult to accurately analyze pre-1654 Athonite literary life in great detail. We do know that, aside from being the leading artist of monumental church murals among seventeenth century Bulgarians, Pimen Zografski was also a writer-copyist of some note. Other aspiring *literati* traveled to Zograf from various regions of the Bulgarian lands over the course of the seventeenth century to further their literary studies in the free and living cultural atmosphere found on Mount Athos. Among those who migrated to Zograf during this period were men who also produced literary works of their own, either while at Athos or following their return to the Bulgarian lands. The regions of Sofia, Vratsa, Rila, Etropole and Karlovo were represented in their ranks.

The flow of Bulgarian pilgrims to Zograf was steady and numerous. The beadroll of the monastery was begun in the early sixteenth century, and it was later recopied in 1709 by the monk, Kiril.[18] It listed the names of all Orthodox Christians who donated ten or more silver pieces to the monastery. Significantly for our study, the beadroll was organized by dividing the lists of names into sections headed by titles representing the various lands from which the donors originated. Thus donors to Zograf were officially listed as originating in the Bulgarian, Greek, Serbian or other "lands." These major headings were subdivided into geographic regions. Under the heading, "Bulgarian lands," were listed the regions of "Zagorie" (the westcentral and northcentral lands, including the towns of Tŭrnovo, Lovech, Etropole, Vratsa and Vidin), "Sredets" (the western lands around Sofia, including Samokov, Dupnitsa and Rila), "Znepole" (the western lands surrounding Trŭn and Kyustendil), "Visok" (the region of Pirot), "Peflagoniya" (the Macedonian lands), "Razlog" (the western lands in the regions of Razlog and Nevrokop), and "Plovdiv kadilŭk" (the southcentral lands of Northern Thrace, including Plovdiv, Pazardzhik and Kuklen). The names of donors to the monastery were entered into the roll under the suitable land and region from whence they came to Zograf. Oftentimes, the date of the donor's visit was also noted. Since female names were also entered, and females were forbidden to set foot on the Holy Mountain, it is probable that *taxidiots* of Zograf entered into the roll the names of persons who gave them donations for the monastery during their travels in the Bulgarian lands.

Should any of the pilgrims who entered their own names into the beadroll have been curious enough to glance through it, they would have realized that they were not only adding their names to a list of patrons but that the book itself was a document of great historical and cultural note. At the head of the roll, on the very first page, were listed the names of medieval Bulgarian tsars. A second such listing appeared on the third page as well.[19] In the beadroll of Zograf the monks at the monastery possessed a remembrance of the Bulgarian past, its history, and its geographic location. One might posit that the cultural activity undertaken by the Zograf monks reflected that awareness of the past, and that their impact on the population of the Bulgarian lands transmitted to some degree a glimmer of Bulgarian historical perception.

Hilendar Monastery, the second largest Bulgarian-inhabited monastery on Mount Athos during the seventeenth century after Zograf, was originally of Serbian origin. The traditional date of its founding was 1197-1198. At that time the son of the Serbian *župan* Stefan Nemanja (1159-1195), Rastko-Sava, lived as a monk on Athos. Sava persuaded his father to renounce the throne and worldly existence for the cell of an Athonite monk. As *monah* Simeon the former ruler later persuaded the Byzantine Emperor Alexios III Angelos (1195-1203) to grant him a ruined Athonite monastery that had once been the property of Vatopedi Monastery. Simeon and Sava then set about constructing Hilendar Monastery from the ruins of their imperial grant. Serbian monks from their native lands or other monasteries on the Holy Mountain colonized the new establishment. During the thirteenth and fourteenth centuries Hilendar developed into a major center of Serbian Orthodox culture, richly endowed by medieval Serbian rulers and one of the wealthiest of all Athonite monasteries.

With the fall of the independent Balkan states to the Ottoman invaders during the late fourteenth and early fifteenth centuries, Hilendar gradually lost its exclusively Serbian character and the ethnicity of its inhabitants grew increasingly Bulgarian. The Serbian lands lay far to the north of Athos, while those of the Bulgarians lay relatively closeby. The northern Balkans became a military frontier region separating the aggressive Turks and their European enemies, and with the unsettled conditions accompanying such a situation travel on the region's highways grew hazardous and difficult. As a result, few Serbs made the long trek to the Holy Mountain for the purpose of embracing the monastic way of life at Hilendar, and the monastery largely became a preserve of the neighboring Bulgarians.[20]

THE BULGARIANS

Bulgarians had begun taking an active interest in Hilendar as early as the first quarter of the fourteenth century. In 1322 the Bulgarian Tsar Georgi Terter II (1322-1323) donated a beautifully inscribed gospels to the monastery. The Hilendar library also acquired original charters granted to the Bulgarian monasteries of Virpino and Orehovo (1347) by tsars Konstantin Asen Tih (1270-1287) and Ivan Aleksandŭr, respectively.[21]

Throughout the fifteenth and sixteenth centuries the library at Hilendar was enriched by donations of other medieval Bulgarian manuscripts. These documents were presented by both pilgrims from the Bulgarian lands who visited the monastery and by Hilendar *taxidiots*, who purchased or received them as donations during their travels between the various *metohs* and the parent monastery.[22] The most noted, and historically-minded as well, of those manuscripts was the oldest known Slavic copy of a twelfth century Greek chronicle written by Konstantin Manasses, which extensively dealt with the historical relations between Byzantium and medieval Bulgaria.[23]

A school was opened at Hilendar shortly after the one founded at Zograf in the fifteenth century. It was still in operation during the seventeenth century. Unfortunately, once again, the rapaciousness of the Russian monk Suhanov has made the literary, artistic and educational picture of Hilendar during the seventeenth century somewhat cloudy. Few exemplars of such activity at Hilendar during the century are extant. Those that do exist demonstrate the close ties maintained between the monastery and the Bulgarian lands, especially its connections with the regions of Sofia and Plovdiv.[24] Hilendar did not rise to a level of cultural influence in the Bulgarian lands equal to that enjoyed by Zograf Monastery until the mid eighteenth century with the important work of its most notable Bulgarian resident, Paisii Hilendarski.

Living Slavic Orthodox cultural traditions flourished and grew in the Slavic monasteries of Mount Athos because of their relative isolation and the measure of respect for the mountain's sacredness exhibited by the Ottoman authorities. These living Athonite traditions served as models to be followed in similar activities in the Bulgarian lands. The unbroken contacts maintained by the Bulgarians with the Slavic monasteries of Athos ensured the continued expression of a living Slavic Orthodox culture in the Bulgarian-inhabited lands of the Ottoman Empire.

4. Slavic Education: The Foundation for Cultural Expression

By its very nature Slavic education formed the most basic foundation for the Orthodox cultural life of the seventeenth century Bulgarians. Without a system of education that reinforced and propagated the Slavic forms of Orthodoxy, the Bulgarians of that period may well have been assimilated into Greek Orthodox culture, a process that would have been difficult to resist, given the dominance of Greeks in the church administration with the consent and support of the Muslim Turkish civil authorities. This situation was analogous to that which had brought about the original development of the Slavic liturgy in Bulgaria during the early tenth century. Just as the adoption of the work of Cyril and Methodius and its subsequent adaptation to contemporary realities had assisted the medieval Bulgarians in fending off eventual incorporation into the essentially Greek Byzantine state, so too did the preservation of their Slavic form of Orthodoxy aid them in maintaining their cultural identity in the face of a renewed cultural threat posed by the privileged Greek Orthodox hierarchy within the Ottoman Empire.

The traditions of Slavic education among the Bulgarians extended back to the time when the Cyrillic alphabet was created in Bulgaria by the disciples of Cyril and Methodius. During the ninth and early tenth centuries schools were founded at the palace of Tsar Simeon in Preslav and in the religious center of Ohrid, as well as in the monasteries of the surrounding regions. The apex of medieval Bulgarian education was attained in the final quarter of the fourteenth century at the patriarchate and in the monasteries of the last medieval Bulgarian capital, Tŭrnovo. This period has been identified with the work of Evtimii Tŭrnovski, patriarch of the Bulgarian Orthodox church and the greatest spiritual, literary and pedagogical figure produced by the Second Bulgarian Empire. Under his outstanding guidance Tŭrnovo developed into a leading center of Slavic Orthodox culture not only in Bulgaria but in the entire Balkan Peninsula. The traditions established by Evtimii's Tŭrnovo School of grammar, literature and the fine arts were destined to have a lasting impact on all elements of Bulgarian Orthodox culture until the late eighteenth century and the rise of modern Bulgarian nationalism.[1]

The Ottoman conquest put an end to the Tŭrnovo School. Students of Evtimii, such as Grigorii Tsamblak (d. 1418) and Konstantin Kostenechki Filosof (b., *c.a.*, 1380), fled beyond the borders of the fatally smitten Bulgarian state to escape the Muslim avalanche. Orthodox education within the Bulgarian lands came to a halt during the early, unstable years of the Ottoman conquest. The cultural shock involved in the superimposition of a foreign, anti-Christian system of domination over the Orthodox Bulgarians was not conducive to the overt expression of Christian cultural activities by the subjugated people.

A number of Bulgarian refugees found their way to Mount Athos and the Bulgarian monasteries of Zograf, Hilendar and, also at that time, "St. Panteleimon." In the peace and security offered by Athos the disciples of Evtimii opened schools during the early years of the fifteenth century in which instruction was furnished in the manner of their mentor. For the most part, their students were other fugitives from conquered Bulgaria. Somewhat later, Bulgarian pilgrims to the Holy Mountain began attending classes at the monasteries. Nourished by the unfettered atmosphere of Athos and the material support enjoyed by the monasteries because of their extensive network of *metohs* and *taxidiots,* the Athonite schools became models for those later established within the Bulgarian lands.[2]

By the middle of the fifteenth century Slavic education was beginning to find its way back into the Bulgarian lands. The intermediaries in this process were the Athonite *metohs* and certain direct links that some Bulgarian monasteries, especially that of Rila, forged with those on the Holy Mountain. A spate of literary activity erupted at Rila Monastery during the second half of the century, suggesting that a school was also operating within its walls at that time. By the close of the century Rila maintained *metohs* of its own scattered throughout the Bulgarian lands. These houses later formed nuclei for literary endeavors during the seventeenth century.[3]

Over the course of the sixteenth century the number of monastery schools in the Bulgarian lands increased. Known sites of Slavic schools during that period were the monasteries of "St. Georgi," near the town of Pleven, Cherepish, Boboshevo and "Yastreb" (near Lovech, destroyed by the Turks in the early years of the seventeenth century and rebuilt some 50 years later). By the close of the sixteenth century the monasteries in the Bulgarian lands were firmly established as the leading strongholds of Slavic education.

The *raison d'être* for the monastery schools was the education of young men from the local Bulgarian population for the priesthood or the monastic way of life. One of the many repercussions of the Ottoman conquest was a sharp decline in the number of native Bulgarian priests to serve the spiritual needs of the local faithful in the face of a rising influx of Turkish colonists and foreign, especially Greek and Dubrovnik, traders.[4] Quite commonly, a single priest was forced to care for five, ten or even 20 villages in turn. To supply the villagers with an adequate number of local clergy, youths were often selected from among the regional villages and sent off to the nearest monastery to train for the priesthood.

Monasteries located in regions densely populated by Bulgarians tended to preserve and disseminate Slavic forms of Orthodox cultural traditions. By the close of the sixteenth century almost every monastery in question serviced both the spiritual and educational needs of the general Bulgarian population, although the type and quality of the education offered often varied. Usually, each literate resident of a monastery took on one or more students, termed *dyaks,* sent by the local villagers. The teacher, whose title was *daskal,* instructed his young pupils within his own living quarters, or cell. From this fact has been derived the now common designation of "cell schools" for the schools operating in the Bulgarian lands prior to the nineteenth century era of national revival.

Two types of students populated the monastery schools. The first type consisted of those who took up actual residence at the monastery in the cells of their *daskals.* These young men usually sought a monastic vocation. This group of student also included those who traveled a great distance from their native villages to study at a particular monastery. Aside from their studies, resident students were charged with learning and performing all of the mundane tasks that punctuated life within monastery walls.

The second type of student lived at home in the village with his family and traveled daily to the monastery for instruction in the cell of his *daskal.* His was usually the vocation of the village priest, for whom knowledge of the world was as important as any sort of formal education. Obviously, this latter type of student was one who lived within relatively easy commuting distance of the monastery. He thus was able to live a much less restricted life while engaged in his studies than were the resident *dyaks,* who lived under the constant supervision of their *daskals* and the strict authority of the monastic officers.[5]

Although the monastery schools possessed no formally organized system of education, the curricula offered at the schools can be considered to constitute both elementary and advanced levels of instruction. The actual levels available at any particular school appear to have depended largely on the abilities of the monks in residence at any given time. If the *daskal* was merely literate and familiar with the intricacies of Orthodox liturgical ritual, he was usually incapable of providing instruction beyond the elementary level. If, on the other hand, the *daskal* was highly skilled in the fundamentals of Church Slavonic grammar, the art of calligraphy and the craft of copying accurately (such a person often bore the title of *gramatik*), or was a master *(maistor)* of Orthodox iconography and artistic technique, he most certainly was qualified to provide advanced instruction in his areas of specialty to those capable students willing to pursue such studies.

The elementary course of instruction was of relatively short duration. The actual length of time involved was dependent on the individual student's ability to master the basic materials presented by the *daskal.* The curriculum at this level consisted of the most rudimentary elements of Slavic literacy, such as learning the Cyrillic alphabet, reading and, usually (though not necessarily always), writing.

The student was also taught to recognize the alphabetical equivalents of numerals that were commonly used in texts for expressing dates and other quantities. Because the fundamental reason for education was training for the religious life, the elementary level of instruction included the inculcation in the students of a basic understanding of Orthodox divine services and the various rituals involved in their performance.[6]

For those students whose abilities and desire led them to look beyond the level of elementary education, the monastery schools were able to make accommodation. Not every monastery, however, served as a font of advanced learning. Such a level of instruction usually was found only in the larger, more wealthy establishments, such as in Zograf or Rila or in their *metohs*. The term of advanced study was limited only by the abilities of the available instructors and of the students themselves. The student was required to assume full-time residence with his master *daskal*. During that period of residency the student was exposed to the most intensive training then available in the intricacies of the Orthodox Slavic liturgy, literature and art.

Advanced education commenced by delving into reading and mastering such complex works of liturgical literature as the book of hours and the psalter. The student received instruction in the art of singing the requisite sections of the liturgy and in all other fine points of Orthodox ritual in Church Slavonic. The entire program of studies was regulated by the precepts of Konstantin Kostenechki Filosof, one of the foremost students of Evtimii at the Tŭrnovo School, as outlined in his early fifteenth century philological treatise, *The Saga of the Alphabet*. In essence a philosophy of grammar, the *Saga* expounded Kostenechki's theory of Slavic learning. The system of prayers studied by the student represented a ladder of grammatical complexity, the mastery of which resulted in the student's evolution into the full expertise of the *gramatik*. Great emphasis was placed on learning the Cyrillic characters by name and not merely by order or visual recognition, as was taught at the elementary level. The student was required to learn the characters forward and backward, and to distinguish them from their Greek forms.[7]

After mastering the Cyrillic alphabet and the liturgical prayers, the advanced *dyak* received instruction in Slavic phonetics, learning the individual and combined sounds of letters, before beginning the construction of words and, finally, sentences. At that point he began to put pen to paper and actually to write. Mastering writing without committing grammatical errors was strongly emphasized.[8] There then followed instruction in the arts of calligraphy, illumination and the techniques of producing black and colored inks from a variety of common ingredients, the knowledge of which was orally transmitted from teacher to student over the course of centuries. The student attaining this level of instruction received practical experience by copying manuscripts housed in the library or church at the monastery. Because many of those manuscripts dated from times prior to the Turkish conquest of the Balkans, the monastery schools played a decisive role in preserving and continuing the traditions of medieval Bulgarian literature.[9]

For those students desiring a vocation in the field of religious art, the regimen was similar to that undertaken by those studying literature. They too were compelled to master Slavic phonetics and calligraphy so as to properly identify and inscribe the images they were being trained to create. They were also obliged to serve terms of apprenticeship with their arts *maistor,* from whom they learned the necessary techniques, such as manufacturing and mixing the required pigments in the painter's palette, in much the same way that the would-be grammarian learned to make inks from the *gramatik*. The course of artistic studies involved mastering the correct hierarchy of forms in the medieval Orthodox system of iconography, and used as a text the standard Orthodox artist handbook (*ermeniya*) found on Mount Athos.

Obviously, advanced education under such a system entailed a number of years and much practical experience. The student terminated his studies when his mentor decided that there was nothing further that could be imparted to him. The student was thus adjudged to have mastered all that had been taught him by his *daskal*. There was, of course, no ceremony surrounding the completion of studies. The student simply ceased using the title of *dyak* and took up that of *gramatik, zograf,* or *maistor*. As of that moment the former student was deemed qualified to furnish instruction to other students in his field of expertise.[10]

Such was the nature of the system of education that existed in the monasteries of the Bulgarian lands over the course of the fifteenth and sixteenth centuries. It afforded an elementary level of instruction that emphasized fundamental Slavic literacy while also offering, at certain of the larger monasteries, opportunities for advanced learning in the fields of literature and art. All of the system, of course, lay within an Orthodox religious context, thus demonstrating both its strengths and its weaknesses.

The system's strength lay in its role of preserving Bulgarian Orthodox cultural traditions possessing lines of descent extending back to the Tŭrnovo School of Evtimii through the intermediacy of Konstantin Kostenechki Filosof. The constant copying and recopying of medieval exemplars of liturgical literature and art in the cell schools maintained the traditions and techniques that had developed in the Bulgarian lands during that period, and served to preserve actual works produced in medieval Bulgaria that otherwise might have been forever lost. Furthermore, within the walls of the monasteries students from all strata of Bulgarian society and every region of the Bulgarian lands came and lived together on an equal footing for the purpose of learning. The monastery cell schools thus represented fortresses of Slavic Orthodox culture in the face of foreign Muslim political and Greek ecclesiastical domination, while in some degree they also managed to impart a cultural sense of unity to the Bulgarians populating the regions of the central Balkans.

The weakness of the cell school system lay in the fact that the scope of education was narrow and generally isolated from the mundane interests of the vast majority of the Bulgarian population. The monastic schools set as their goal the training of youths for religious vocations. The curriculum, therefore, was strictly liturgical in content. Moreover, the monastery schools in the Bulgarian lands were generally able to serve only those villages that lay relatively closeby. As the monasteries usually were located in sites offering worldly isolation, youths who desired an education but not the concomitant religious vocation or, on the other hand, were otherwise unable to take up residency or make the long daily trek into the hills to reach the monastery, found it difficult to impossible to attend instruction held in the cells. As a result, the educational needs of the Bulgarian urban population went virtually unexploited, except for the few schools operated by *metohs* of the larger monasteries, such as Zograf and Rila, and those run by the Greek metropolitanates in the larger towns, such as in Sofia.[11]

Throughout the period of the fifteenth to the late sixteenth centuries the relatively narrow import of the monastery cell schools was a factor of no great significance, for that time was one of social and economic instability among the subjugated Bulgarians because of the unsettling repercussions of the Ottoman conquest. It was enough that the monasteries managed to preserve pockets of Slavic Orthodox culture during those harrowing times. By the second half of the sixteenth century, however, the initial upheavals caused by the conquest had ended, and relatively normal conditions had been reestablished within the Bulgarian lands of the Ottoman Empire. Under these new conditions the Bulgarians began playing an active role in the economic life of the empire. Relative freedom was granted to large numbers of Bulgarian villagers, who acquired small privileged niches within the ruling economic system in exchange for supplying the conquerors with military and commercial necessities that the Muslims were unable, or disinclined, to furnish on their own. Urban Bulgarians slipped comfortably into the artisan and merchant *esnafs*, enjoying rights and privileges extended to those organizations by the authorities, as well as the monetary benefit that they ensured.

The offshoot of the new conditions operating in the Bulgarian lands by the late sixteenth century was that, once they came to realize the worldly advantages open to an educated layman, the Bulgarians were then in a position to support schools in their midst. Rather than sending a few young men off to a distant monastery, they were now financially able to provide an education to a greater number of youths at a location closer to their homes. Thus the advantages of education then became potentially more readily available to those who plied their trades in the secular world, as well as to those who were still desirous of a religious vocation.

The end of the sixteenth and the beginning of the seventeenth centuries witnessed the earliest expansion on any great scale of cell school education out of the monasteries and into the towns and villages. The new local schools of the seventeenth century were opened in churches, *metohs* and, in cases of villages having no church or *metoh,* in private residences. *Taxidiots* from some of the larger monasteries were usually called upon to serve as the first *daskals* in the new schools. Such men were readily available for service since Rila and Athonite *taxidiots* were constantly traversing the Bulgarian lands collecting alms, caring for the parent monasteries' business affairs on their far flung properties, selling liturgical books and icons to town and village churches, and performing various sorts of tasks as preachers and confessors.

In a scenario common for the establishment of a local town or village cell school, the parents of the local youths would pool their resources to finance the new school. They hired and paid the *daskal* a small sum of money, and bestowed upon him a variety of gifts. They also furnished the necessary educational materials, including the space for the classroom and supplies for the students. Later, they would often purchase for the local church those works of liturgical literature and art copied by the students at the school over the course of their studies. Eventually, the local priest came to play a leading role in the conduct of classes at the school. Many of these men received their own educations at the hands of the visiting *taxidiots*.[12]

The ultimate development in the new seventeenth century Bulgarian cell schools was the education of young men who took up the vocation of *daskal* without entering the priesthood or becoming monks. Such men represent the first instances among the Bulgarians of educators who pursued their vocations in the secular world and not within the parameters of the Orthodox hierarchy. The lay teachers of the seventeenth century usually were forced to divide their time between the schools in which they taught and some other sort of worldly livelihood.[13]

The expansion of education during the seventeenth century was a phenomenon dependent upon the economic conditions of the Bulgarians in any given locale. In villages, the limited number of inhabitants, who were usually engaged in a single primary occupation (such as livestock-breeding or some other agricultural pursuit), commonly could support only one school in any particular village. Many of these village schools led intermittent existences since they lay at the mercy of both local socio-political conditions and the availability of teachers to staff the classrooms. Village schools often lay dormant for long periods of time after their initial founding because of the absence of a *daskal* or as a result of periodic acts of vandalism perpetrated by local Muslim authorities or inhabitants. Village schools were constantly pressured by the villagers' ability to pay for their upkeep. A *daskal* taught at a school only as long as the parents of the students were able to pay for his services. When the funds were no longer forthcoming he moved on. Thus local economic conditions played a significant role in maintaining rural education among the Bulgarians during the seventeenth century, and determined that the life of a teacher was that of an itinerant.[14]

Unlike the villages, urban centers, such as Sofia and Vratsa, often supported more than a single school. Bulgarian townsmen, who during the seventeenth century comprised the minority of the urban population in the Bulgarian lands, were concentrated in certain *mahalles* of the towns. Within those urban quarters Bulgarian guildsmen, merchants, miners, clergy and visiting *taxidiots* lived in close conjunction with each other, and their varied incomes permitted them to support educational efforts to an extent often unrealizable in the countryside. Also, because more wealth was available for investment in urban schools, the curricula at such schools offered both elementary and advanced instruction to a far greater degree than did schools in the villages. The relatively dense concentration of the Bulgarian population in the towns also ensured that urban schools suffered far less than those in the villages from periodic disruptions. *Daskals* were more readily available from the *metohs* commonly found in all major urban centers. Furthermore, the urban schools were a constant source of new teachers, either clergy or laymen, capable of conducting courses of instruction for the local youths and elders inhabiting the *mahalles*.

Enrollments in seventeenth century cell schools, whether they were located in villages or towns, usually averaged some 20 to 30 students.[15] The pupils' studies encompassed a curriculum similar to that of the earlier monastic schools: the basic elements of Slavic literacy, singing and liturgical ritual. Again, advanced education was available in only a limited number of urban schools and at certain of the larger monasteries. For the most part, village education remained on an elementary level throughout the century.[16]

To meet the practical needs of a slowly expanding pool of students, seventeenth century Bulgarian cell schools may have added new subjects to the traditional curriculum. It has been reported that some rural *daskals* offered instruction to the local population in methods of agricultural field work, and that in both rural and urban areas they gave married women lessons in methods of housework.[17]

A significantly new element emerged in the seventeenth century cell school curriculum as a direct result of the practical needs of the Bulgarian population. This novel development was instruction in a new literary language, known to philologists as "New Bulgarian," which was largely based on the Bulgarian vernacular of the western lands, as opposed to instruction in the traditional

IN THE SEVENTEENTH CENTURY

Church Slavonic literary language of the Orthodox liturgy, which was virtually unintelligible to the average Bulgarian of the time. The importance of education in the vernacular, or at least in a language that approximated the vernacular, was obvious. For the first time since the fall of the medieval Bulgarian state Bulgarians once again began to learn a literary language that was generally intelligible, and seventeenth century literary works transcribed in the new language became readily comprehensible to the literate elements beginning to emerge within Bulgarian society.

Marginalia evidence left in extant seventeenth century manuscripts indicates that, as the century opened, schools were operated in the large monasteries of Rila, Etropole and "The Holy Trinity" near Vratsa, as well as in some smaller monasteries lying in close proximity to the larger ones (*i.e.*, Boboshevo, Teteven and Glozhene). The towns of Sofia and Vratsa exhibited significant educational activity during the late sixteenth and early seventeenth centuries, supporting at least one or two schools within the town limits and a number of individual ones in nearby monasteries (*i.e.*, Dragalevtsi, Eleshnitsa and Dolni Lozen near Sofia; Cherepish and Gradeshnitsa near Vratsa). Scattered throughout the western Bulgarian lands were schools in such locales as Samokov, Chelopechane and Adzhar.

From these early centers education diffused further outward into the countryside. It is estimated that by the close of the seventeenth century Bulgarian cell schools operated, or had operated, in approximately 69 locations throughout the Bulgarian lands. Of these, 28 were monasteries, 30 were villages and 11 were towns. (See Table 14) Their geographical diffusion would seem to indicate that seventeenth century Bulgarian education flourished predominantly in the mountainous regions of the western Bulgarian lands, particularly around Sofia, in the Rila Mountains and in the western and central Balkan Mountains, with a very few sites located on the northern fringes of the Rhodope Mountains. Few schools were founded on the lowlands or on the Thracian Plain. This particular dispersion of educational sites indicates that, for the most part, Bulgarian education was most active in areas where ethnic Bulgarians formed the bulk of the population, especially in isolated locations away from the major highways used by the Ottoman armies and administration. The schools in Sofia were an exception because, although the town was a major Ottoman administrative, military and commercial center, it served as the hub for the most populous and prosperous concentration of Bulgarian inhabitants in the western Bulgarian lands.

A number of *daskals* who worked in the seventeenth century Bulgarian schools are known. Probably the most influential of them was Daniil Etropolski (Mazach), who studied in Sofia and later taught at the monastery of "The Holy

Trinity" near Vratsa and at Etropole Monastery. In the latter place he played the leading role in the formation of the Etropole School of literature and calligraphy, the most active and influential school of its kind in the Bulgarian lands during the seventeenth century. Other *daskals* of note were Nedyalko and his son, Filip, from the Sredna Gora village of Adzhar, Avram Dimitrievich from Karlovo, Krŭstyu Gramatik at Kuklen Monastery in the northern Rhodopes, and Pimen Zografski, the noted and prolific painting *maistor* from Sofia. Viewed *in toto,* the activities of these leaders in education spanned the entire century, lending a note of continuity to Bulgarian education during the period.

In addition to the recognized masters noted above, other men, perhaps less influential in their impact but no less dedicated to their vocation, actively staffed the numerous schools that sprang up in the Bulgarian lands over the course of the seventeenth century. *Daskals* Dragan and Yakim worked in Sofia. Koyu worked in both the Teteven and Etropole monasteries, while Kalinik taught at the latter as well. Zhivko, the village priest of Adzhar, established a school that would play a role of significance under Nedyalko and Filip in mid century; Sidor was active near the close of the century in Kuklen Monastery. Four known Vratsa *daskals* were *pop* Todor, Rashko, *pop* Nikola, and Mihail. The latter eventually left Vratsa to work in a school in Razlog. There were others as well, most of whom must remain anonymous because they left no extant traces of their personal lives.[18]

Slavic education played an important cultural role among the Bulgarians living in the seventeenth century. It preserved and produced works of literature and art that bore distinct ties to the traditions of the medieval Tŭrnovo School. Moreover, education expanded beyond the confines of the monasteries into villages and towns on a scale hitherto unknown. Such a development reflected the growing need of the Bulgarian population for literacy that could be put to practical use. The act of acquiring an education thus no longer exclusively meant a commitment to the religious life as it had in the past. Hand-in-hand with this development, the schools of the century furnished literacy not only in the traditional liturgical literary language of Church Slavonic but also in the newly evolving New Bulgarian language, which was principally based on the Bulgarian vernacular of the period. Thus the first tentative steps along the road toward general lay education were taken. The level and form of literacy were of the most rudimentary kinds, and the number of individuals who directly benefited from them was relatively small. Yet the work of the seventeenth century cell schools made advanced forms of culture, such as literature and art, more readily accessible to greater numbers of Bulgarians than ever before in their history, and created the foundation for future cultural advances.

5. The Forms of Orthodox Culture

The question can be raised: Is there such a thing as Orthodox culture, and if so, of what does it consist? Modern religious scholarship has concluded that Orthodox Christianity does indeed possess a distinct culture that is exhibited through its liturgical literature and fine art. Moreover, given the tradition of toleration for national autonomous ecclesiastical organizations within the general Orthodox world (*e.g.*, the Greek, Russian, Serbian, Romanian and Bulgarian churches, to cite the primary examples), ethnic or national manifestations of Orthodox culture constitute a valid topic for historical investigation. It is, therefore, in the fields of Orthodox literature and art that we must seek evidence of significant Bulgarian cultural development during the seventeenth century. In fact, these were the only avenues open to the Bulgarians of that period for expressing their Slavic Orthodox culture and self-identity.

Writing and Literature

A direct correlation existed between education, particularly on the advanced level, in the Bulgarian lands during the seventeenth century and Slavic literary activity among the Bulgarians. Given the nature of the cell school system, the *daskals* who furnished literary instruction were also accomplished *gramatiks*, and were well-versed in the traditions of medieval Bulgarian literature. To call such men writers, in the true sense of the term, would be an overstatement. They were mostly expert copyists and calligraphers. Within the context of the period in which they worked, one during which original, creative writing was sadly repressed because of the stultifying effects of foreign domination and in-bred Orthodox conservatism, their prodigious efforts in painstakingly, often beautifully, creating new exemplars of older literary works for the benefit of posterity may be justifiably construed as a form of literary activity.

Although the number of original literary works produced during the seventeenth century by Bulgarian authors was deplorably small, the extensive copying of older works of Orthodox literature demonstrated a marked vitality in educational efforts and in calligraphical development. With regard to the latter aspect of literary activity among the Bulgarians of the century, it should be noted that Slavic traditions of calligraphy extended in an unbroken line back to the second half of the thirteenth century. At that time a unique, non-Byzantine style of calligraphy had developed in Bulgaria and during the following century had established itself securely both there and in Serbia. Highly ornamental and geometrical in its motifs, that writing style came to characterize most of the manuscripts produced in the regions of the central Balkans until the rise of the Tŭrnovo School in the late fourteenth century. Because of its widespread use, the style has come to be designated "Balkan calligraphic letters."

The Tŭrnovo School of Evtimii was influenced by the ascetic precepts of the mystical Hesychist movement then playing an important role in Orthodox circles of the Balkan states and Byzantium. Splendid manuscript decoration was thus set aside for an austere sense of spirituality, squelching the concept of ornate calligraphy. A further blow to decorative calligraphy was dealt by the Ottoman conquest soon after the rise of the Tŭrnovo School. Thus not only was the Balkan style of calligraphy undermined by the rise of Hesychist asceticism but Bulgarian literary activity was also effectively ended within the fallen Bulgarian lands for most of the fifteenth century.

In regions outside the stricken Bulgarian lands, the Balkan style of calligraphy continued to enjoy use by Orthodox writer-copyists, and particularly by those working in the Romanian Principalities and Serbia. In those lands the Balkan form of script interacted with artistic and other aesthetic influences that emanated from the West, as well as with Islamic anthropomorphic motifs that were permeating the Balkan Peninsula in the wake of the Ottoman advance.[1]

The further development of the Balkan style of calligraphy that occurred in Wallachia and Moldavia over the course of the sixteenth and seventeenth centuries played a role of significance in the stylistic development of a number of Bulgarian literary centers (*i.e.*, Etropole Monastery, Sofia and Rila Monastery) that were beginning to revive at the close of the sixteenth century. At that time, Cyrillic manuscripts produced in the Romanian lands were finding their way south of the Danube to Bulgarian monasteries and churches. Such a development was not surprising because a large number of Bulgarian *literati* had fled north into the Principalities seeking refuge following the fall of Tŭrnovo. There they recommenced their literary activities, perpetuating the writing of Slavic works in the Balkan and Tŭrnovo scripts. Throughout most of the fifteenth and sixteenth centuries, with the exception of Mount Athos and Rila Monastery, works written in the language and styles of medieval Bulgaria were to be found only in the Romanian Principalities. There, under the impact of the Western Renaissance and Baroque influences that seeped into the region from Hungary and the living traditions of Byzantine manuscript decoration preserved among the Romanians, the austere Tŭrnovo style of calligraphy underwent a transformation that retained the simple geometric forms of the individual letters but infused them with a variety of highly decorative motifs.[2]

IN THE SEVENTEENTH CENTURY

Perhaps no other literary center in the Bulgarian lands was more receptive to the stylistic influences slowly making their way south of the Danube than Etropole Monastery, situated on the northern slopes of the Balkan Mountains. During the late sixteenth and early seventeenth centuries the monks working in Etropole's monastery scriptorium created a uniquely new form of calligraphy that combined elements found in the medieval Tŭrnovo, Serbian, and Romanian scripts. Their creation was destined to exert a powerful influence on a great many of the Slavic manuscripts produced during the seventeenth century in the Bulgarian lands. So unique was the style of writing developed at the monastery that it has come to be known among modern philologists as the "Etropole calligraphic style."[3]

Briefly, the Etropole style was grounded on two basic principles. The first involved embellishing the geometric initial letters of the page with embroidered designs and anthropomorphic images, while decorating those letters that formed the initial line of a page or chapter with floral motifs. The second principle lay in harmonizing the graphics on a particular page by paralleling the components in vertical and horizontal planes. With the emergence of this style, as exemplified in the works of Etropole's finest calligrapher, Daniil Etropolski, Bulgarian manuscript illumination once again acquired a quality of intricate artistic design, with anthropomorphic and zoomorphic decorative techniques used within an ingenious graphic scheme, that had been absent from literary works produced in the Bulgarian lands since the fourteenth century.[4]

The impact of Etropole calligraphy was felt almost immediately by writer-copyists working in the smaller centers of literary activity located in the Balkan Mountains closeby Etropole, such as in the monasteries of Teteven and Glozhene. Before long, the new writing style appeared in regions of the Sredna Gora Mountains lying to the south of the Balkan range. Students who came to the school at Etropole Monastery from various regions of the Bulgarian lands, and especially from the areas to the south of the Balkan Mountains, carried their familiarity with the new style with them upon their return to their native villages or towns. In such manner Etropole calligraphy was propagated in places such as Karlovo and Adzhar, in the southern Balkan Mountains and the eastern Sredna Gora, respectively, and as far south as the region around Plovdiv, especially in Kuklen Monastery in the northern foothills of the Rhodope Mountains.

The influence of the Etropole style became so widespread in the Sredna Gora during the seventeenth century that it has been argued that the style of calligraphy common to that region, which past scholars had identified as a separate form, termed "Sredna Gora letters," was in actuality a modified version of the Etropole style. To be sure, a unique style of letters characterized the literary works produced in the Sredna Gora during the late sixteenth century. It was greatly influenced by works that had originated in Rila Monastery to the west. The form of letters utilized by that style, known as "lamb's-tailed" letters, found currency in manuscripts written in the Sofia, Vratsa and Etropole regions. By the seventeenth century, however, the Sredna Gora style had been incorporated into that of Etropole, so that throughout the rest of the period the Etropole style reigned supreme in the central and western regions of the Bulgarian lands.[5]

Of more significance than calligraphy for seventeenth century Bulgarian literary activity was the form of Slavic literary language used by the *gramatiks* and *daskals*. Two literary languages became current in the Bulgarian lands over the course of the century. The primary language was the traditional Church Slavonic, which enjoyed reverential usage since the ninth century among the limited number of educated Bulgarians, and which literally maintained the legacy of Evtimii's Tŭrnovo School. By the seventeenth century the nature of Church Slavonic in the Bulgarian lands was varied and complex. Far from representing a monolithic vehicle of literary expression, it exhibited three different variants: the Bulgarian form, frequently referred to as Middle Bulgarian; the Serbian form, also termed "Resava;" and the Russian form, which modern scholars commonly designate as Church Slavic. One or more of these variants could be found in any given Bulgarian Orthodox Church Slavonic manuscript produced during the seventeenth century.

The variant possessing the least currency in the Bulgarian lands during the seventeenth century was the Russian. Slavic Orthodox culture, particularly its alphabet and literary traditions, had been twice transplanted to Russia from Bulgaria during the Middle Ages. The first transfer occurred in the tenth-eleventh centuries and basically involved the corpus of works produced by such noted medieval Bulgarian Orthodox writers as Kliment Ohridski, Chernorizets Hrabŭr, Konstantin Presbyter, Ioan Ekzarh and Kozma Presbyter. Originally Bulgarian in language, the works transported to Russia following her conversion to Orthodox Christianity in the late tenth century experienced a gradual transformation over time as Russian linguistic elements entered the written vocabulary of the Russian *literati* who worked at copying the Bulgarian originals. During the early fifteenth century a new influx of Bulgarian literary influence made itself felt in the Russian Orthodox world as Bulgarian refugees from Tŭrnovo, most notably Grigorii Tsamblak, found their way into the Muscovite lands. The literary and philological works of Tsamblak, who eventually was raised to the seat of the Kievan metropolitanate (1415), helped initiate a new wave of Bulgarian literary influence on the Russian literary language. As a disciple of Evtimii, Tsamblak propagated the tenets of the Tŭrnovo School in Russian literature and introduced the Russian church to the life and works of Evtimii himself.

By the late sixteenth century the Russians were issuing printed editions of medieval Bulgarian literary works in Russian Church Slavic. At that time as well, a number of Bulgarian and Athonite monasteries were in close contact with the

Muscovite court and various notable Russian monasteries, usually out of the necessity for the Bulgarian establishments to seek financial assistance from their relatively wealthy Russian coreligionists. Some Bulgarian monasteries, such as Rila, Bilintsi and Cherepish, and the Bulgarian Athonite monasteries of Zograf and Hilendar, sent delegations to Muscovy in search of aid at various times during the seventeenth century.[6] Through the connections established between the Bulgarians and Russians by means of such delegations, their coexistence in the Athonite monasteries, and other more indirect contacts, such as *via* the Romanian Principalities, a number of Russian language liturgical books found their way into the Bulgarian lands and were used in many monastery and parish churches for the purposes of divine worship or textual instruction in the cell schools. Only a few Bulgarian writer-copyists, such as *pop* Peshov from Kostenets and Todor Pirdopski, however, produced manuscripts in the Russian Church Slavic variant during the seventeenth century.[7]

Somewhat surprisingly, the native Bulgarian variant of Church Slavonic was only slightly more utilized than the Russian in seventeenth century Bulgarian cell schools and works of literature. As noted earlier, the destruction of the Tŭrnovo literary center and the subsequent diaspora of Bulgarian *literati* resulted in the preservation of Bulgarian literary traditions in regions outside the former frontiers of the fallen Bulgarian state. In those regions where Slavic Orthodox culture flourished within a native Slavic *milieu*, as, for example, in the Russian and Serbian lands, Bulgarian traditions transported there by the refugees from Tŭrnovo underwent a rather swift process of assimilation into the local Orthodox cultures. This did not occur, however, in the Romanian Principalities. Throughout the twelfth through fourteenth centuries the Orthodox Romanians maintained strong cultural links to the Second Bulgarian Empire, and their Orthodox cultural life was essentially an extension of the Bulgarian, despite certain elemental variations. Some fugitive Bulgarian *literati* from Tŭrnovo found new homes in Romanian monasteries (*e.g.*, Suseava, Gorova, and Neamți), where they continued to conduct literary activity in the language and traditions of the defunct Tŭrnovo School.[8]

Middle Bulgarian works of church literature written in the Romanian Principalities began to filter back into the Bulgarian lands during the late sixteenth century, eventually finding their way to the active literary and educational centers located in the Balkan Mountains and in the western Bulgarian highlands. Most of the Middle Bulgarian manuscripts circulating in the Bulgarian lands during the seventeenth century were thus products of Romanian monasteries. Only a few were produced within the Bulgarian lands themselves, and only one writer-copyist, K. Pahomie from the monastery of "Koziya" near Dupnitsa, has been positively identified as working in the Bulgarian variant.[9]

Some Middle Bulgarian manuscripts were circulated in the Bulgarian lands during the seventeenth century by persons who had acquired them from points outside the Romanian lands, such as from the Athonite monasteries. An example of such a circulating work was a Bulgarian book of Lenten offices that originally had been written at Hilendar Monastery in the sixteenth century and during the seventeenth century was found in the villages of Bzovnik (1662) and Prisyan (1689?).[10]

An important exception to the picture of dearth regarding activity in the native Bulgarian Church Slavonic variant was Rila Monastery, whose library housed a number of Middle Bulgarian manuscripts predating the fall of Tŭrnovo. Perhaps like no other location in the Bulgarian lands, the traditions of medieval Bulgarian literature never completely died out in Rila. During the seventeenth century these old Bulgarian works were avidly studied by the students attending the monastery's cell school.[11] Yet no seventeenth century writer-copyist from Rila chose to work in Middle Bulgarian.

By far, the most widely used Church Slavonic variant current in the Bulgarian lands during the seventeenth century was the Serbian (or Resava) literary language. Its origins stemmed from the philological work of the Bulgarian student of Evtimii, Konstantin Kostenechki Filosof. After the fall of Tŭrnovo he fled to the lands of the Serbian despot, Stefan Lazarović, where under that ruler's patronage Kostenechki established a school in the Serbian monastery of Manasija (also called Resava, after the small river that flowed nearby) during the early years of the fifteenth century. While in residence at that monastery he developed a philological reform of literary Serbian that was firmly grounded in the similar efforts of Evtimii with regard to Bulgarian. Kostenechki's reforms were popularized in his *Saga*. For this reason, the designation, "Resava," was lent to the Serbian form of Church Slavonic propagated by Kostenechki.[12]

Kostenechki's work made an almost immediate impact on the educational and literary centers located in the Macedonian lands of the Ottoman Empire. From these centers the Serbian variant formalized by Kostenechki was diffused into the western Bulgarian lands, either directly or by way of Mount Athos. A number of Macedonian monasteries (*e.g.,* Lesnovo, Osogovo and "Matejče") maintained contact with those in the regions of Rila, Sofia and Etropole. In fact, Serbians constituted a large proportion of the population in those areas of the Bulgarian lands because of their intimate involvement in the ore mining industry. From Athos, Rila, Sofia and Etropole the Serbian variant spread throughout the western and northcentral regions of the Bulgarian lands, becoming the overwhelmingly dominant form of the traditional Church Slavonic literary language by the seventeenth century.[13]

A prodigious number of Bulgarian *gramatiks* from the period worked in the Serbian variant, the most notable of whom were Daniil Etropolski, Avram Dimitrievich and Krŭstyu Gramatik. Many writer-copyists of lesser prominence also used the Serbian in their works. Among those whose work deserves particular attention were *daskal* Dragan from Sofia, Ioan Gramatik, Rafail and Zaharii (the contemporaries of Daniil at Etropole Monastery), *daskals* Nedyalko and Filip from Adzhar, and *dyak* Dragul at "The Holy Trinity" Monastery near Vratsa.[14]

All three of the Church Slavonic variants possessed a common link to the Tŭrnovo School of Evtimii Tŭrnovski, not only in terms of his philological reforms, as applied to the Russian and Serbian variants by Grigorii Tsamblak and Konstantin Kostenechki Filosof, respectively, but also in terms of literary content, especially in the realm of Orthodox hagiography.[15] Evtimii was perhaps the greatest of medieval Bulgarian hagiographers. His subject matter was drawn from the historical past of the Bulgarians, and his works intentionally emphasized Bulgarian historical topics. At the time of his elevation to the Bulgarian patriarchal throne (1375), the Bulgarian state, under Tsar Ivan Shishman (1371-1395), was faced with the threat of impending Ottoman onslaught. An army composed of allied Balkan states, led by the Serbian despot, Jovan Uglješa (1365-1371), was thoroughly defeated on the banks of the Maritsa River by the Turks in the Battle of Çirmen on 26 September 1371. Uglješa was among the many victims of the ensuing carnage, and the way into the heart of the Balkan Peninsula was flung open before the victorious Ottoman forces.

Shishman's Kingdom of Tŭrnovo was forced into vassalage to the Ottoman sultan as a consequence of the debacle. Evtimii apparently assumed the leadership of the Bulgarian patriotic reaction against the humbled political position of the state and the inevitable destruction that such a condition portended. His hagiographical works thus focused on the temporal and spiritual greatness of medieval Bulgaria. They appear to have been written both to commemorate native saints and to inform the common Bulgarian worshipers of the past glories of their threatened country.

The most outstanding and influential of Evtimii's hagiographical works was his *Life* of the ninth-tenth century Bulgarian hermit-saint, Ivan Rilski.[16] Ivan was born in the western Bulgarian village of Skrino (*ca.*, 876), in the area of Dupnitsa, to parents beset by the poverty common to the Bulgarian peasantry of the period. His birth occurred during the reign of Prince Boris, barely 15 years after that astute ruler had adopted Orthodox Christianity. The years of Ivan's youth coincided with the so-called "Golden Age" of medieval Bulgaria that was initiated by Boris' son, Tsar Simeon. It was a period of blossoming Orthodox culture in Bulgaria, but it was also a time of deep social unrest because of the vast gulf that separated the *bolyar* ruling class, with its wealth and power, from the struggling class of peasants, who were beset with the heavy burden of rising feudal-like obligations to their aristocratic overlords. As a result, a current of worldly escapism permeated the Bulgarian lower classes in the midst of Simeon's shining reign of culture. Worldly pessimism found its release in either the Christian dualistic heresy of Bogomilism or Orthodox anchoritism. On the deaths of his parents, young Ivan, aged 20 or 25, chose the renunciation of the world offered by Orthodox monasticism.

Ivan entered the monastery of "St. Dimitrii" in the Osogovo Mountains of western Bulgaria with the intention of dedicating his life to the service of God. Not long afterward he concluded that monastic life was too worldly for one so devoted to serving the Lord, so he forsook the monastery and set off into the mountains seeking a totally secluded existence dedicated to complete spiritual devotion. He lived for a time in the deserted regions of the upper Struma River near Pernik. Later he moved into the southern foothills of Mount Vitosha. Yet even in those isolated locales he was unable to find the utter seclusion that he so fervently sought.

Following an episode in which he was attacked by bandits, Ivan again set out on continued searches for a place of perfect worldly isolation. Almost naturally, he was drawn to the wild and virtually inaccessible Rila Mountains, the highest and most forbidding massif in the Balkans. Following the Rila River eastward into the heart of the Rilas, Ivan finally arrived at a site that seemed to offer the requisite seclusion for which he had searched so long. He made his first living quarters high up in a hollow tree trunk. Later he displaced some wild animals in a cave they had been using as a den. There Ivan lived for a number of years alone, fasting and struggling against demons in his mind that continually tempted him to renounce his ascetic, anchoritic life.

Despite all of Ivan's tireless efforts to rid himself of the world, the world sought him out. His hermit's abode was eventually discovered by shepherds who grazed their flocks in the area. Before long, local villagers from the Rila lowlands were visiting the hermit and soliciting his advice on an assortment of personal problems. Rumors of the holy man who inhabited an animal's cave in the Rila Mountains, living a saintly life of pure spiritual devotion, spread throughout the western regions of Bulgaria. Luka, Ivan's nephew, traveled to the cave to take up the life-style of his uncle. Others soon followed, and a small anchorite community grew up around the cave of Ivan, who then realized that further flight from worldly acclaim was futile.

The disciples of Ivan carved out living quarters of sorts from the rocky terrain surrounding his cave. A small church was extemporized in another nearby den. The men sat at Ivan's feet and absorbed the tenets for the ascetic life that he expounded. Among that small group of apostles were Ioakim Osogovski, Gavril Lesnovski and Prohor Pshinski, men who would later leave the Rilas to form similar anchorite communities of their own in the mountains of the Macedonian lands, and who would eventually share the same posthumous honor as their mentor in being elevated to sainthood by the Bulgarian Orthodox church.

The fame of the saintly Ivan was such that word of his holy existence reached the Bulgarian court at Preslav and Tsar Petŭr (927-970). During a trip to the Sofia region Petŭr dispatched royal emissaries into the Rila Mountains to seek out the cave of Ivan and to request that the hermit grant the ruler an interview. Ivan refused to receive them, and they were forced to return to their sovereign and report the failure of their mission. They related how they had been miraculously fed when suffering from hunger while in the mountains near the reported site of Ivan's cave. Petŭr then attempted to go himself into the mountains but was forced to return by the inhospitable environment. He later sent Ivan money and fruits but the hermit returned them with a letter declaring that men dedicated to God had no need of such worldly luxuries as money and fine foods.

Ivan lived out the remaining days of his life in his cave close to the cells of his disciples. Upon his death at the age of 70 (18 August 946), his body was buried outside that cave. Not long afterward, however, new rumors circulated in the western Bulgarian lands claiming miraculous powers for his remains. Petŭr then had Ivan's bones disinterred (950) and carried to Sofia, where a stone church was eventually erected to house his sacred relics. In that same year, Ivan was canonized a saint by the Bulgarian Patriarch. Following the rise of the Second Bulgarian Empire and the liberation of Sofia from Byzantine control (1188), the relics of Ivan were ordered brought to the new Bulgarian capital at Tŭrnovo (1195) by Tsar Ivan Asen I (1190-1196).[17]

Further subjects for Evtimii's hagiographical treatment were Ilarion Müglenski, a twelfth century bishop of Müglen who was a staunch warrior against Christian heresies, and Filoteya Temnishka, a twelfth century female anchorite from southern Thrace. Both of those Christian notables were buried in Tŭrnovo at the time Evtimii wrote their commemorative *Lives*. Both had had their relics brought to the capital by Tsar Kaloyan.

Ivan Shishman requested that Evtimii write a fourth *Life*, that of Petka (Peraskeva) Tŭrnovska. Much like Filoteya, Petka was a twelfth century female anchorite. She was born of wealthy Bulgarian parents in the Thracian town of Epivatos, which was situated on the coast of the Sea of Marmara between Selymbria and Constantinople. Her brother took the tonsure and eventually rose to the seat of an archbishopric. According to the *Life*, one day while praying in church Petka was struck by the words of Christ in the gospels concerning the need for selling all worldly goods and taking up the cross to follow Him. She left the church and straight away gave her rich clothing to the poor of the city. Following the deaths of her parents, Petka decided to forsake the world completely for a life of Christian asceticism. She turned over her extensive properties to the poor and spent the next five years of her life in prayer at a church outside the city of Heraclea. Petka then made the pilgrimage to the Holy Land, where she visited all the sacred sites, walking barefooted in the footsteps of her savior. Finally, she ventured into the Jordanian desert and assumed a life of abject self-deprivation, scratching out a meager existence from the desert until she grew old. A day came, however, when it was revealed to her that God did not wish her to perish alone in that wasteland but, rather, desired her to return to her native soil and to serve as an example of the pure Christian life for others. Petka obeyed the message from God and returned to Epivatos, where she died two years later.

Numerous miracles were said to have occurred at her grave site, and eventually she was canonized. In 1238 the powerful military tsar of the Bulgarians, Ivan Asen II, had her relics disinterred and brought to Tŭrnovo, where they were laid to rest in a church dedicated in her honor.[18]

Although none of the hagiographies written by Evtimii were entirely original, for he utilized numerous existing sources, many of which were Greek, he did infuse what can be construed as a unique sense of Bulgarian patriotism into each tale. He consistently unfolded the essentially spiritual narrative that he related by stressing historical and realistic details referring to either the Bulgarian people or the Bulgarian state. The reader was thus informed of the names of villages and towns located within the borders of the Bulgarian state during the period in which the central characters lived; often those locales lay outside the perimeter of late fourteenth century Bulgaria. Evtimii stressed the Bulgarian ethnicity of the parents of those saints born outside the borders of Bulgaria. In each work he emphasized the existence and glory of the Bulgarian tsardom through his depiction of those particular tsars who played important roles in the narratives. They were presented as men renowned for their spirituality or for their military prowess, and were, therefore, considered national heroes.[19] By his frequent use of the possessive when referring to the central protagonists of his tales (*e.g.*, "our Petka," "our tsar Petŭr"), Evtimii may have sought to invoke in his readership a sense of some common link between themselves, their church, their state and the Bulgarian people, church and state of the past.

Evtimii made use of similar techniques in a number of his other literary works, such as his eulogies for various Orthodox saints.[20] Given the close relationship that existed between the church and the state in the tradition of Byzantium that existed in Evtimii's time, the only medium for the propagation of patriotic themes lay within the realm of religious edification. Through his hagiographical writings Evtimii attempted to reinforce the national dignity of the Bulgarians in the face of the Muslim Ottoman menace through descriptions of Bulgarian spiritual and temporal heroes. Perhaps he was trying to imbue his Bulgarian audience with the idea that God had often shown favor to "His" people in the past and might well do so again. Yet despite his efforts to strengthen a national front against the Turks, those rapacious enemies of the Christians proved victorious. Bulgaria ceased to exist as an independent entity, and its patriotic patriarch, deemed by the Turks too dangerous to be permitted to remain in Tŭrnovo, was sent into exile (1394).

IN THE SEVENTEENTH CENTURY

The hagiographical style of Evtimii did not die with the destruction of the medieval Bulgarian state. It was kept alive by his disciples and students in the lands to which they dispersed following the national disaster. In Russia, Tsamblak wrote a fifteenth century continuation of Evtimii's *Life* of Petka Tŭrnovska that described the transfer of her relics to Vidin from Tŭrnovo in 1393, while Evtimii's *Lives* of Ivan Rilski and Ilarion Mŭglenski became popular in the monasteries surrounding Moscow and Kiev, where sixteenth and seventeenth century copies were included in manuscripts and printed books. Likewise in Serbia, Konstantin Kostenechki Filosof produced a *Life* of his patron, Stefan Lazarević, in the mold of Evtimii's hagiographies. Upon Mount Athos there appeared the earliest extant copies of Evtimii's *Lives* of Ivan Rilski, Petka Tŭrnovska and Ilarion Mŭglenski. It is highly probable that the copy of Ivan Rilski housed in Zograf Monastery was an original work penned by either Evtimii himself or by one of his contemporary associates.[21]

Even within the Bulgarian lands the hagiographical tradition of Evtimii was not totally expunged by the catastrophic destruction of the medieval Bulgarian state. The works of Vladislav Gramatik from the mid fifteenth century demonstrated an indebtedness to those of Evtimii. Although the bulk of his activity occurred at "Matejče" Monastery in the Macedonian lands, Vladislav maintained close contacts with the western Bulgarian lands, especially with Rila Monastery, where he spent some time following its refounding in the mid fifteenth century.

In 1479 Vladislav copied an extensive panegyric for Rila Monastery to commemorate the return of the relics of Ivan Rilski to the monastery from Tŭrnovo (1469) after an absence of nearly 500 years. The work was written in Middle Bulgarian and included Evtimii's *Life* of Ivan Rilski, as well as his eulogies for Nedelya and Constantine and Helena. It also included an original *Life* of Ivan Rilski written by the Bulgarized Greek writer-copyist and friend of Vladislav, Dimitrios Kantakuzinos. Yet of most significance in the work was an original piece written by Vladislav himself and appended to the conclusion of Evtimii's *Life* of Rilski. This work, known as the *povest* (novelette) of the transfer of Rilski's relics to Rila Monastery, was firmly grounded in the hagiographical traditions of Evtimii. Not only did it describe the transfer of the relics in narrative fashion but it also encompassed a much broader scope, in that it included a description of Bulgarian society during the first century of Ottoman domination. As in Evtimii's works, Vladislav placed great emphasis on the Bulgarian character of the people and places mentioned in the narrative. That Vladislav consciously patterned his work on that of Evtimii was virtually stated outright in the manuscript by the location of the *povest* as a direct continuation of Evtimii's *Life*.[22]

In the following century the traditions of Evtimii were again demonstrated to be alive within the Bulgarian lands in the original works written by two men from Sofia, *pop* Peio and Matei Lambadarii Gramatik. Peio served as a priest in the metropolitan church of "St. Marina." Born in or near Sofia, Peio traveled throughout the Serbian and Macedonian lands and visited Mount Athos before taking up his position at the Sofia metropolitanate. At some point prior to February 1515 a young Bulgarian goldsmith named Georgi, from the western town of Kratovo, briefly resided in Peio's home. Later that same young man was burnt to death in front of the old church of "The Holy Wisdom" (11 February 1515), a victim of Muslim mob fanaticism. Peio was inspired to write a *Life* of young Georgi, who had been 18 years of age at the time of his execution. Georgi was eventually canonized by the Bulgarian Orthodox church under the name of Georgi Novi Sofiiski. In his *Life*, Peio utilized the standard techniques of Evtimii, noting that Georgi had been born of Bulgarian parents, citing Bulgarian place names, and the like. Interestingly, Peio noted the fact that Georgi had received an education to prepare himself for a career in the goldsmithing craft.[23]

Muslim reaction also contributed to the creation of another original hagiography, that of Nikolai Novi Sofiiski, written by Matei Gramatik. Throughout the narrative of the life and martyrdom (1555) of that Bulgarian shoemaker from Iannina, Matei demonstrated the common techniques of Evtimii in emphasizing the Bulgarian elements in the story. The similarities that existed between the works of Peio and Matei spoke for the operation of a small literary school in Sofia during the sixteenth century that actively expounded the hagiographical tenets of Evtimii's Tŭrnovo School.[24]

Although copies of the works of Evtimii, Vladislav and Peio appeared in many seventeenth century works of literature, few original Slavic works in the tradition of Evtimii, or in that of any other for that matter, were produced in the Bulgarian lands over the course of the period. (See Table 19) There were, however, two works that did bear marked influences of the Tŭrnovo School. One was an original *Life* of Ivan Rilski that was included in a work written in 1636 by Ioan Gramatik, in collaboration with *daskal* Koyu from Teteven, while Ioan was in residence at Etropole Monastery. Ioan added his *Life* to copies made of Vladislav's Rilski *povest* and a Slavic *Life* of Ivan Rilski written by the Greek, George Skylitzes. The other original seventeenth century Evtimii-like hagiography was that of the celebrated Bulgarian monk and master painter, Pimen Zografski, written in Middle Bulgarian by his former student at Zograf Monastery, *monah* Pamfilii, during the second half of the century.[25]

For the most part, Slavic Orthodox literary activity conducted in the Bulgarian lands during the seventeenth century consisted of copying older Slavic works. (See Table 18) The majority of the manuscripts penned during the period were works that revolved around the celebration of Orthodox divine services, such as gospels, missals, sermons and suchlike. The period also witnessed the revival of an older category of religious writing that simply strove to satisfy the believers' spiritual edification, and that would eventually have a significant impact on the

IN THE SEVENTEENTH CENTURY

development of a decidedly Bulgarian form of Orthodox literature. That literary form was the *sbornik* (collection).

The term *sbornik* described the general content of the work itself. It represented a miscellany of religious and secular writings that apparently were gathered together under one cover at the discretion of the work's compiler. Any given compiler was free to choose the materials that would be included in his collection from a wide variety of hagiographies, writings of the early church fathers, popular tales of an historical, apocryphal or legendary nature, sermons or any of the other types of stories available to him at the time. No two *sborniks* were exactly similar in terms of content, and no single *sbornik* contained selections from all the categories of available materials.

One may suggest that the socio-economic conditions within the Bulgarian lands that helped bring about the broadening of education during the seventeenth century also assisted in the reemergence of the *sbornik* as a popular literary vehicle. Now that literacy began to spread beyond the walls of monasteries and was growing accessible to a portion of the secular population, the new readership that was forming had need of reading material with a broader appeal than strictly liturgical writings used in Orthodox ritual. In turn, the didactic purposes thus opened to Bulgarian writer-copyists as a consequence of this new situation contributed to the development of a second, more practical literary language for use in works primarily aimed at a secular audience, rather than at clergy for recitation in celebrating divine services. So there arose the New Bulgarian literary language, which found personification in the literary genre of the *damaskin* that came into full bloom during the seventeenth century.

In essence, the *damaskin* represented the same sort of literary work as the *sbornik* but with one critical difference — it was written in the New Bulgarian language. While remaining within the realm of religious literature, the *damaskin* demonstrated a close affinity to the secular world in that it was written in a language resembling the vernacular of its intended readership, thus being potentially accessible to the majority of Bulgarians through that element of the population enjoying the benefit of any sort of education.

The *damaskin* received its name from the originator of the literary form, the sixteenth century Greek preacher from Thessaloniki, Damaskin Studit. He had come to the realization that it was futile to attempt sermonizing to a population that could not understand the language in which the sermons were written. In Studit's case, the problem lay in the divergence between the High Greek of the Byzantine tradition and the Greek *koine* spoken by the common people. He set about transcribing 36 homilies from Byzantine to *koine* Greek, which he then had published in Venice (1558) under the title: *The Treasury*. Before his death in 1577 Studit's book underwent four additional editions. Two posthumous editions appeared prior to the close of the sixteenth century, leaving little doubt as to the popularity that the work enjoyed among Orthodox Greek believers.[26]

The great success of *The Treasury* and the reason for its widespread popularity were not lost upon the non-Greek Orthodox *literati* of the Balkans. The fact that the work was written in a language comprehensible to the common believer was obviously the primary factor. By the close of the sixteenth century Serbian and Bulgarian translations of *The Treasury* made their appearance in the Macedonian and western Bulgarian lands.

The road taken by the new literary genre into the Bulgarian lands ran through Rila Monastery. The monks at Rila possessed Greek, as well as Slavic, works in their library. They also maintained lively ties with Greek monasteries on Mount Athos and in Istanbul. It is highly probable that they possessed a copy of the original Greek version of *The Treasury* and thus were placed in a very advantageous position for creating a Bulgarian translation. This they did in the latter years of the sixteenth century. The language of that work was a mixture of Bulgarian and Resava Serbian, and did not as yet represent a truly new, more conversational form of Bulgarian literary language. The Rila *damaskin,* however, did represent a step taken in the direction of creating the New Bulgarian literary language. The transformation of the mixed language of the Rila copyists into the New Bulgarian was a process that began in earnest during the seventeenth century, and that was only completed in the century that followed.[27]

Copies of the Rila *damaskin* spread throughout the regions of the Sredna Gora and the Balkan Mountains through the intermediation of Rila Monastery's network of *metohs* and *taxidiots.* In the process of the *damaskin's* dissemination an interesting transformation occurred. The earliest *damaskins* were complete translations of the original 36 sermons found in *The Treasury*. With the passage of time, the Bulgarian versions grew less interested in the original sermons and came to resemble the Church Slavonic *sborniks,* with content left to the discretion of the compilers. The Rila *damaskin* contained 26 translations of the original sermons of Damaskin Studit, while only one sermon was not found in the Greek prototype. On the other hand, the late seventeenth century "Popstoikov" *damaskin* contained only two of the original sermons from *The Treasury,* and only one of those was copied *in toto.*[28]

Despite the apparently eclectic nature of the work, the selections found in seventeenth century Bulgarian *damaskins* demonstrated a definite profile. They were all didactic or moralistic works of one sort or another. As in the *sborniks,* the prominent selections were hagiographies, sermons for Orthodox feast days, didactic tales and, though rarely, apocryphal or historical writings. A notable tie to the *sbornik* tradition, and through it to the traditions of the Tŭrnovo School, was the frequency with which Evtimii's *Life* of Petka Tŭrnovska found its way into the contents of seventeenth century *damaskins*. In one such work, the "Koprivshtitsa" copy, Evtimii was identified as the "Patriarch of Tŭrnovo."

Interestingly, in earlier copies of the *Life* of Petka no such identification was made.[29]

Evtimii's *Life* of Petka, with its concluding section that spoke of the victorious Bulgarian tsar, Ivan Asen II, his royal capital at Tŭrnovo, native *bolyars* and the Bulgarian Patriarchate, was but one example of a noticeable Bulgarian slant to the *damaskins*. There were also other, more subtle reminders of the past glories of the former Bulgarian state and the sad condition to which the Bulgarians had been reduced by foreign conquest. No *damaskin* blatantly attempted to instill in its readership a modern sense of national consciousness. They did, however, often make reference to the natural enemies of that readership. In the sermon known as "The removal of the Cross" (by Constantine and Helena from the Holy Land), found in four extant seventeenth century Bulgarian *damaskins,* the "impious barbarians" faced by Constantine on the Danubian frontier of his empire were transformed by the writer-copyists into Turks. This sermon went on to relate that Constantine was defeated by the Turks, who then crossed over onto the Bulgarian Danubian Plain, an area of intensive Turkish colonization by the seventeenth century. After Constantine's mother, Helena, discovered the "true cross" of Christ's crucifixion in the Holy Land, he once more marched against the Turks, cross in hand, and totally routed them in battle. The allegories of the cross (Christianity), Constantine (the Christian emperor), and the contested region along the Danube (the Bulgarian lands) were obvious to the Bulgarian readers of those *damaskins*.[30]

Only one seventeenth century Bulgarian *damaskin,* the "Popstoikov" copy, contained Peio's *Life* of the native Bulgarian saint, Georgi Novi Sofiiski. Another, the "Drinov," included a list of medieval Bulgarian tsars, as well as historical tales concerning the Bulgarian Orthodox church from the time of the ninth century Christianizer, Prince Boris.[31]

A number of Bulgarian *damaskins* produced during the century contained secularly oriented material, speaking well for the emerging existence of an audience that was not strictly relegated to the ranks of the clergy. There were sermons against drunkenness, sorceresses and soothsayers. Others admonished evil women. So too were there instructional tales, such as, "For the woman who, out of love for her husband, murdered her two children." Other commonly found selections dealt with instructions for properly raising children, maintaining friendships, and the importance of education. The "Lukovit" *damaskin* provided its readers with instructional quotations from ancient philosophers. In most cases, the didactic messages were colorfully presented, sometimes in verse. Scientific works, naive and primitive by modern standards (and by those of the seventeenth century West, for that matter) but representative of the level of knowledge enjoyed by the subject populations of the Ottoman East, found their way into a number of Bulgarian *damaskins*. Usually, such works told simple stories of animals or gave highly inaccurate lessons in geography.[32]

Accessibility and reader comprehension seem to have been the primary concerns of the *damaskin* compilers, not only in the form of language used but also in terms of technique. In transcribing the selections chosen for inclusion in their works, the writer-copyists freely made digressions from the original models and often simplified the phrasing. It was not uncommon for them to insert explanatory notations to help the reader through difficult passages, or even for them to paraphrase entire passages. Simplified phrasing was intended to strengthen the narrative aspect of the work so as to maintain the reader's attention. Compilers of *damaskins* often resorted to including explanatory notes directly within the body of the text itself, and frequently explained archaic or foreign textual elements by references to contemporary expressions or usages. Many compilers, therefore, used Turkish terms for political and military matters related within the text. Such interpolations may have been used to draw analogies concerning the contemporary conditions of the Bulgarians under Ottoman subjugation Outright anti-Turkish sentiment was infrequently expressed openly and directly. Such was the case with *daskal* Todor, who in a note written in the "Protopopintsi" *damaskin* termed the Turks *dyavoli* (devils), the exact expression that was commonly used when referring to the minions of the Anti-Christ in Bulgarian Orthodox literature.[33]

Such merging of religious and ethical sermons with contemporary realities demonstrated that *damaskin* compilers were not reclusive monks who copied their works in the isolation afforded by monastery walls. The content and form of their works indicate that they were alive to the needs and conditions of contemporary life in the Bulgarian lands. They reached beyond the frontiers of traditional Orthodox literary tradition to touch the wider reading public created by the expansion of education during the seventeenth century. They attempted to instruct that new, secular, educated audience in the ethics of Orthodox Christianity while providing it with materials that would be both useful in their everyday lives and of interest, even entertaining, as literature.

A number of Bulgarian writer-copyists were active in the seventeenth century. (See Table 21) The more renowned of those men, such as Daniil Etropolski and his circle at Etropole Monastery, Avram Dimitrievich of Karlovo, Nedyalko and his son, Filip, from the village of Adzhar, and Krŭstyu Gramatik at Kuklen Monastery, will be dealt with in detail later in this study. At this point, a brief discussion of a few lesser known literary personalities from the period may well be in order.

Three Bulgarian Athonite monks produced works of some note. Pamfilii, as noted earlier, wrote an original *Life* of Pimen Zografski during the latter half of the century. Another Bulgarian inmate at Zograf, Stefan Svetagorets ("the Bulgarian"), a contemporary of Pamfilii, produced a noteworthy work, entitled: *The Saga of the Holy Mountain of Athos,* in which, for the first time in Bulgarian literature, Athos was described as a major Orthodox cultural center in the Balkan world.[34] The most productive of the seventeenth century Athonite Bulgarians, however, was Makarii *ieromonah*. He resided in the monastic *skete* of "St. Anna" during the second half of the century. There he copied the five extant works attributable to his hand. They ranged in date from 1668 to 1701. In his 1701 work, Makarii copied a eulogy for Saint George that had originally been written by Grigorii Tsamblak. Four other works tentatively have been attributed to Makarii but no extant copies of them have been located to date.[35]

Two Bulgarians who worked outside of the Bulgarian lands during the century but deserving of attention were Melentii Makedonski and *ieromonah* Stefan Ohridski. Those two men operated a Russian variant Church Slavonic printing press in the Moldavian monastery of Gorova under the auspices of *voevoda* Matei Basarab (1633-1654). Melentii, the abbot at the monastery, and Stefan, the printer at the press, produced printed Slavic psalters in 1637 and 1638.[36]

Finally, there was *pop* Bogdan, a productive man-of-letters from the small Bulgarian village of Slavovitsa near the town of Pleven. Aside from his duties as the village priest, Bogdan also pursued writing and bookbinding. Exactly where he received his education is unknown but his style of calligraphy betrayed a close affiliation to that of the Etropole School, so he may have studied at Etropole Monastery. Five works by Bogdan are extant. Only one was dated (1641). In another, Bogdan included prayers originally written by the Byzantine Orthodox patriarch, Philotios (1353-1354, 1364-1376), in which was mentioned the Bulgarian tsar, Ivan Shishman. Also of significance was the stylistic parallel drawn by Bogdan between the presentation of Philotios' prayer and that of "To the Virgin," which was originally written in the Middle Bulgarian language during the fifteenth century by Dimitrios Kantakuzinos at Rila Monastery. A third work by Bogdan, also written in the Etropole style, contained copies of Evtimii's *Lives* of Ivan Rilski, Petka Tŭrnovska and Ilarion Mŭglenski. That work was bound in 1692. Bogdan produced a fourth work and then filled in a missing page of a book printed in Cetinje, Montenegro, that had been written by *ieromonah* Makarii in 1494.[37]

Writer-copyist and reader notations made in the pages of manuscripts dating to the seventeenth century furnish a general picture of the origin, circulation and uses of a great many of the works of literature available to the Bulgarians during the period. (See Tables 15, 16, 17 and 20) Oftentimes, the writer-copyist would sign the finished work, give the date, and mention the place where the work was produced. Sometimes he would make mention of the work's patron(s). If the work was performed in a monastery, the abbot was often identified. The original recipient of the manuscript, usually a monastery or village church, was frequently named. More infrequently, the intention underlying the donation to the church was stated.

Once the manuscript was deposited in its initial resting place, it was often read by whomever was interested or instructed to do so. Many readers would commemorate their use of the work by signing their names and, frequently, the date (usually merely the year) of its use. Readers often included the name of their native village or town, or noted their monastic affiliation. Further notations could be made if the manuscript was purchased for, or donated to, another church or monastery, and the note often disclosed the sum of money involved if purchased, as well as often identifying the profession(s) of those who financed the transaction. If the work was used as a school text, the *daskal* would often write his signature and title in the manuscript, as would his students. In short, any event that occurred in the life of a manuscript could be immortalized on its pages by the people involved. Such marginalia evidence that has survived makes it clear that manuscripts available to the seventeenth century Bulgarians received a much wider geographic circulation, and were annotated far more frequently, than was common for those in earlier centuries, indicating that education had, indeed, begun to broaden its base within Bulgarian society in general, and that a great many more Bulgarians were literate than at any time in their past history.[38]

Beyond furnishing information concerning the life of a particular manuscript, seventeenth century marginalia at times rose to the level of short chronicles of contemporary events. These were usually brief and concerned with mundane occurrences, such as local droughts or famines. Chronicle notes often dealt with historical, especially military, events, for which they often constitute the only known sources, such as for Ottoman military musters or for *haidut* raids.[39] One such note dating to the latter part of the century, however, was exceptional in that it constituted a rather lengthy, detailed account. A short historical essay rather than a mere note, the account written by *pop* Petŭr from Mirkovo (1690) related the heavy lot experienced by the Bulgarian population under Ottoman control during a time when Turkish power was falling into decline.

The progression found in manuscript marginalia during the seventeenth century, from simple statements of names, dates and places to lengthy descriptive accounts of contemporary events of a wholly secular, historical nature, appears to demonstrate a growing historical awareness among at least certain literate elements of the Bulgarian population over the course of the century. That awareness was reflected in the common human urge to immortalize even the most insignificant events in their lives, such as reading a book. Yet a number of notations made in the same book, possibly by readers from different locales, could form a story unto itself. The book was given a life beyond its pages, in which the annotator, by the simple fact of penning his own personal notation, was able to participate in that life and to make his participation known to others. He became a part of the story. Eventually, that story was expanded upon not only by the name and date of the annotator but also by events that he had witnessed or heard of in his personal mundane world. That this evolution was a process that developed over time can be seen from the fact that nearly all of the chronicle-like notations were written during the second half of the century, while the simplest notations were found from the period's beginning to its close.

It would seem that the broadening of education beyond the monastery walls and the growth of a rudimentary historical awareness among those who were the recipients of that education were complimentary developments. In such a *milieu*, the patriotic aura found in works of the Tŭrnovo School must have had at least a subliminal impact. If the popularity of the works of Evtimii and his disciples among the writings produced within the Bulgarian lands during the seventeenth century can be viewed as a sort of barometer for such a phenomenon, then it can be suggested that such was indeed the case.

Religious Art

Similar to the *literati*, after the fall of Tŭrnovo in 1393 a great many Bulgarian artists fled the country to seek shelter in regions less threatened by the Muslim invaders. The majority eventually found new homes and work in the Romanian Principalities, particularly in Moldavia, or on Mount Athos.[40] Those artists who remained in the Bulgarian lands earned their livelihood by adopting itinerant lives amid the commonplace economic and social disturbances forming the wake of the conquest. With the elimination of the two primary patrons of the arts, the native church and state, and the economic dislocation caused by the conquest, no individual region of the Bulgarian lands, let alone any single town or village, was able to offer artists steady employment during the years immediately following that event.

Even more adverse than such economic considerations was the imposition of a foreign, antagonistic ruling class, which made the overt expression of high Christian art unwise during the period of militant Islamic consolidation in regions recently wrested from Christian enemies at sword's point. On the other hand, many Bulgarian villages managed to retain their church buildings but were unable to renovate those that had been damaged by the passage of Turkish or Christian troops.

For the Bulgarian artist, however, the Ottoman conquest of nearly the entire Balkan Peninsula created a large common field of opportunity and creative exchange. Thus the itinerant life that was imposed upon them also resulted in a widescale interaction of artistic influences from among all reaches of the Balkan Orthodox world and from the now dominant Islamic world as well. In his search for employment, the Bulgarian artist of the early period of Ottoman domination in the Balkans often traveled a road that led from the Bulgarian lands to Mount Athos and back. The road also often could take him to the lands of the Serbs and Romanians as well, and if he was truly adventurous, that road might extend as far as Muscovite Russia. Every point on that long highway potentially offered new artistic inspirations and techniques, often the native creations of some particular region, that could be incorporated into whatever Bulgarian elements that the artist already possessed in his palette for expressing Orthodox artistic ideals. Such a broad interaction of local artistic styles makes the discernment of specifically Bulgarian elements within extant works by Bulgarian artists of the Ottoman period somewhat problematic.[41]

Under the Hanafite school of law operating in the Ottoman Empire, conquered non-Muslim subject peoples were forbidden to build new or to enlarge old places of worship. The law did, however, permit non-Muslims to repair or renovate existing religious buildings so long as the local authorities agreed that the work was necessary. By taking advantage of this legal loophole, as well as by appealing to the essentially theocratic mentality of the Ottoman rulers, the Orthodox Bulgarians were able to maintain their Orthodox cultural expression and, in many cases, to expand it by erecting completely new religious facilities, primarily in or near newly established village settlements. Permission had to be first obtained from the local Ottoman authorities through the intercession of a healthy bribe. This relaxation of restrictions on Christian subjects was reflected in the rather large number of churches and monasteries built or restored in the western Bulgarian lands during the opening quarter of the seventeenth century.

With the crushing of the Western crusaders led by Władysław Jagiełło (1440-1444), king of both Poland and Hungary, in the Battle of Varna (10 November 1444) and the capture of Byzantine Constantinople (29 May 1453), the Ottoman military frontier in Europe was pushed outward from the Bulgarian lands and nearby vicinities into Bosnia, Albania, northern Serbia and the Danubian Principalities. A period of relative peace descended on the Bulgarian lands during the second half of the fifteenth century. As the Muslim overlords turned their attentions to the expanding European frontier, the chaotic conditions that had reigned in the Bulgarian lands since the turmoil of their conquest began to subside. During the social and economic stabilization within those lands that accompanied the northern extension of the Ottoman European military frontier, the Bulgarians once again were able to devote some attention to the finer arts.

IN THE SEVENTEENTH CENTURY

The revival of monumental religious art that occurred during the latter half of the fifteenth century was a limited affair. A wealthy native Orthodox church organization did not exist at that time; high ecclesiastical offices had become the monopolies of foreign, Greek prelates. With the advent of more peaceful times, however, the Orthodox Bulgarians felt the need for the spiritual comforts that accompanied the outward practice of their religion. Despite the limitations imposed by foreign rulers in both the political and spiritual spheres, and despite the great depletion of wealth among the Bulgarian population in general, efforts were made to restore and rededicate as many of the abandoned or partially ruined church buildings as discretion and finances would permit. For the most part, the churches restored in the late fifteenth century were those attached to monasteries located in the highlands outside of urban centers and at some distance from major, heavily traveled highways. In a few cases, some structures were totally rebuilt.

Church renovation, by its very nature, involved the decoration of the structures' interiors with paintings, since mural art played an integral part in Orthodox iconography and ritual. As the ravages of time, fire or axe were erased, or as new structures rose, artists were summoned by local clergymen to execute the proper iconographic scenes on the buildings' ceilings and walls. Funds for such renovations were supplied by the treasuries of the larger monasteries, such as Rila and Dragalevtsi, or by the few wealthy Bulgarian merchants and *bolyars* who had managed to survive the initial shocks of the Ottoman conquest. In general, the activity of this early revival of monumental religious art in the Bulgarian lands following the conquest was confined to those regions surrounding Sofia, Rila and Kyustendil.[42]

A notable feature of the late fifteenth century artistic revival among the Bulgarians was its dependence on local Bulgarian notables or monastery coffers for financial support. The resulting regionalism in artistic production caused by this development led to a division of art in the Bulgarian lands between that produced for the benefit of Greek worshipers and that produced for the Slavic Bulgarians. It is the latter segment that most concerns the discussion that follows.

Toward the end of the sixteenth century a number of Bulgarian monastery and village churches were built or renovated over a period spanning the final decade of the century and the first half of the seventeenth. That period of artistic activity in the Bulgarian lands was primarily centered in the western Bulgarian lands, and most particularly in the regions of Sofia, Kyustendil and Pernik. Between the years 1590 and 1650 nearly 40 now wholly or partially extant churches in the western lands were newly constructed or renovated, both of which activities required extensive decoration of all kinds. (See Table 23.)

Certain common elements are discernible in the artistic revival that characterized the first half of the seventeenth century. Of first note was the architectural style of the church structures themselves. They were small, simple stone structures with tiled or shingled gable roofs and almost totally lacking in any overt elements of traditional church architecture except for an apse, which usually protruded from the eastern-most wall of the building. Their thick walls were pierced by narrow, slit-like windows, and a single door was cut in the wall opposite that with the apse. There usually were no cupolas or domes, nor were there bell towers. The interiors of the structures were sometimes divided into a narthex and a nave, with the latter commonly being of the single-aisle variety. Quite often, the church building was surrounded by high courtyard walls. The entire architectural conception was designed so as to be as unobtrusive as possible to the social and religious sensibilities of the ruling Muslim class, while affording the maximum amount of privacy for the conduct of the Orthodox rituals that took place within.[43]

Despite a repressed form of architecture, certain subtle innovations were made in church design during the seventeenth century. An attempt was made to add elements of aesthetic design in the stonework of the thick church walls. Varying sizes of stone were used to achieve pleasing decorative patterns by builders of some of the new churches, such as those, for example, in the village of Maritsa and in Kurilo Monastery (1596). Another innovation in church architecture made during the period was the construction of an exterior arch in the gable of the wall sporting the doorway. This device was used in the churches built in the monasteries of Bilintsi, Malo Malovo and Alino (1626). In some isolated mountainous regions, at a distance from direct Ottoman surveillance, a few church structures built during the early seventeenth century displayed marked deviations from the typically small, single-apsed structures so commonly found in regions closer to urban centers. For example, those built in the villages of Dobŭrsko (1614) and Vukovo (1598) were of larger than usual size for churches of the time, and they possessed apses in both their northern and southern walls, in addition to the one that faced east, thus affecting a more traditional cruciform type of design. It is possible that the architectural scheme of those churches reflected the influence of Athonite architectural concepts, but its application on a large scale in the Bulgarian lands during the seventeenth century was limited.[44]

The interiors of churches involved in the artistic revival of the seventeenth century were lavishly decorated with mural paintings depicting portraits of Christ and the Virgin, Christian martyrs and church fathers, prophets, and archangels. Numerous events from the Old and New Testaments were portrayed in scenes on the ceiling, walls and apse. The entire decorative scheme was conceived of as an integral supplement to, even an extension of, the liturgical rituals enacted within the church. Every scene, every portrait was carefully regulated by the strict rules of Orthodox iconography, which, for the most part, determined the order, position and the individual elements contained in the compositions found in the decoration. The models for the system and its numerous components used by the

IN THE SEVENTEENTH CENTURY

Bulgarian artists of the period had been developed in the post-iconoclastic period in Byzantium during the ninth and tenth centuries. They had subsequently gained the official recognition of the Orthodox church of Constantinople, and had thereafter been propagated by individual artists and eventually codified through the development of artist handbooks on Mount Athos.[45]

The iconographic uniformity imposed by the almost universal use of the Athonite artist handbooks tended to suppress overt artistic innovations, in terms of images or scenes represented by the artists. New artistic trends were expressed, perforce, through either deviations from or variations within the accepted iconographic schemes. In essence, Orthodox art became a universal art in the Balkan lands under Ottoman rule, and virtually all national artistic distinctions were checked.[46]

Even though religious art produced in the Bulgarian lands during the seventeenth century possessed a generally denationalized character, certain specific artistic influences and trends were discernible. In terms of style, the impress of Mount Athos was unmistakable. The Athonite style of the period was one of compositional tranquility. Figures were rendered by sharp but flowing lines that engendered them with a rather rude and severe quality. Yet the attitude of the figures and the movement depicted within scenes reflected a naturalness and profundity reminiscent of the Palæologian period in Byzantine art (thirteenth-fifteenth centuries). Furthermore, the linear depiction of figures and the abstraction used in representing scenic backgrounds reflected the mystical and ascetic character of worldly renunciation that emanated from Athos during the period. Such austere mysticism was but a reflection of a conscious attempt by the Eastern Orthodox church in general to combat Western religious and artistic influences that were attempting to intrude into the Balkan world, particularly from Italy. The gaunt, ascetic Athonite style, however, was also paralleled by another Athonite movement that emphasized sumptuousness in the use of color and in the clothing depicted worn by the figures portrayed. Both styles were reflected in works produced in the Bulgarian lands during the seventeenth century revival.[47]

Bulgarian artists during this period increasingly made use of floral and geometric decorative motifs in spaces on the surfaces of scenes that were not otherwise covered by regulated scenic elements, such as figures or specified backgrounds, and possibly reflecting Islamic artistic influences. This development seems to have had its twin manifestation in the field of calligraphy with the advent of the decorative style expounded by the Etropole School. Of more concern to this study than style, however, was the appearance of certain elements within decorative schemes themselves that reflected a particularly Bulgarian ethnic character in Bulgarian religious art of the seventeenth century.[48]

The most obvious Bulgarian element that attained widespread popularity in works of art created during that period of artistic revival was the inclusion of native Bulgarian saints within the iconographic scheme. This development was not especially unique unto itself. The earliest extant representation of a Bulgarian saint within the Bulgarian lands has been dated to the year 1259, at which time the image of Ivan Rilski was included in the murals of the narthex in the small church at Boyana. As the most popular of native saints, Rilski's image quite frequently appeared in exemplars of Second Empire Bulgarian art. A few other Bulgarian saints were represented in paintings executed between the early fourteenth and late sixteenth centuries in the Bulgarian lands. During the period spanning the late sixteenth and first half of the seventeenth centuries, however, images of native Bulgarian saints became common elements in the iconographic schemes of Bulgarian artists. In Alino Monastery, the three artists who decorated the church created images of Ivan Rilski, Ioakim Osogovski and Prohor Pshinski garbed in monastic dress. Ivan Rilski was also depicted in the churches of Dragalevtsi Monastery, "St. Nikolai" in Vukovo (1598), Seslavtsi Monastery and Dobŭrsko (1614). Also depicted in Dobŭrsko were Ioakim Osogovski and Prohor Pshinski.[49]

The paintings in two particular churches dating to the early seventeenth century were significant in that for the first time in Bulgarian churches were depicted the images of Bulgarians martyred at the hands of the Muslim Turks. The image of Nikolai Novi Sofiiski in Kurilo Monastery (1596) represented the earliest rendition of a Bulgarian victim of Turkish execution.[50] A few years after the Kurilo Monastery church was decorated, the church at Seslavtsi Monastery underwent interior renovation. As part of the new mural paintings at Seslavtsi the artists included images of Georgi and Nikolai Novi Sofiiski, both of whom were murdered by the Turks of Sofia during the sixteenth century.[51]

Seslavtsi Monastery was remarkable not only for the two images of relatively contemporary Bulgarian martyrs but also for the total number of native Bulgarian saints portrayed within its decorative scheme. Both Georgi and Nikolai were to be seen in the decorations of the nave, in the company of Naum, a ninth-tenth century Bulgarian disciple of Methodius and contemporary of Kliment Ohridski, and an early father of the Cyrillic Orthodox liturgy as well. In the narthex of the monastery church were portrayed the early monastic native saints of the ninth-eleventh centuries — Ivan Rilski, Ioakim Osogovski, Gavril Lesnovski and Prohor Pshinski. Never before had so many native saints been included within the iconographic scheme of a church in the Bulgarian lands.[52]

Another first for church mural paintings in the Bulgarian lands arising from the artistic revival of the seventeenth century was the portrayal of the saintly brothers, Cyril and Methodius, who first established the validity of the Slavic liturgy during the mid ninth century. Their images were painted among those of the church fathers in the apse of the Dolna Beshovitsa Monastery church, "Holy Arhangel Mihail," perhaps by *maistor* Pavel from the nearby village, who worked in the church at some time during the early seventeenth century. In this earliest of painted renditions of the missionary saints in the Bulgarian lands, the brothers were depicted in the robes of Orthodox bishops.

Saints who figured prominently in the hagiographies and eulogies of Evtimii Tŭrnovski also found representation in the iconographic schemes of seventeenth century Bulgarian artists. The image of Petka Tŭrnovska was included in the decoration of the church at Kurilo Monastery, and her likeness was also portrayed in two western Bulgarian churches dedicated to her in the villages of Balsha and Vukovo (1598). In the latter church, Nedelya also figured in the decorative iconography. Her image was further rendered in the mural paintings in the narthex of the church at Karlukovo Monastery (1602). Ilarion Mŭglenski was portrayed in the village church, "St. Nikola," of Maritsa.

The representation of native saints formed but one element of a pictorial system that paralleled the development of didacticism in Bulgarian Orthodox literature during the seventeenth century. It would seem that the artists who worked in the western Bulgarian churches during the first third of the century made efforts to create iconographic scenes that were readily comprehensible to the local worshipers. They used two techniques to accomplish that task. The first, and most obvious, was the use within the scenes of identifying inscriptions in Cyrillic script. The second was the depiction of contemporary native articles (*e.g.,* clothing, furnishings, tools, and the like) that were familiar to the general population . Both of those techniques had their roots deeply embedded in medieval traditions of Bulgarian Orthodox art, but during the seventeenth century their use became more widespread than previously had been the case.

With few exceptions, all extant monuments of art in the western Bulgarian lands dating to the early seventeenth century bore Slavic identifying inscriptions. Slavic had been used for this purpose within the region since the medieval period, but with the expansion of education that began in the seventeenth century the inscriptions became more readily understandable to a broader segment of the Bulgarian population.[53]

Contemporary native ethnographic details were commonly depicted by the Bulgarian artists of the seventeenth century. Again, the use of contemporary models for details within religious iconography possessed a lengthy tradition in the Bulgarian lands. During the period of the Second Bulgarian Empire such details were found in the more rural art monuments of the western lands, such as at Zemen Monastery (*ca.* 1360) and the small church of Berende (fourteenth century). It would appear that the inclusion of folk elements in religious paintings depended on the location of the work and the artistic education of the artist(s) involved. As a rule, rural works created by local artists who possessed training but were little influenced by formal schools of art demonstrated a greater freedom in the use of ethnographical elements within scenes than did works produced by artists living and trained in urban centers. This is not to infer that the quality of the rural artists was any less striking than those from the cities, with their formal schools of art. Rural, often termed "village," artists created some of the most notable works of Orthodox monumental art in the western Bulgarian lands during the early seventeenth century, such as those at the monasteries of Bilintsi and Alino. On the whole, rural artists seemed to place great emphasis on the didactic, narrative nature of the scenes they created, and demonstrated a lesser concern for strict adherence to the traditional Orthodox iconographic system. Thus in rural monuments of art not only were native folk elements made an important part of the decorative scheme but innovations were commonly made in the religious iconography itself.

The mural paintings in the Bilintsi Monastery church, executed at some time in the last decade of the sixteenth or first decade of the seventeenth century, were masterful examples of rural religious art in the western Bulgarian lands at the opening of the seventeenth century.[54] The monastery lay three kilometers north of Bilintsi village. The date of its founding is unknown but it may have been established at some time in the eleventh-twelfth centuries. The first piece of historical evidence for the monastery dates from 1586, when a priest named Stefan, who resided at the monastery, accompanied the Kyustendil metropolitan, Visarion, on an alms-seeking mission to Muscovy.[55] Within a decade of that event the small monastery church was decorated for the first time with mural paintings under the patronage of an unknown donor, who was depicted in monastic garb among the images painted on the south wall but whose name is no longer decipherable.

A few of the scenes painted at Bilintsi demonstrated marked resemblances to those executed at Hilendar Monastery on Athos in 1621. Stylistically, the mural paintings also closely resembled those produced in the western Bulgarian lands during that same period (*e.g.,* those at Maritsa, Dobŭrsko and Alino, among others). For the most part, traditional Orthodox iconography was followed but a few of the cycles representing church feasts, and the cycle of the passion of Christ, were incomplete. In some of the scenes the Bilintsi artists broke completely with traditional representations and created their own original compositions.[56]

Realism and elements of an ethnographic nature played prominent roles in many of the compositions at Bilintsi. A number of realistic elements were included in the representation of the Last Supper, which was a scene that traditionally offered artists an opportunity to demonstrate their powers of observation by depicting items commonly present in the everyday lives of the worshipers. Among the rich native ethnic details found in the Bilintsi murals were colorful veils and embroideries, decorative carpets, long-sleeved cloaks, pottery jars, and other village items that the contemporary Bulgarian villagers encountered daily.[57]

The portrait of the donor for the paintings at Bilintsi was rendered in a realistic fashion. He was portrayed as an austere monk with a plasticity that was lacking in all the other figures found in the church's religious scenes. In fact, realism became the common element in the donor portraits painted in early seventeenth century Bulgarian churches. The period was one in which the traditional donor portrait experienced widespread inclusion within the iconographic scheme. By mid century portraits of 16 patrons appeared as single individuals or in groups in the churches for which they had provided the funds for construction or renovation. They were represented in garb appropriate to their occupations in life. Thus the monks who were the patrons at Bilintsi and Karlukovo monasteries were portrayed arrayed in their monastic habits, while secular donors, such as five of the six patrons at Dobŭrsko, were depicted in secular robes befitting their stations as relatively wealthy *celeps*. Most often, the treatment of the faces of the donors was realistic in its attempt to render a primitive form of portraiture. A donor, however, could also be rendered in the stylized manner reserved for standard iconographic figures, as was Abbot Agapii at Karlukovo Monastery (1602).[58]

A common feature of the inscriptions identifying donor portraits from that period was a brief biographical notation, similar to the notes found in Orthodox literary works at that time. If an actual donor portrait was lacking, an inscription was often painted commemorating those who were responsible for funding the completed artwork. At Dobŭrsko, Hasiya, the principal donor, had the tale of his pilgrimage to the Holy Land and his subsequent efforts to gather funds for the construction of the church from the other five donors, one of whom was his priestly son, Bogdan, noted in the inscription to the general donor portrait, in which all six men are shown offering a model of the completed church to Christ. At Alino Monastery, four of the five patrons were priests residing in the monastery, while the fifth was a notable from the nearby village. The patrons of Kurilo Monastery were notables from the villages of Dobroslavtsi and Kumaritsa, as well as members of a bread-bakers guild in Sofia. Another Sofia notable was responsible for funding the redecoration of the exterior narthex at Kremikovtsi Monastery in 1611. In this monastery, as well as in that of Dragalevtsi, the newer paintings produced during the seventeenth century supplemented those that had been executed at earlier dates and also included donor portraits, thus rendering an historical painted record of past Bulgarian men-of-note for the seventeenth century Bulgarian worshippers.[59]

After the mid seventeenth century artistic activity within the Bulgarian lands declined. The artistic decline roughly coincided with the period in which the Ottoman Empire became hopelessly embroiled in a series of wars that occupied nearly the entire second half of the century. That was a time of great unrest in the Balkan heartlands of the empire. The Turks showed signs of strain over the drawn out war with Venice for possession of Crete (1645-1670), as well as over attendant conflicts with Venice's ally, Habsburg Austria, in the northern Balkans and in Transylvania (1658-1670). Aggression followed upon aggression, and the Turks became involved in successive campaigns against Poland (1672-1676), Russia (1677-1681), and Austria (1682-1699). The near continuous struggle against Christian enemies wore thin any sense of Ottoman religious toleration. Being the Christian population nearest the core of the empire, the Bulgarians suffered greatly.

A few monuments of art created during the troubled period of the later seventeenth century survived. Most extant exemplars were located in the northwestern Bulgarian lands, on the northern slopes of the Balkan Mountains, and on the Danubian Plain. In the mountain village of Vŭrbovo the church of "St. John the Baptist" was erected within the span of a single month (July 1652) under the auspices of two village notables, Petka and Podruzie. It was later decorated in the style common to western Bulgarian churches. Similar to Vŭrbovo was the church in the village of Gorni Lom, "St. Paraskeva," which had been destroyed by the Turks following their late fourteenth century conquest of the Vidin region. During the middle of the seventeenth century the villagers were finally able to reconstruct and redecorate their long-ruined church. Two churches in Vidin, "St. Panteleimon" (1642) and "St. Petka", were decorated near mid century. Likewise, in the Danubian town of Svishtov the church of "SS. Petŭr and Pavel" was given new murals in 1644. All of the art monuments in the northwestern Bulgarian lands fell heavily under the influence of artistic developments taking place in the Romanian Principalities at that time. The Romanian influence was so strong and direct that donor portraits of Romanian *voevodas* were represented in the churches of Svishtov and Vidin ("St. Petka").[60]

Elsewhere, a scattered number of churches in the western and southern Bulgarian lands were decorated during the second half of the seventeenth century. As a rule, these also followed the trends established earlier but demonstrated little or no distinguishing characteristics.[61]

The most significant trends in seventeenth century Bulgarian religious art were overtly manifested in monumental church art. Such art was complex and, being so, was flexible. It offered the artist the freedom necessary for innovation. The more minor genre of icon painting was far less flexible because of its specific liturgical purpose and compact, limited treatment of subject. Innovations in the icon were expressed in extremely subtle fashion, such as in facial molding and color schemes. Externally, the seventeenth century Bulgarian icon retained its centuries-long traditional appearance, which was rigidly regulated by the models furnished in the artist handbooks. Some innovation, however, was expressed in the earliest appearance of artists' signatures on the paintings and the notation of the date of the works' completion, as well as of donor inscriptions. Of all the native Bulgarian saints, only Ivan Rilski received any particular attention by seventeenth century icon painters. All of the icons produced by Bulgarians during the century bore Slavic inscriptions.[62]

In the genre of woodcarving, especially in decorating the wooden frames and screens of church iconostases, the geometric and floral motifs evident in seventeenth century manuscript illumination and calligraphy found a parallel. So too did the movement toward realism in the portrayal of figures noted in mural paintings of the period. Extant examples of seventeenth century woodcarving expertise are today found in the southwestern Bulgarian lands in the region of Melnik, especially at Rozhen Monastery.[63]

Metalworking, especially goldsmithing, was also a minor but popular field of Orthodox art in the seventeenth century. Orthodox church ritual demanded such pieces of art as crosses, chalices, cyboria and the like, and certain insignia of clerical rank were metalware articles, such as the staff carried by bishops. The earliest extant seventeenth century exemplar of religious goldsmithing was the cross over the altar in the metropolitan church in Vratsa created by two Vratsa master goldsmiths, Nikola and Pavla, in 1601. During the 1640s a certain Velo was an active goldsmith in Sofia, and produced a number of items for some of the surrounding monasteries.[64]

The leading center for the art of goldsmithing in the Bulgarian lands during the seventeenth century was Chiprovtsi, which despite its predominantly Catholic orientation still included a significant number of Orthodox Bulgarians among its inhabitants. In fact, the Orthodox population maintained two churches in Chiprovtsi itself, both of which were rebuilt or restored during the century, and they supported a nearby Orthodox monastery in Gushavo. Orthodox Bulgarians were on intimate terms with their Catholic neighbors and were often the craftsmen hired by the Catholics to construct their religious edifices. Thus the Chiprovtsi Orthodox Bulgarian artisans and artists were exposed to the Western cultural traditions adhered to by their Catholic conationals.[65]

Besides the ferrous metals mined in the region surrounding Chiprovtsi, the mountains yielded precious metals. Chiprovtsi silver was highly prized in Venice, and gold was abundant in the region. The Catholic connection with Italy, Dubrovnik and the West in general provided extensive markets for the gold and silver products of the region's metalsmithing artisans, who, although they cannot be considered artists in the sense of those who worked at decorating churches or painting icons, can be viewed as the most artistic of the various groups of craftsmen. In return, he Chiprovtsi Bulgarians were kept abreast of the latest artistic trends and tastes prevalent in the West. The smithing artisan *esnafs* of Chiprovtsi were thus wealthy and strong, serving as trading partners of Dubrovnik merchants throughout the Balkans and as creditors for commercial operation as far afield as Transylvania.

The Chiprovtsi School of goldsmithing was one of the most productive and famous in the Bulgarian lands. It was renowned throughout the Balkans, and its products were sought by churches and monasteries in Russia and in the Serbian and Romanian lands. The work of the Chiprovtsi goldsmiths was patronized by high church prelates, as well as by local notables. A *mahalle* of Chiprovtsi was called the "silver quarter" after the gold and silversmithing craft pursued by most of its inhabitants. The goldsmithing activity of Vratsa was a subsidiary of the main industry in Chiprovtsi. Thus between 1601 and 1671 products of the Chiprovtsi School reigned supreme in the Bulgarian lands. Ten master goldsmiths of the School are known through extant works. All used Church Slavonic in the inscriptions left on their products.[66]

Mining in Chiprovtsi experienced a decline in the second quarter of the seventeenth century, as did other mining areas in the Bulgarian lands, caused by a drop in Western demand for eastern ores after the opening of new sources in the Western Hemisphere, and by the internal decline of the Ottoman Empire, which resulted in a contraction of investment capital for the industry, an inability to maintain existing mining facilities, and a lack of modern, more efficient mining techniques. By the third quarter of the century the Chiprovtsi School of goldsmithing was waning, and the uprising in 1688 provided its death knell.

Regarding the traditional Bulgarian artists themselves, during the seventeenth century their lives were no longer those of itinerants. Internal social stability played a normalizing role in artistic activity, as it had in the field of literature. The surge of artistic activity during the first half of the century was stimulated by the availability of a relatively wealthy group of Bulgarian guildsmen, merchants and *serviteurs,* who acted as patrons of the arts. Artists were able to take up regional, even local, existences for the first time since the late fourteenth century. The formerly itinerant artists could now settle into a locale and hire apprentices, who they instructed in the techniques that they had already mastered, as well as in the rules set down by the artist handbooks. In such manner, modest groups of village artists formed in the rural regions of the western Bulgarian lands, usually centered around local monasteries because of the close relations those establishments maintained with social elements within the general population that could fund artistic endeavors. In western urban centers, with their Athonite *metohs,* rich monasteries and large, compact Bulgarian artisan and merchant populations, more formal schools of art were able to develop. This was especially true for Sofia, where the formal traditions and classical Orthodox iconography held sway. Although the groups of seventeenth century artists to some extent resembled the other artisan organizations, they did not constitute official *esnafs*. They were, however, tolerated by the Turkish authorities.[67] (See Table 24)

The late sixteenth and early seventeenth centuries produced the most talented Bulgarian artistic predecessor of Zaharii Zograf (1810-1853), the noted nineteenth century master of Bulgarian national revival artists. Pimen, often surnamed Sofiiski but more commonly called Zografski, was born in Sofia near the mid sixteenth century. He studied as a youth in the cell school operated at that city's church of "St. Georgi." Pimen expressed a particular talent for art and received his early artistic training from *pop* Toma, under whom he spent six years in study. Realizing that his opportunities for further schooling in Sofia were limited, Pimen set out for Mount Athos, the foremost center of Orthodox art at that time. He enrolled in Zograf Monastery, where he was exposed to the unbroken artistic traditions and techniques of medieval Byzantium and Bulgaria. His talents in both art and literature lent him an aura of a Renaissance-type man, and he was soon entrusted with administering all construction and art projects at Zograf. Pimen's reputation was such that monasteries from all corners of the Holy Mountain sought out his advice and aid for every sort of problem, artistic or otherwise.[68]

At some time during the final decade of the sixteenth century Pimen requested, and received, the reluctant permission of the Zograf superiors to relinquish his duties at the monastery and to return to his native Sofia to commence a vast and ambitious art project. Upon his return, Pimen began working in as many churches in the Sofia region as was possible, financially and otherwise. His fame was such that requests for his services were submitted by patrons from all regions of the western Bulgarian lands. Pamfilii, Pimen's seventeenth century biographer, credited him with decorating 300 churches and 15 monasteries in the western lands.[69] Among these were the monasteries of Cherepish, in the region of Vratsa and where he was elected abbot by the monastic brotherhood residing there, and Suhodol (1606). After leaving Suhodol Pimen worked at Dorostol Monastery, located near Cherven. By 1618 he was at Seslavtsi Monastery outside Sofia, where he wrote a menologion for the month of November. He then returned to Cherepish Monastery, where he died and was buried in the church that he had constructed and decorated. According to Paisii Hilendarski, the relics of Pimen were disinterred many years after his death and transferred to Suhodol Monastery.[70]

Most of the finer monuments of art that date to the period of Pimen's activity in the western Bulgarian lands have been attributed to him. He has been credited with the decorations in the monasteries of Kurilo, Seslavtsi, Eleshnitsa, Ilientsi, and Bilintsi, as well as those in the Sofia church of "St. Petka of the Saddlemakers."[71] All bore some stylistic similarities to each other and to churches known to have been the work of Pimen. To have personally performed the task of decorating the numerous edifices with which he has been credited over the course of nearly three decades would have required a superhuman effort on his part. Of course, Pimen had assistants who either were apprenticed to him or were artistic *maistors* in their own right. With his group of assistants in tow, Pimen was able to perform a complete renovation of a church in a surprisingly short span of time. He completely decorated the church in Suhodol Monastery in just two months. If he was the master artist at Kurilo, the project likewise required little more than the same amount of time to complete.[72]

The number of trained assistants and *maistors* in Pimen's entourage is unknown, but the stylistic similarities among monuments of art executed during the early seventeenth century in the western Bulgarian lands would seem to indicate that Pimen Zografski, through the work of his own hands and those of his assistants and disciples, both under his personal guidance and after his death, represented the single most important force in the revival of Orthodox art in the Bulgarian lands. For his outstanding contributions to the field of Bulgarian art, Pimen was eventually canonized a saint by the Bulgarian Orthodox church.

Although no new genre of significance emerged in the religious art of the Bulgarians during the seventeenth century, that field of Orthodox culture demonstrated certain elements, such as decorative motifs in architecture and painting and a willingness to experiment within iconographic schemes, that were to persist throughout the period preceding the nineteenth century national revival of the Bulgarians.

Three.

Seventeenth Century Bulgarian Orthodox Culture:

Expression

6. Major Centers of Orthodox Cultural Activity

Although seventeenth century manifestations of Slavic Orthodox culture were far-flung within the Bulgarian lands of the Ottoman Empire, such cultural activity was focused upon certain primary locations. Those foci were essentially either monastic or urban centers that provided the inspirational or economic wherewithal for cultural expression over broad areas of their surrounding regions. None of those centers operated in a vacuum but, rather, maintained active contacts among themselves and with the cultural wellspring of Mount Athos, thus lending a sense of organic continuity to the cultural activity of the Bulgarians during the century. (See Table 22)

Rila Monastery

Perhaps no other site in the Bulgarian lands could claim pride of place as a center of Bulgarian Orthodox culture as could the monastery dedicated to the medieval Bulgarian hermit-saint, Ivan Rilski. Tucked away in a forested recess in the heart of the Rila Mountains some 120 kilometers south of Sofia, Rila was traditionally believed to have been the direct descendant of the small anchorite community that had arisen near the cave of that noted holy man during the early tenth century. Yet despite the tradition, the earliest extant documentary evidence for the existence of Rila Monastery has been dated to the mid fourteenth century. At that time the monastery formed part of the holdings of Hrelyo, a local feudal lord of the Serbian ruler, Stefan Dušan. If the monastery had been originally founded near the cave of Ivan Rilski, as tradition relates, then Hrelyo moved the site of his holding a bit to the west, where he proceeded to construct a stone fortress-like edifice sometime between 1335 and the year of his death, 1343. The new structure was apparently dictated by necessity arising from Hrelyo's convoluted political alliances, as he deftly attempted to retain his social and political station through intriguing with both Dušan and the Byzantine emperor, John VI Kantakuzenos (1341-1355). In the end, Hrelyo failed in his efforts and was forced into retirement at his monastery in the Rila Mountains, where he was tonsured and, eventually, strangled (27 December 1343) on the orders of Dušan.[1]

Following the murder of Hrelyo, Rila Monastery passed into the possession of the Bulgarian tsar, Ivan Aleksandŭr, whose successor, Ivan Shishman, granted it a charter in 1378. Through that charter Shishman guaranteed the monastery certain tax exemptions, and conferred upon it large tracts of land in the western regions of Bulgaria, which included villages, forests, pastures, meadows, grainfields, mills, vineyards and fishing rights.[2] As a result of such royal generosity, Rila Monastery grew into a wealthy monastic establishment during the twilight years of the medieval Bulgarian state. By an ironic quirk of fate, the monastery experienced its initial flowering as an Orthodox cultural center precisely at the time when the independent Bulgarian state was falling into the hands of the Muslim Ottoman Turks.

More ironic than the timing of its cultural flowering was the fact that Rila Monastery was permitted to conduct Slavic Orthodox cultural activity throughout the initial period of the Ottoman conquest of the Balkans through the intercession of a local Bulgarian military vassal of the conquerors, Konstantin, from Kyustendil, who served as a Christian *sipahi* in the Turkish ranks at the decisive battle against the Serbs and other Balkan Christians fought at Kosovo Pole (15 June 1389). The monastery formed part of Konstantin's *timar* holdings. Most likely through his intercessions at the Porte, the sultans Bayezid I (1389-1402) and Mehmed I granted Rila Monastery *fermans* that, in essence, confirmed the rights and properties guaranteed it by the charter of Shishman.[3] Those *fermans*, combined with the protection of Konstantin and the relative inaccessibility of the monastery in its location deep within the Rila Mountains and far from the commonly traveled invasion routes of the Ottoman forces, consorted to spare Rila Monastery the disruptive effects of the initial Turkish conquest.

The idyllic situation enjoyed by Rila Monastery was, however, short-lived. Sometime during the second quarter of the fifteenth century the monastery was assailed by roving bands of marauders. By mid century it lay deserted. A bit later, prior to 1466, three monastic brothers from the village of Granitsa near Kyustendil, David (who later became the monastery's abbot), Ioasif, and Teofan — the sons of the Krupnik Orthodox bishop, Yakov — rebuilt Rila Monastery on the site established by Hrelyo and enlisted new inhabitants and patrons. Soon after its rededication the monastery once again evolved into a major Slavic Orthodox cultural center, and continued to function as such uninterruptedly into the twentieth century.[4]

The monastery experienced a great spiritual uplifting soon after its reestablishment when, in 1469, the relic remains of Ivan Rilski were brought from their resting place in Tŭrnovo and once again interred in the soil of the Rila Mountains at the monastery dedicated to their memory. This event bestowed on Rila Monastery a place of honor among the Orthodox Bulgarians that was unrivaled by any other religious establishment within the Bulgarian lands. It became the object of pilgrimages made by pious Orthodox Bulgarians, who ventured into the Rila wilds to visit and worship at the site made holy by their beloved native saint.

IN THE SEVENTEENTH CENTURY

The notoriety of the monastery resulted in the rapid growth of its monastic population during the second half of the fifteenth century. It swiftly became a flourishing cultural center, in which operated a school and an active group of *literati*. Most renowned of the resident men-of-letters at the monastery during that time was Vladislav Gramatik. His original work (1479) describing the return of Ivan Rilski's relics from Tŭrnovo to the monastery was of historical, as well as religious, importance.[5]

Throughout the sixteenth century Rila Monastery continued to operate as an important Bulgarian religious cultural center protected, to some degree, by *fermans* granted it by a succession of Ottoman sultans and the confirmation of *vakıf* status upon its properties.[6] During that century the monastery expanded its direct contacts with Orthodox centers beyond the frontiers of the Bulgarian lands. Monks from Rila were received in the monastic establishments on Mount Athos, in those of the Serbian lands, in the Romanian Principalities, and at the court of Muscovy. Through its contacts with the broader Orthodox world Rila Monastery received spiritual and material aid while, concomitantly, it spread the cult of Ivan Rilski and an awareness of the Bulgarians as an ethnic entity among the Orthodox peoples at large.

As the seventeenth century opened Rila Monastery lay in a sorry material state despite the seeming protection afforded by the Ottoman authorities. The monastic lands and fiscal privileges were not exempt from increasing inroads made by greedy local Ottoman *sipahis* and wandering bands of brigands as the internal repercussions of the late sixteenth century Ottoman decline began to make themselves apparent. In 1635 the Turks themselves described the monastery as damaged, with its buildings toppling over as if they had not been repaired for many years. Meanwhile, the Ottoman authorities gradually began leveling new and increased taxes upon the monastery as part of an effort to raise revenues for the shrinking state treasury. In 1612 a local official attempted to force the Rila monks into paying tithes and tribute, duties from which earlier *fermans* had exempted the monastery. In the resulting legal complaint filed by the monks, the local Dupnitsa *kadı* upheld the monastery. Prior to that ruling, Sultan Ahmed I had granted a new *ferman* to Rila Monastery (1604), partly as a result of complaints lodged by the monks against the ravages perpetrated on some of the monastery's properties by a local *sipahi*.[7]

Despite the renewed overt protection of the central authorities, the inroads into the rights and properties of the monastery continued. Sultan Ibrahim (1640-1648) was forced to issue Rila a new *ferman* in 1640 because of numerous complaints made by the monks against local authorities who were demanding larger sums as tithes from some of the monastery's fields. Ibrahim's new charter failed to curb the avarice demonstrated by the local Turkish authorities, and once again, in 1660, the Dupnitsa *kadı* heard another quarrel over the payment of tithes from the monastery's lands. Finally, in 1685 Sultan Mehmed IV issued Rila yet another *ferman,* in which he attempted to place the monks in an unassailable position *vis-à-vis* the local Turkish authorities, acknowledging that past orders had not been fulfilled and had thus created "intolerable" conditions for the monastery.[8]

In the face of the worsening financial conditions created by the decline in the Ottoman socio-economic system, Rila Monastery somehow managed to remain a relatively large and wealthy monastic community throughout the seventeenth century. In 1635 the Rila monks received permission to repair and rebuild the monastery buildings after paying a large fee to the authorities. Later, in 1685, the abbot, Ioanikii, was able to purchase additional lands for the monastery. At that time Rila Monastery possessed seven meadows, six vineyards, 101 beehives, 500 sheep, 15 head of cattle, ten horses, eight grain fields, one samokov and three water mills. Thirty monks resided within the monastery's walls.[9]

In their efforts to maintain their many properties and to remain financially afloat, the Rila monks resorted to the common practice of soliciting alms from the Orthodox faithful to help defray the operating costs of the monastery. Rila's numerous *metohs* located in various towns and villages throughout the Bulgarian lands collected funds for the parent establishment. *Taxidiot* monks from Rila were despatched for the purpose of gathering donations for the monastery treasury. Letters petitioning for alms were sent to various Bulgarian parishes.[10]

The reputation enjoyed by the monastery of Ivan Rilski enabled it to seek financial aid from as far afield as the Muscovite court with good hopes for success. In 1628 a delegation of five Rila monks, headed by their abbot, Stefan, presented a petition to the Russian Tsar Mihail Feodorovich Romanov (1613-1645) at his court in Moscow. In their letter of petition the monks reminded Mihail of charters and donations granted Rila Monastery during the previous century by tsars Ivan IV Groznyi (1533-1584) and Feodor I Ivanovich (1584-1598). The monks requested that Mihail equal his predecessors in generosity, and informed him that the monastery was in such need of funds that they had been forced to pawn the monastery valuables. To strengthen their petition, the delegation included copies of the older charters in their presentation, and as an added entreaty assured the tsar that his aid to Rila Monastery would serve as an act of devotion to Ivan Rilski. A similar appeal was made to the Muscovite Orthodox patriarch.[11]

A further Rila delegate, Arsenii, was despatched by the monastery to Russia in 1632. Because of strict Muscovite regulations on the number of delegations to the court and the outbreak of an epidemic, Arsenii was stopped at the Russian border and prohibited from entering the country. He eventually was forced to return to the monastery empty-handed.[12]

Thanks to official Ottoman protection, active fund raising, and the enormous spiritual prestige enjoyed by Ivan Rilski among the Orthodox faithful, Bulgarian and non-Bulgarian alike, Rila Monastery survived throughout the seventeenth century as one of the largest monastic establishments in the Bulgarian lands. As such, it played a significant cultural role in the lives of the local Bulgarian population through the activities of the numerous Bulgarian monks who lived within its walls.

Because of the periodic plundering of the monastery and the cumulative effects of extensive post-seventeenth century renovations and reconstructions, few works of seventeenth century monumental art produced at Rila Monastery have survived. No known major church construction or renovation was attempted during the century. Icon images of Ivan Rilski, however, were produced. Three such works are extant. One appeared at the end of the petitional letter to Tsar Mihail. Another was a full-length portrayal of the saint in monastic garb. The third also presented Ivan Rilski in a similar pose but the central image was surrounded by a border of ten smaller scenes from the saint's hagiographical life. Within these latter scenes the medieval Bulgarian ruler, Petŭr, figured prominently and was identified in Slavic script as a Bulgarian tsar.[13]

Happily, the literary output of the seventeenth century Rila monks fared a bit better than did their works of art. Literary activity flourished at the monastery throughout the century and well into that which followed. The earliest extant seventeenth century exemplar was penned in 1602 by *ieropop* Nikifor. His work was a hagiography of Ivan Rilski that he translated and copied into Slavic from a twelfth century Greek work by George Skylitzes. Nikifor deposited his manuscript in the monastery church, where it was later (1739) bound by *pop* Atanas from the village of Boboshevo. Most likely, Nikifor was also the copyist of a *sbornik* that contained three hagiographical lives of Ivan Rilski, and which was later acquired by Etropole Monastery.[14]

Two Slavic menologions, for the months of February and November, were produced in 1653 under the auspices of abbot Atanasii *hadzhi*. Both were despatched to Zograf Monastery in the hands of *pop* Milente, who was sent to Athos to further pursue his education. Later, in 1656, a certain Arsenii copied a *sbornik* of saints' canons that especially included those of Ivan Rilski. Arsenii noted his desire that the book be used in the monastery church and school.[15]

The only other extant manuscript produced at Rila Monastery bearing a seventeenth century date was an *otechnik* copied by *pop* Viktor in 1696.[16]

Two undated works believed to have been seventeenth century Rila Monastery products were a gospels, written during the term of office of abbot Ioasif, and a menologion for the month of August, which contained hagiographies of Ivan Rilski and Ioakim Osogovski. Although the date of the latter manuscript's production is unknown, it was bound, together with a number of others at the monastery, at the order of abbot Visarion *hadzhi* in 1693.[17]

During the seventeenth century, the most significant cultural role of Rila Monastery lay in the field of education. The monastery's impact was felt not only on the local Bulgarian level but on the international stage as well.

A cell school had been established at the monastery during the second half of the fifteenth century and it continued to operate well into the eighteenth. The students at the school during the seventeenth century were able to make advantageous use of the well-stocked monastery library, which at that time housed literary works produced both at the monastery and in other locations that dated to the fifteenth and sixteenth centuries, as well as works produced at the monastery during their period of study.[18] In a note (1656) made in a *sbornik* written in Rila Monastery, Arsenii stated that his reason for having the work produced was to benefit students in their studies at the monastery.[19] The extensive library and the number of works either produced or annotated at the monastery during the seventeenth century leave little doubt that Rila Monastery operated a large school of Slavic letters during that period.

Education as conducted at the monastery served two purposes. The first emphasized the maintenance of Slavic literacy and was primarily aimed at the local population of the Bulgarian lands. In that regard, the teachers at Rila instructed their students in both the traditional Church Slavonic and in the newly developing New Bulgarian literary language of the *damaskins*. One might posit that traditional education, with its emphasis on basic literacy and the liturgical works of medieval Bulgarian writers, such as Evtimii, constituted the primary course of instruction at the elementary and advanced levels. Most of the works produced at the monastery during the century lay in the mainstream of traditional Orthodox liturgical literature, including the hagiographies of Bulgarian saints, Ivan Rilski, Ioakim Osogovski and the sixteenth century martyr-saint, Georgi Novi Sofiiski. Instruction in the New Bulgarian literary language most likely was reserved for the more advanced level students.

Rila Monastery had been instrumental in the initial formulation of the New Bulgarian literary language during the latter years of the sixteenth century. A *damaskin* produced there at that time proved to be the earliest prototype of the new literary genre to appear in the Bulgarian lands. Although no new work of that kind was produced at Rila during the seventeenth century, the New Bulgarian literary language was undoubtedly familiar to the teachers and monks working at the monastery. Rila *taxidiots* traveling between the monastery and its numerous *metohs* located throughout the Bulgarian lands spread the knowledge of the new literary language. In many regions of those lands where Rila *metohs* existed, especially in the Sredna Gora Mountains, the seventeenth century saw the emergence of *damaskins* written in New Bulgarian.[20]

The second purpose placed on education at Rila Monastery was the propagation of the cult of Ivan Rilski, which was directed toward both native Bulgarian and non-Bulgarian Orthodox believers. The widespread prestige accorded the monastery by the Orthodox world at large testified to the success the Rila monks enjoyed in cultivating and sustaining the cult of veneration directed toward their patron saint. The monks' devotion to their patron over the course of centuries appears to have bordered on obsession. All known seventeenth century icons produced at the monastery were images of Ivan Rilski. Nearly all of the extant Rila literary works of that period contained hagiographies of that Bulgarian saint.

No opportunity for spreading the cult of Ivan Rilski was lost upon the monks of Rila. Through the activities of Rila *metohs* and *taxidiots*, literary works from the seventeenth century containing hagiographies of the saint proliferated in a number of other Bulgarian cultural centers (*e.g.*, the Sofia monasteries, Etropole Monastery and the monasteries in the region of Vratsa). The Rila delegations sent to Muscovy in the sixteenth and seventeenth centuries actively propagated the cult of Ivan Rilski among the Russians. The Rila petitional letter of 1628 to Tsar Mihail contained not only a request for material aid but also stressed the sacredness of the Rilski cult.

Partly in response to such propagandizing by Rila monks, the cult of Ivan Rilski gained widespread popularity in seventeenth century Russia. Hagiographies of the saint appeared in a number of Russian literary works of that period. The most notable example was the first printed version of the hagiography produced at the Kievan Monastery of the Caves in 1671. The printer was *ieromonah* Antoniy Radivilovskiy, whose patron for the work was a Bulgarian living in Moldavia, Raicho Dimitrashko.[21]

Significantly, the emphasis placed on spreading the Rilski cult by the monks of Rila perforce included the transmission of an awareness of the greatness of the Bulgarians' medieval past. The life of Ivan Rilski, as related in his hagiography, was intimately linked to historical personages and places in the medieval Bulgarian state. Thus Ivan's dealings with Tsar Petŭr and the transfer of his remains from Rila to Sofia, and eventually to Tŭrnovo, the capital of the Second Bulgarian Empire, were indivisible elements of the saintly cult. By their indefatigable efforts to honor their patron saint, the monks of Rila Monastery played an important role in preserving the memory of the Bulgarians' past among the population of the Bulgarian lands subject to Ottoman authority, while they also stirred interest in their contemporary fellow Bulgarians among foreign populations, especially in Russia.[22] The efforts of the Rila monks to sustain veneration of Ivan Rilski among the Bulgarian population of the Ottoman Empire during the seventeenth century were successful, as evidenced by the numerous exemplars of Rilski hagiographies that appeared in seventeenth century Bulgarian literary products. Such success undoubtedly assured that Rila Monastery enjoyed pride of place among similar religious establishments in the Bulgarian lands. For the Orthodox Bulgarians, Rila Monastery represented a direct and living link to their lost past.

In terms of geographic breadth, no other seventeenth century Orthodox cultural center located in the Bulgarian lands was as well-known and influential as was Rila Monastery. Its impact was felt in all other major Bulgarian centers of Orthodox culture and as far afield as Russia. It is not surprising, then, that cultural activity conducted in regions lying in close proximity to the monastery (*e.g.,* in the regions of Samokov, Dupnitsa, Kyustendil and Razlog) were noticeably influenced by forces emanating from Rila Monastery. (See Map 4)

The iron processing town of Samokov, which lay to the northeast of Rila Monastery on the far side of the Rila Mountains, had long benefited from its proximity to the monastery. Prior to the Ottoman conquest, the Samokov region had possessed the highest level of literacy in medieval Bulgaria, and it had furnished one of the most astute students of Evtimii Tŭrnovski in the person of Konstantin Kostenechki Filosof. By the seventeenth century the level of literacy among the local clerics had experienced a decline. Yet during that period cell schools operated in the town and in a number of *metohs* belonging to Rila, Zograf, Hilendar and other large monasteries. Two works produced in Samokov during the seventeenth century are extant. One was copied by *pop* Nikola in 1601. The other was produced in 1639.[23]

Artistic activity flourished in the Samokov region during the seventeenth century. In 1626 Alino Monastery, in the Plana foothills of Mount Vitosha and lying northwest of Samokov, was erected and decorated, possibly by students of Pimen Zografski. Also of note were the mural paintings in the small church of "St. Nikola" in the village of Maritsa, which were executed sometime during the closing years of the sixteenth or opening years of the seventeenth century. The Maritsa paintings exhibited a strong link with the medieval Bulgarian tradition of monumental art in both style and iconography. Their high level of quality indicates that the anonymous artists responsible for the decoration in the church must have been talented and extensively trained. Other such work in the region, as in the church of "St. Petka" in the village of Belchin and the village church in Mala Tsŭrkva, demonstrated noticeable affinities to the paintings in both Alino and Maritsa, and they may have all been the work of the same group of artists.[24]

The Dupnitsa region, beyond the mountains northwest of Rila Monastery in the valley of the Struma River, was also active in the realm of Slavic literature during the seventeenth century. In 1613 a service menologion was copied in Dupnitsa by one K. Pahomie. Later, in 1634, the Dupnitsa furrier, Dimitre Popov, purchased a sixteenth century gospels and donated it to the church of "The Holy Arhangel Mihail." A year afterward, in 1635, a certain Petŭr copied another gospels for the church of "St. Nikola" in the town. This evidence speaks of two churches operating in Dupnitsa during the seventeenth century, and both were probably active in the literary and educational fields.[25]

IN THE SEVENTEENTH CENTURY

Villages in the Kyustendil region demonstrated activity in the fields of education (*e.g.,* Boboshevo, Tŭrvarishta and Tavalichevo) in close association with Rila Monastery, Dupnitsa and Razlog.[26] In the field of art, village churches in Boboshevo ("St. Iliya"), Goranovtsi ("Holy Arhangel Mihail"), Vukovo ("St. Petka" and "St. Nikolai"), Pastuh ("St. Ivan") and Tavalichevo ("St. Petka"), among others, were decorated with mural paintings during the period spanned by the final years of the sixteenth and the first decade of the seventeenth centuries.

In the region of Razlog, little evidence for seventeenth century cultural activity survived the ravages of time. There is, however, some meager evidence for Slavic education in Razlog during the century.[27] Also, in the field of art, some of the most skillful seventeenth century mural paintings were produced in 1614 in a church dedicated to saints Teodor Tiron and Teodor Stratilat located in the village of Dobŭrsko, which lay some 12 kilometers northeast of Razlog on a local mountain road that connected Razlog with Rila Monastery. Among the saints depicted in the paintings were the Bulgarians, Ivan Rilski, Prohor Pshinski and Ioakim Osogovski. The wooden iconostasis of the church was carved and decorated at the same time. The character of the Dobŭrsko paintings showed the artists to have been schooled masters in the medieval Bulgarian traditions, indicating ties with Mount Athos. As Dobŭrsko was a village mentioned in the charter of properties granted Rila Monastery by Ivan Shishman in 1378, it is likely that the village continued to maintain close ties with the monastery during the seventeenth century.[28]

Rila Monastery was an important focus for seventeenth century Bulgarian Orthodox culture. It was a stronghold of Slavic traditions during a period of increasing socio-economic turmoil and rising levels of Muslim reaction. The monastery library was, perhaps, one of the largest existing in the Bulgarian lands at the time, and it housed Slavic works of church literature and royal charters spanning the history of the monastery itself. Through its extensive network of *metohs,* Rila Monastery was able to influence a wide area of the Bulgarian lands, having its greatest impact in the fields of education and literature. Such a broad field of operations contributed to its instrumental role in the development of the New Bulgarian literary language and in the propagation of the cult of Ivan Rilski. The latter development not only made an impact on the fields of Bulgarian literature and art but also stirred the Bulgarians' interest in their own past, and it created among them a consciousness of their unity in devotion.

Sofia

Modern studies treating with seventeenth century Sofia have tended to dwell on the demographic, social and economic aspects of the city, and to discuss Bulgarian Orthodox cultural life there primarily in terms of the Greek-dominated church hierarchy resident in the city. Sofia was, in fact, a large Ottoman administrative and commercial center, and the city served as the capital of the empire's extensive European province of Rumeli. Its population was overwhelmingly Turkish and rigidly organized *via* strong artisan and merchant *esnafs*. Greek prelates sat upon the metropolitan throne. Over the course of the 200 years following the Ottoman conquest Sofia played a significant role in Ottoman internal affairs.[29]

The disadvantageous demographic situation of the Bulgarian inhabitants of the city, however, did not prohibit the efflorescence of Sofia into a major center of Bulgarian Orthodox culture during the sixteenth century. Among the known cultural figures who worked in the city during that time were the teachers and writer-copyists, *pop* Peio and Matei Lambadarii Gramatik. The revival by Peio and Matei of Slavic Orthodox literature in the city for the first time since the Ottoman conquest was paralleled in the monasteries located in the surrounding countryside.

Stefan Gerlach, a German Anabaptist pastor who traveled through Sofia in the final quarter of the sixteenth century, left a note in his diary under the date 25 June 1578 in which he confirmed the flourishing Slavic cultural life in the city:[30]

> ...I went with...our buyer to the Metropolitan...His [the metropolitan's] main church is "St. Marina," newly arched and entirely repainted; the icons have been restored. In a coffin near the altar door lies the body of St. Stefan [Uroš II Miljutin, Serbian ruler (1282-1321)] who was a Bulgarian [*sic*] tsar [*sic*] who had become a monk. His hands were exposed, but the face and the rest of the body were covered. On his waist was set a bowl, in which the people who look at him leave aspers [*akçes*]. Next to him is a tall candle. In this church there is a Bulgarian school. In the city there is one other school, where children are taught to read. There are no Greek schools, and from these two schools come most of the Bulgarian priests [for the region of Sofia]. The Bulgarians and the Greeks here [Sofia] attend the same church, because they have similar religious services. When many Bulgarians are in attendance, the liturgy is read in Bulgarian [Slavonic]. Next to our [Gerlach's travel party's] house stands a tall circular tower that forty years ago [*ca.* 1538] the Bulgarians possessed as one of their churches ["St. Georgi," a fifth century structure and oldest building standing in Sofia], but the Turks took it over and converted it into a mosque, that

is, a Turkish [sic] church. There are, as well, twelve priests [in Sofia], and so [there are] twelve churches: 1. the aforementioned main, or cathedral, church, St. Marina; the three churches of St. Nicholas ["St. Nikola"]; two — St. Paraskeva [also known as "St. Petka" (Tŭrnovska)]; . . . 7. Kiriaki — meaning the church of the Lord [also known as "St. Nedelya"]; 8. St. Archangel; 9. the Ascension [also known as "The Holy Savior"]; 10. Filled with Grace ["Vseh svetih," also known as "The Presentation of the Blessed Virgin Immaculate"]; 11 . St. John the Baptist [often identified by scholars as "St. Ivan Rilski," the church mentioned in the hagiography by Evtimii]; 12. St. Luke ["St. Luka"]. Falling under [the authority of] this metropolitan are over three hundred villages or churches.

Sixty-two years after Gerlach, in 1640, the Bulgarian Catholic bishop, Petŭr Bogdan, painted a somewhat more somber picture of Bulgarian Orthodox cultural life in Sofia as part of a report dated 20 May 1640 filed with the Vatican:[31]

> There are five [Orthodox] churches [in Sofia]; two [others?] were demolished by the Turks in the past [few] years. Here is the seat of their [the Orthodox faithful of the Sofia metropolitanate] schismatic [Orthodox] archbishop [metropolitan]. The archbishops [metropolitans] are always Greeks, but the people are of the Bulgarian nationality. In the metropolitan [cathedral] there are human relics, which are called the Holy King [Stefan Uroš II Miljutin]. It appeared to me that this ruler had been embalmed. But they [the Orthodox authorities] do not permit this to be seen, other than one hand, for the rest [of the body] remains covered. This [the Orthodox] archbishop [metropolitan] has under his authority in his archbishopric [metropolitanate] 1500 [sic] priests, outside of the monasteries and [their] churches, which have no priests [sic]. Close to the city can be seen a church in a high and pleasant locale; there, it is said, met the Œcumenical Council of Sardica [A.D. 343-344]. In the Bulgarian language this place [Sofia] is called Triaditsa.

The descriptions of Sofia made by Gerlach and Bogdan have been used by some scholars as comparative evidence for the cultural decline of the city during the seventeenth century. While Gerlach noted that schools and churches flourished, Bogdan made no mention in his report of schools or cultural activity of any kind, and by his time the number of functioning churches in Sofia had decreased. Yet a critical examination of the details contained in the two descriptions reveals that they were essentially in agreement on all points other than the number of churches in operation. Both men noted that the ecclesiastical hierarchy was in Greek hands and that the Orthodox congregations, as well as the parish priests, were predominantly Bulgarian. Likewise, both Gerlach and Bogdan noted the confiscation or destruction of Orthodox religious structures by the Muslim Turks.

A decline in the number of functioning churches in the city cannot of itself serve as an absolute index for the decline of Orthodox culture in Sofia during the seventeenth century. That the church in Sofia suffered materially during the years that separated the visits of Gerlach and Bogdan is, perhaps, understandable in view of the events that occurred in the region of the city during that time.

Between the years 1593 and 1606 the Ottoman Empire was engaged in an extensive struggle with the Habsburg Empire and its Danubian and Transylvanian allies known as the Long War. The repercussions of that conflict within the Ottoman Empire were significant. During the course of the war the first obvious signs of Turkish military decline came to the fore, marking the incipient degeneration of the empire's feudal socio-administrative organization. Concurrently, the Western enemies of the Turks, notably Vienna and Rome, carried out revolutionary agitation within the empire *via* their Dubrovnik intermediaries. These factors in combination succeeded in creating widespread unrest in the Bulgarian lands, resulting in the ill-fated first Tŭrnovo Uprising (1598) and, more significantly for the Sofia region, the growth of bands of Bulgarian *haiduts*. Throughout the first two decades of the seventeenth century such bands operated with apparent impunity in the Sofia countryside, preying on the commercial traffic traveling the Belgrad-Istanbul highway and other secondary routes in the region. At times the bandits made so bold as to attack even open and covered market places in the town.[32] The Ottoman authorities eventually were able to restore order in the region but in doing so perpetrated some retaliatory acts upon the local Christian population. Although no direct evidence exists describing such acts with regard to church structures in Sofia, Bogdan's comment concerning the demolition of church edifices by the Turks most likely refers to acts of retaliation against the *haidut* activity resulting from the Long War.[33]

It is difficult to determine exactly how detrimental this period of internal agitation was for Bulgarian cultural activity in Sofia. The available evidence suggests that those cultural activities that had abounded during the sixteenth century to a large extent weathered the storm. Precisely during the anarchistic times of the early seventeenth century Pimen Zografski was active in the field of religious art throughout the region of Sofia, and a number of church structures were decorated under his supervision. Furthermore, such artistic activity, whether conducted by Pimen or by other artists, was given official Ottoman sanction by the authorities in Sofia. Thus in 1617 the Bulgarians in the nearby village of Kurilo received permission from the Sofia *kadı* to renovate the church in the village monastery, "St. Father Ivan Rilski." Later, during the middle of the century, at a time when Muslim reactionary sentiment ran high among the Turkish population of the empire, the right of the Sofia Christians to build or renovate their churches and monasteries was confirmed in a *ferman* (1669) issued by Sultan Mehmed IV to the Sofia metropolitan. In that decree Mehmed stipulated that, in order to build or renovate religious edifices, the Christians were obliged first to seek and obtain the written permission of their local authorities or that of the High Divan (Council) in Istanbul. Mehmed further required that the Christian structures could not be constructed so as to offend Muslim sensibilities. Under such conditions Bulgarian Orthodox art in Sofia was able to exist throughout the seventeenth century, even during the early decades of heavy Muslim reaction.[34]

A large number of churches in the Sofia region were built or decorated during the early decades of the seventeenth century by Pimen or his students. Among the sites of such artistic activity were Kurilo Monastery (1596-1617), Kremikovtsi Monastery (1611), Dragalevtsi Monastery (which also received six icons as gifts from devout patrons in 1617 and 1620), Seslavtsi Monastery, Eleshnitsa Monastery and Ilientsi Monastery. Following this spate of activity connected with Pimen and his students, however, artistic life in the Sofia region slackened, although minor efforts continued to be made during the remaining years of the century. For example, the north exterior wall of the church at Dragalevtsi Monastery was decorated with murals, probably by a certain Kalist, prior to the year 1689. Smaller works, such as icons, were produced for various churches in the region.[35]

Turning from the field of Bulgarian art to that of education, the evidence suggests that Slavic education did not die out in Sofia during the seventeenth century. Schools existed both within the city and in certain of the nearby monasteries. Direct evidence for the existence of Slavic schools was furnished by manuscript marginalia written throughout the century. A few writers of such glosses identified themselves with the title of *daskal*. For example, *daskal* Dragan, born in the village of Novoseltsi near Sofia, noted in a manuscript originally produced at Hilendar Monastery (1623) that he had received his education in Sofia. The anonymous author of a psalter (1639) written in the Sofia region described himself as a "*daskal* from Sofia." A certain [I]Ovan (1617) made note of the fact that he had studied at Eleshnitsa Monastery. In a manuscript dedicated to the hagiography of Ivan Rilski, Nikola Gramatik from the village of Gorni Lozen stated that he had studied in Sofia under the priest, Yakim. An undated gloss penned in a *sbornik* (*ca.* 1664) by one Stefan Singel (?) noted that he had studied under a certain Ivanika from Niš. Whether Ivanika taught in Niš or in Sofia is unclear in Stefan's note.[36]

The marginalia evidence also suggests that Slavic literacy was maintained among elements in the Bulgarian population of the Sofia region who were not members of the clergy or of monastic communities. This, as well as the widespread circulation enjoyed by many of the manuscripts glossed by Sofia Bulgarians, speaks for the continued existence of education in the Sofia region throughout the seventeenth century. In fact, during the final quarter of the century a book market operated in the city's Solni bazaar, suggesting that not only did a literate clientele exist in Sofia and the surrounding countryside, but that the city served as a center for the distribution of Slavic works of literature throughout the western Bulgarian lands.[37]

Two schools certainly functioned in the Sofia region during the seventeenth century, and the number may have been as high as five. Both Dragalevtsi and Eleshnitsa monasteries maintained large, well-known schools. Inscriptions carved on the exterior walls of the church at Dragalevtsi Monastery spoke of the school and its curriculum, which consisted of instruction in basic Cyrillic reading and writing, and of advanced studies in copying and writing religious texts. Petŭr Bogdan made mention of the school at Dragalevtsi in his correspondence. The school at Eleshnitsa Monastery was first mentioned in the previously noted annotation by [I]Ovan in 1617. Eleshnitsa appears to have been a thriving enterprise during the seventeenth century, and it maintained contacts with other Bulgarian educational and literary centers, most especially with Etropole Monastery.[38]

It is possible that Slavic schools existed at three other sites in the region of Sofia during the seventeenth century. In the city itself, the most likely location for such a school was the church of "St. Nikola." This church was mentioned in three separate sources from Sofia during the century. A 1563 manuscript written by the noted Bulgarian writer, Ioan Kratovski, bore six seventeenth century notations, four of which were dated. The earliest note mentioned *pop* Kostadin of "St. Nikola," his brother Petko, Nikola Vranko and Tsona Manov, who donated the manuscript to the church in 1622. Another of the notes was penned by a certain Ivan (1646), which stated that the manuscript was placed in the church. *Ieromonah* Nikodima from Zograf Monastery left a gloss in the work in 1668. The final dated notation was made by one Stancho, mentioning *pop* Stefan of "St. Nikola" (1680).[39]

Our second source for a possible school at "St. Nikola" is a Bible originally produced in Russia (1581) that contained a note explaining that the book was donated to "St. Nikola" in 1647. A second notation (1690) stated that Todor from Sofia later donated the Bible to Kuklen Monastery, near Plovdiv.[40]

The third source, a psalter (1598), was copied by *monah* Danail, Stoyan and Vladko, three brothers from Sofia. An undated note in this manuscript stated that Danail and Stoyan commenced work on the manuscript in the church of "St. Nikola," and that *dyak* Vladko completed it in Dragalevtsi Monastery.[41]

The Ioan Kratovski manuscript offers a strong suggestion that a Slavic school operated at "St. Nikola," as does the 1598 psalter. The presence of an Athonite monk, the relatively high number of marginalia and the possession of a work produced by a leading sixteenth century Bulgarian writer whose works were widely known, studied and imitated, would seem to indicate that "St. Nikola" conducted educational activity within the city during the seventeenth century.

Schools may also have operated in the monasteries of Buhovo and Dolni Lozen, but the evidence in those cases is not wholly convincing.[42]

Despite the known conduct of some cultural activity within the limits of the city, and because of the intense presence of Muslim civil and Greek religious authorities within the city itself, Bulgarian Orthodox cultural life in the Sofia region during the century flourished primarily in the numerous monasteries located in the highlands surrounding the Sofia Plain. Since the mid tenth century Sofia served as the focal point for intense Orthodox monastic activity. This situation began when Tsar Petŭr I had the relics of Ivan Rilski transferred from their grave in the Rila Mountains to a new church that Petŭr ordered erected in Sofia. Thus the city acquired a popular sacred patron who soon commonly became known as the "Saint of Sredets [Sofia]." Thereafter, Sofia evolved into a center for the extremely widespread cult of veneration directed toward Ivan Rilski. The mountains of the region sprouted numerous monastic communities founded and populated by Bulgarians who sought to emulate the beloved native anchorite.[43]

Throughout the thirteenth and fourteenth centuries monasticism in the region of Sofia thrived to such an extent that some modern scholars have applied the descriptive term "Little Mount Athos" to the phenomenon.[44] The fall of the area to the Turks in the late fourteenth century, however, dealt monastic activity a heavy blow, and monasticism in the Sofia region only began to recover after a lapse of some 100 years. By the end of the sixteenth century monastic activity in the region had regained its feet, and in the early seventeenth century 13 separate monastic communities functioned in the immediate vicinity of the city. Two, Dragalevtsi and Boyana, lay on the northern slopes of Mount Vitosha just to the south of Sofia. German and Dolni Lozen monasteries were situated in the Lozen foothills east of Sofia. In the Plana foothills of Vitosha, southeast of Sofia, stood Kokalyane. Lyulin (Gorna Banya) Monastery was situated in the western Lyulin foothills of Vitosha. A few kilometers northwest of Sofia on the Sofia Plain lay Ilientsi Monastery, and on the southern slopes of the Balkan Mountains to the north of the city, the monasteries of Kurilo, Kremikovtsi, Seslavtsi, Buhovo, Zhelyava and Eleshnitsa stretched off to the east. Of all these establishments, two, Boyana and Lyulin, suffered at the hands of the Turks during the early years of the seventeenth century and by mid century lay deserted. The 11 remaining monasteries all played roles of varying note in the Slavic Orthodox cultural life of the Sofia Bulgarians during the century. (See Map 5)

Eleshnitsa Monastery, "The Assumption of the Blessed Virgin (Immaculate)," often referred to in the sources as "Yakovishtitsa" because of its proximity to a small rivulet bearing that name, was one of the largest and most active monasteries in the region in the field of Slavic literature. It lay some seven kilometers northeast of the village of Eleshnitsa and 30 kilometers east-northeast of Sofia in a small valley of the Balkan Mountain massive known as Murgash. The monastery was originally founded in the final years of the fifteenth century, and it played an active role in the sixteenth century cultural efflorescence of the Sofia region. During the seventeenth century Eleshnitsa Monastery was rich in fertile lands, possessed a newly constructed church (erected in the final years of the preceding century), to which was added a narthex with mural decoration, and served as a center for a Slavic school and literary workshop.[45]

The earliest seventeenth century reference to Eleshnitsa Monastery was made in 1604 In that year three persons from the village of Vrazhdebna, Petra, Stoina and Vulcha, banded together and purchased one of the manuscripts produced at the monastery (1603) for the purpose of making a donation to the monastery church. The abbot of Eleshnitsa at the time was *ieromonah* Kalist, and working under him was the writer-copyist, *ieromonah* Nikifor. Nikifor produced a menologion in 1604 and sold it to a certain Miliya from Eleshnitsa village, who likewise promptly donated the manuscript back to the monastery. Thirteen years later (1617), concrete evidence for the school at Eleshnitsa was furnished by the marginal gloss of [I]Ovan in a fourteenth-fifteenth century psalter used as a school text. The school at the monastery survived through the seventeenth century, for in 1702 a note was left in one of the monastery's manuscripts stating that *monah* Kralcho, Mati Stano and "the reader," Ioan, studied in the monastery at the time. The numerous references to local villages (*e.g.*, Vrazhdebna, Eleshnitsa and Dolni Kamenartsi) in the marginalia pertaining to Eleshnitsa Monastery make it evident that the monastery played an important role in the Slavic cultural life of the nearby village populations.[46]

Three other active Bulgarian monasteries lay in the Murgash highlands in close proximity to Eleshnitsa Monastery. Little is known about the history of Zhelyava Monastery, "St. Petka." It appears in three sources, all of them undated marginalia, but internal evidence seems to indicate that the monastery was in operation before 1624. Two extant literary works were produced at Zhelyava. That monastery, however, was overshadowed by the one of Buhovo, "The Holy Arhangel," another Murgash establishment. Quite possibly, Zhelyava was a lesser, affiliated house of Buhovo. One of the manuscripts copied at Zhelyava was purchased in 1624 by Nesho Doblishko from Chelopechane and donated to Buhovo Monastery. There is evidence that a school functioned in the monastery, as notations made by the laymen, Stotse Mladen from "Krikotsi" (Kremikovtsi?) and Nesho Obreshkov from Chelopechane, spoke of using the 1624 manuscript.

IN THE SEVENTEENTH CENTURY

An undated book of Lenten offices, most likely produced during the seventeenth century, is the only extant work known definitely to have been copied at Buhovo Monastery. The marginalia found in the three manuscripts that involved both Zhelyava and Buhovo monasteries demonstrated the close relations they maintained with the Bulgarian villages on the Sofia Plain, especially with Chelopechane, Birimirtsi, Zhelyava, Buhovo and Kremikovtsi.[47]

The fourth Murgash monastery, that of Seslavtsi, "St. Nikolai," lay in a small ravine, high upon the southern slopes of that massive some two kilometers north of Seslavtsi village and approximately 20 kilometers northeast of Sofia. According to local legend, the monastery was founded by the Bulgarian *bolyar,* Seslav, who reportedly also erected a fortress in the area at some time prior to the Ottoman conquest. The monastery church was built during the sixteenth century and was redecorated with mural paintings during the early seventeenth century by two artists, a master (possibly Pimen Zografski) and his assistant. These two men created on the walls of the nave and narthex the most striking visual statement of Bulgarian Orthodox consciousness found in the western Bulgarian lands during the seventeenth century. Among the standard Orthodox iconographic images were prominently portrayed the likenesses of seven Bulgarian saints, all identified by Slavic inscriptions (Ivan Rilski, Georgi and Nikolai Novi Sofiiski, Ioakim Osogovski, Gavril Lesnovski, Prohor Pshinski and Naum). The possibility that the master artist responsible for these efforts was Pimen Zografski is heightened by the fact that the monastery possessed a menologion (1618) copied by Pimen. Except for a 1605 gloss in a sixteenth century manuscript produced at the monastery, no further literary evidence for Seslavtsi during the seventeenth century is extant.[48]

On the wooded lower southern slopes of the Balkan Mountains to the west of Seslavtsi, some 17 kilometers northeast of Sofia, lay Kremikovtsi Monastery, "St. Georgi." It was one of the oldest, largest and most famous of the monastic communities in the region of Sofia, and it was closely bound to the Slavic cultural life of the Bulgarians living in both the city and the local villages. The monastery was founded by the Bulgarian Tsar Ivan Aleksandŭr during the fourteenth century. Razed at the end of that century, Kremikovtsi was left deserted for a century, until it was rebuilt (1493) under the auspices of the Bulgarian *bolyar* from Sofia, Radivoi, and the Greek metropolitan, Kalevit. The mural paintings executed at that time rank among the masterpieces of Bulgarian religious art prior to the nineteenth century national revival. An exonarthex was added to the monastery church in 1611 and decorated with wall paintings.

From the time of its refounding by Radivoi and Kalevit Kremikovtsi was continuously inhabited as a monastic community. One can safely assume that visitors to the monastery were able to view the paintings in the church and to read (or have read to them) the Slavic inscriptions that identified Radivoi as a rich Bulgarian from Sofia, as well as that which announced the image of Petka Tŭrnovska. Radivoi later (1497) donated an illuminated manuscript originally written in Dragalevtsi Monastery by Peyu and Petko to Kremikovtsi in honor of the renovation of the church. Since that time the manuscript acquired the title of the "Kremikovtsi Gospel." Its pages were heavily annotated throughout the sixteenth and seventeenth centuries.[49]

A legend persisted among the villagers of Kurilo that Ivan Rilski had actually been born in their village rather than in Skrino, and that he had resided in the nearby monastery prior to his journey to the Rila Mountains. Resting at the foot of the Balkan Mountains near the southern mouth of the Iskŭr River gorge, Kurilo Monastery, "St. Father Ivan Rilski," was, to be sure, an old establishment. The exact date of its founding is unknown but the monastery certainly existed during the second half of the tenth century at the time Tsar Petŭr brought the relics of Ivan Rilski to Sofia. The legend linking Rilski with Kurilo eventually resulted in the monastery being commonly dedicated to that saint. During its reconstruction in the late sixteenth and early seventeenth centuries, the monastery was referred to simply as "St. Father." The paintings created on the church walls during the renovation, under the patronage of two men named Stoyan, bakers from Sofia, and abbot Teodosii, were the work of Pimen Zografski. They included an image of Petka Tŭrnovska.

At approximately the same time as the renovation of the monastery church, a gospel was produced in the Kurilo scriptorium. Sometime later, abbot Iosif created another such work of all four gospels, introducing each of them with a passage from the writings of the medieval Bulgarian bishop of Ohrid, Teofilakt (*ca.* 1090-1118). Another Bulgarian Slavic version of the gospels, begun in Moldavia during the sixteenth century, eventually found its way to Kurilo sometime prior to the close of the seventeenth century, where sections of the manuscript were completed after its arrival.[50]

Information regarding Ilientsi Monastery, "St. Iliya," is sparse. It was located near Sofia, and it was the only monastic community in the region standing directly on the Sofia Plain rather than in the surrounding highlands. Apparently, Ilientsi had evolved into a monastic community from a village church sometime during the final days of the medieval Bulgarian state. The monastery contributed to the sixteenth century cultural flowering of Sofia by producing a manuscript of the acts of the apostles. The only known cultural activity conducted at Ilientsi during the seventeenth century was the decoration of the church's endonarthex, possibly by Pimen, near the opening of the century.[51]

IN THE SEVENTEENTH CENTURY

The largest and most famous of the Sofia monasteries was Dragalevtsi, "The Blessed Virgin of Vitosha," located in a forested fold in the lower northern slopes of Mount Vitosha approximately ten kilometers south of Sofia. Its popularity was such that even foreign travelers on the Belgrad-Istanbul highway were able to identify it by name.[52] Since its founding by Bulgarian Tsar Ivan Aleksandŭr, Dragalevtsi played a leading role in the Slavic culture of the Christian Bulgarians inhabiting the region of Sofia. The original charter granted the monastery by its founder is no longer extant, but that one issued by his royal son, Ivan Shishman, in 1376 alluded to the fact that it reaffirmed the rights and privileges granted the monastery by the founder. One of the charter's articles removed Dragalevtsi Monastery from the control of the Greek Patriarchate and placed it directly under the authority of the metropolitan of Sofia. So it remained throughout the course of its history.[53]

Dragalevtsi was probably plundered at the time of the Ottoman conquest and left deserted until the middle of the fifteenth century. Life returned to the monastery about 1469, when under abbot Pavel a gospels was produced there by a certain *pop* Nikola. Seven years later (1476) a noted Sofia *bolyar*, Radoslav Mavŭr, and his sons, Nikola Gramatik and Stahna, sponsored the renovation and decoration of the monastery church. The cultural activity conducted at Dragalevtsi was ever afterward strongly supported by the Bulgarian *esnafs* of Sofia and by prominent city residents, including, ironically, Sofia Roman Catholic archbishops.[54]

As were so many other monastery churches in the Sofia region during the early seventeenth century, that at Dragalevtsi was redecorated with mural paintings both inside and out. The patron for the work at Dragalevtsi was one Kalist, who may also have served as the chief artist in the endeavor. Among the new images placed on the exterior walls at that time were those of Ivan Rilski and Kiril Filosof. The paintings were retouched by another artist in 1689.[55]

The exterior walls of the church at Dragalevtsi also constitute an historical document concerning cultural activity at the monastery during the seventeenth century for reasons other than works of mural art. Numerous inscriptions were carved into the surface of the walls by visitors to the monastery. We have already noted the importance of these inscriptions for documenting the presence of a Slavic school at Dragalevtsi. Unfortunately, only a single manuscript produced in the monastery scriptorium during the seventeenth century is extant.[56]

The wall inscriptions at Dragalevtsi also illustrate the fact that the monastery enjoyed widespread fame as a religious center, particularly during the second half of the seventeenth century. Visitors, both lay and clergy, visited the monastery in droves. Many of them have been immortalized in carvings of their names and the dates of their visits in the plaster and stone of the church wall. Some of the carved graffiti were written in Latin letters and probably were the handiwork of

Dubrovnik merchants who were members of the small Dubrovnik merchant colony of Sofia.[57]

Dragalevtsi's popularity among the local Orthodox population was reflected in the large number of inscribed religious articles that were donated to the monastery, including numerous icons (two dated 1617 and 1620, and others undated but considered products of the seventeenth century), a beautifully worked gold and silver bookcover for a 1534 gospels crafted by Velo from Sofia in 1646, and an organ (1620), most likely a gift from foreign Westerners since organs are rarely used in Orthodox ritual, the acappella human voice being deemed the most spiritual method of musical devotion.[58]

Two seventeenth century abbots of Dragalevtsi are known by name. One was *hadzhi* Avram (1646), under whom Velo created his magnificent bookcover. The other was Eremiya, who was known to have held the office in 1647 and to have died in a fire 16 years later (1663).[59]

Kokalyane Monastery, "Holy Arhangel Mihail," lay some 17 kilometers southeast of Sofia on the easternmost fringe of Vitosha's Plana foothills overlooking the Iskŭr River valley that separated the Plana and Lozenska ranges. The area of its location was steeped in legend concerning Tsar Ivan Shishman and his futile struggle to stem the Ottoman invasion during the late fourteenth century. Across the valley from the monastery once stood the Bulgarian fortress of Urvich and its affiliated monastery, "St. Nikola." According to legend, at the first approach of the Ottoman armies Shishman placed all of his valuable treasures in the Urvich Monastery following his flight from the capital at Tŭrnovo. He and his troops offered battle to the Turks near the fortress in a desperate attempt to retain the Sofia Plain and the Iskŭr Valley but they were crushed by their Muslim adversaries (1395?). The treasures were then hurriedly transferred from Urvich to Kokalyane Monastery to prevent their falling into the hands of the victors.

Both the fortress of Urvich and its monastery were dismantled by the conquerors. Kokalyane housed the treasures for some period of time and possibly still retained a few objects during the seventeenth century.[60] If such were the case, the numerous Bulgarian visitors to the monastery were treated to a rich visual glimpse of their medieval past. That such visitors existed during the seventeenth century is verified by the only written document pertaining to Kokalyane Monastery from that time, the Urvich *sbornik*. Although written in the previous century, the *sbornik* evolved into a monastery beadroll. The earliest entries were dated 1645 and list the names of Sofia residents and their respective city *mahalles* (*e.g.*, Sungular and Tabahana), as well as a number of artisan and non-artisan professions that were in the hands of Bulgarians in Sofia at that time (*e.g.*, children's hat-makers, furriers and some others). Also listed were the names of

IN THE SEVENTEENTH CENTURY

numerous villages in the regions of Sofia and Samokov, as well as the monasteries of Dolni Lozen and Alino.[61]

The last two monasteries that must be considered in this survey of the Sofia region lay on the northern slopes of the Lozenska foothills southeast of the city. German Monastery, "St. Ivan Rilski," was founded on the northwest fringes of the Lozenska range at some time during the tenth century. Because it bore the dedicatory title of Ivan Rilski, the monastery's origins have been commonly associated with Tsar Petŭr. That the monastery existed during the late eleventh century was verified in a charter granted it by the Byzantine emperor, Alexios I Komnenos (1081-1118). Under the Second Bulgarian Empire German Monastery led a flourishing cultural existence but, as were so many of the other Sofia monasteries, it was ruined by the Ottoman conquest.[62]

Monastic activity revived at German in the sixteenth century, and by the opening of the seventeenth the monastery ranked as one of the leading centers of Bulgarian Orthodox culture in the Sofia region. Its library contained one of the oldest printed Slavic books, a psalter that had been published in Cetinje by Đord Crnojević (late fifteenth century) and containing a codex of Bulgarian saints among its listings of those venerated by the Serbs. The Bulgarian saints listed in that work were Petka Tŭrnovska, Ivan Rilski, Ilarion Mŭglenski and Ioakim Osogovski. In the closing years of the sixteenth century German's scriptorium produced a psalter, while a menologion was copied there near the mid to late seventeenth century, with additions made to it (1694) by Roman Zagorets. Nikola Gramatik, who left evidence for educational activity in the Sofia region, worked at German Monastery in 1671. Among the hagiographies contained in Nikola's work were two for the Bulgarian saints, Ivan Rilski and Ioakim Osogovski. Given Nikola's title, it is possible that at least a small cell school existed at German during the second half of the seventeenth century.[63]

Dolni Lozen Monastery, "The Holy Savior," was located ten kilometers southeast of German and five kilometers above the villages of Gorni and Dolni Lozen in a small ravine of the peak called Poluvrak. The monastery was founded during the thirteenth century, was razed by the Turks in 1382, and left to languish for the next 200 years. The Athonite monastery of Zograf possessed numerous properties within the city of Sofia and in the surrounding countryside, including the villages of Gorni and Dolni Lozen.[64] The reestablishment of Dolni Lozen Monastery was most likely the work of *taxidiots* from Zograf, who rededicated the monastery at some time during the first half of the seventeenth century as a *metoh* of their parent establishment. By 1645 the monastery was definitely active, as it was mentioned in the Urvich *sbornik* for that year. During the closing years of the seventeenth century *pop* Mladen Mali of the Sofia church, "The Holy Arhangel" wrote a brief account of the life of Pimen Zografski in a manuscript housed at Dolni Lozen Monastery. Adjoining the signature of Mladen was that of *pop* Dovrena from the village of Birimirtsi, illustrating that the monastery was frequented by members of the local Bulgarian village populations from the eastern Sofia Plain.[65]

Despite the documented literary activity that took place in the monasteries surrounding Sofia, no literary figures of the stature of Peio or Matei Gramatik emerged during the seventeenth century. As a consequence, the reputation of Sofia as a Slavic Orthodox cultural center during the period has suffered at the hands of most scholars of Bulgarian history. Quite unfortunate for the cultural reputation of Sofia was the fact that those Sofia-trained writer-copyists who did manifest literary talent a cut above the average did so in regions outside of Sofia. Such was the case with *daskal* Dragan, who wrote in the Athonite monastery of Hilendar (1626), with Todor (1690), who left Sofia for Kuklen Monastery, near Plovdiv, at the close of the century, as well as with Vasilii Sofiyanets (1640-1642), who worked at Etropole Monastery and later at Zograf, and with the most talented of the lot, Daniil Etropolski, who was the greatest Bulgarian literary figure of the seventeenth century.[66]

The reasons for the flight of these men from Sofia are unknown. Perhaps the atmosphere of the city was too heavy with Muslim reaction or, possibly, they left because of more personal reasons. As they themselves left no written statements disclosing their motives for leaving Sofia, any attempt to explain their flight must be relegated to the realm of conjecture.

That the sixteenth century Sofia cultural center did not collapse at the turn of the sixteenth-seventeenth centuries can be amply illustrated. Education, the foundation of any such center, continued to prosper throughout the seventeenth century and may have been even more widespread than during the preceding period. The sixteenth century Sofia Literary School and its traditions, which extended back to the time of the Second Bulgarian Empire and the Tŭrnovo School of Evtimii, affected all the literary works produced by seventeenth century Sofia *literati*, whether they remained in Sofia or traveled elsewhere. In that sense, the literary products of seventeenth century Sofia formed a continuum of the Sofia Literary School, and the dispersion of writer-copyists from Sofia over areas outside the Sofia region only served to broaden the influence of Sofia in the field of Bulgarian Orthodox literature. Of the fields of Orthodox culture, only that of monumental religious art seems to have suffered a decline in Sofia after the first quarter of the century, and that phenomenon may be linked to the death of the greatest Sofia artist of the period, Pimen Zografski.

All forms of Orthodox culture in Sofia during the seventeenth century were unmistakably Bulgarian in character. Education was exclusively Slavic in nature, and Church Slavonic served as the vehicle of literary expression, including inscriptions in the field of art. Bulgarian themes were frequently present in both literature and art, where hagiographies and images of expressly Bulgarian saints commonly appeared within the accepted Orthodox iconographic schemes.

If the sixteenth century witnessed the rise of Sofia as a Bulgarian cultural center during the period of Ottoman rule, the seventeenth century served to continue the work begun at that time and to diffuse its traditions throughout the Bulgarian lands. The volume of works produced in the city, both literary and artistic, and in its monasteries, the elements in those works that were decidedly Bulgarian in nature, the literary and artistic links to the city's cultural flowering during the sixteenth century, and the evidence for Sofia's relations with other major Bulgarian Orthodox cultural centers (*e.g.,* Athos, Vratsa, Etropole and Kuklen) all demonstrate that Sofia was an important seventeenth century center of Bulgarian Orthodox culture.

Etropole Monastery

Approximately five kilometers east of the small town of Etropole, nestled in the midst of a travertine terrace on the northern slopes of the Balkan Mountains, lay Etropole Monastery, "The Holy Trinity."[67] Throughout most of the seventeenth century this monastic community constituted the single most important and productive Slavic Orthodox literary center in the Bulgarian lands. The educational and literary activities that flourished within its limestone walls developed to such a degree that the influence of Etropole was felt in all other major centers of Bulgarian Orthodox culture.

The town of Etropole had been a center of some note since medieval times because of geographic and economic factors. Geographically, the town guarded the northern mouth of Etropole Pass through the Balkan range. The Etropole-Zlatitsa road that wound through the pass served as a major trans-Balkan line of communications, linking the Bulgarian Danubian regions of the northwest to the Thracian Plain and its vital military and commercial highways. So important was the route through Etropole Pass that the medieval settlement of Etropole had been heavily fortified. Although the fortifications had disappeared by the seventeenth century, possibly as a result of the Ottoman conquest, the town retained its role of importance as a link in a major communications artery for as long as Turkish rule lasted in the Bulgarian lands and enjoyed *dervenci* status.[68]

Of more significance than geography was the economic position of Etropole. The town thrived because it served as the chief urban center for the rich mineral mining industry of the region. Although lead, silver and gold were extracted from the numerous mines that bore into the surrounding highlands, iron was of primary importance. During the second half of the sixteenth and throughout the seventeenth centuries, the Etropole mines were in intensive operation, producing much needed iron for Ottoman military efforts. Consequently, the town flourished and the population of the region, composed of local Bulgarians and foreign Saxon and Serbian mining colonists who enjoyed a privileged existence at the behest of the Ottoman authorities, thrived.[69]

Economic vitality contributed to the growth of an active cultural life for the inhabitants of Etropole that was manifested through their Orthodox faith. A number of Etropole natives were able to afford the long and expensive pilgrimage to Jerusalem. Three Slavic rite churches were constructed in the town — "St. Georgi," "Holy Arhangel Mihail" and "St. Paraskeva." The parish priests of those churches were often active in the fields of literature and education. Those men received their training at the nearby monastery of "The Holy Trinity." Although Orthodox cultural life within the town during the seventeenth century was lively, the monastery was the primary focus of activity.[70]

The exact year in which Etropole Monastery was founded is unknown. Legend linked the event to the life of Ivan Rilski but such legends abound for numerous Bulgarian monasteries that were actually established only during the Ottoman period, long after the saintly hermit had died. No written evidence for Etropole Monastery can be dated to any time earlier than the mid sixteenth century, although a note entered into the monastery's beadroll by abbot Hrisant (1864) spoke of the existence of a stone slab built into the old monastery church that bore inscriptions from as early as 1158. The oldest icon housed in the monastery church was the work of Nedyalko Zograf from Lovech, and it was painted in 1598. By the closing years of the sixteenth century Etropole Monastery was a large monastic community within the episcopal diocese of Lovech, Tŭrnovo metropolitanate.[71]

Because the local mining population provided generous patronage, Etropole Monastery blossomed into an Orthodox establishment of great size and widespread renown. Pious Christians from every region of the Bulgarian and Macedonian lands, as well as from the Principality of Wallachia, traveled to Etropole throughout the seventeenth century to visit the monastery. Both the local population and the pilgrims from more distant regions donated money and valuables to the monastery church. The rich donations, such as crosses and reliquaries worked in precious metals, made to the monastery permitted abbot Misaila to carry out a renovation of the church in 1682-1683.[72]

Many of the manuscripts copied in the monastery scriptorium were purchased by patrons and subsequently deposited in the monastery church or in the parish churches of the town. Likewise, the monastery library grew rich in Slavic manuscripts and printed books. The majority of those acquisitions were sixteenth century products of western Bulgarian literary centers, such as Sofia, Rila

IN THE SEVENTEENTH CENTURY

Monastery and Vratsa. The printed books represented some of the earliest editions of South Slavic works published by the fifteenth century press in Cetinje. All told, over the course of the seventeenth century a *milieu* was created and maintained at Etropole Monastery that favored the development of a Slavic Orthodox cultural center.[73]

The center that emerged at Etropole found its singular form of expression in the field of Slavic literature. Between the latter years of the sixteenth and the close of the seventeenth centuries such a large volume of Slavic literary work was produced by the residents and students at the monastery, all bearing a distinctive style of calligraphy, that one may speak of a veritable literary school existing at Etropole Monastery. Under the guidance of such gifted abbots as Andronii, Zaharii and Rafail, the Etropole School experienced its most productive period during the first half of the seventeenth century. Although a decline in literary activity characterized the second half of the century, probably as a result of the turmoil surrounding the military efforts of the Ottomans in Europe and the chaos caused by the Tatar incursion in the Danubian regions of the Bulgarian lands in behalf of their beleaguered Turkish allies, Etropole continued to train and produce new *literati* throughout.

Forty-one individual works of Orthodox literature are known to be extant products of the Etropole School. Paleographic studies of those manuscripts have revealed that all were western Bulgarian versions of Orthodox liturgical works that were heavily influenced by Serbian and Wallachian literary examples. As a large proportion of the mining population in the Etropole region consisted of Serbian colonists, Serb influence on the literary activity conducted at the monastery was rather direct and well documented.[74]

Etropole's contacts with Wallachia were apparently strong but less well documented. That Serbia and Wallachia should have exerted significant influences on Bulgarian literature in the seventeenth century, whether directly or indirectly, was not surprising since both had served as havens for Bulgarian *literati* following the fall of medieval Bulgaria to the Turks. The traditions of the original Bulgarian writers-in-exile were preserved on their soils and experienced continued development under the influx of Western and Russian influences throughout the fifteenth and sixteenth centuries. At some point during the latter years of the sixteenth century, Slavic manuscripts from those foreign havens began to seep back into the Bulgarian lands, bringing new literary influences in their train. Apparently, Etropole Monastery served as one of the primary gateways in that phenomenon.[75]

Fortunately, the authorship of all but ten of the extant exemplars of the Etropole School has been established with some degree of certainty. The 31 identifiable manuscripts have been attributed to the pens of 11 men. Three of those men, *ieromonah* Rafail, Ioan Gramatik and abbot Zaharii, each produced four works. Rafail worked in the monastery between the end of the 1630s and the early 1640s. His earliest work, a menologion for May (1637), was purchased by the monks of Eleshnitsa Monastery near Sofia. He later produced three other menologions, one for April (1639), a second for May (1641) and the last for June (1642). Sometime prior to 1643 Rafail made the pilgrimage to Jerusalem and returned to the monastery to assume the duties of abbot.[76]

Both Ioan Gramatik and Zaharii were contemporaries of Rafail. Ioan produced his first work, a prologue (1635), as a young student at the monastery school. In 1636 he co-authored a prologue in verse with *daskal* Koyu from Teteven, which contained an original hagiography of Ivan Rilski. Three years later (1639), by which time Ioan was a parish priest in the town of Etropole, he produced a book of services that was sold to the church of "St. Nikola" in the village of Chelopechane near Sofia. Ioan's final extant work was a gospels that he copied in 1658.[77]

The four works attributed to Zaharii were all menologions for the months of October (1638), January (1641), February (1630s-1640s) and September (1630s-1640s).[78]

Seven of the Etropole writers can be credited with producing single works or notations in single works. *Daskal* Koyu from Teteven shared the authorship of the 1636 verse prologue with Ioan Gramatik, as noted above. Vasilii Sofiyanets, a native of Sofia, worked at Etropole Monastery during the time Zaharii was abbot. Although Vasilii produced a number of menologions during the 1640s, only that for the month of September (1642), subsequently donated to the Athonite monastery of Zograf, has survived. The copyist, *pop* Stoyu, a priest in the town of Etropole, sold a manuscript prayer book that he penned to *pop* Yancho from Pirdop in 1618. Yankul Gramatik from "Beligrad" (Byala?) produced a doxology under the monastery's abbot, Varlaam, in which were contained short *Lives* of the Bulgarian saints, Ivan Rilski, Ioakim Osogovski, Gavril Lesnovski and Petka Tŭrnovska. The remaining three men, Teodosii (1648), the Romanian *gramatik*, Naum Matei, and Sevlad Gramatik (1674), have reached posterity only through penning marginal glosses in extant manuscripts.[79]

The primary impetus for the development of the Etropole School was lent by the unusually productive work of the monastery's most renowned man-of-letters, Daniil Mazach, who is more commonly designated Daniil Etropolski. Thirteen extant manuscripts bear his signature, and three others, unsigned, have been attributed to his pen. All of these works reveal Daniil to have been a master writer, calligrapher and illuminator, possessing the exceptional ability to combine all three elements into an harmonious whole. The style of calligraphy found in his writings, which was highly ornamental and embroidered for both title and common letters while possessing a regular and geometric character, demonstrated that Daniil was the originator of the so-called "Etropole" style of calligraphy, which characterized virtually all the works produced by Etropole *literati*. His style of manuscript illumination, which expressed great freedom in the use of floral motifs and possessed some elements of a primitive folk nature, also became standard in the works of the Etropole School.[80]

Very little is known of Daniil's life other than that which can be gleaned from the few personal references he included in his manuscripts. The documented dates of his notations range between the years 1616 and 1644. Most likely, Daniil was born in or near Sofia sometime during the final quarter of the sixteenth century. There he received his education and the monastic tonsure. From Sofia he traveled to the Vratsa monastery of "The Holy Trinity," where in 1616 he produced his first known work at the insistence of abbot Varlaam. At that time, Varlaam had established a lively literary center at "The Holy Trinity," of which Daniil became a part. He copied a second work there in the same year as his first.[81]

By 1620 Daniil had arrived at Etropole Monastery where, under the guidance of the abbot, Andronii, and the rich patronage of the monastery's visitors, literary life was beginning to fully blossom. In the year of his arrival at Etropole, Daniil produced an illuminated prologue for the months of September through February that contained a brief service for Ivan Rilski. The manuscript was soon purchased for 1,400 *akçes* by a certain Gino, a Greek butcher from the town of Etropole, and donated to the monastery church.[82]

Daniil's initial stay at the monastery was brief, for in 1622 he was summoned to Tŭrnovo by the Greek metropolitan, Gavriil. There, between October 1622 and March 1623, Daniil produced one of his most important works, a panegyric *sbornik* containing copies of Evtimii Tŭrnovski's hagiographies of the Bulgarian saints, Petka Tŭrnovska, Ivan Rilski and Ilarion Mŭglenski. Daniil apparently enjoyed good relations with the Greek ecclesiastical authorities in Tŭrnovo since he remained in the city for a number of years after completing the sbornik. In 1625 Gavriil once again commissioned him to produce an illuminated gospels. Gavrill died the following year but his successor on the metropolitan seat, Makarios, retained Daniil's services. The third Tŭrnovo manuscript by Daniil, a *sbornik* of Orthodox religious holidays commissioned by Makarios (1626), was sold for 1,900 *akçes* to an Athonite monk, Mihail.[83]

The length of Daniil's stay in Tŭrnovo is unknown. In 1628, however, he produced two manuscripts. A book of services, its place of origin unnoted, was sold to a certain Pasho from the village of Dolni Dŭbnik. The second work, probably written by Daniil in Glozhene Monastery, was a student's reader, which was sold to Staru, the son of the village priest in Glozhene. Following the completion of this latter work, Daniil returned to Etropole Monastery, where he took up residence for nearly two decades.[84]

Daniil's second period of residence at Etropole coincided with the most productive period of the Etropole School. *Ieromonah* Rafail abbot Zaharii, Ioan Gramatik, *daskal* Koyu Tetevenski, Vasilii Sofiyanets, and others whose names have been lost worked at the monastery between 1630 and 1649. All of the manuscripts produced by those men were noticeably affected by the calligraphical and ornamental styles used by Daniil in his earlier works. Under Daniil's influence the definitive forging of the Etropole School's style of letters and decoration occurred. Undoubtedly, Daniil served as the School's principal progenitor and patriarch.

In 1632, while Varlaam was abbot, Daniil produced a hymnal. Six years later, in 1638, he sold a book of Lenten offices that he copied to a certain *pop* Pavel. Under abbot Rafail, in 1643, Daniil copied a menologion for July in which he noted that in that same year the Ottoman authorities commenced a census of "homes" that caused the Christian population of Etropole a certain amount of uneasiness and dread. The following year (1644), Daniil produced the final two of his extant works, a menologion for August and an acts of the apostles. The former was purchased by two artisans, Nedko Stainov and Spas Georgov, who then donated the manuscript to the monastery church. The latter work was sold to one Raiko Stoiov, who deposited it in the church at Teteven Monastery. This final work of Daniil bore an interesting notation by him, in which he termed the currently reigning Ottoman sultan, Ibrahim, the "unhonored tsar."[85]

Nothing further is known of Daniil after 1644.

Despite the scantiness of biographical information for Daniil, an evaluation of his work *in toto* reveals him to have been a highly skilled professional writer-copyist with great and original talents in the areas of calligraphy and manuscript illumination. He was a man for whom Slavic literature constituted a lifework. The inclusion of decidedly Bulgarian themes in some of his works (*e.g.*, hagiographies of Bulgarian saints, copies of medieval Bulgarian writers, and a few pointedly anti-Ottoman notations) indicates that Daniil most likely entertained some awareness of his Bulgarian ethnicity. Finally, if one may judge by the impact he made on contemporaries at the Etropole School, Daniil must have been a gifted teacher who was dedicated to the highest ideals of Slavic literary traditions.

Given the extraordinary literary activity conducted at Etropole Monastery, education there was extremely active and long-lived. The numerous notations left in virtually all Etropole manuscripts by their lay and religious users suggest that the school at Etropole not only trained *literati* but also provided education on the elementary level for a significant portion of the local population. Yet the school seemed to specialize in providing education on the advanced level. A book of hours written in 1634 by *pop* Zhivko in the village of Adzhar bore an author's note stating that he had received his education in Etropole Monastery. The signature of Koyu Tetevenski, found in the verse prologue that he co-authored with Ioan Gramatik, was preceded by the title of *daskal*. In his doxology (1678), *gramatik* Yankul noted that he had studied at Etropole Monastery under *monah* Kalinik.[86]

Etropole Monastery held precedence in the field of manuscript illumination among the Bulgarian literary centers of the seventeenth century. The early style of ornamentation found in Etropole works dating to the period 1595-1620 was geometric. That style made extensive use of single- or multi-lined interlacing circular designs. Later, during the zenith of the Etropole School (1630-1658), manuscript decoration acquired zoomorphic motifs that made use of human faces or birds as ornamental elements for individual lettering. Another decorative device utilized by Etropole illuminators throughout the seventeenth century was the "cross" motif, which centered the ornamentation on a cross-like design. This motif, in particular, became the central feature of Etropole illumination, and it was used with great freedom of interpretation. Oftentimes, cross motifs were combined with circular medallions and other geometric designs. Eventually, design elements originating in local folk art (*e.g.*, locally found flora and fauna, particular colors, and certain painting techniques) appeared in the illuminations and were often used in combination with sophisticated figural scenes. All of the styles and motifs found in Etropole manuscripts, except for the local folk elements, had their roots in Byzantine and medieval Bulgarian artistic traditions that were preserved, following the demise of Bulgaria, in the scriptoria of Serbia and the Romanian Principalities.

Many of the seventeenth century Etropole manuscripts were illuminated by their writer-copyists. Daniil, Ioan Gramatik, Vasilii Sofiyanets and Zaharii were expert illumination artists. A number of manuscripts, however, were illuminated by hands other than those of the author. The Etropole *sbornik* (mid seventeenth century), a product of more than a single author, was decorated by *pop* Uroš, a Serbian priest residing at the monastery. Nikola Gramatik, the son of a certain Nedyalko from Etropole, and *pop* Ioan performed the illumination for an anonymously produced menologion sometime during the early seventeenth century.[87]

Bookbinding, an ancillary craft to manuscript production, was actively pursued at Etropole Monastery, especially during the middle and later years of the seventeenth century. The earliest known Etropole bookbinder was *pop* Vlŭcho, who bound a book of prayers to the Virgin in 1616. Ioan Gramatik bound the verse prologue that he co-authored with Koyu Tetevenski. In 1639 Daniil bound one of the fifteenth century hymnals that had been printed in Cetinje and was housed in the monastery library. A sixteenth century psalter, also the possession of the library, was rebound twice during the seventeenth century. The first rebinding was performed by Sevlad Gramatik in 1674, and the second, by *monah* Onufrii in 1699, was paid for by the furrier, Lazar. *Pop* Vlaio, who bound a work at the monastery in 1704, was probably also active in that craft during the final decade of the seventeenth century but no evidence of his work dating to that earlier time has survived.[88]

All the literary works produced by the Etropole School lay within the mainstream of traditional Slavic Orthodox liturgical literature — gospels, acts of the apostles, psalters, monthly prayer missals, hagiographies, books of hours or services, prologues and the like. The writing style of Etropole manuscripts was grounded in the traditions of the fourteenth century Tŭrnovo School with the addition, as noted above, of more recent influences acquired *via* Serbia and Wallachia.

Within the Orthodox context of their works, the writer-copyists of the Etropole School often demonstrated their apparent awareness of themes that were expressly Bulgarian in nature. This awareness was most vividly expressed in hagiographical works. The *Lives* and services of Bulgarian Orthodox saints, such as Petka Tŭrnovska, Ilarion Mŭglenski, Gavril Lesnovski, Ioakim Osogovski and, of course, the most popular saint, Ivan Rilski, found their places on the pages of numerous Etropole manuscripts. Oftentimes, these hagiographies were copies of works originally written by notable Bulgarian writers from the pre-Ottoman period (*e.g.*, Kliment Ohridski, Evtimii Tŭrnovski and Grigorii Tsamblak). The interest of the Etropole writer-copyists in Bulgarian saints and writers has led some modern scholars to discover the nascent origins of a Bulgarian national consciousness in the works of the Etropole School.[89]

Surprisingly, Etropole Monastery produced no works in the *damaskin* genre. The period of greatest literary productivity at the monastery roughly coincided with the flowering of the New Bulgarian literary language in the Sredna Gora regions of the Bulgarian lands. That new literary language found its initial expression in the *damaskins*. It is believed that one of the earliest Bulgarian *damaskins*, the Sredna Gora version (late sixteenth century), was quite possibly written at Etropole Monastery. If such were the case, Daniil was probably familiar with the work, and he may have been influenced by it in terms of his letters' graphics. Although the Etropole *literati* remained faithful to the Church Slavonic traditions, their graphics and orthography exerted a strong influence on the writers of *damaskins* in the nearby Sredna Gora regions over the course of the seventeenth century. The literary style of the Etropole School was used as a model to be imitated by the early *damaskin* compilers.[90]

The immediate impact of the Etropole School was felt throughout the western and central Bulgarian highlands. (See Map 6) Perhaps this impact was felt no more strongly than in the monasteries of Teteven, "St. Iliya," and Glozhene, "St. Georgi," which lay to the northeast of Etropole on the slopes overlooking the Vit River.

IN THE SEVENTEENTH CENTURY

Teteven Monastery was built on the shoulder of the peak called Ostrech in the Balkan Mountains just a kilometer north of the village of Teteven. It was probably founded prior to the Ottoman conquest. The origins of Glozhene Monastery are steeped in legend. According to the story, the monastery was founded in the early thirteenth century by the Kievan Prince Glozh, who had fled to the newly reconstituted medieval Bulgarian state ruled by the Asen brothers because of the Tatar invasion of the Ukraine. He was granted asylum by the Bulgarians and as a gesture of thanks he founded the monastery and village that afterward bore his name. Glozhene was often referred to as the "Kievan" monastery by the local population as late as the seventeenth century. Both Teteven and Glozhene monasteries served as locations for schools that taught Slavic reading and writing. Likewise, both maintained such close ties with each other and with Etropole that, in studying them, one may treat the two as a single literary satellite of "St. Varovitets."[91]

A Church Slavonic missal, copied in Teteven by *ieromonah* Vasilii in 1600 and later acquired by the monastery of Cherepish in the Vratsa region, as well as a gospels, tentatively dated to the late sixteenth or early seventeenth century, represent the earliest extant pieces of evidence for literary activity in Teteven-Glozhene during the seventeenth century. Within a decade of the work by Vasilii, a second regional writer-copyist of some merit, Koiko Gramatik from the village of Bresnitsa near Teteven, produced a hymnal (1609) in a style that later became characteristic of the Etropole School. Ten years later (1619), while in residence at Glozhene Monastery, Koiko penned a book of Lenten offices at the insistence of the monastery's abbot, Gavril.[92]

During the decades of the 1620s and 1630s Teteven-Glozhene demonstrated its intimate interrelationships with Etropole Monastery by the sojourn of Daniil Etropolski in Glozhene Monastery (1628) and the residence of the Teteven *daskal*, Koyu, at Etropole (1636). Both men conducted literary activity during their respective stays.

Slavic literary and related activity continued in Teteven-Glozhene throughout the remaining years of the seventeenth century, although all but one of the later works were the products of anonymous men. The influence of the Etropole School was discernible in all.

From Sofia and Vratsa in the west to Karlovo and Adzhar in the east, from Tŭrnovo and Pleven in the north to Kuklen Monastery in the south, works produced by the Etropole School found avid readers and imitators. Students were attracted to Etropole from towns and villages throughout the Bulgarian lands and from as far afield as Wallachia. If and when they returned to their places of origin, the Etropole-trained *literati* took with them the principles and instruction that they acquired at the monastery. Thus after the decline of literary productivity experienced by the Etropole School during the latter years of the seventeenth century had set in, works bearing the unmistakable stamp of the Etropole School continued to appear outside the monastery throughout the remaining years of the century.[93]

Vratsa

As the seventeenth century opened, the inhabitants of Vratsa were in the process of rebuilding their town following the devastation wrought upon it and the surrounding countryside in 1596 by the troops of the Wallachian Prince Mihai Viteazul the Brave (1593-1601). Mihai's foray south of the Danube formed part of his activities in behalf of his Habsburg allies in their common struggle against the Ottoman Empire during the Long War. Prior to the town's destruction in the 1596 campaign, Vratsa was predominantly populated by Bulgarians. One may assume that the rebuilt settlement retained its Bulgarian character. Undoubtedly, the demographic preponderance of the Bulgarians in the region greatly assisted Vratsa in its development into a major center of Bulgarian Orthodox culture as the century wore on.[94]

Within the town itself four Orthodox churches served the spiritual needs of the Bulgarian inhabitants. The largest church was that of "St. Nikola," and it was probably the beneficiary of rich donations granted by some of the town's more wealthy merchants and artisans. Thus "St. Nikola" acquired the common local sobriquet of the "*Bolyar* church." It became the site of the first Slavic school established in Vratsa during the early years of the seventeenth century. A second school, its site now uncertain, was founded at some time during mid century. The names of four teachers who worked in the Vratsa schools have been preserved. These were *pop* Todor (1632), Rashko (*ca.* 1640), *pop* Nikola (1654), and *daskal* Mihail (d. 1666).[95] Only a few of the literary works copied in the Vratsa schools are extant, but the students at those schools left a number of marginalia in older Orthodox liturgical works that they used in their studies, suggesting that Slavic educational and literary life were firmly established in the town during the seventeenth century.[96]

Despite the Slavic cultural activity that took place within the confines of the town limits, the more significant efforts were conducted in the monasteries located in the countryside surrounding Vratsa, and especially in the monastery of "The Holy Trinity," which lay some three kilometers southeast of the town in an area known as Monastery Ravine. (See Map 7)

Built on the site of a medieval Bulgarian fortress, "The Holy Trinity" was probably founded just prior to the Turkish conquest of the region in the late fourteenth century.[97] The monastery blossomed into a major Slavic literary center during the first quarter of the seventeenth century under the guidance and inspiration of its abbot, Varlaam. He was first mentioned in 1605 by *dyak* Dragul, from the village of Kameno Pole, in a notation made in a manuscript housed in the monastery. Varlaam himself possessed a talent for literary work and produced a menologion for the month of March in 1608. He apparently also exhibited a desire to create an active literary school at "The Holy Trinity" by drawing other talented writer-copyists to the monastery. At Varlaam's bidding liturgical manuscripts were produced by *dyak* Dragul and Iov Shishatovats while they were residents of "The Holy Trinity." Credit must also be rendered Varlaam for sparking the distinguished and influential literary career of the greatest seventeenth century Bulgarian literary figure, Daniil Etropolski, who arrived at "The Holy Trinity" from Sofia sometime prior to 1616. During his sojourn at the monastery Daniil produced at least four Orthodox liturgical works under the patronage of Varlaam.[98]

By 1620 the literary school at "The Holy Trinity" had ended. Daniil departed the monastery for that of Etropole. Iov Shishatovats took to a career of *taxidiot* monk, visiting Transylvania and Wallachia before returning to Sofia in 1612, after which he disappeared all together from the pages of history. Varlaam left the monastery in 1618 on a pilgrimage to Jerusalem. As no further works of literature originating at "The Holy Trinity" are extant, the departures of Varlaam and Daniil must have marked the closing of concentrated literary activity at the monastery for the remaining years of the seventeenth century.[99]

Although the "The Holy Trinity" literary school was short-lived, it was influential enough to have an impact on other monastic communities in the Vratsa region. The most fertile recipient of that influence was Cherepish Monastery, "The Assumption of the Blessed Virgin." The name Cherepish is derived from the Bulgarian word, *cherep,* meaning skull. Legend has it that the troops of Tsar Ivan Shishman fought a fierce battle with the Turks in the gorge of the Iskŭr River in the area where the monastery was later founded. After the battle the ground was littered with the decapitated heads of warriors killed in the struggle. When the monastery was established in that same area soon after the battle, it quickly acquired the name Cherepish.[100]

Founded in the late fourteenth century (*ca.* 1390-1396) on the right bank of the Iskŭr in the most picturesque part of the gorge cut by the river through the Balkan Mountains, Cherepish Monastery was plundered and burnt during the general conflagration that accompanied the campaign of Mihai the Brave against the Turks during the final decade of the sixteenth century. It was subsequently reconstructed at the turn of the century under the supervision of Pimen Zografski. Orthodox liturgical works were needed to replace those lost in the razing of the monastery. One of the monks, Makarie, was, therefore, dispatched to "The Holy

Trinity" Monastery, where he purchased the 1616 gospels that had been copied by Daniil. The Cherepish Monastery library later acquired a second work by Daniil, his panegyric *sbornik* (1623) that contained copies of hagiographies of the Bulgarian saints, Petka Tŭrnovska, Ivan Rilski, and Ilarion Mŭglenski, which Daniil had produced while in Tŭrnovo. Cherepish's search for liturgical materials for the purposes of worship and study extended to Teteven Monastery, from which a missal written by the monk, Vasilii, in 1600 was acquired.[101]

Unfortunately, only two original seventeenth century manuscripts produced in Cherepish Monastery have survived. One is a book of psalms written by *ieromonah* Gerasim in 1682. This manuscript was used and copiously annotated by residents and visitors to the monastery, thus furnishing some interesting historical data. For example, a note from 1684 reveals that the principal, most frequent patrons of Cherepish Monastery were residents of Etropole. In fact, a certain Stoyan from that town, who was probably an iron ore miner, made annual donations to the monastery in the form of ten iron ingots, each weighing one-and-one-quarter kilograms.[102]

The other extant Cherepish work, an acts of the apostles produced by an anonymous copyist in 1630, was purchased by a certain Yakov from Zograf Monastery and subsequently deposited in the Athonite monastery's library.[103]

Slavic Orthodox literary activity was pursued at two other monasteries in the Vratsa region — Kalugerovo (Chikotino), "The Holy Arhangel Mihail," and Gradeshnitsa, "St. John the Precursor." In 1646 *ieromonah* Kalinik, a resident of Kalugerovo Monastery, produced a psalter. At Gradeshnitsa a *nomokanon*, which had probably originated at that monastery, was annotated by an unknown hand in 1689. This anonymous notation was historically interesting. It spoke of the deaths of a number of local villagers and monks as a result of a famine. It also noted that in the autumn of 1689 all of the "birds" in the area were slaughtered by the "half-wild" *haiduts* led by Golcha Voivoda from Glavanovtsi, who operated in the region during the disturbances of the Chiprovtsi Uprising and the Habsburg military efforts along the Danube.[104]

Turning from literary activity to the field of Orthodox art, there is a paucity of extant works from the town of Vratsa itself. Slavic Orthodox art, however, was well represented in the villages and monasteries of the region's countryside. The reconstruction of Cherepish Monastery by Pimen Zografski most likely involved the decoration of the new church with mural paintings, icons and other works of liturgical art. Unfortunately, none of the art from that effort has survived. The church at Strupets Monastery, "The Prophet Iliya," a *metoh* of Cherepish, was possibly decorated with mural paintings near the time of Cherepish's reconstruction.[105]

An impressive exemplar of early seventeenth century Bulgarian church decoration was created in the church of Karlukovo Monastery, "The Blessed

Virgin." The entire interior of the church, including the narthex, was covered with murals that, for the most part, bore Slavic inscriptions. Interestingly, the iconographical scheme used in the decoration departed from the traditional in that three allegorical scenes were included. Three artists worked in the church and all of them exhibited a degree of skill that spoke for their having been schooled in the techniques of mural painting.[106]

The donor's inscription at Karlukovo, painted on the east wall of the narthex, was dated 1602, but it is possible that the actual work was conducted a bit earlier. On the wall opposite the narthex was placed the portrait of the monastery's abbot at the time of the renovation, Agapii, who was depicted dressed in white monastic garb. Agapii was one of a number of patrons responsible for making the decoration of the church possible. Other benefactors mentioned in the inscription were *pop* Naiden and Petka Pavlova. Besides the image of Agapii, a second donor's portrait painted on the south wall of the narthex represented *ieromonah* Ioan. Finally, the inscription that accompanied this second portrait mentioned a certain *daskal* Nedelko, suggesting that a school was established either at the monastery or in the village of Karlukovo. More direct evidence for a Karlukovo school, however, is lacking.

The church of "St. Nikolai" in the village of Tsarevets was decorated with mural paintings at some uncertain time during the seventeenth century. All inscriptions in the scenes were written in Slavic. The work was undertaken by two anonymous artists.

Perhaps the most significant work of art produced in the region of Vratsa, in terms of expressing Bulgarian cultural awareness, was painted in the church of Dolna Beshovitsa Monastery, "The Holy Arhangel Mihail." The earliest known images of Cyril and Methodius, the saintly missionary brothers to the Slavs, to be found within the confines of present-day Bulgaria were painted in the apse of the monastery church at some time during the early seventeenth century. The two saints, so venerated by the Bulgarians as the progenitors of their alphabet and the Slavic form of their Orthodox literary culture, were portrayed in the garb of Orthodox bishops and placed among the images of the fathers of the church found in the apse. In their hands were clutched manuscripts bearing Slavic letters. No other images of Cyril and Methodius appeared in the Bulgarian lands during the seventeenth century.[107]

One further shred of evidence concerning minor works of religious art at Dolna Beshovitsa was left in a marginal note written in a sixteenth century psalter that the monastery had acquired from the Sofia monastery of Eleshnitsa. In 1634 *monah* Haritoniya of Dolna Beshovitsa bound and refurbished this work in the monastery library and proudly noted his accomplishment. The fact that bookbinding was a craft practiced at the monastery may suggest that literary activity, for which there is no other explicit extant documentation, was undertaken at Dolna Beshovitsa.[108]

Vratsa and its environs constituted an important Bulgarian Orthodox cultural center during the seventeenth century. In the field of education, Slavic schools existed within the town and in the regional monasteries of "The Holy Trinity," Cherepish, Kalugerovo and Karlukovo. Evidence for the widespread impact of educational activity in Vratsa can be seen in the fact that a Vratsa teacher, Mihail, traveled as far south in the Bulgarian lands as Razlog to establish a Slavic school in the cell of a certain *pop* Filipa.[109]

Slavic literary activity flourished in the town and in "The Holy Trinity," Cherepish, Kalugerovo and Gradeshnitsa monasteries. Vratsa, "The Holy Trinity," and Dolna Beshovitsa maintained literary contacts with Sofia, while contacts between Etropole, on the one hand, and "The Holy Trinity" and Cherepish monasteries, on the other, were firm and frequent. So too were interactions between Zograf Monastery and Vratsa, "The Holy Trinity," and Cherepish Monastery.

Bulgarian Orthodox artistic activity was well represented at Cherepish, with Pimen Zografski, as well as at Dolna Beshovitsa and Karlukovo.

All told, Vratsa and the region roundabout lay in the active mainstream of seventeenth century Bulgarian Orthodox culture.

Karlovo, Adzhar and Kuklen Monastery

Perhaps the literary and calligraphical influences of the Etropole School were no more deeply assimilated into the cultural activity of the Bulgarian lands during the seventeenth century than in the three literary centers of Karlovo, Adzhar, and Kuklen Monastery, "The Sacred Healer." These three locales constituted the most active Bulgarian literary centers during the second half of the century, and they produced two of the most significant seventeenth century Bulgarian literary figures, Avram Dimitrievich and Krŭstyu Gramatik. (See Map 8)

The first of the three centers to arise was the village of Adzhar. A small community, Adzhar was nestled in the Sredna Gora Mountains 22 kilometers southeast of Karlovo, and was populated by Bulgarian metal craftsmen and herders. Unlike most of the other villages in the surrounding countryside, which were predominantly inhabited by Turks, the villagers of Adzhar were exclusively Bulgarian, who steadfastly adhered to their Orthodox faith and Slavic traditions. Their stand against the encroaching foreign influences from the countryside roundabout was reflected in their active support of the village church, "St. Georgi," where in 1630 *pop* Zhivko, the most educated man in the village at the time, established a Slavic school.[110]

Because of Zhivko's school, a number of literate villagers began to copy Slavic liturgical works or to commission such works for deposit in the village church. Sometimes a writer-copyist from outside the village was sought out and invited to the village for the purpose of creating new copies of liturgical works. Such a man was *pop* Iovko from Etropole. He arrived in Adzhar during the early 1630s. There he produced a book of hours in 1634. Two years later (1636) another of Iovko's works was purchased by one of the villagers and then donated to the village church. Following this event, a 16-year hiatus in extant literary activity at Adzhar ensued.[111]

At about the time that Iovko was active in Adzhar, a priest in Karlovo, Avram Dimitrievich, embarked upon a long and productive literary and pedagogical career. Apparently, Avram was the son of a prominent Karlovo merchant named Dimitriev. Whether he was educated in Karlovo or at nearby Sopot Monastery is uncertain, but the former location appears to have been the most likely.[112]

The earliest known work by Avram, a psalter, was completed in 1638. All told, he produced a total of six extant, dated works. Ten other manuscripts have been tentatively attributed to his pen. Unfortunately, Avram left posterity very little information concerning his personal life other than his name and place of birth. We may infer from notations made in his works that *ierei* Avram visited and worked in the monasteries of Sopot and Troyan. In 1656 *ieromonah* Iosif of Sopot Monastery, "The Holy Savior," acquired a book of services copied by Avram. Four years later (1660) Iosif, by then abbot of Sopot, commissioned Avram to produce a menologion for the month of October. Funding for the work was supplied by Iovan Draganov from the village of Sopot and *monah* Peika. It is highly probable that soon after completing Iosif's commission Avram left Sopot Monastery for that of Troyan, "The Blessed Virgin," where he then spent some years. The two seventeenth century Troyan *damaskins* have been stylistically attributed to him. Quite possibly, Avram then traveled to the town of Elena, where he may have produced the Elena *damaskin*. By 1666 Avram had returned to Karlovo.[113]

Avram's stay in Karlovo following his return was short-lived. In 1669 he deposited a psalter that he copied in the Zograf Monastery library on Mount Athos. Upon completing his pilgrimage to Athos, Avram once again returned to Karlovo, where in 1674 he produced his last dated extant work, a *sbornik*, which included monthly services for the Bulgarian saints, Petka Tŭrnovska and Ivan Rilski. He then most likely set out for Kuklen Monastery, where he taught writing and manuscript illumination during the latter years of the seventeenth century. The date and place of Avram's death are unknown.[114]

Examined *in toto*, the work of Avram Dimitrievich demonstrated that he was a master calligrapher and illuminator. So prominent was the Etropole style displayed in his work that it appears highly likely that Avram actually studied in Etropole at some point in his life.[115] His work also demonstrated that he was a writer-copyist comfortable in both the Church Slavonic and the near conversational New Bulgarian *damaskin* languages. As such, Avram was the most versatile literary figure to emerge in the Bulgarian lands during the seventeenth century.

The literary influence of Avram was felt in a number of regions throughout the central and southcentral Bulgarian lands because of his extensive travels and, perhaps more importantly, his work as a teacher. Among his students was *daskal* Nedyalko from Adzhar. One may surmise from his title that Nedyalko was a teacher in the Adzhar village school at "St. Georgi." He also was a writer-copyist of some note, whose earliest extant work was written in Adzhar (1652), in which the author signed himself as a *ierei*. Nedyalko at that time must have been a young village priest. His next extant work was produced some 30 years later (1686), in which the title of *daskal* appeared before his name. In the interim, Nedyalko had studied under Avram, married, and fathered a son who, in turn, became his finest student.[116]

The 1686 *damaskin* by Nedyalko was written in collaboration with his son, Filip, who was also a *daskal*. Together, Nedyalko and Filip formed an active literary partnership that produced and sold Slavic liturgical manuscripts in Adzhar and in other Bulgarian Sredna Gora villages. This unique father and son literary team was responsible for seven, and possibly ten, extant works produced during the final quarter of the seventeenth century. Their 1686 Adzhar *damaskin* revealed stylistic links to those works written by Avram Dimitrievich, and it was so markedly similar to one found in Kostenets that this, too, may have been their handiwork. Among the contents of the Adzhar *damaskin* was a copy of Evtimii's *Life* of Petka Tŭrnovska, in which the copyists referred to the saint as "our Petka." One may suggest that Nedyalko and Filip were aware of medieval Bulgarian literary traditions and may, in fact, have consciously demonstrated to their readers their awareness of being Bulgarians through the use of the possessive adjective when mentioning Petka in the work. In an undated menologion, however, Filip once again included a service for Petka but did not make use of the possessive adjective.[117]

Through the work of Nedyalko and Filip, Adzhar developed into a noted center of Bulgarian literature, calligraphy and education. Both men were active as teachers in the village, and if the content of their own literary efforts can be taken as evidence, both must have imparted to their students a knowledge of the medieval Bulgarian literary traditions of Evtimii's Tŭrnovo School, as well as the stylistic traditions of the Etropole School, which they had imbibed *via* Iovko and Avram Dimitrievich. Their prodigious writings, many of which probably disappeared over the course of the following centuries, reflected their solid literary grounding in the traditional Church Slavonic and in the newly born *damaskin* New Bulgarian literary language. A wide audience was given their work as a result of their vending their manuscripts in local Sredna Gora Bulgarian villages. Original copies of their works eventually found their way to Mount Athos, Rila Monastery and the Sofia region.

Aside from Karlovo and Adzhar, Avram Dimitrievich also made a profound impact on Kuklen Monastery, primarily through his term of residence there as an aging teacher near the close of the seventeenth century.

Kuklen Monastery was situated in the northern foothills of the Rhodope Mountains four kilometers above the village of Kuklen and some 16 kilometers south of Plovdiv. It may have been originally founded during the eleventh century by two Byzantine feudal lords, the brothers Gregorios and Aspazios Pakurina, who also founded the nearby large and famous monastery of Bachkovo. At the time of its founding, Kuklen formed part of the lands granted Gregorios by the Byzantine emperor in Constantinople. Archaeological studies have revealed that fragments of the present altar in Kuklen Monastery church bear striking similarities to altars known to have been erected in the earliest churches at Bachkovo. From its founding, Kuklen Monastery played an active Orthodox cultural role under the Second Bulgarian Empire, but it may have undergone conversion into a Muslim establishment during the early years of the Ottoman conquest, as had many other Orthodox monasteries in the Rhodopes.

At some point during the late sixteenth or early seventeenth centuries Kuklen Monastery was rechristened as an Orthodox monastic community, following which it commenced to develop into a large, wealthy religious establishment. Since Kuklen was a Bulgarian, not a Greek, community, unlike so many of the other monasteries near Plovdiv (*e.g.*, Bachkovo and Gorni Voden), it can be assumed that it served to attract a large number of Rhodope friars. As a result, Kuklen grew into the largest and most important seventeenth century Bulgarian Orthodox cultural center in the Rhodope-Plovdiv region.[118]

Kuklen Monastery was a wealthy community, enjoying the abundant patronage of numerous Bulgarians from nearby villages. In 1632 the monastery, under the care of its abbot, Nikodim, possessed a number of rich religious vestments, vessels and other liturgical accoutrements that had been donated by the local villagers. Active local patronage of the monastery continued throughout the century, as can be seen by the painting of new murals in the narthex and on the exterior facades of the monastery church. Likewise, the later addition of a fountain in the monastery courtyard in 1695 was accomplished through the financial and material aid of the local village laity and clerics. Obviously, Kuklen Monastery played an active role in the spiritual lives of the local Bulgarian villagers.[119]

A school of Slavic reading and writing was established in the monastery at the time of its rededication, sometime in the late sixteenth or early seventeenth centuries. Nearly all of our evidence for the school at Kuklen, however, dates to the final quarter of the seventeenth century. By that time the wealth and fame of Kuklen Monastery were known throughout the Bulgarian lands, and many men were drawn to the monastery to teach, to study or to write. Todor arrived at Kuklen from Sofia in 1690, bringing with him a printed Russian Bible. Avram Dimitrievich went to Kuklen as a teacher at some time prior to 1695, as did Sidor, who arrived in the company of *ieromonah* Simeon in 1695. Finally, a young layman from the western Bulgarian lands, Krŭstyu Gramatik, was also attracted by the literary light that shown at Kuklen Monastery, arriving there about the same time as did Avram. Thus, the stage was set for the final flowering of seventeenth century Bulgarian literary activity that took place at Kuklen Monastery during the last decade of the century under the enlightened guidance of its abbot, Teofan *ieromonah*.[120]

Sidor, who identified himself as a *daskal-gramatik,* and Simeon produced a menologion for the month of November in 1695.[121] Avram probably kept himself busy writing and copying while at the monastery but none of those works have survived. His style of writing, however, so highly reminiscent of the Etropole School, was predominant at Kuklen Monastery. The style was amply reflected in the works of Avram's able student and most prolific of the Kuklen *literati,* Krŭstyu Gramatik.

Three, possibly four, extant works were produced by Krŭstyu in the years 1695-1696. All were menologions, for the months of May (1695), June (1695), September (1696), and April (undated). Each exemplified the consummate skill of its author in the fields of calligraphy and illumination. The traditions of the Etropole School and of Avram were unmistakable in all of Krŭstyu's manuscripts. Unfortunately, nothing further is known of Krŭstyu or of any other of his works.[122]

As has been noted above, Kuklen Monastery maintained contacts with most of the major seventeenth century Bulgarian cultural centers (*e.g.,* Sofia, Etropole and Karlovo). Relations were also established with Zograf Monastery and with Orthodox lands beyond the confines of Bulgaria.[123]

The educational and literary activity conducted in Karlovo, Adzhar and Kuklen Monastery formed an extension of the work developed at Etropole Monastery during the first half of the seventeenth century. After the mid century decline of Etropole as a literary center, the traditions of its literary school were taken up by those three centers, preserved and expanded upon by the writer-copyists working at them, and continued for the remainder of the century. Through Avram Dimitrievich, Nedyalko and Filip, the Etropole School made a definitive impact on *damaskin* literature, while the Church Slavonic works of Krŭstyu Gramatik brought the art of Etropole calligraphy and illumination to its pinnacle.

Conclusions

Overview of Extant Evidence

In the early sixteenth century the total population of the Ottoman Empire numbered some 12 million people, of which the five million inhabitants of the empire's Balkan possessions comprised 41.7 percent. The 4.1 million Christians living in those possessions represented 81 percent of the Ottoman Balkan population and 34.2 percent of all Ottoman subjects. The population of the empire's Bulgarian *sancaks* accounted for 19.2 percent of its total and 46.1 percent of its Balkan subjects. In the Bulgarian *sancaks* the 1.7 million Christians constituted the overwhelming majority of the local (73.9 percent), a third of the Balkan, and a significant share (14.2 percent) of the total Ottoman population. (See Table 1.)

By the late sixteenth century the empire's demographic picture had changed. Ottoman conquests of territories in Central Europe, Asia and Africa swelled the population to nearly 22 million people. Most of the newly incorporated subjects were Muslims. Assuming that the proportions of Christian to Muslim subjects in the older, European possessions of the empire remained relatively stable, the Christian population of the Ottoman Balkans fell to an 18.6 percent share of the total (a decline of 45.6 percent), while the Christians of the Bulgarian *sancaks* dropped to a mere 7.7 percent of the Ottoman population (a 45.8 percent decrease). The changed demographic situation of the empire had important consequences for the Christians of the Ottoman Empire, since the swollen population placed great strains on the state's antiquated economy and fiscal systems, contributed toward transforming socio-political relationships (*e.g.,* the nature of the *devşirme*), and facilitated the rise of Muslim anti-Christian reaction.

In the Bulgarian *sancaks* of Paşa, Sofia, Kyustendil, Vidin, Nikopol, Viza and Çirmen an estimated one million Christians were subject to the Ottoman Porte at the opening of the seventeenth century. By the close of the period, their numbers had declined to less than 760,000 (a loss of 24.3 percent) because of the demographic ravages of warfare, famine and disease, migratory movements and conversions to Islam. (See Tables 2 and 3.) It can be stated that, on average, the Christian population of the Bulgarian lands during the seventeenth century numbered some 882,000 persons, most of whom were Orthodox Bulgarians. (See Table 4.)

Although the theocratic nature of the Muslim Ottoman state relegated all Christian *reaya* to the level of second class subjects, certain groups within the Christian population were granted specific, primarily fiscal, privileges that elevated them slightly above the low social level of the common element. Bulgarian historical demographers have estimated that as many as an additional 59.5 percent of the registered Christian inhabitants of the Bulgarian lands enjoyed some sort of privileged status within Ottoman society. Given such a situation, the average Christian population of the Bulgarian lands in the seventeenth century comprised some 553,000 common and 329,000 privileged Ottoman subjects. (Again, see Table 4.)

In official Ottoman documents the subject population was organized under regional state administrative (*sancaks*) and taxation (*vilayets*) units. Within the population itself, a more traditional regional organization was recognized. Thus the Bulgarian lands of the seventeenth century were divided into regions, each centered on a town or village that either economically or traditionally held pride of place for the population settled in surrounding areas. An estimated near 3,400 settlements (towns and villages) in the Bulgarian lands were inhabited by Christians, 99 percent of which were villages, while only a meager one percent constituted urban centers. The region of Sofia, with 286 settlements listed in Ottoman tax registers (or 13.9 percent of all such registered settlements), was the single most densely settled of all the Bulgarian lands. In fact, of the ten most densely settled regions, six (*i.e.*, Sofia; Kyustendil, with 132 such settlements [6.4 percent]; Gorna Dzhumaya, 122 [5.9 percent]; Pernik, 117 [5.7 percent]; Kutlovitsa, 93 [4.5 percent]; and Vidin, 90 [4.4 percent]) comprised nearly 41 percent of all population settlements in the Bulgarian lands, and they were all located in the western Bulgarian lands. Two other regions, both considered central Bulgarian lands — Plovdiv, with 106 such settlements, and Tŭrnovo, with 105 (together totalling 10.2 percent of all settlements in the Bulgarian lands) — were among the ten most densely settled regions. Only two regions of the ten (Burgas, with 137 registered settlements [6.7 percent], and the region surrounding Razgrad, Shumen and Tŭrgovishte, with 110 settlements [5.3 percent]) lay in the eastern Bulgarian lands, which were exposed to heavy Turkish colonization. (See Table 5.)

The seventeenth century Christian Bulgarian population of the Ottoman Empire was almost completely rural. Village size among those Christians averaged 164 persons for all the Bulgarian lands, but significant regional differences existed. Whereas the western lands were generally the most densely settled regions, the average size of the settlements was usually small (ex., average village size in the region of Vratsa was 82 persons; in the Lovech region, 84; and in the Vidin region, 86). Even in the densely settled Sofia and Kyustendil regions, villages averaged only 117 persons. The eastern lands, on the other hand, contained the largest sized villages, with those in the regions of Razgrad-Shumen-Tŭrgovishte (264 persons), Varna (240) and Burgas (214) among the largest. It appears most likely that geography played the deciding role in this situation. The western Bulgarian lands were quite mountainous and thus demographically confining and divisive, while the eastern lands were mostly plain regions with broad open spaces conducive to fewer but more numerous village habitations. (See Table 6.)

What little urban population that did exist in the Bulgarian lands during the seventeenth century did so in the 35 towns spread throughout the 25 documented regions. Ten of those towns (29.4 percent) were located in the western Bulgarian lands, among which was Sofia, the primary Ottoman administrative center for most of the Balkan Peninsula. The Orthodox Bulgarian urban population averaged 586 persons per town, with the Danubian commercial ports of Silistra (3,075 persons), Nikopol (2,345) and Svishtov (2,100) the largest, and the heavily Turkified and hellenized administrative centers of Burgas (55 persons), Berkovitsa (50) and Provadiya (90) among the smallest Bulgarian urban settlements. The estimated 22,000 urban Bulgarians constituted only 2.5 percent of the average seventeenth century Orthodox Bulgarian population. (See Table 7.)

As were all the possessions of the Ottoman Empire, the Bulgarian lands were classified and divided along lines regulated by Islamic precepts of landholding. Technically, all possessions acquired through military conquest were considered *miri*, or government owned properties, which in reality meant the property of the Ottoman sultan. The revenues from most of such lands, based on taxes paid by the settlements located on them, were conditionally bestowed in pseudo-feudal fashion as benefices to support the Turkish military and administrative classes. Some of the very largest properties, however, termed *has*, were retained as the personal income-producing possessions of the sultan, his family and the highest ranking state officials. Other properties were originally bestowed on high military and administrative officials as private possessions (*mülk*) outright. It became common for owners of *mülk* to designate some or all of their properties as perpetual endowments (*vakıfs*) to various Muslim religious establishments, such as mosques or Islamic schools. By the seventeenth century some of the holders of *miri* benefices had succeeded in transforming their conditional income-producing holdings, which they technically did not own personally, into *mülk* possessions, the majority of which represented medium or large sized farm properties (*çiftliks*).

In the Bulgarian lands of the seventeenth century, at most nearly three-quarters of all settlements located on registered lands were *miri* (74.3 percent). Of the remaining 25.7 percent of the settlements, 8.2 percent (88 settlements) were *has*, 14 percent (124 settlements) were *vakıf*, and only 3.5 percent (36 settlements) were registered as *çiftlik*. (See Tables 8., 9. and 10.) Over half (53.8 percent) of the *has* properties were located in the western Bulgarian lands (in the regions of Vratsa, Vidin, Lovech, Petrich, Kutlovitsa, Gorna Dzhumaya and Sofia), and these generally contained the largest concentrations of the type. (See Table 8.) The relatively low share of property holding in the Bulgarian lands enjoyed by *çiftliks* demonstrates that, despite the commonly held generalization of Balkan scholars that the seventeenth century was a time of rapid transformation of the Ottoman landholding system from state to privately owned holdings, in the Bulgarian lands at that time the process was slow and relatively insignificant in the overall scheme of things. The transformation actually gained momentum in the Bulgarian lands in later centuries of Ottoman rule. Less than two percent of total *çiftlik* properties were located in the western Bulgarian lands. (See Table 10.) The largest share of non-*miri* Bulgarian land was involved in *vakıf* holdings. Few of these properties were established in the western lands but, rather, they were primarily concentrated in the eastern Thracian, Danubian and Black Sea coastal regions, regions that experienced widescale Muslim colonization. (See Table 9.)

The regional distribution involved in the questions of settlement density and landholding types discussed above has been emphasized because they appear to have been important factors in the overall geographic distribution of Bulgarian Orthodox cultural activity during the seventeenth century. Extant Orthodox literary and art evidence from the period has been found for 17 of the 25 documented regions of the Bulgarian lands (68 percent), which encompassed 71.4 percent of all documented Bulgarian settlements. Literary activity has been found in 94.1 percent of those 17 regions with evidence for cultural activity, while art activity was a bit less widespread (over 70 percent of those same regions). The regions that displayed no extant evidence for cultural activity during the century were all located in the highly islamized and hellenized eastern lands (*i.e.*, Eastern Thrace, the Black Sea coast and hinterland and the eastern Danubian Plain). (See Table 11.) It is interesting to note that of the 184 sites for which extant literary or art evidence for cultural activity during the seventeenth century exist, the majority were located in the western Bulgarian lands (69.6 percent), which were precisely those regions of greatest settlement density and of the most *has* and least *vakıf* landholding. (See Table 12.) It might also be pointed out that the largest concentration of privileged settlements (*e.g., voynuk* and *celep* settlements) were located in the western lands as well. (See Map 9.)

The overwhelming majority of seventeenth century Bulgarian Orthodox cultural sites were villages, or more precisely, village churches (67.4 percent of all cultural sites). Monasteries, the fountainheads of Orthodox culture, comprised a little over a quarter of all Bulgarian Orthodox cultural sites, while towns represented only 7.1 percent, although the 13 towns found in the extant evidence constituted well over a third (38.2 percent) of all urban settlements in the Bulgarian lands. (See Table 13.)

IN THE SEVENTEENTH CENTURY

In the field of seventeenth century Slavic Orthodox education among the Bulgarians, evidence is extant for 69 locations that served as educational sites at one time or another during the period. Not surprisingly, given the monastic origins and strong traditions of an educational system that stressed religious vocational training, monasteries played an important role in the field, representing 40.6 percent of all educational sites, 59.6 percent of known monastic cultural sites and 15.2 percent of the total number of cultural sites. Interestingly, villages proved just as numerous as locations for education during the century, having shares of 43.6, 24.2 and 16.3 percent, respectively. Education was particularly active in those towns that served as cultural sites, 84.6 percent of which supported schools during the period, although they represented only 16 percent of the total educational sites and a mere 6 percent of all Bulgarian cultural sites for the time. (See Table 14.)

The field of literary culture was the best documented Orthodox cultural activity among the Bulgarians during the seventeenth century. All told, evidence gleaned from 285 citations made in manuscript marginalia exists for 142 sites of literary activity during the period, which ranged from the merest work of manuscript annotation to full-fledged literary school production. In terms of number of sites in this field, the western regions of Sofia and Lovech led all others (19.6 and 10.9 percent of total literary cultural sites, respectively), closely followed by the regions of Plovdiv and Vratsa (8.2 and 7.1 percent, respectively). Those four regions of the Bulgarian lands together accounted for 45.8 percent of the known literary cultural sites among the Bulgarians of the century. (See Table 15.)

Examining the Orthodox literary cultural sites in closer detail, 47.4 percent of the extant marginalia citations referred to activity that occurred in villages. Monastic activity was mentioned in 39.6 percent of the citations, and urban activity received only 13 percent of the notices. (See Table 16.) Yet an interesting fact arises when the average number of citations per type of site (*i.e.*, village, monastery or town) is considered. The average number of citations for village sites was 1.1 per village. Monastic sites averaged 2.4 citations per site (or 2.2 times the village average), and urban sites enjoyed the highest average of all, 2.8 citations per site (or 2.5 times the village average). It thus would appear that while literary activity was extensive among the rural population it was not as intensive or as long-lived as the literary work conducted in the monasteries (as one would expect) and, especially, the towns (which at first glance is somewhat of a surprise, since the urban sector represented such a small element in the total Bulgarian population). (See Table 17.)

Turning to the extant products of seventeenth century Bulgarian Orthodox literary culture, the first obvious observation is that there were no printed books. Printing presses did not start to operate in the Bulgarian lands until the nineteenth century. The second obvious fact is that all the 261 extant manuscripts were religious in nature. Menologions, missals, *damaskins,* and the Christian gospels (representing 19.9, 10.7, 10.4 and 9.2 percent of the extant manuscripts, respectively) were the most common products, totalling just over 50 percent of extant literary production during the century. It is significant that *damaskins,* which were highly eclectic, didactic and in many cases secular in content, and which were the only literary works written in the partially vernacular New Bulgarian literary language, were so popular. Their Church Slavonic counterpart, the *sborniks,* were also popular (6.5 percent of literary production) but less so, probably because of the arcane literary language used. (See Table 18.)

Because the literary culture was wholly encompassed by the Orthodox religion, which by ritualism, convention and tradition imposed severe limitations on its content, when one seeks to discern literary expressions of such secular conceptions as ethnic awareness or historical consciousness one must examine religious works that provide a degree of latitude for such expression (*e.g.,* specific hagiographies or ritual prayer services to specific Orthodox saints) and the non-religious annotations and assorted marginalia left in the manuscripts by various copyists and other users. In 46 (17.6 percent) of the 261 extant seventeenth century Bulgarian manuscripts can be found religious works dealing with specific Bulgarian saints, in which their *Bulgarian* natures were stressed. The Bulgarian female anchorite, Petka Tŭrnovska, appeared in 69.6 percent of those manuscripts, followed closely by Ivan Rilski (52.2 percent). Both of these most popular saints' lives were intimately tied to periods of past medieval Bulgarian independence and glory, either in the cultural or military fields, and those facts were intrinsic elements in their identities. (See Table 19.)

With regard to extant annotations and other marginalia dating to the seventeenth century, in the 261 extant manuscripts examined there have been left 253 such notations, which, in turn, were found to contain 471 citations treating with individual topics. Over 74 percent of the extant notations provided biographical information of cultural patrons, monastery abbots, parish priests, Ottoman sultans and church prelates. Sixty percent of the notations were autobiographical in nature. Social topics (*e.g.,* commodity prices, educational activity and reactionary acts carried out by the Ottoman authorities) were found in nearly 35 percent of the notations, and entries of a chronicle nature, ranging from bewailing natural calamities to extended, detailed accounts of the repercussions of Ottoman military campaigns on the local Bulgarian population, were written into 16.9 percent of the extant notations. (See Table 20.) It is such marginalia that provides much of the specific evidence for Bulgarian Orthodox cultural activity during the seventeenth century.

Such marginalia also furnishes the information necessary for identifying the social backgrounds of many who engaged in literary activity of assorted kinds. All told, the social backgrounds of 93 of the 114 persons known to have been active in the literary field during the seventeenth century can be established. Of those, 62.3 percent were from the ranks of the church (*i.e.*, priests, 35.1 percent; monks, 27.2 percent) and 19.3 percent were from the laity. Those with unknown backgrounds comprised 18.4 percent. Those who worked as writer-copyists represented 41.2 percent of all involved, while those who simply worked as annotators (42.1 percent) slightly outnumbered the writer-copyists. (See Table 21.)

The five major centers of seventeenth century Bulgarian Orthodox literary cultural activity — Rila Monastery, Sofia, Etropole Monastery, Vratsa and Karlovo-Adzhar-Kuklen Monastery — together accounted for 44.2 percent of all manuscript notations and 39.4 percent of all citations found in the notations. Etropole, with 14.4 and 16.2 percent of the notations and citations, was indisputably the leading seventeenth century Bulgarian literary center. (See Table 22.)

In the field of Orthodox religious art during the period, 72 sites located throughout 12 regions of the Bulgarian lands demonstrated activity. Once again, Sofia was the leading region in the cultural field with 14.5 percent of the known sites of artistic activity. The regions of Pernik, Kyustendil, Kutlovitsa, Vratsa and Lovech, all regions of the western lands, each owned a 4.4 percent share in such activity. (See Table 23.) Most of the art cultural activity occurred during the first half of the century.

Extant inscriptions left on the products of artistic activity play a role similar to that of literary marginalia in providing information on the social backgrounds of the artists involved, although the information is far less complete. Of the 24 identifiable known artists, only a third (8) can be placed with any kind of certainty. Of those, 20.8 percent were from the clergy and 12.5 percent from the laity. The high percentage with unknown background (66.7) makes any conclusion based on the previously noted figures highly conjectural. (See Table 24.)

Overall, 138 persons were known to be involved in the Bulgarian cultural intelligentsia during the seventeenth century. Those in literary endeavors accounted for 82.6 percent of all involved. The clergy provided 55.1 percent of the cultural workers, and the laity 18.1 percent. Those with unknown social backgrounds comprised the remaining 26.8 percent. (See Table 25.)

One last topic must be considered before closing this brief analysis, and that is the social backgrounds of those persons who served as the patrons for Bulgarian Orthodox cultural activity during the seventeenth century. The extant evidence has provided 158 cultural patrons for the period. Of those, 79.7 percent patronized the literary field and 20.3 the fine arts. This proportion appears natural in that literary activity involved less expense than did most art activity, and that the Bulgarians were naturally relegated to the lower socio-economic rungs of the

Ottoman social ladder by their Muslim overlords. The majority of cultural patrons were from the ranks of the laity (65.2 percent), which appears to indicate that by the seventeenth century social classes were emerging among the Bulgarians able and willing to fill the void in cultural patronage left by the Ottoman conquest two centuries previous. The clergy still retained a significant role in cultural patronage (31 percent of all patrons). (See Table 26.)

General Summary

In the preface to his *Slaveno-Bulgarian History* written in 1762, Paisii, the Bulgarian Athonite monk, declared that the Bulgarians were considered a people without a history by their Serbian and Greek neighbors. His argument turned on the fact that the Bulgarians had been drawn into a foreign cultural orbit that, if left unchecked, would lead the Bulgarians down the road toward ethnic, hence national, oblivion. In Paisii's view, by the mid eighteenth century the Bulgarians were perched on the verge of cultural assimilation. His was a perception that was due, in large measure, to the Bulgarians' position within the Ottoman social system. Yet despite their hazardous position within the Ottoman empire, by the time Paisii composed his ground breaking nationalist work the Bulgarians had managed to survive as a distinct people through a period that had posed some of the most mortal threats to their continued independent existence — the seventeenth century. Most of the credit for their survival was due to their retention of the Orthodox faith in its Slavic forms. The Bulgarians' accomplishment was truly a grass-roots success earned in spite of both the official Orthodox church organization, and its position within the Ottoman administration, and the social and cultural pressures exerted upon them by their Muslim Turkish overlords.

Prior to the reigns of sultans Selim I the Grim and Süleyman I the Magnificent the European possessions of the Ottoman Empire represented nearly half of the state's territories and population. Of those possessions, the population of the core Bulgarian lands, encompassing the classical Balkan provinces of Mœsia and northern Thrace, formed a significant part, accounting for close to one-half of the European and a fifth of the total population of the empire.

By the opening of the seventeenth century the situation had changed. The conquests of large regions in the Islamic Middle East and northern Africa during the reigns of Selim and Süleyman transformed the demographic nature of the empire. The population of the empire nearly doubled, and the overwhelming majority of the new subjects was Muslim. The European Balkan Christians dropped to less than a fifth of the total population and the Christians in the Bulgarian lands were reduced to an insignificant share in the overall demographic picture.

IN THE SEVENTEENTH CENTURY

The new Muslim majority in the population demanded a share in the administration of the empire that until the sixteenth century had been reserved for slaves of the sultan. Under Islamic sacred law (the *Şeriat*) it was forbidden to enslave Muslims. Pressure from the Muslim majority finally succeeded in corrupting the traditional slave administrative system of the empire by the middle of the sixteenth century with disastrous long-term results. As the military decline that was a consequence of the corruption of the Janissary standing forces set in, following the death of Süleyman the Magnificent (1566), especially in the European theater of operations, the Christian minority in the empire's population was exposed to a growing Muslim reaction against the changing fortunes of the Islamic state. Nowhere were these changes experienced more fully than in the Bulgarian lands, which lay in closest geographic proximity to the heart of the Ottoman Empire, Istanbul and its environs.

The eastern Thracian, Black Sea coastal and eastern Danubian plain regions of the Bulgarian lands had experienced serious Turkish colonization in the early centuries of Ottoman rule. In the mountainous western lands, which were less amenable to the Turkish semi-nomadic way of life, the Muslim presence was fairly confined to urban settlements that served as imperial administrative centers. The Christian Bulgarians who inhabited the core Bulgarian lands were overwhelmingly Orthodox in religion. Large numbers of Orthodox Bulgarians assimilated into the Muslim ranks in the regions of the Rhodope Mountains (in the central Bulgarian lands), the Pirin Mountains (in the southwestern lands) and in the above mentioned regions of the eastern Bulgarian lands. Assimilation occurred because of social pressure on individuals or groups primarily exerted by the possibility of tax relief, the attraction of military and syncretic Muslim religious institutions or by random bouts of Muslim reactionary violence.

Orthodox Bulgarians were thus predominantly inhabitants of the western Bulgarian lands. They managed to retain their self-identity as Christians and Bulgarians because of their Orthodox faith, and they fortified this identity through expressions of Orthodox culture. The regions of the core Bulgarian lands where Orthodox cultural expression was manifest during the seventeenth century were located in the rugged western and central lands, which demonstrated the highest share of *has* landholding. This was understandable, since the imperial owners had little to gain by decreasing the taxpaying Christian inhabitants and thus diminishing their personal incomes.

As we have seen, Ottoman rule in the Bulgarian lands had the effect of eliminating the two major supports of Bulgarian Orthodox culture, namely the native aristocracy and the native-controlled church organization. Lands that had been formerly held by Bulgarian *bolyars* under the medieval Bulgarian state were confiscated by the Ottoman conquerors and transformed into military fiefs that were conditionally held by *sipahi* cavalrymen of the Turkish land forces, by important Ottoman administrative officeholders or owned outright by members of the Turkish imperial family. Bulgarian cities that had once formed the administrative and commercial underpinnings of the medieval Bulgarian state were transformed into similar centers for the Turks. Again, the former leading Bulgarian urban elements were brushed aside in favor of the Ottoman conquerors.

A similar process occurred in the control of the Bulgarian Orthodox church. Through the imposition of the *millet* system for administering non-Muslim affairs within the Ottoman Empire following the conquest of Bulgaria, the autonomous medieval Bulgarian church was eliminated and its administration turned over to the Greek Patriarchate of Constantinople. Because the hierarchy of the Orthodox church in the Bulgarian lands was totally controlled by Greek prelates, the Bulgarians had only a small stake in the official church organization, forming the lowest echelons of parish priests and local monks. The Orthodox cultural activity in towns that served as Orthodox ecclesiastical centers was primarily Greek, so that in places such as Plovdiv and the Black Sea coastal towns Bulgarian cultural expression was virtually nil. This situation also was detrimental to general Bulgarian Orthodox cultural activity in that it precluded the application of a large portion of church funds toward the support of Slavic (Bulgarian) cultural endeavors. What had once been a Bulgarian church, which had conducted all of its ritualistic and cultural activities in the native Slavic tongue and traditions of its membership, became an organization controlled by Greeks and Greek-speakers, and thus foreign to the majority of its membership in the Bulgarian lands.

The general social inferiority of the Bulgarians within Ottoman society significantly affected the range, type and quality of their Orthodox cultural life. In the first place, the conduct of Slavic (*i.e.,* Bulgarian) Orthodox cultural activity was totally in the hands of native monks and parish priests, who were forced to seek financial support for such activity from amongst the poorest elements in the Ottoman social system. Such a situation could not but limit the quantity and the quality of the products of Slavic Orthodox cultural endeavor among the Bulgarians. The burden of taxation levied on the seventeenth century Bulgarian population constantly increased because of the inflationary Ottoman economy and the enormous sums involved in the requisite bribes that served as normal procedural steps in any form of civil or ecclesiastical transaction. As members of the poorer social classes in the Ottoman state, the Bulgarians, as a whole, possessed a limited amount of funds that could readily be applied toward cultural activity after meeting the rising demand for state and ecclesiastical taxes, as well as for their own mundane expenses.

IN THE SEVENTEENTH CENTURY

Fortunately for the maintenance of the Bulgarians' Slavic form of Orthodox culture, the Ottoman social system unintentionally created new Bulgarian social elements that were able to lend native cultural activity their financial support in place of the vanished *bolyars* and church administrators. These patrons were inhabitants of the small but numerous villages and towns of the western and central Bulgarian lands, who funded schools, literary production and artistic activities connected with their local churches or nearby monasteries. Although such activity was widespread in the villages of the western and central lands, it was most intensive in the monasteries and the towns located in those regions, places where the funds and the cultural intelligentsia were concentrated because of traditional and economic reasons.

In the urban centers of the Bulgarian lands, the *esnaf* system, although under strict Turkish control, offered Bulgarian artisans and merchants a limited form of autonomy and unity *via* the corporate nature of the individual guilds, and, at least, a relatively stable income based on the commercial market that exceeded that of the average rural peasant class, the members of which often operated at little above the level of subsistence. On average, urban Bulgarians were able to support more than one parish church or monastic *metoh*, along with accompanying cultural activity, while the average Bulgarian village could manage to support only a single church and, possibly, join with inhabitants of other villages in supporting a nearby monastery.

Because major urban centers usually served as Turkish civil and Greek ecclesiastical administrative centers, the Slavic cultural life of the urban Bulgarians was rather limited. Quite often, Bulgarian members of urban guilds, or guilds composed completely of Bulgarian members, gave their financial support to cultural activity conducted in the countryside surrounding the cities and towns. Such was particularly the case for the Bulgarian inhabitants of Sofia, of whom we possess the most complete available documentation for urban participation in Bulgarian cultural life during the seventeenth century. Sofia Bulgarians were instrumental in providing funds to the monasteries lying, on average, some seventeen kilometers outside the city, in the foothills of the mountains ringing the Sofia Plain. A similar situation held true for the regions surrounding the towns of Vratsa and Etropole, although neither was a major administrative center for the Turkish and Greek authorities. Though the data are sparse, such was probably also the case for all the urban centers throughout the Bulgarian lands. During the seventeenth century, therefore, urban centers were able to serve as economic bases for Bulgarian Orthodox cultural activity, but such activity was, for the most part, conducted in the surrounding rural regions because of the predominantly urban presence of the Bulgarians' foreign masters.

The essentially rural nature of Bulgarian Orthodox culture was further reinforced by the creation of relatively large numbers of Bulgarian corporate rural service groups that were granted certain fiscal and social privileges by the Ottoman authorities. In return for rendering a variety of professional services required by the central government and its military forces, those groups were extended the right to live in local village autonomy, free from the discriminatory taxation usually levied on the non-Muslim subjects of the empire (*i.e.,* the *cizye* and *haraç*). Of the privileged service corporations, the most numerous, in terms of membership, were the Bulgarian *voynuks, celeps* and ore-miners, who inhabited the regions of the western Bulgarian lands and who commonly comprised the entire populations of numerous villages and small towns. *Voynuk* and *celep* villages were particularly numerous in the regions of Sofia, Kyustendil and the Sredna Gora Mountains. The privileged mining populations, the majority of whom had originally been foreigners but by the seventeenth century had become assimilated into the local Bulgarian population, were likewise concentrated in the western lands in the regions of Etropole, Samokov and Kyustendil. As a consequence of the social and economic privileges extended to the service corporations of the western regions of the Bulgarian lands, their village populations were relatively free of continuous and direct Ottoman supervision and possessed higher than average amounts of wealth. Such conditions were conducive to the lively conduct of Orthodox cultural activity on the part of the local Bulgarian populations. As we have noted, the regions of the Bulgarian lands most active in the field of Orthodox culture during the seventeenth century were precisely those that were inhabited by populous privileged Bulgarian service corporations (*i.e.,* Sofia, Etropole, Vratsa, Kyustendil, Samokov [Rila Monastery] and the Sredna Gora [Adzhar]).

The Bulgarian Orthodox cultural intelligentsia of the seventeenth century displayed the traditional dominance of the clergy in cultural affairs but lay participants were on the rise, comprising nearly a fifth of all persons involved. The predominance of the laity in cultural patronage and the growing number of laymen actually participating in cultural activity were trends that would continue into the century that followed, eventually erupting into a full-blown Bulgarian cultural and national revival in the early years of the nineteenth century. By that time cultural activity had burst the bounds of Orthodox religious culture and had entered into the mainstream of modern European nationalism.

The social system imposed by the Muslim Ottoman authorities throughout the Bulgarian lands not only affected the means of support for Bulgarian Orthodox culture during the seventeenth century but also played a role in determining the nature of Bulgarian cultural activity. Because the Bulgarians were reduced to the lowest levels on the civil and ecclesiastical social scales, the conduct of Orthodox cultural activity was placed into the hands of local monks and priests. The role of cultural leadership in such a situation fell upon the

Bulgarian-populated monasteries for a number of reasons. In the first place, monasticism had played a leading role in the formation and conduct of cultural affairs in the Orthodox world since the ninth century. Centuries of tradition had entrenched Orthodox monasteries in their position of cultural leadership. Nowhere was that fact more evident than in the monastic communities of Mount Athos, with which Bulgarian monasteries historically maintained close and continuous relationships. In the second place, the monasteries in the Bulgarian lands tended to be located in mountainous regions that were isolated from the areas that were densely colonized by Muslims (*e.g.*, the Thracian, Danubian and the Dobrudzhan plains), and from the main Ottoman military and commercial highways. In the third place, as we noted in our discussion of Rila Monastery, the Ottoman central authorities tended to extend *vakıf* status to properties owned by the monasteries, thus guaranteeing them, insofar as that was possible, given the unstable political and economic climate within the Ottoman Empire during the seventeenth century, a relatively stable income that could be used to finance cultural activity conducted inside their walls. In the last place, the Bulgarian monasteries possessed a developed network of intercommunication among individual establishments, the local population, and the Orthodox world that lay beyond the frontiers of the Ottoman Empire through the activities of *taxidiot* monks. Seventeenth century Bulgarian Orthodox culture was, therefore, essentially monastic in nature.

All three of the cultural factors that we have examined — education, literature and art — bore the imprint of their monastic origins.

Cell schools, the only form of education available to the Bulgarians of the period, were conducted in the cells of individual teachers, usually either monks or priests, and possessed a tradition that was rooted in the period of the medieval Bulgarian state. When during the seventeenth century education expanded outward from the monasteries into the villages and towns of the Bulgarian lands for the first time on any kind of large scale, it retained its "cell" nature. Although seventeenth century education was admittedly still limited to a small portion of the general Bulgarian population, its expansion signaled the beginnings of a transformation in its purpose. Schooling no longer merely constituted the preparation for a religious vocation, as it had in the past, but now acquired a measure of practicality that future, post-seventeenth century developments were to amplify. Thanks to the growing needs of the urban guilds and rural corporations, didactic and secular subjects slowly crept into the heretofore exclusively religious curriculum offered in the schools. The annotations left in hundreds of manuscripts during the period demonstrated that the small but expanding literate element in the population had an awareness of their social and economic situation within the Ottoman Empire. They also revealed a growing sense of historical perspective of the Bulgarians as a people separate from both the Turks and the Greeks. Perhaps education might have enjoyed a more widespread impact on the general Bulgarian population had it not been for the relative poverty of the Bulgarians as a social class and the periodic ravages perpetrated on the *reaya* populations of the empire by the Muslim authorities and anarchists, which made the existence of most village schools intermittent at best.

A key factor in the Bulgarians' success in maintaining their ethnic self-awareness during the seventeenth century was their recognition of themselves as Slavs and not as Greeks or as Turks. In this regard, language, in both its spoken and written forms, was of primary importance. Language also proved to be one of the thorniest problems for the Bulgarians themselves until the mid nineteenth century precisely because of its Orthodox religious literary traditions. For both defining and differentiating the Bulgarians from other ethnic groups, the vernacular remained the fundamental means: all other factors being relatively equal, if a given person's speech was understood, then that person was a fellow Bulgarian; if not, the person was a foreigner. The literary language, however, which was wholly encompassed within an Orthodox liturgical context, was not so fundamentally successful in drawing such ethnic distinctions.

Orthodox literature never shook itself free from its monastic origins. For the most part, literary works remained highly liturgical in content and quite unoriginal in nature throughout the seventeenth century. The production of such literature was the traditional preserve of monastic scriptoria. As with education, however, literary production expanded into the villages to some degree, and in the process it acquired certain new, didactic and narrative qualities. This evolution was accompanied by the development of the New Bulgarian literary language, for which the seventeenth century served as the period of consolidation. Here again, for the first time since the period of the medieval Bulgarian state, works of literature were produced that were written in a language that approximated the Bulgarian vernacular of their intended readership. The development of New Bulgarian closely paralleled the rise in popularity of *sborniks* and *damaskins,* two separate but similar literary genres. Both types of works, which came to characterize the new road taken by religious literature during the seventeenth century, emphasized a certain awareness of the Bulgarians' past through hagiographies of Bulgarian saints in the traditions of medieval Bulgarian religious literature, and especially those of Evtimii Tŭrnovski. Because of the expansion of education from the monasteries, a literate segment, albeit still small, was created in secular Bulgarian society, and its existence created novel demands for less strictly liturgical reading matter. Such a development may help explain the evolution of New Bulgarian as a literary vehicle. That efforts were made to make an essentially religious literary culture more appealing to its secular patrons and general audience was demonstrated by the large popularity enjoyed by *sborniks* and *damaskins,* which contained highly secularized, narrative and didactic materials, such as moral tales, helpful hints, excerpts from the writings of ancient philosophers and other nonliturgical, and often nonreligious, topics.

Bulgarian religious art demonstrated the least amount of growth during the seventeenth century of all the three cultural fields. Orthodox art was, by its very nature, highly regimented by traditions that had been codified in artist handbooks that laid down the law regarding correct Orthodox iconography and artistic forms. Moreover, monuments of art were usually highly visible (*e.g.,* church buildings) and, therefore, also greatly susceptible to destruction by fanatical Muslims, who might take an inkling to harass the Christian *reaya* by any possible means. Indeed, the seventeenth century did not lack outbreaks of such violence. Those artistic monuments from the period that did survive demonstrated marked adherence to traditional Orthodox artistic forms. A few new elements, however, such as the increased use of floral and geometric decorative motifs and the inclusion of contemporary ethnographic elements within traditional iconographic schemes, which formed part of a Balkan Orthodox artistic tradition in its own right beyond the iconographical traditions of Byzantium, have been discerned. On the whole, art was used by the Bulgarians to reinforce the didactic and narrative aspects of education and literature during the seventeenth century.

All of the new developments formed within Bulgarian Orthodox culture during the seventeenth century were to be expanded on and further transformed during the period of the Bulgarian national revival of the mid eighteenth through nineteenth centuries.

The Orthodox Bulgarians managed to maintain, defend and further develop their religious culture in the face of a number of simultaneous foreign cultural threats. That which was posed by Roman Catholic missionary activity in the Bulgarian lands, although the most studied topic of seventeenth century Bulgarian history, was easily fended off because of the deep-seated, centuries-long animosity and distrust that separated the two major branches of medieval Christianity. The Catholics were unable to overcome Orthodox opposition and made virtually no cultural impact on the general Orthodox population within the Bulgarian lands. The Catholics, with their contacts with the West, could have provided the spark for creating a sense of modern nationalism among the seventeenth century Bulgarians, but since they were considered hated "Latins" by the Orthodox Bulgarians, their modern national message went virtually unheeded while they operated within the Bulgarian lands and was rapidly forgotten following the debacle of Chiprovtsi.

Some of the earliest expressions of mutual hatred between Bulgarians and Greeks were recorded during the seventeenth century. Although the seeds of antagonism were present, the religio-cultural struggle between the two peoples, which was to characterize most of the eighteenth and nineteenth centuries, had not as yet developed during the seventeenth. Contrary to the surmises of nonspecialists, Greek cultural aggression against Slavic cultural expression was not greatly in evidence within the Bulgarian lands during the seventeenth century. Lists of former Bulgarian rulers or gazetteers of the "Bulgarian lands" could appear in Bulgarian monastery beadrolls but none would appear in Bulgarian metropolitan cathedrals, where the Greek hierarchy fostered a Greek cultural *milieu*. Images of Bulgarian saints could appear on the walls of local parish churches or in those of isolated Bulgarian monasteries but little of the work would be funded by official church treasuries. On the contrary, the ever increasing monetary demands made on the Bulgarian Orthodox faithful by their Greek prelates for satisfying the financial debts of the nepotistic and simonious *millet* system were detrimental to the cultural self-expression of the Bulgarians and eventually resulted in instigating ethnic animosities between Bulgarians and Greeks. The Greek threat to Bulgarian Orthodox culture remained almost exclusively confined to the monopoly of the Orthodox *millet* and to fiscal extortions.

The most serious threat to the Bulgarians' Orthodox culture was that exerted by the Muslim Ottoman ruling establishment. The conversions in the Rhodope Mountains and in the central and eastern Danubian Plain, combined with those that occurred in scattered fashion throughout the Bulgarian lands, constituted a heavy blow to Orthodox cultural life among the Bulgarians because of the religio-political nature of the Ottoman *millet* system. The converts were forever lost to the body of the Bulgarian Orthodox population. Muslim pressures, through active discriminatory policies and through the colonization of Muslims in the rolling lowlands of the Bulgarian lands, resulted in the virtual confinement of Bulgarian Orthodox culture to the mountainous western Bulgarian lands. Scattered pockets of Orthodox Bulgarians remained in other regions inundated by the Muslims, such as Adzhar, Kuklen and a few Rhodope villages, which later would serve as the bases for the Bulgarians' cultural reconquest of much of the territory lost during the seventeenth century. The cultural demography that existed during the seventeenth century, however, had effects that have lasted to the present time. The cultural and political heart of present-day Bulgaria still resides in the western lands and is centered on Sofia. Large Muslim populations still inhabit the Rhodope Mountain, Thracian and Dobrudzhan regions of the country.

The Bulgarians faced and repulsed these cultural threats by fortifying their sense of self-awareness through Slavic literary and artistic cultural activity. Both existed within the context of a Slavic Orthodox culture that, given the condition of foreign Turkish political and Greek religious domination, could only operate on a local level. Although ethnic awareness never completely died out among the Bulgarians thanks to the cultural activity of those who worked within the Orthodox church, that activity existed in a state of continuous poverty right through the nineteenth century and the eruption of western-style nationalism.

IN THE SEVENTEENTH CENTURY

That it managed to exist at all was more a matter of the *Orthodoxy* of the Bulgarians — their belief in the Orthodox form of Christianity and the preservation of its Slavic cultural traditions — than of the established Orthodox church organization and the advantages afforded by the Orthodox *millet*. Orthodoxy ensured that the Bulgarians were able to distinguish between themselves and non-Orthodox peoples (*e.g.*, Muslims, Jews and Catholics) and between themselves and other non-Slavic Orthodox Christians (*e.g.*, Greeks and Armenians). Differences between themselves and other Slavic Orthodox peoples (*i.e.*, the Serbs) were less well defined in the Orthodox context. It took Paisii and his exposure to western and Russian historical literature to commence the last phase of conceptual development within Orthodox tradition that would lead to a definitive Bulgarian self-identity as an ethnic and, ultimately, national entity. By the time that identity matured, it had moved beyond the purely Orthodox context into the realm of modern European nationalism.

Appendix I: *Glossary*

A

Aba	Course woolen homespun cloth.
Akçe	Basic silver monetary unit in the Ottoman Empire.
Akıncı	Ottoman irregular strike cavalry, also used for scouting and raiding.
Avaris	Ottoman extraordinary tax, often collected on a regular basis.

B

Ban	"Leader;" title of a Bulgarian village commune official.
Bashtina	a.) Autonomous peasant farmstead; b.) tax-free grant of land by Ottoman authorities in partial return for services rendered the state.
Berat	Ottoman imperial warrant conferring dignities or privileges.
Bey	a.) Ruler; b.) governor; c.) gentleman.
Beylerbey	Highest ranking Ottoman provincial governor.
Bolyar	Medieval Bulgarian aristocrat.
Boza	Fermented millet drink.

C

Celep	Livestock-breeder or dealer; deliverer of food to Istanbul or to military depots.
Celepkeşan	Livestock breeder-dealer (see *Celep*).
Cherep	Bulgarian for skull.
Cizye	Ottoman poll-tax levied on non-Muslim subjects.

Ç

Çaribaşı	*Voynuk* village elder (see *Voynuk*).
Çarşi	Market street, usually devoted to a single craft industry; primary urban marketplace.
Çavuş	Ottoman *esnaf* (which see) official who assisted the *ustabaşı* (which see also).
Çeltukçı	Producer of rice.
Çift	Land plot on military fiefs reserved for the holders' personal use.

Çift resmi	"Yoke tax;" payment in lieu of labor services.
Çiftlik	Privately owned Ottoman farm or estate
Çiftlikbey	Owner of a *çiftlik* (which see).

D

Damaskin	Orthodox literary genre; a didactic book having an eclectic contents and written in a language approximating the vernacular of its intended readership.
Daskal	Bulgarian teacher.
Dervenci	Mountain pass and road guard.
Derviş	Wandering Muslim holy man.
Devşirme	Periodic Ottoman child-levy.
Dime	Local land-use tax in Bulgarian village communes.
Ducat	Ottoman gold monetary unit.
Dyak	Bulgarian student.
Dyavol	Bulgarian term for minion of the Anti-Christ; "devil."

E

Ecclesiarch	Athonite superintendant of the central church at Karyes.
Emvatikon	Orthodox ecclesiastical tax paid to the Patriarchate of Constantinople by newly appointed church prelates.
Ermeniya	Orthodox artist's iconographical handbook.
Esnaf	Ottoman artisan or merchant guild.
Eyalet	Largest Ottoman provincial administrative unit, governed by a *beylerbey* (which see).

F

Ferman	Ottoman imperial edict.

G

Gramatik	Bulgarian master grammarian, usually active in literary production and education.
Groş	Ottoman silver monetary unit representing a sum of *akçes* (which see).

H

Haci	Muslim title granted to a person who completed the pilgrimage to Mecca.
Hadzhi	Orthodox title granted a Christian who completed the pilgrimage to the Holy Lands.
Haidut	Bandit; sometimes an anti-Ottoman resistance fighter.
Han	Ruler of the Crimean Tatars; ruler of Tatar-Mongol peoples.
Hane	Household constituting the smallest Ottoman tax unit, estimated to average five persons in size; "hearth."

Haraç	Ottoman land-use tax; sometimes used synonymously for *cizye* (which see).
Has	Largest type of Ottoman privately owned property, usually imperial lands.
Hisba	Islamic religious injunction against undue profiteering, fraud and speculation in the artisan economic sphere.
Hoca	Muslim teacher; a learned man or wise elder.
Hospodar	Title held by a Romanian ruler.

I

Ierei	Orthodox priest.
Ieromonah	Orthodox priest-monk.
Ieropop	Orthodox priest in charge of other priests.
Iltizam	Ottoman tax farm.
Imam	Muslim prayer leader.

K

Kadı	Ottoman judge.
Kaza	Smallest Ottoman provincial administrative unit.
Kethüda	Head official of an Ottoman *esnaf* (which see).
Kmet	"Mayor;" title for leading Bulgarian village commune official.
Knez	"Headman" or elder; title of a Bulgarian village commune official.
Kocabaşı	Ottoman title for chief elders, often used by Bulgarian village commune elders.
Koine	Vernacular form of the Greek language.

L

Lonca	General assembly of an Ottoman *esnaf* (which see).

M

Madancı	Metal ore miner or processor.
Mahalle	Residential quarter; borough.
Maistor	Master artist, often a teacher.
Maktu	Annual Ottoman fixed tax levied on certain *vakıf* properties (see *Vakıf*).
Manastir resmi	Annual dues paid by monasteries to the Patriarchate of Constantinople.
Martolos	Local militiaman.
Metoh	Satellite monastic establishment owned, administered and staffed by a larger monastery.

Millet	Nation; a group of Ottoman subject people considered by the authorities as a legal administrative unit, based on religious affiliation.
Miri	Government owned properties, usually divided and conditionally bestowed as benefices supporting members of the Ottoman ruling institutions.
Monah	Monk; friar.
Mukataa	Special state levy of considerable size collected by taxfarmers.
Mülk	Ottoman private property, usually land.
Mültezim	a.) Ottoman tax collector; b.) holder of an *iltizam* (which see).
Müsellem	Ottoman free peasant, landholding light cavalry.

N

Nomokanon	a.) Orthodox book of rules and regulations concerning the order in the church; b.) manual for confessors containing prescribed penances for given sins.

O

Ocak	*Yürük* military company or platoon; "hearth" (see *Yürük*).
Oikonomos	Athonite steward assistant of the *Protos* (which see).
Otechnik	Orthodox book of prayers to God the father.

P

Paşa	High, honorific Ottoman title of rank; high military rank (*e.g.*, a general).
Pavlikyani	Bulgarian descendents of medieval Paulician and Bogomil Orthodox heretics.
Peşkeş	Pseudo-legal bribe paid to higher authorities in return for an appointment to an office.
Philotimon	Cash gift due a newly appointed Orthodox prelate by all monastic and parish clergymen placed under the prelate's authority.
Piastre	Ottoman silver monetary unit representing a sum of *akçes* (which see), synonymous with *groş* (which see).
Pomagach	Bulgarian term for helper.
Pomak	Christian convert to Islam.
Pop	Orthodox priest.
Povest	Novelette; short story, usually hagiographical in nature.
Pronoia	Byzantine form of military feudalism.
Protos	Athonite chief political representative, head of the Karyes Assembly.

R

Rakiya	Plum or grape brandy.
Reaya	"Flock;" originally all subjects of the Ottoman state, later restricted to non-Muslims only.

S

Sancak	Ottoman provincial administrative unit forming a major subdivision of an *eyalet* (which see).
Sancakbey	Governor of a *sancak* (which see).
Saski	A professional metallurgist or miner from the area of Chiprovtsi; "Saxon."
Sbornik	"Collection;" Orthodox prayer book containing a miscellany of liturgical and didactical writings.
Sipahi	Cavalryman in the Ottoman military, either feudal or salaried.
Sipahilık	Ottoman pseudo-feudal system, primarily military in nature.
Skete	Small monastic cell or group of cells belonging to but separate from a larger monastery.
Sokolar	Raiser of falcons for the Ottoman nobility.
Sübor	Village fair held in honor of the local Orthodox patron saint.
Sufi	a.) Muslim mystic; b.) mystical school of the Muslim faith.
Sultan	Ottoman imperial title.
Sunni	Muslim belief based upon the four recognized "orthodox" legal schools.

Ş

Şeriat	Islamic sacred law.
Şeyh	Muslim spiritual leader in any of a number of religious, political and socio-economic fields.

T

Tapu	Tenant's lease; title deed to land.
Taxidiot	Itinerant monk, often a teacher, writer or artist.
Thaler	Western European monetary unit.
Timar	Ottoman *sipahilık* fief (see *Sipahilık*).
Tsar	Slavic imperial title.
Tüccar	Merchant involved in international and interregional trade.
Tuzcı	Producer of salt.

U

Ustabaşı	Head official of an Ottoman *esnaf* (which see); "First master."

V

Vakıf — Income-producing property bestowed by the Ottoman authorities or landholders on religious establishments as personal endowments.

Vali — Highest ranking provincial Ottoman commander-in-chief of professional military forces, replacing the *beylerbey* (which see).

Varosh — Christian quarters in an Ottoman urban center.

Vezir — Ottoman title for a governor-general or commander-in-chief, with the privilege to use the title, *paşa* (which see).

Vilayet — Ottoman regional taxation district.

Voevoda — Romanian princely title.

Voivoda — a.) Bulgarian *voynuk* village elder; b.) Bulgarian *haidut* leader (see *Voynuk* and *Haidut*).

Voynuk — Horse-breeder for the Ottoman imperial stables and for the military.

Y

Yamak — An auxiliary Janissary.

Yaya — Ottoman fief-holding infantry.

Yiğitbaşı — Second ranking official in an Ottoman *esnaf* (which see).

Z

Zeamet — Medium-sized Ottoman *sipahilik* fief (see *Sipahilik*).

Zimma — Guarantee of protection granted by Muslim authorities to their non-Muslim subjects under the *Şeriat* (which see).

Zimmi — "Protected persons;" non-Muslims subject to Muslim rule and protected by *zimma* (which see), usually denoting an inferior status.

Zitiye — Orthodox special "voluntary" tax assessed on the occasion of a metropolitan visitation.

Zograf — Painter; artist.

Ž

Župan — Serbian princely title.

Appendix II: *Statistical Tables*

Table 1. Population of the Ottoman Balkans by Religion, Early 16th Century

Religion	All *Sancaks*			Bulgarian *Sancaks**		
	Hane	Persons	% Total	*Hane*	Persons	% Total
Christian	814,777	4,073,885	81.0	333,909	1,669,545	33.2
Muslim	186,952	934,760	18.6	127,067	635,335	12.6
Jewish	4,134	20,670	0.4	3,243	16,265	0.3
Total	1,005,863	5,029,315	100.0	464,219	2,321,145	46.1

Source: Todorov and Velkov, Table 6, p. 31.
* Paşa, Sofia, Kyustendil, Vidin, Nikopol, Silistra, Viza and Çirmen *Sancaks*.

Table 2. Estimated Bulgarian Population During the 17th Century

Tax Class	Early 17th Century		Late 17th Century	
	Hane	Persons	*Hane*	Persons
Common	125,915	629,575	95,270	476,350
Privileged*	74,919	374,595	56,686	283,430
Total	200,834	1,004,170	151,956	759,780

Source: Grozdanova, Българската народност, Table 160, pp. 694-97, and regional tables, *passim*.
* It is estimated that as many as an additional 59.5% of common Bulgarian *hane* enjoyed privileged status.

Table 3. Estimated Bulgarian Population Change, 17th Century

	Change (Early to Late 17th Century)	
Tax Class	Hane	Persons
Common	-30,645	-153,225
Privileged	-18,233	-91,165
Total	-48,870	-244,390
% Change	-24.3	-24.3

Source: Table 2, above.

Table 4. Average Estimated Bulgarian Population, 17th Century

Tax Class	Hane	Persons
Common	110,593	552,965
Privileged	65,803	329,015
Total	176,396	881,980

Source: Data given in Table 1, above.

Table 5. Estimated Number of Bulgarian Settlements, 17th Century

Region	Documented Urban (% Region)	Documented Rural (% Region)	Documented Total (% All)	Projected* Rural (% Region)	Projected* Total[#] (% All)
Burgas	5 (3.6)	132 (96.4)	137 (6.7)	211 (97.7)	216 (6.6)
Gabrovo	—	32 (100.0)	32 (1.6)	51 (100.0)	51 (1.6)
Gorna Dzhumaya	1 (0.8)	121 (99.2)	122 (5.9)	193 (99.5)	194 (5.9)
Haskovo	—	63 (100.0)	63 (3.1)	100 (100.0)	100 (3.1)
Kŭrdzhali	—	71 (100.0)	71 (3.5)	113 (100.0)	113 (3.5)
Kutlovitsa	2 (2.1)	92 (97.9)	94 (4.4)	147 (99.3)	148 (4.5)
Kyustendil	2 (1.5)	130 (98.5)	132 (6.4)	207 (99.0)	209 (6.4)
Lovech	2 (7.7)	24 (92.3)	26 (1.2)	38 (95.0)	40 (1.2)
Pazardzhik	1 (1.3)	77 (98.7)	78 (3.8)	123 (99.2)	124 (3.8)
Pernik	—	117 (100.0)	117 (5.7)	187 (100.0)	187 (5.7)
Petrich	2 (6.7)	28 (93.3)	30 (1.4)	45 (95.7)	47 (1.4)
Pleven	2 (7.1)	26 (92.9)	28 (1.3)	41 (95.3)	43 (1.3)
Plovdiv	2 (1.9)	104 (98.1)	106 (5.1)	166 (98.8)	168 (5.1)
Razgrad-Shumen-Tŭrgovishte	2 (1.8)	108 (98.2)	110 (5.3)	172 (98.9)	174 (5.3)
Ruse	1 (2.2)	45 (97.8)	46 (2.2)	72 (98.6)	73 (2.2)
Silistra	2 (9.5)	19 (90.5)	21 (1.0)	30 (93.8)	32 (1.0)
Sliven	1 (1.2)	82 (98.8)	83 (4.0)	131 (99.2)	132 (4.0)
Smolyan	—	30 (100.0)	30 (1.5)	48 (100.0)	48 (1.5)
Sofia	2 (0.7)	284 (99.3)	286 (13.9)	453 (99.7)	455 (13.9)
Stara Zagora	1 (1.9)	51 (98.1)	52 (2.5)	81 (98.8)	82 (2.5)
Tŭrnovo	2 (1.9)	103 (98.1)	105 (5.1)	164 (98.8)	166 (5.1)
Varna	2 (2.8)	70 (97.2)	72 (3.5)	112 (98.2)	114 (3.5)
Vidin	1 (1.1)	89 (98.9)	90 (4.4)	142 (99.3)	143 (4.4)
Vratsa	1 (2.2)	44 (97.8)	45 (2.2)	70 (98.6)	71 (2.2)
Yambol	1 (1.2)	84 (98.8)	85 (4.1)	134 (99.3)	135 (4.1)
Total	35 (1.7)	2,086 (98.3)	2,121 (100.0)	3,332 (99.0)	3,366 (100.0)

Source: Grozdanova, Българската народност, regional tables, *passim*. Data lacking for three regions: Etropole, Zlatitsa and Ihtiman.

* Based on estimated 59.5% added of existing Bulgarian *hane* excluded from tax registers because of privileged status.

[#] Includes documented settlements.

Table 6. Average Size of Bulgarian Rural Settlements, 17th Century

Region	Documented Settlements	Average Settlements/ Tax Register*	Documented Hane [a]	Average Hane/ Tax Register*	Average Size/ Settlement Hane (Persons)	
Burgas	132	43.5	2,058	1,860.3	42.8	(214)
Gabrovo	32	22.8	782	545.5	23.9	(120)
Gorna Dzhumaya	121	47.4	2,026	1,733.8	36.6	(183)
Haskovo	63	17.8	592	545.4	30.6	(153)
Kŭrdzhali	71	32.0	1,381	1,309.3	40.9	(205)
Kutlovitsa	92	27.5	2,250	769.0	28.0	(140)
Kyustendil	130	40.0	1,604	932.7	23.3	(117)
Lovech	24	15.3	337	257.7	16.8	(84)
Pazardzhik	77	65.5	2,786	2,493.5	38.1	(191)
Pernik	177	32.7	1,045	743.7	22.7	(114)
Petrich°	28	28.0	405	1,347.5	48.1	(241)
Pleven	26	15.5	423	355.0	22.9	(115)
Plovdiv	104	72.0	2,144	1,652.5	23.0	(115)
Razgrad -Shumen - Tŭrgovishte	108	38.3	4,677	2,021.0	52.8	(264)
Ruse	45	12.8	505	414.8	32.4	(162)
Silistra	19	8.7	1,910	600.0	69.0	(345)
Sliven	82	43.7	2,054	1,755.0	40.2	(201)
Smolyan	30	12.0	366	253.7	21.1	(106)
Sofia	284	197.0	5,894	4,589.5	23.3	(117)
Stara Zagora	51	23.3	869	643.0	27.6	(138)
Tŭrnovo	103	66.5	3,306	2,829.5	42.5	(213)
Varna	70	25.8	2,831	1,236.0	47.9	(240)
Vidin	89	28.5	1,320	497.0	17.1	(86)
Vratsa	44	23.0	403	374.2	16.3	(82)
Yambol	84	32.5	1,691	1,018.3	31.3	(157)
Total	2,086	972.1	43,659	30,777.9	819.2	(4,103)
Average		83.4	38.9	1,746.4	1,231.1	32.8 (164)

Source: Grozdanova,Българската народност, regional tables, *passim*.

* Statistical average, based on extant information per settlement over total number of extant tax registers per region.

[a] Highest number of *hane* given over total number of extant tax registers per region.

° Data based on extrapolations made from that furnished in Table 65, Grozdanova, *Ibid.*, pp. 262-70.

Table 7. Average Size of Bulgarian Urban Settlements, 17th Century

Region	Number of Towns Total	Number of Towns w/Known Pop.	Towns	Estimated Bul. Population Hane	Estimated Bul. Population Persons
Burgas	5	4	Ahtopol	*172	860
			Burgas	*11	55
			Nesebŭr	—	—
			Pomorie	*300	1,500
			Sozopol	*298	1,490
Gorna Dzhumaya	1	1	Nevrokop	96	480
Kutlovitsa	2	1	Berkovitsa	10	50
			Chiprovtsi	—	—
Kyustendil	2	1	Dupnitsa	—	—
			Kyustendil	49	245
Lovech	2	—	Lovech	—	—
			Etropole	—	—
Pazardzhik	1	1	Pazardzhik	149	745
Petrich	2	1	Melnik	—	—
			Petrich	62	310
Pleven	2	1	Nikopol	469	2,345
			Pleven	—	—
Plovdiv	2	1	Plovdiv	*194	970
			Stanimaka	—	—
Razgrad- Shumen- Tŭrgovishte	2	2	Razgrad	40	200
			Shumen	169	845
Ruse	1	1	Ruse	213	1,065
Silistra	2	1	Silistra	615	3,075
			Tolbuhin	—	—
Sliven	1	1	Sliven	81	405
Sofia	2	2	Samokov	225	1,125
			Sofia	*164	820
Stara Zagora	1	1	Stara Zagora	50	250
Tŭrnovo	2	2	Svishtov	420	2,100
			Tŭrnovo	*170	850
Varna	2	2	Provadiya	18	90
			Varna	*355	1,775
Vidin	1	1	Vidin	70	350
Vratsa	1	—	Vratsa	—	—
Yambol	1	1	Yambol	31	155
Total	35	25		#4,431	22,155
Average Size	—	—		177.2	586

Source: Grozdanova, Българската народност, regional tables, *passim.*
* Documented *hane* halved to account for presence of non-Bulgarian Christian inhabitants.
\# This figure represents 2.5% of average total 17th century Bulgarian population given in Table 4, above.

Table 8. Registered* Has Settlements in the Bulgarian Lands, 17th Century

Region	Total Settlements	*Has* Settlements	% Total Settlements
Vratsa	45	28	62.2
Vidin	90	20	22.2
Lovech	25	5	20.0
Silistra	21	4	19.0
Pleven	28	3	10.7
Petrich	30	3	10.0
Kutlovitsa	93	9	9.7
Ruse	46	4	8.7
Razgrad - Shumen - Tŭrgovishte	110	5	4.5
Varna	72	3	4.2
Tŭrnovo	105	1	1.0
Gorna Dzhumaya	122	1	0.8
Sofia	286	2	0.7
Total	1,073	88	8.2

Source: Grozdanova, Българската народност, regional tables, *passim.*

* In *cizye* registers, includes only those liable for *cizye*.

Table 9. Registered* Vakıf Settlements in the Bulgarian Lands, 17th Century

Region	Total Settlements	Vakıf Settlements	% Total Settlements
Varna	72	24	33.3
Haskovo	63	21	33.3
Kŭrdzhali	71	23	32.4
Burgas	137	20	14.6
Sliven	83	12	14.5
Yambol	85	9	10.6
Smolyan	30	2	6.7
Pazardzhik	78	4	5.1
Plovdiv	106	5	4.8
Stara Zagora	52	2	3.8
Razgrad - Shumen - Tŭrgovishte	110	2	1.8
Total	887	124	14.0

Source: Grozdanova, *Българската народност*, regional tables, *passim.*

* In *cizye* registers, includes only those liable for *cizye*.

Table 10. Registered* Çiftlik Settlements, Bulgarian Lands, 17th Century

Region	Total Settlements	Çiftlik Settlements	% Total Settlements
Ruse	46	7	15.2
Varna	72	8	11.1
Razgrad - Shumen - Tŭrgovishte	110	6	5.5
Silistra	21	1	4.8
Tŭrnovo	105	4	3.8
Burgas	137	3	2.2
Stara Zagora	52	1	1.9
Sofia	286	4	1.4
Sliven	83	1	1.2
Plovdiv	106	1	0.9
Total	1,018	36	3.5

Source: Grozdanova, Българската народност, regional tables, *passim.*

* In *cizye* registers, includes only those liable for *cizye.*

Table 11. Distribution of Bulgarian Cultural Sites,* 17th Century

Type of Region	Regions			Settlements		Cultural Sites		
	Number	% Total	% w/ Sites	# in Region	% Total	Number	% Tot. Settles.	% Tot. Cul.Site
With Cultural Sites	17	68.0	100.0	1,531	71.4	184	8.6	100.0
w/Literary Cultural Sites	16	64.0	94.1	1,505	70.2	142	6.6	77.2
w/Art Cultural Sites	12	48.0	70.6	1,305	60.9	72	3.4	39.1
Without Cul. Sites¹	8	32.0	—	613	28.6	—	—	—
Total	25	100.0	100.0	2,144	100.0	184	8.6	100.0

Source: Data given in Table 5, above, and author's research.

* Settlements for which there exists extant literary and/or art evidence.

¹ Those regions are: Burgas, Haskovo, Kŭrdzhali, Razgrad-Shumen-Tŭrgovishte, Ruse, Smolyan, Varna and Yambol.

Table 12. 17th Century Bulgarian Cultural Sites by Region

Region	Settlements[#]	Cultural Sites	% Settlements	% Total Cultural Sites
Sofia	303	50	16.5	27.2
Lovech	41	20	48.8	10.9
Vratsa	58	16	27.6	8.7
Plovdiv	113	16	14.2	8.7
Pernik	122	13	10.7	7.1
Kyustendil	135	12	8.9	6.5
Pleven	36	12	33.3	6.5
Kutlovitsa	100	11	11.0	6.0
Tŭrnovo	108	10	9.3	5.4
Pazardzhik	81	5	6.2	2.8
Gabrovo	33	3	9.1	1.6
Gorna Dzhumaya	124	3	2.4	1.6
Sliven	83	3	3.6	1.6
Vidin	90	2	2.2	1.1
Stara Zagora	54	2	3.7	1.1
Silistra	20	1	5.0	0.5
Petrich	30	1	3.3	0.5
Unknown	—	4	—	2.2
Total	1,531	184	12.0	100.0

Source: Table 5, above

[#] Numbers of settlements per region modified by literary and art evidence.

Table 13. Types of Bulgarian Cultural Sites by Region, 17th Century

Region	Monastery	(% Sites)	Village	(% Sites)	Town	(% Sites)
Sofia	16	(32.0)	32	(64.0)	2	(4.0)
Pernik	3	(23.1)	10	(76.9)	—	—
Kyustendil	2	(16.7)	9	(75.0)	1	(8.3)
Vidin	—	—	1	(50.0)	1	(50.0)
Kutlovitsa	1	(9.1)	10	(90.9)	—	—
Vratsa	6	(37.5)	9	(56.3)	1	(6.2)
Pleven	—	—	10	(83.3)	2	(16.7)
Lovech	7	(35.0)	12	(60.0)	1	(5.0)
Gabrovo	1	(33.3)	2	(66.7)	—	—
Tŭrnovo	3	(30.0)	5	(50.0)	2	(20.0)
Silistra	—	—	—	—	1	(100.0)
G.Dzhumaya	—	—	3	(100.0)	—	—
Petrich	1	(100.0)	—	—	—	—
Plovdiv	4	(25.0)	11	(68.7)	1	(6.3)
Pazardzhik	3	(60.0)	1	(20.0)	1	(20.0)
S. Zagora	—	—	2	(100.0)	—	—
Sliven	—	—	3	(100.0)	—	—
Unknown	—	—	4	(100.0)	—	—
Total	47	(25.5)	124	(67.4)	13	(7.1)

Source: Author's research.

Table 14. Bulgarian Educational Activity by Type of Site, 17th Century

Type of Site	Educational Sites	% Total Site Type*	% Total Cultural Sites[#]
Monastery	28	59.6	15.2
Village	30	24.2	16.3
Town	11	84.6	6.0
Total	69	—	37.5

Source: Author's research.
* See Table 13, above.
[#] Total cultural sites = 184.

Table 15. Literary Evidence for Bulgarian Cultural Sites by Region, 17th Century

Region	Total Cultural Sites	Cultural Sites w/Lit. Evidence	% Cultural Sites Regional	(Total)	Extant Literary Citations
Sofia	50	36	72.0	(19.6)	67
Pernik	13	5	38.5	(2.7)	5
Kyustendil	12	7	58.3	(3.8)	24
Vidin	2	2	100.0	(1.1)	4
Kutlovitsa	11	6	54.5	(3.3)	9
Vratsa	16	13	81.2	(7.1)	27
Petrich	1	0	0.0	(0.0)	0
Pleven	12	12	100.0	(6.5)	16
Lovech	20	20	100.0	(10.9)	60
Gabrovo	3	3	100.0	(1.6)	3
Tŭrnovo	10	6	60.0	(3.3)	9
Silistra	1	1	100.0	(0.5)	1
G. Dzhumaya	3	2	66.6	(1.1)	3
Plovdiv	16	15	93.8	(8.2)	37
Pazardzhik	5	5	100.0	(2.7)	6
Stara Zagora	2	2	100.0	(1.1)	5
Sliven	3	3	100.0	(1.6)	5
Unknown	4	4	100.0	(2.2)	4
Total	184	142	—	(77.2)	285

Source: Author's research.

Table 16. Literary Evidence by Type of Cultural Site, 17th Century

Type of Site	Literary Citations	% Total Citations
Village	135	47.4
Monastery	113	39.6
Town	37	13.0
Total	285	100.0

Source: Author's research.

Table 17. Average Number of Citations per Type of Cultural Site, 17th Century

Type of Site	Total Sites	Total Citations	Average Citations/Site
Village	124	135	1.1
Monastery	47	113	2.4*
Town	13	37	2.8#
Total	184	285	2.1

Source: Author's research.

* Represents 2.2 times the village average.
# Represents 2.5 times the village average.

Table 18. 17th Century Bulgarian Literary Culture, Manuscript Types

Type of Ms	Manuscripts	% Total Mss
Menologion	52	19.9
Missal	28	10.7
Damaskin	27	10.4
Gospel(s)	24	9.2
Services	20	7.7
Sbornik	17	6.5
Lenten Offices	16	6.1
Psalter	15	5.7
Hymnal	14	5.4
Book of Hours	13	5.0
Prologue	7	2.7
Canons	6	2.3
Acts of the Apostles	5	1.9
Others	17	6.5
Total	261	100.0

Source: Author's research.

Table 19. Bulgarian Subjects in Bulgarian Literary Culture, 17th Century

Subject	Type of Literary Work				Total Citations	%Base*	%Total Cits.
	Life	Service	Antiphon	Canon			
Petka Tŭrnovska	11	7	14	—	32	69.6	40.0
Ivan Rilski	11	6	6	1	24	52.2	30.0
Kiril Filosof	—	2	6	—	8	18.0	10.0
Ilarion Mŭglenski	4	—	3	—	7	15.2	8.6
Ioakim Osogovski	1	2	2	—	5	10.9	6.3
Mihail Voin	3	—	—	—	3	6.5	3.8
Georgi Novi Sofiiski	1	—	—	—	1	2.2	1.3
Total	31	17	31	1	80		
% Base*	67.4	37.0	67.4	2.2			
% Total Citations	38.7	21.3	38.7	1.3			

Source: Author's research.

* Base = 46 manuscripts = 17.6% of total extant 17th century Bulgarian literary products (261).

Table 20. Contents of 17th Century Bulgarian Manuscript Notations

Type of Content	Citations		% Ms Notations*	
Autobiographical	152		60.0	
Biographical	188		74.3	
Cultural Patrons		85		33.6
Monastery Abbots		35		13.8
Parish Priests		27		10.7
Ottoman Rulers		22		8.7
Church Prelates		19		7.5
Social	88		34.7	
Cultural/Social Activity		38		15.0
Commodity Prices		22		8.7
Educational Activity		17		6.7
Muslim Reactionary Acts		11		4.3
Chronicle	43		16.9	
Military Events		16		6.3
Benign Natural Phenomena		12		4.7
Famines & Disease		12		4.7
Extended Accounts		3		1.2
Total	471		186.2	

   Source: Author's research.
   * Total extant Ms notations = 253.

Table 21. Social Position of 17th Century Bulgarian Literary Intelligentsia*

Type of Literary Field	Persons (% Total)	Monks (% Type)	Priests (% Type)	Lay (% Type)	Unknown (% Type)
Writer -Copyist	47 (41.2)	13 (27.7)	19 (40.4)	4 (8.5)	11 (23.4)
Annotator	48 (42.1)	10 (20.8)	20 (41.7)	10 (20.8)	8 (16.7)
Bookbinder	19 (16.7)	8 (42.1)	1 (5.3)	8 (42.1)	2 (10.5)
Total	114 (100.0)	31 (27.2)	40 (35.1)	22 (19.3)	21 (18.4)

Source: Author's research.

* Based on extant positive identification.

Table 22. Major Centers of Bulgarian Literary Culture, 17th Century

Cultural Site	Site Citations	% Total Citations*	% Total Notations#
Rila Monastery	16	5.6	6.3
Sofia	17	6.0	6.7
Etropole	41	14.4	16.2
Vratsa	15	5.3	5.9
Karlovo - Adzhar - Kuklen Monastery	23	8.1	9.1
Total	112	39.4	44.2

Source: Author's research.

* Total citations = 285.

Total notations = 253.

Table 23. Bulgarian Art Cultural Sites, 17th Century

Region	Total Cultural Sites	Cultural Sites w/Art Evidence	% Cultural Sites Regional	(Total)
Sofia	50	23	44.0	(14.5)
Pernik	13	7	53.8	(4.4)
Kyustendil	12	7	58.3	(4.4)
Vidin	2	1	50.0	(0.6)
Kutlovitsa	11	7	63.6	(4.4)
Vratsa	16	7	43.8	(4.4)
Lovech	20	7	35.0	(4.4)
Tŭrnovo	10	6	60.0	(3.8)
Petrich	1	1	100.0	(0.6)
Gorna Dzhumaya	3	1	33.3	(0.6)
Plovdiv	16	4	25.0	(2.5)
Pazardzhik	5	1	20.0	(0.6)
Total	159	72	—	(45.3)

Source: Author's research.

Table 24. Social Position of Bulgarian Artists, 17th Century

Field of Art	Persons (% Total)	Clergy (% Field)	Lay (% Field)	Unknown (% Field)
Mural Painting	6 (25.0)	3 (50.0)	2 (33.3)	1 (16.7)
Icon Painting	5 (20.8)	1 (20.0)	—	4 (80.0)
Metalworking	13 (54.2)	1 (7.7)	1 (7.7)	11 (84.6)
Total	24 (100.0)	5 (20.8)	3 (12.5)	16 (66.7)

Source: Author's research.

Table 25. Social Position of Total Bulgarian Cultural Intelligentsia, 17th Century

Cultural Field*	Persons (% Total)	Clergy (% Field)	Lay (% Field)	Unknown (% Field)
Literature	114 (82.6)	71 (62.3)	22 (19.3)	21 (18.4)
Art	24 (17.4)	5 (20.8)	3 (12.5)	16 (66.7)
Total	138 (100.0)	76 (55.1)	25 (18.1)	37 (26.8)

Source: Author's research.
* Educational activity included within listed fields.

Table 26. Social Position of Bulgarian Cultural Patrons, 17th Century

Cultural Field	Persons (% Total)	Clergy (% Field)	Lay (% Field)	Unknown (% Field)
Literature	126 (79.7)	37 (29.4)	83 (65.8)	6 (4.8)
Art	32 (20.3)	12 (37.5)	20 (62.5)	—
Total	158 (100.0)	49 (31.0)	103 (65.2)	6 (3.8)

Source: Author's research.

Appendix III: *Chronology*

Seventeenth Century Events in the Ottoman Empire and the Bulgarian Lands

Ottoman Empire		Bulgarian Lands	
1588-1612	War with Safavid Persia		
		1590-1650	Period of extensive church renovation throughout western Bulgarian lands
1593-1606	Long War with Habsburg Austria and Wallachia		
1595-1603	Reign of Sultan Mehmed III	1595	Catholic Franciscan missionaries arrive in Chiprovtsi
1596-1608	Calali revolt in Anatolia	1596-1617	Renovations of Kurilo Monastery, Sofia region
		1596	Vratsa sacked by Wallachians
		1598	First Tŭrnovo Uprising; church of "St. Nikolai," Vukovo, Kyustendil region
		1601-1674	Life of Petŭr Bogdan Bakshich, Bulgarian Catholic missionary leader
		1601-1671	Flourishing of Chiprovtsi School of goldsmithing
		1602	Renovation of Karlukovo Monastery, Vratsa region
1603-1617	Reign of Sultan Ahmet I		
1603	Popular revolt against the *devşirme* regime in Istanbul		

		1605-1618	Literary activity in "The Holy Trinity" Monastery, Vratsa
1606	Treaty of Zsitvatorok with Austria		
1609	Agrarian laws	1609	Presence of 37,627 registered Janissaries
1611	Greek uprising in Epiros	1611	Renovation of Kremikovtsi Monastery, Sofia region
		1612-1674	Life of Filip Stanislavov, Bulgarian Catholic literary figure
		1614	Village church of Dobŭrsko built
		1616-1644	Extant evidence for life of Daniil Etropolski (Mazach)
		1616-1617	Plague in Plovdiv region
1617-1618	Reign of Sultan Mustafa I	1617-1674	Life of Petŭr Parchevich, Bulgarian Catholic political leader
		1617	New icons in Dragalevtsi Monastery, Sofia region
1618-1622	Reign of Sultan Osman II	1618	Last extant evidence for life of artist Pimen Zografski; *haidut* activity in Sofia region
1620-1621	War with Poland	1620	New icons and an organ at Dragalevtsi Monastery, Sofia region; plague in Sofia and Plovdiv regions
1622	Osman II assassinated by rebellious Janissaries		
		1622	Plague in Sofia and Plovdiv regions
1622-1623	Second reign of Mustafa I		
1623-1640	Reign of Sultan Murad IV		
1624-1630	War with Persia; renewal of Calali revolts; Arab revolts in Egypt, Yemen and Lebanon		

IN THE SEVENTEENTH CENTURY

		1624-1641	Iliya Marinov heads Catholic mission in Bulgarian lands, marking beginning of native Bulgarian leadership in the movement
1624	Loss of Baghdad to Persians		
		1626	Alino Monastery, Sofia region, built
		1627-1628	Plague in Sofia, Kutlovitsa and Nevrokop regions
		1628	Rila Monastery delegation to Muscovite court
1629-1632	Janissary revolts in Anatolia and Istanbul		
		1630-1658	Zenith of the Etropole Monastery Literary School
		1630	Adzhar village school founded by *pop* Zhivko
1633-1634	War with Poland		
1634	Campaign against Persia; capture of Erivan and Tabriz		
		1635	Rila Monastery in state of disrepair
1638	Recapture of Baghdad	1638-1674	Extant evidence for the life of Avram Dimitrievich from Karlovo
1639	Treaty of Kasr-ı Şirin ends 150 years of warfare between Ottomans and Safavids		
1640-1648	Reign of Sultan Ibrahim	1640	*Description of Bulgaria* by Petŭr Bogdan
		1641-1642	Plague in Sofia, Kutlovitsa and Nikopol regions
		1641	Chiprovtsi council of Catholic missionaries concerned with

Appendix III: Chronology 227

			pavlikyani issues; renovation of "St. Panteleimon" church in Vidin
		1644	Renovation of "SS. Petŭr and Pavel" church in Svishtov
1645-1670	War with Venice		
1645	Invasion of Crete	1645	Beginning of beadroll at Kokalyane Monastery, Sofia region
		1646-1674	Political missions of Parchevich to European courts in behalf of Bulgarians
1648-1687	Reign of Mehmed IV	1648	Etropole Monastery beadroll begun by *monah* Teodosii
1650-1657	Venetian blockade of the Dardanelles		
1651	Defeat in naval Battle of Para; rebellion in Istanbul		
		1651	*Abagar* published in Rome by Filip Stanislavov
		1652-1686	Extant evidence for the life of Nedyalko from Adzhar
		1652	Church in village of Vŭrbovo, Kutlovitsa region, built
1653-1656	Political anarchy in Istanbul		
		1655-1725	Life of Georgi Peiyachevich, Bulgarian Catholic and revolutionary leader
1656-1683	Köprülü Grand Vezirate		
1656	Naval defeat near Dardanelles; Venice captures Tenedos and Limnos		
1657	Recapture of Limnos and Tenedos, breaking		

IN THE SEVENTEENTH CENTURY

	the Venetian blockade of the Dardanelles		
1658-1670	War in Transylvania		
1658-1659	Rebellions in Anatolia and Syria		
1663	Austria enters war as Venetian ally		
1664	Defeat by Austria at St. Gotthard; Truce of Vasvár with Austria		
		1666-1699	Period of heightened anti-Christian Muslim reaction
1669	Capture of Iraklion (Candia) on Crete		
1670	Peace with Venice; acquisition of Crete		
		1670	Execution of Bishop Visarion in Smolyan
		1671	Plague in Kutlovitsa region
1672-1676	War with Poland		
1673	Defeat of Hotin	1673-1675	Plague in northeastern and eastern Bulgarian lands
		1674	Plague in Sofia region
1676	Peace of Żurawno (Ottoman Empire reaches its maximum extent in Europe)		
1677-1681	First war with Russia		
1681	Peace of Radzyń (Ottoman Empire loses Eastern Ukraine — first permanent territorial loss)		
1682-1699	War with Austria	1682-1683	Renovation of Etropole Monastery
1683	Second siege of Vienna		
1684	Formation of Third Holy League against the Turks (Austria, Venice and Poland)		
1685	Approximate end of the *devşirme*		

		1685	Rila Monastery expands properties; last *devşirme* of note
1686	Defeat by Austria at First Battle of Zenta; loss of Buda to Austria; loss of most of the Morea to Venice		
		1686	Second Tŭrnovo Uprising; Adzhar *damaskin* of Nedyalko and his son, Filip
1687-1691	Reign of Sultan Süleyman II		
1687	Defeat by Austria at Second Battle of Mohács; First Russian siege of Azov		
		1687	Presence of 70,394 registered Janissaries
1688	Loss of Belgrad to Austria	1688	Chiprovtsi Uprising
1689	Loss of Vidin and Niš to Austria		
		1689	March of Crimean Tatars across northern Bulgarian lands, resulting in mass Islamic conversions in northeastern, eastern and northwestern Bulgarian lands; flight of Chiprovtsi Catholic survivors to Wallachia and Transylvania, ending Catholic mission in Bulgarian lands; *haidut* activity in Kutlovitsa, Plovdiv and Pazardzhik regions; renovation at Dragalevtsi Monastery, Sofia region
		1690-1696	Flourishing of Kuklen Monastery, Plovdiv region, as literary center

IN THE SEVENTEENTH CENTURY

1690	Recapture of Belgrad, Niš and Vidin; defeat of Austria in Transylvania		
		1690	Chronicle note of *pop* Petŭr from Mirkovo; *haidut* activity in Vidin and Pleven regions
1691-1695	Reign of Sultan Ahmet II		
1693	New tax laws make male individual, rather than *hane*, basic taxation unit		
1695-1703	Reign of Sultan Mustafa II	1695-1696	Extant evidence for life of Krŭstyu Gramatik at Kuklen Monastery
1696	Loss of Azov to Russia		
1697	Defeat by Austria at Second Battle of Zenta		
		1698	*Haidut* activity in Vidin and Pleven regions
1699	Treaty of Sremski Karlovci (Karlowitz) — loss of the Morea and most of Dalmatia to Venice; loss of most of Hungary to Austria; loss of Podolia to Poland		

Notes

Introduction

¹ This introductory essay of conditions in the Balkans under Ottoman rule is based extensively on material found in the following studies: P.F. Sugar, *Southeastern Europe under Ottoman Rule, 1354-1804* (Seattle, 1977); D. Kosev, *et. al.,* [eds.], Историята на България [History of Bulgaria], IV, Османско владичество, XV-XVIII в. [Ottoman Rule, 15th-18th Cen.] (Sofia, 1983); M. Macdermott, *A History of Bulgaria, 1393-1885* (New York, 1962); H. Inalcik, *The Ottoman Empire: The Classical Age, 1300-1600* (London, 1973); H.A.R. Gibb and H. Bowen, *Islamic Society and the West*, I, *Islamic Society in the Eighteenth Century,* 2 pts (London, 1965-67 [2nd. ed.]); T.H. Papadopoullos, *Studies and Documents Relating to the History of the Greek Church and People under Turkish Domination* (Brussels, 1952); L.S. Stavrianos, *The Balkans Since 1453* (New York, 1958); A.H. Lybyer, *The Government of the Ottoman Empire in the Time of Suleiman the Magnificent* (Cambridge, 1913); and S.J. Shaw, *History of the Ottoman Empire and Modern Turkey,* I, *Empire of the Gazis: The Rise and Decline of the Ottoman Empire, 1280-1808* (Cambridge, 1976).

Chapter 1. The Social Position of the Bulgarians

¹ E. Grozdanova, Българската народност през XVII век. Демографско изследване [The Bulgarian Nationality During the 17th Century. Demographic Study] (Sofia, 1989).
² *Ibid.,* pp. 536-41.
³ *Ibid.,* pp. 542-43.
⁴ *Ibid.,* p. 502.
⁵ *Ibid.,* p. 504.
⁶ For the *tapu* arrangement and its implications, see Tsvetkova, "Typical features of the Ottoman social and economic structure in South-Eastern Europe during the 14th to the 16th centuries," *EH*, IX (Sofia, 1979), pp. 139-41.
⁷ For an outline of the Bulgarians' obligations to the Ottoman central authorities, see V. Mutafchieva, "De l'exploitation féodale dans les terres de population bulgare sous la domination turque aux XVe et XVIe siècles," *EH*, I, (Sofia, 1960), pp. 147-48.
⁸ See H. Inalcik, "The Ottoman Decline and Its Effects upon the *Reaya*," *IIe Congrès international des études du Sud-est européen,* III, *Histoire* (Athens, 1978), p. 75.
⁹ See: *Ibid.,* pp. 75-76; Mutafchieva, "De l'exploitation féodale," p. 149.

[10] See Grozdanova, *Българската народност*, pp. 57f, for a detailed discussion of Ottoman household tax units and their implication on demographic studies. The commonly accepted average size of a Bulgarian *hane* during the seventeenth century is five persons.

[11] *Ibid.*, pp. 682-84.

[12] *Ibid.*, p. 688.

[13] See S. Gerlach, *Дневник на едно пътуване до Османската порта в Цариград* [Daybook of a Journey to the Ottoman Porte in Constantinople], M. Kiselincheva, trans., (Sofia, 1976), p. 68. For documentation concerning Bulgarian *voynuks*, see: D.G. Gŭlŭbov [ed.], «Османо-турски извори за българската история [Ottoman Turkish Sources for Bulgarian History], I, Няколко стари османо-турски държавни документи относно войниганите» [Some Old Ottoman Turkish State Documents Regarding the *Voynuks*], *ГСУифф*, XXXIV (1937-38), [offprint], 70 p.; *id.* [ed.], «Османотурски извори за българската история [Ottoman Turkish Sources for Bulgarian History], III, Три стари закона и други османотурски документи относно войниганите» [Three Old Laws and Other Ottoman Turkish Documents Regarding the *Voynuks*], *ГСУифф*, XXXIX (1942-1943), [offprint], 98 p.; and B. Tsvetkova [ed.], *Извори за българската история* [Sources for Bulgarian History], XX, *Турски извори за българската история* [Turkish Sources for Bulgarian History], V, (Sofia, 1974), which is devoted to documents pertaining to the *voynuks*.

[14] See Grozdanova, *Българската народност*, pp. 427-28.

[15] For the mining industry in the Bulgarian lands, see: V. Nikolaev, *Характерът на минните предприятия и режимът на рударския труд в нашите земи през XVI, XVII и XVIII в.* [The Character of Mining Enterprises and the Regime of Ore Mining in Our Lands During the 16th, 17th and 18th Cen.] (Sofia, 1954); O. Davies, "Ancient Mining in the Central Balkan," *Revue internationale des études balkaniques*, III (1953), pp. 405-18; G.K. Georgiev, *Старата железодобивна индустрия в България* [The Old Metallurgical Industries in Bulgaria] (Sofia, 1978); and S. Draganova, «Неизвестен турски документ за положението на рударското население в Самоковската каза през първата половина на XVII век» [An Unknown Turkish Document for the Position of the Ore-mining Population in Samokov *kaza* During the First Half of the 17th Century], *ИДА*, XX (1970), pp. 189-95.

[16] The standard study of the Bulgarian *celeps* is B. Tsvetkova, "Le service des *celep* et le ravitaillement en bétail dans l'Empire ottoman (XVe-XVIIIe s.)," *EH*, III, (Sofia, 1966), pp. 145-72. Also see her "Les *celep* et leur role dans la vie économique des Balkans a l'époque ottomane," *Studies in the Economic History of the Middle East* (London, 1970), pp. 172-92.

[17] Tsvetkova, "Le service des *celep*," p. 158.

[18] On average, "free" *hane* paid about 30 *akçes* less in yearly taxes than did common *hane*. See Grozdanova, *Българската народност*, p. 693.

[19] *Ibid.*, p. 688.

[20] *Ibid.*, 685.

[21] Tsvetkova, "Typical Features," pp. 136-37.

²² S. Dimitrov, E. Grozdanova and S. Andreev, [eds.], *Извори за българската история* [Sources for Bulgarian History], XXVI, *Турски извори за българската история* [Turkish Sources for Bulgarian History], VII, (Sofia, 1986), p. 14.

²³ Grozdanova, *Българската народност*, pp. 684-85.

²⁴ The Bulgarian village commune has received a good deal of attention by Bulgarian scholars. The undisputed specialist in this topic is E. Grozdanova. Her studies: *Българската селска община през XV-XVIII век* [The Bulgarian Village Commune During the 15th-18th Centuries] (Sofia, 1979); "Les fondements économiques de la commune rurale dans les regions bulgares (XVe-XVIIIe s.)," *EB*, 1 (1974), pp. 30-45; «Ролята на традиционната селска община за опазване на българската народност и народностното самосъзнание» [The Role of the Traditional Village Commune for Protecting the Bulgarian Nationality and National Self-Consciousness], *Българската нация през Възраждането. Сборник от изследвания* [The Bulgarian Nation During the Revival. Collection of Studies], H. Hristov, ed., (Sofia, 1980), pp. 139-77; and «Същност и роля на българската селска община през XV-XVIII век» [The Nature and Role of the Bulgarian Village Commune During the 15th-18th Centuries], in *България 1300. Институции и държавни традиция* [Bulgaria 1300. Institutions and State Traditions], II, (Sofia, 1982), pp. 407-12, have been consulted extensively for our study. See also Ts. Georgieva, «Ролята на българските социални институции в условията на османското владичество» [The Role of Bulgarian Social Institutions under the Conditions of Ottoman Rule], in *България 1300*, III, (Sofia, 1983), pp. 511-18.

²⁵ See: Georgieva, *Ibid.*, p. 514; Grozdanova, «Същност и роля,» pp. 407-08; *id.*, "Les fondements économiques," p. 44. Communal elder titles in privileged service group villages might also vary. For example, *voynuk* elders often used the terms *voivoda* or *çaribaşı*.

²⁶ Collective responsibility went further than tax collection. It also applied to criminal activity. For example, in 1617 a *sipahi*, Mehmed *bey*, was assassinated on lands belonging to the village of Birimirtsi, near Sofia. During the investigation and hearings, the inhabitants of the village were held responsible by the authorities, and the village's communal officials were incarcerated until the actual murderer was found. See Grozdanova, "Les fondements économiques," p. 34.

²⁷ See G.D. Gŭlŭbov [ed.], *Турски извори за историята на правото в българските земи* [Turkish Sources for the History of Law in the Bulgarian Lands], I, (Sofia, 1961), pp. 78-79, 129, 140, 157, 249.

²⁸ See Grozdanova, "Les fondements économiques," pp. 34-37. On *voynuk* or *vakıf* lands, the commune had the legal right to reclaim and redistribute vacant *bashtina* plots up to a year after they fell vacant. If the lands were not so claimed within that time, outsiders could buy them, granted that the required permission of the authorities was received.

²⁹ Gŭlŭbov [ed.], *Турски извори за историята на правото*, pp. 140, 157.

³⁰ Grozdanova, "Les fondements économiques," p. 35.

³¹ B. Tsvetkova, "L'évolution du régime féodal turc de la fin du XVIe jusqu'à milieu du XVIIIe siècle," *EH*, I, (Sofia, 1960), p. 177.

³² For studies on the effects of the inflation on the Ottoman Empire, see: S. Razaj, "Counterfeit of Money on the Balkan Peninsula from the XV to the XVII Century," *Balcanica*, I (Belgrad, 1970), pp. 71-79; and H. Inalcik, "L'empire ottoman," *Actes du Premier congrès international des études balkaniques et Sud-est européenes*, III, (Sofia, 1969), pp. 94f.

³³ An insightful summary of growing Ottoman administrative corruption can be found in Inalcik, "The Ottoman Decline," pp. 77-78.

³⁴ E. Radushev, «Институции на османския феодализъм на Балканите XVII-XVIII век» [Institutions of Ottoman Feudalism in the Balkans 17th-18th Centuries], in *България 1300*, II, p. 456.

³⁵ Inalcik, "The Ottoman Decline," pp. 87-88.

³⁶ Grozdanova, *Българската народност*, p. 682.

³⁷ Radushev, p. 456.

³⁸ Ts. Georgieva, «Развитие и характер на кръвния данък в българските земи» [Development and Character of the Blood Tax in the Bulgarian Lands], *ГСУфиф*, LXI, 3 (1968), pp. 48-49. Her major study, *Еничарите в българските земи* [The Janissaries in the Bulgarian Lands] (Sofia, 1988), constitutes the standard work on the subject.

³⁹ P.H. Petrov, *Съдбоносни векове за българската народност. Края на XIV век—1912 година* [Fateful Centuries for the Bulgarian Nationality. The End of the 14th Century-1912] (Sofia, 1975), p. 76.

⁴⁰ See: Inalcik, "The Ottoman Decline," p. 86; Tsvetkova, *Извънредни данъци и държавни повинности в българските земи под турска власт* [Extraordinary Taxes and State Services in the Bulgarian Lands under Turkish Rule] (Sofia, 1958), pp. 20-22, 37.

⁴¹ Inalcik, *Ibid.*, pp. 73, 75, 86.

⁴² Mutafchieva, "De l'exploitation féodale," pp. 154-55.

⁴³ Tsvetkova, "L'évolution du régime féodal," p. 201.

⁴⁴ For conditions in the Bulgarian countryside at this time, see: S. Fischer-Galati [ed.], *Man, State, and Society in East European History* (New York, 1970), pp. 72-75; E. Grozdanova, «Турски документи за данъка джизие през XVII-XVIII в. като извори за историята на балканските страни» [Turkish Documents for the Tax *Cizye* During the 17th-18th Cen. as Sources for the History of the Balkan Countries], *ИДА*, XVIII (1970), pp. 289-303; R. Stoikov, «Български селища с населението им в турски регистри за джизие от XVII в.» [Bulgarian Settlements with Their Inhabitants in Turkish Registers for *Cizye* From the 17th Cen.], *ИДА*, VIII (1964), pp. 147-64; and N. Todorov [ed.], *Положението на българския народ под турско робство. Сборник с документи и материали* [The Position of the Bulgarian People under the Turkish Yoke. Collection of Documents and Materials] (Sofia, 1953), *passim*.

⁴⁵ D.I. Polivyanni, *Средновековният български град през XIII-XIV век. Очерци* [The Medieval Bulgarian City During the 13th-14th Centuries. Essays], I. Ilieva, trans, (Sofia, 1989), provides the latest serious study of the pre-Ottoman Bulgarian urban environment.

[46] For a good, brief general overview of the material orientalization of Bulgarian society under the Turks, see N. Genchev, *Българската култура XV-XIX в. Лекции* [Bulgarian Culture 15th-19th Cen. Lectures] (Sofia, 1988), pp. 134-35.

[47] Urban population statistics for the seventeenth century can be found in Grozdanova, *Българската народност, passim;* Evliya Celebi, *Пътепис* [Travel Account], S. Dimitrov, trans., (Sofia, 1972), *passim;* and P. Dŭrvingov [ed.], *Евлия Челеби и западните български земи. Евлия Челеби и книжовните му трудове. Турция и българите в XV, XVI, XVII в.* [Evlia Celebi and the Western Bulgarian Lands. Evlia Celebi and His Literary Works. Turkey and the Bulgarians in the 15th, 16th, 17th Cen.] (Sofia, 1943), *passim.* The standard work on Ottoman urban society in the Balkans is N. Todorov, *The Balkan City, 1400-1900* (Seattle, 1983), and although he furnishes no data for the seventeenth century, he provides data from the sixteenth on pp. 53-55.

[48] See G. Tankut, "The Spatial Distribution of Urban Activities in the Ottoman City," in *Structure sociale et développement culturel des villes Sud-est européennes et adriatiques aux XVIIe-XVIIIe siècles* (Bucharest, 1975), pp. 245-65.

[49] Grozdanova, *Българската народност,* pp. 649-54.

[50] *Ibid.,* pp. 649, 654-56.

[51] S. Pŭrveva, «Към демографския облик на град Никопол през 1693 г.» [On the Demographic Aspect of the City of Nikopol During 1693], in *300 години Чипровско въстание (Принос към историята на българите през XVII в.)* [300 Years Chiprovtsi Uprising (Contribution to the History of the Bulgarians During the 17th Cen.)] (Sofia, 1988), pp. 26-27.

[52] See Grozdanova, *Българската народност,* pp. 655-56; V. Paskaleva, «Общинското самоуправление в българските земи и други балкански провинции на Османската империя от XV в. до Берлинския конгрес» [Communal Self-Government in the Bulgarian Lands and Other Balkan Provinces of the Ottoman Empire From the 15th Cen. to the Congress of Berlin], in *България 1300,* II, p. 502. *Mahalles* were not exclusively an urban phenomenon in the Bulgarian lands of the seventeenth century. They were sometimes found in larger villages, especially in those with a mixed Christian and Muslim population, in which case each would possess its own *mahalle.* Village *mahalles* were usually designated as "upper," "middle" (if present) and "lower" followed by the name of the common village (for example, Gorni and Dolni Lozen in the Sofia region). See *Ibid.,* p. 649. Village *mahalles* could also develop when the size of the village population became too large to permit smooth operation of the village commune, or to differentiate two or more clans, in which case the *mahalles* were frequently subdivided into smaller ones along family lines. See Grozdanova, *Ibid.,* p. 658.

[53] H. Inalcik, "The Foundations of the Ottoman Economic-Social System in Cities," *Studia balcanica,* III, *Le ville balkanique, XV-XIX ss.* (Sofia, 1970), p. 22.

[54] *Ibid.,* pp. 22-23.

[55] For *esnaf* administration, see K.H. Stoyanov, *Българските еснафи през турското робство (История, организация дейност)* [Bulgarian *Esnafs* During the Turkish Yoke (History, Organizational Effort)] (Varna, 1943), pp. 35-38. Also see Todorov, *The Balkan City,* pp. 113f.

⁵⁶ See Stoyanov, *Ibid.*, p. 33; Todorov, *Ibid.*, p. 115; Georgieva, «Ролята на българските социални институции,».p. 515.

⁵⁷ Z.S. Plyakov, «Градското занаятчийско производство в българските земи през XV-XVII в.» [Urban Artisan Production in the Bulgarian Lands During the 15th-17th Cen.], *ИПр*, 6 (1973), pp. 74f.

⁵⁸ *Ibid.*, pp. 70-72, 74.

⁵⁹ *Ibid.*, pp. 77, 79-80.

⁶⁰ *Ibid.*, p. 81.

⁶¹ For the general position of the Ottoman merchant, see Inalcik, "The Foundations of the Ottoman Economic-Social System," pp. 18f.

⁶² For the regional trade role of the merchants in the Bulgarian lands during the seventeenth century, see the standard work on the subject by S. Panova, *Българските търговци през XVII век* [Bulgarian Merchants During the 17th Century] (Sofia, 1980), pp. 40-42.

⁶³ The economic role played by Dubrovnik merchants in the Bulgarian lands during the sixteenth and seventeenth centuries has been studied profusely. *Ibid.*, pp. 55f, provides an excellent overview for the seventeenth century. An early but still valuable general study is Iv. Sakŭzov, *Стопанските връзки между Дубровник и българските земи през 16 и 17 столетие* [Commercial Relations Between Dubrovnik and the Bulgarian Lands During the 16th and 17th Centuries] (Sofia, 1930).

⁶⁴ Panova, pp. 59-60.

⁶⁵ *Ibid.*, p. 64.

⁶⁶ *Ibid.*, pp. 75f, 91.

⁶⁷ *Ibid.*, pp. 90-91; T. Stoianovich, "The Conquering Balkan Orthodox Merchant," *Journal of Economic History*, XX (Summer, 1960), p. 281.

⁶⁸ See the data in Todorov, *The Balkan City*, pp. 89-91, which, unfortunately, dates from the sixteenth century and not from towns within the Bulgarian lands.

⁶⁹ Pŭrveva, pp. 29f.

⁷⁰ N. Todorov, "The Socio-Economic Life of Sofia in the 16th and 17th Centuries," in *La ville balkanique sous les Ottomans (XV-XIXe s.)* (London, 1977), pp. 10-13, and the table on p. 11.

⁷¹ Todorov, *The Balkan City*, p. 83.

⁷² *Ibid.*, p. 89.

⁷³ *Ibid.*, pp. 70-71. The new artisan migrants often created tension between themselves and the members of established *esnafs*. Apparently, not all newly arriving artisans were immediately entered into the appropriate guilds but, rather, set up shops in competition with the guild shops. This situation often took the decision of the city *kadı* in response to guild complaints to resolve, usually with the new artisans being merged into the existing guilds. See *Ibid.*, pp. 116f.

⁷⁴ *Ibid.*, pp. 72-73; Tsvetkova, "Typical Features," p. 140.

⁷⁵ For this transformation of the role of the church among the Bulgarians, see H. Gandev, «Демократизация на българската църква (XV-XVII в.)» [Democratization of the Bulgarian Church (15th-17th Cen.)], *Векове* [Centuries], 1 (1984), pp. 5-6.

⁷⁶ See Grozdanova, *Българската народност*, pp. 594-96, 601.

⁷⁷ See: Georgieva, «Ролята на българските социални институции,» p. 514; E. Floreva, *Средновековни стенописи. Вуково. 1598 г.* [Medieval Wall Paintings. Vukovo. 1598] (Sofia, 1987), p. 13; Grozdanova, «Ролята на традиционната селска община,» pp. 155-59.

⁷⁸ O. Todorova, «Православието в българските земи през XVII в.» [Orthodoxy in the Bulgarian Lands During the 17th Cen.], in *300 години Чипровско въстание*, pp. 144-45.

⁷⁹ Grozdanova, *Българската селска община*, pp. 86f; Gandev, «Демократизация,» p. 8.

⁸⁰ See: G. Neshev, «Православните институции през XV-XVIII в.» [Orthodox Institutions During the 15th-18th Cen.], *Православието в България* [Orthodoxy in Bulgaria] (Sofia, 1974), p. 134; M. Bur-Markovska, «За връзките между християнското население и манастирите» [On the Relations Between the Christian Population and the Monasteries], in *България 1300*, II, p. 420.

⁸¹ For the economy of Bulgarian monasteries during the Ottoman period, see Iv. Sakŭzov, «Манастирското стопанство през турско време» [The Monastic Economy During Turkish Times], *Духовна култура* [Spiritual Culture], XXVI and XXVII (1925). [offprint], pp. 18f.

⁸² Gandev, «Демократизация,» p. 8.

Chapter 2. Threats to Bulgarian Orthodox Culture Posed by Ottoman Society

¹ B. Tsonev, *Опис* I, #433. Petŭr's note was also published in its entirety by M. Drinov in his «Български летописен разказ от края на XVII век» [Bulgarian Chronicle Tale from the End of the 17th Century], *Избрани съчинения* [Collected Works], II, (Sofia, 1971), pp. 344-48. Other marginalia describing Muslim violence in the Bulgarian lands during the century can be found in: Tsonev, *op. cit.*, #225; *id., Опис Пловдив*, #18, 66, 84; and E. Sprostranov, *Опис Св Синод*, #63. For Stanislavov's letter, see N. Milev, *Католишката пропаганда в България през XVII век* [The Catholic Propaganda in Bulgaria During the 17th Century] (Sofia, 1914), p. 136. For the travelers' accounts, see those, for example, given in: *Чужди пътеписи за Балканите* [Foreign Travel Accounts of the Balkans], I, *Френски пътеписи за Балканите, XV-XVIII в.* [French Travel Accounts of the Balkans, 15th-18th Cen.], B. Tsvetkova, ed., (Sofia, 1975), pp. 188, 252; F. Babinger, "Robert Bargrave in Bulgarien," *ИИДв*, XIV-XV (1937), pp. 147-48; Iv. Shishman, «Стари пътувания през България в посока на римския военен път от Белград до Цариград» [Old Travels Through Bulgaria in Line with the Roman Military Road from Belgrad to Istanbul], *СбНУ*, IV (1891), p. 459; and Drinov, «Нови паметници за историята на българите и на техните съседи» [New Monuments for the History of the Bulgarians and of Their Neighbors], *Избрани съчинения* [Collected Works], I, (Sofia, 1971), pp. 160-62.

² *По следите на насилието* [On the Traces of Violence], I, P.H. Petrov, ed., (Sofia, 1987), pp. 142, 228-29; *id. [ed.], По следите на насилието*, II, (Sofia, 1988), pp. 251-52; and G.D. Gŭlŭbov [ed.], *Турски извори за историята на право*, I, p. 138. Also see Petrov, *Съдбоносни векове*, p. 61.

³ Milev, pp. 58-59.

⁴ *По следите*, II, pp. 188-91; P. Rycaut, *The Present State of the Ottoman Empire* (London, 1687), p. 38.

⁵ For the *derviş* orders, see H. Inalcik, *The Ottoman Empire*, esp. pp. 188f.

⁶ A study of the role of the *derviş* orders in converting Christians to Muslims in the Bulgarian lands can be found in S. Dimitrov's, "Some Aspects of Ethnic Development, Islamization and Assimilation in Bulgarian Lands in the 15th-17th Centuries," *Aspects of the Development of the Bulgarian Nation* (Sofia, 1989), esp. pp. 41-47.

⁷ *Ibid.*, pp. 47-48.

⁸ See *Ibid.*, pp. 48-49; N. Todorov and A. Velkov, *Situation démographique de la Péninsule balkanique (fin du XVe s. début du XVIe s.)* (Sofia, 1988), pp. 33-34. In 1543 the number of *ocaks* stationed in the Bulgarian lands totalled 639, each mustering from 10 to 40 men. When the dependent families of the *yürüks* are considered, the estimated population figure for them alone may have approached 128,000 Muslims. Their numbers were augmented by an additional 76 *ocaks* of Tatars, providing as many as 3,000 effective troopers and a total dependent Muslim population of nearly 15,000. According to Todorov and Velkov, *Ibid.*, the number of *yürük ocaks* in the Bulgarian lands declined during the seventeenth century to near 422, representing a possible settled population of 84,400 individuals, all Muslims.

⁹ Contemporary seventeenth century accounts of such premeditated policy were furnished by two Englishmen who resided in Istanbul during the early to mid years of the century, Sirs Paul Rycaut, *op. cit.*, pp. 37-39, and Richard Knolles, *The Turkish History*, II (London, 1687), p. 920.

¹⁰ For the story of the sixteenth century mass conversions, see Petrov, *Съдбоносни векове*, pp. 91f, 412 and *passim*. M. Kiel, in his study of Bulgarian art history during the Ottoman period, *Art and Society of Bulgaria in the Turkish Period* (Maastricht, 1985), makes the case that no such official efforts existed during the Ottoman period. Perhaps Bulgarian nationalist historians do exaggerate the official policy aspect of the question but there appears little doubt that ordinary Orthodox Bulgarians suffered during periodic bouts of Muslim reaction among the Ottoman authorities in the sixteenth and seventeenth centuries.

¹¹ Kiel, pp. 33f, provides a good overview of both the Bulgarian nationalist and modern Turkish and Western sides in the scholarly debate over the nature of the Ottoman conquest on the subject Christians' existence. The Bulgarians view the conquest and rule of the Turks as intrinsically negative, anti-Christian and destructive, while the modern Turks and some western scholars argue that such was not the case. The literature spawned by this arguement can be found in the extensive footnotes to the text of the chapter. Kiel strongly espouses the modern Turkish cause.

¹² *Pomak* means "helper," from the Bulgarian word, *pomagach*. See S.N. Shishkov, *Помаците в трите български области: Тракия, Македония, и Мизия* [The *Pomaks in Three Regions: Thrace, Macedonia, and Moesia*], I (Plovdiv, 1914), pp. 19f, for the origin and use of the term, *pomak*, as well as for the use of others acquired by Bulgarian Muslims (*i.e.*, *ahryanin, torbesh, apovnik, mŭrvak*, and *poganik*).

¹³ First published in S. Zahariev, *Географико-историко-статистическо описание на Татар-Пазарджишката кааза* [Geographical-Historical-Statistical Description of Tatar-Pazardzhik *kaza*] (Vienna, 1870), pp. 67-68. Modern transcriptions can be found in: I. Ivanov, *Старобългарски разкази. Текстове, новобългарски превод и бележки* [Old Bulgarian Tales. Texts, New Bulgarian Translation and Notes]. (Sofia, 1935), pp. 80-81; and in *По следите*, II, pp. 357-58, where the approximate date of the note is discussed, p. 358n.

¹⁴ The Pazardzhik note was originally published in G. Dimitrov, *Княжество България в историческо, етнографическо отношения* [The Principality of Bulgaria in Historical, Ethnographical Perspectives], I (Plovdiv, 1894), p. 111, and a modern transcription is found in *По следите*, II, p. 359. The Golyamo Belovo note was originally published in N. Nachov, «Лист от хроника, намерен в с. Голямо белово» [Page From a Chronicle, Located in the Village of Golyamo Belovo], *Български преглед* [Bulgarian Review], V, 2 (1898), pp. 149-51, and a modern transcription is in *По следите*, II, pp. 359-60.

¹⁵ Draginov's figures are 218 churches and 33 monasteries. Both the other accounts give the same number of churches but only 32 monasteries.

¹⁶ See my brief study, "Seventeenth century Bulgarian *Pomaks:* Forced or Voluntary Converts to Islam?," *Society in Change Studies in Honor of Béla K. Király*, S.B. Várdy and A.H. Várdy, eds., (Boulder, 1983), pp. 305-14. Also see Kiel, p. 5n, for a good historiographical discussion of the issue.

¹⁷ The tale of Visarion, as related in the *Historical Notebook* written by Athonite monks working in the central regions of the Rhodopes during the eighteenth century, is given in *По следите*, II, pp. 361-63.

¹⁸ *Ibid.*, II, pp. 365-67, 385-86.

¹⁹ Petrov, *Съдбоносни векове*, pp. 412-13, summarizes the regional statistics contained in the body of the text to that work's chap. 2. No exact figures exist for the total percentage of seventeenth century Bulgarian Christians who were lost to Orthodox culture through conversion to Islam. Petrov's regional data, though incomplete, reveal a variation between 10 and 100 percent per region, depending on the intensity of Muslim pressure. For a study of the effects of islamization in two regions of the Bulgarian lands during the century, see S. Dimitrov, «Демографски отношения и проникване на исляма в Западните Родопи и долината на Места през XV-XVII в.» [Demographic Relationships and Penetration of Islam in the Western Rhodopes and the Valley of the Mesta During the 15th-17th Cen.], *Родопски сборник* [Rhodope Collection], I (1965), pp. 63-114.

²⁰ For the history of the Ohrid Archbishopric-Patriarchate see the work by Iv. Snegarov, *История на Охрид архиепископия (от основаването й до завладяването на Балканския полуостров от турците)* [History of the Ohrid Archbishopric (From Its Founding to the Turkish Conquest of the Balkan Peninsula)], 2 v., (Sofia, 1924-1932). Also of interest is T. Sŭbev, *Самостойна народностна църква в средновековна България* [The Independent National Church in Medieval Bulgaria] (Sofia, 1987), Chap. 6, pp. 264f.

²¹ H. Gandev, *Проблеми на българското възраждане* [Problems in the Bulgarian National Revival] (Sofia, 1976), p. 78.

[22] Seventeenth century Bulgarian artists also worked in other Greek churches that later were used as models for revivalist artists. Among those churches located in the Bulgarian lands were "St. Stefan" (1599), "The Holy Savior" (1609) and "St. Kliment" in the essentially Greek Black Sea city of Nesebŭr, and the church at Rozhen Monastery, in the Melnik region of the southwestern Bulgarian lands, whose iconostasis is one of the earliest extant examples of complex woodcarving in the Bulgarian lands.

[23] P. Mutafchiev, *Избрани произведения* [Collected Works], D. Angelov, ed., II, (Sofia, 1973), p. 139.

[24] Kiril Lukaris held the patriarchal throne six individual times between 1612 and 1637. His chief rival, Kiril Kontaris, acquired the position three times during the same period. Between the years 1650 and 1652 there were six patriarchs! Documents concerning patriarchal debts are given in M. Vaporis, *Some Aspects of the History of the Ecumenical Patriarchate of Constantinople in the Seventeenth and Eighteenth Centuries* (published by the author [Boston], 1969). Patriarchs were often held responsible for the debts of their predecessors.

[25] For the amounts noted, see J. Kabrda, *Le système fiscal de l'église orthodoxe dans l'empire ottoman* (Brno, 1969), p. 60, and Mutafchiev, *Избрани произведения*, II, pp. 141-42.

[26] See Mutafchiev, *Ibid.*, pp. 131-35, for data concerning the debts of the Sofia Metropolitanate as of 1652. In Sofia, a loan of 50,000 *akçes*, lent to Metropolitan Eremia (1615) by local Turkish notables, was guaranteed by a number of parish priests from six districts of the metropolitanate. The ecclesiastical income from those districts represented by the guarantors was held as collateral for the loan. See D.A. Ihchiev, «Турски документи за Софийската епархия» [Turkish Documents for the Sofia Bishopric], *Преглед* [Review], I, 6-7 (1908), pp. 318-19. It was not uncommon for a metropolitan to pawn most of his church valuables in an effort to pay or defray interest payments due on his debts. See Vaporis, docs. #XI, XII, XIV, XV, XVII, XXVIII, XXXIII, XXXVII, XXXVIII, and LX, for some of the debts incurred by the Tŭrnovo and Plovdiv metropolitanates during the seventeenth century.

[27] Mutafchiev, *Избрани произведения*, II, pp. 143-44. A special tax (*zitiye*) was imposed as a "voluntary" contribution in the event that a metropolitan or one of his personal agents visited the locales under his authority. The money supposedly was used to defray the travel expenses of the visitation. See Kabrda, *Le système fiscal*, p. 93.

[28] Kabrda, *Ibid.*, p. 48.

[29] *Ibid.*, pp. 71f.

[30] «Описание,» pp. 179-80.

[31] Tsonev, *Опис* I, #225, 317, 320; Sprostranov, *Опис Св Синод*, #19.

[32] Until the seventeenth century the *pavlikyani* (Paulicians) living in the Bulgarian lands, who will be discussed in greater detail later in this work, were regarded as heretics by the Orthodox church and, therefore, were not subject to ecclesiastical taxation. Catholic missionary activity among the heretics, however, and the ever increasing demands for new sources of revenues led the Patriarchate to consider the *pavlikyani* liable for taxation by the church, as they were *Orthodox* schismatics after all! Petŭr Bogdan described one effort at taxing the *pavlikyani* by the Tŭrnovo metropolitanate. See «Описание,» pp. 191-92.

³³ For examples of the mutual recriminations, see: V. Zlatarski, *Нова политическа и социална история на България и Балканския полуостров* [Modern Political and Social History of Bulgaria and the Balkan Peninsula] (Sofia, 1921), p. 34; Stojanović I, #1458; and Gandev, *Проблеми*, p. 83.

³⁴ Both cases are found in P. Dorev [ed.], *Документи за българската история* [Documents for Bulgarian History], III, *Документи из турските държавни архиви* [Documents in the Turkish State Archives] *(1564-1908)*, pt. 1, *(1564-1872)*. (Sofia, 1940), #42, 50.

³⁵ Gandev, *Проблеми*, p. 34. During the late eighteenth century Kuklen Monastery was taken over by Greek monks and the Slavic manuscripts were hidden in the ceiling of the monastery church by the frantic Bulgarian residents in an effort to spare them from destruction. The paintings in the monastery church that bore Slavic inscriptions were defaced and covered over by the Greeks, and new ones bearing Greek inscriptions were painted. These latter now have been removed and the older Bulgarian murals lie exposed once again.

³⁶ «Описание,» p. 189; Gandev, *Ibid.*, pp. 44, 92. Greek demography in the Bulgarian lands during the Ottoman period is discussed in B.G. Spiridonakis, *Essays on the Historical Geography of the Greek World in the Balkans During the Turkokratia* (Thessaloniki, 1977), pp. 90f, and map, p. 93.

³⁷ For the political machinations of Rome and Vienna during the final quarter of the sixteenth century, see Tsvetkova, "La situation internationale et le peuple bulgare à la fin du XVIe et début du XVIIe siècle," *East European Quarterly*, VI, 3 (1972), pp. 324f.

³⁸ Milev, pp. 15, 25.

³⁹ *Ibid.*, pp. 64f, 94f.

⁴⁰ Milev's study was the most comprehensive attempt to discuss the Catholic missionaries in the Bulgarian lands in light of the sources published in *Acta Bulgariæ ecclesiastica ab a. 1565 usque ad a. 1799. Collegit et digessit*, E. Fermendžin, ed., (Zagreb, 1887). The first study to use *Acta Bulgariæ* was L. Miletich, «Из историята на българската католишка пропаганда в XVII в.» [On the History of Bulgarian Catholic Propaganda in the 17th Cen.], *Български преглед*, I, 10; 11 (1894-95), pp. 62-82; 146-89. One of the earliest references to Bulgarian Catholics was made in K. Jireček, *История на българите* [History of the Bulgarians] (Sofia, 1978 [4th ed.]), pp. 494f, and in *id.*, *Пътувания по България* [Travels In Bulgaria], v. II of *Княжество България* [The Principality of Bulgaria] (Sofia, 1974 [Reprint of Plovdiv, 1899 ed.]), *passim*. Iv. Duichev, one of the most noted and prolific of twentieth century Bulgarian medievalists, produced such a voluminous amount of studies dealing with the Bulgarian Catholics that many of his Bulgarian and American colleagues sometimes jokingly conjectured that he might have been a secret Catholic! The 300th anniversary of the Catholic-inspired Chiprovtsi Uprising (1988) has resulted in a new round of studies of the Catholic question. Among these newer works, that by S. Stanimirov, *Политическата дейност на българитекатолици през 30-те — 70-те години на XVII век. Към историята на българската антиосманска съпротива* [The Political Activity of the Bulgarian Catholics During the 30s/70s of the 17th Century. Toward the History of the Bulgarian Anti-Ottoman Resistance] (Sofia, 1988), is of great interest.

[41] «Описание,» p. 176. Bogdan's description of Bulgaria's frontiers also has been published in English in *Macedonia. Documents and Materials,* V. Bozhinov and L. Panayotov, eds., (Sofia, 1978), doc. #66, and in *Documents and Materials on the History of the Bulgarian People,* M. Voinov and L. Panayotov, eds., (Sofia, 1969), p. 67. For Bogdan's history, see J. Jerkov, "Un fragment inedit de l'histoire de la Bulgarie de Petar Bogdan Bakšič," *EB,* XIV, 1 (1978), pp. 103-09.

[42] For the life and political activities of Parchevich, see the following studies by Iv. Duichev: «Архиепископ Петър Парчевич. Политическото значение на българското католичество през XVII в.» [Archbishop Petŭr Parchevich. The Political Significance of Bulgarian Catholicism During the 17th Cen.], *Родина* [Motherland], I, 4 (1939), pp. 5-19; and «Политическата дейност на Петър Парчевич за освобождение от турско владичество» [The Political Efforts of Petŭr Parchevich for Liberation from Turkish Domination], *Българо-румънски връзки и отношения през вековете* [Bulgaro-Romanian Contacts and Relations Through the Centuries], I, (Sofia, 1965), pp. 157-93. Also see M. Holban, "Autour de Parchevich," *RESEE,* VII, 4 (1969), pp. 613-46.

[43] For example, see: V. Pundev, «Сборникът Абагар от епископ Филип Станиславов» [The Collection *Abagar* by Bishop Filip Stanislavov], *ГНБП,* (1924), [offprint, 1926, 49 p.], p. 2; P. Dinekov, «Българската литература през XVII в.» [Bulgarian Literature During the 17th Cen.], *Литературна история* [Literary History], I (1977), p. 6; and Gandev, *Проблеми,* p. 56.

[44] Iv. Duichev, «Прояви на народностно съзнание у нас през XVII в.» [Manifestations of National Consciousness Among the Bulgarians During the 17th Cen.], *Македонски Преглед* [Macedonian Review], XIII, 2 (1942), pp. 26-52, is the most critically reliable study of the national consciousness developed among the Bulgarian Catholics. For the missionary school in Chiprovtsi, see N. Chakŭrov, *История на българското образование* [History of Bulgarian Education], I, (Sofia, 1955), pp. 110-11.

[45] For the history of the Paulicians and a discussion of their dualistic faith, see: S. Runciman, *The Medieval Manichee* (Cambridge, 1967); and N.G. Garsoian, *The Paulician Heresy* (The Hague, 1967).

[46] For the history of the Bogomils and a discussion of their beliefs, see: D. Angelov, *Богомилството в България* [Bogomilism in Bulgaria] (Sofia, 1969 [3rd. ed.]); and D. Obolensky, *The Bogomils. A Study in Balkan Neo-Manichæism* (Cambridge, 1948).

[47] L. Miletich, «Нашите павликяни» [Our *Pavlikyani*], *СбНУ,* XIX (1903), p. 22. According to Grozdanova's demographic study of the seventeenth century, there were no more than 9,000 Catholics in the Bulgarian lands during the seventeenth century, of which some 7,100 were *pavlikyani.* About 450 of those heretics lived in the Plovdiv region among the villages of Zhitnitsa, Sekirovo, Miromir, Duvanli, and some others. Most, however, were located in the Nikopol *sancak.* See her *Българската народност,* p. 641. According to the population table facing p. 104 in Milev, in 1624 there was a total of 8,000 Catholics in the Bulgarian lands, including the Bulgaro-Saxons and the Dubrovnik merchant colonies. In 1640 the Catholic population had increased to 9,000. By 1667, however, Catholic numbers had fallen to approximately 5,100.

⁴⁸ See Jireček, *Пътувания по България*, p. 198. For a contemporary view of *pavlikyani* practices by one who had great personal interest in their conversion to Catholicism, see Bogdan's «Описание,» pp. 189f. *Pavlikyani* beliefs included legends that the Pope could live for a hundred years and that he had wings and flew, so that he could see everything. See Pundev, p. 4.

⁴⁹ B. Raikov, in one of his introductory studies to his edition of *Абагар на Филип Станиславов. Рим, 1651* [*Abagar* of Filip Stanislavov. Rome, 1651] (Sofia, 1979 [Reproduction ed.]), pp. 25-26.

⁵⁰ Milev, pp. 161-63.

⁵¹ *Acta Bulgariæ*, pp. 114f.

⁵² *Ibid.*, p. 196.

⁵³ Abgar was a first century monarch of the east Syrian kingdom of Osrhœne. He was legendarily credited with being the first Christian king by Christian hagiographic tradition. The history of Osrhœne is spotty, and it seems Christianity did not grow dominant in that state until the second century, under King Abgar VIII (or IX), who may not himself have converted.

⁵⁴ See Pundev, p. 11, and B. Raikov, «Към въпроса за мястото на Абагар в старата българска литература» [Toward the Problem of the Place of *Abagar* in Old Bulgarian Literature], *ИИБЛ*, XVIII-XIX (1966), p. 280. There are 15 extant copies of *Abagar*. Some of those copies were made later expressly for Orthodox readers. There were various copyists. For the locations of those copies and other pertinent information, see Raikov's introduction to his edition of *Abagar*, pp. 24-26.

⁵⁵ M. Iovkov, «За статута на павликяните през XVII в.» [For the Status of the *Pavlikyani* During the 17th Cen.], in *България 1300*, II, pp. 445-46.

⁵⁶ *Ibid.*, pp. 447-48.

⁵⁷ B. Tsvetkova, *Хайдутството в българските земи през 15/18 век* [*Haidut* Activity in the Bulgarian Lands During the 15th/18th Centuries] (Sofia, 1971), pp. 51f. The Orthodox Bulgarians in other regions of the Bulgarian lands were not politically inactive during those troubled times. Russia was engaged in a war with the Ottomans, and a russophil Bulgarian, Rostislav Stratsimirovich, organized a rebellion against the Turks in the region of Tŭrnovo. Stratsimirovich claimed to be a descendant of the very last medieval Bulgarian tsar, Ivan Stratsimir (1365-1396), and he looked to Russia for aid. After his plot was betrayed to the Turks by a Greek in 1686, Stratsimirovich proclaimed the uprising. The expected Russian assistance failed to materialize and the rebels were crushed by military force. Tŭrnovo was devastated and a large number of its inhabitants were slaughtered. Stratsimirovich fled to Moscow.

⁵⁸ The stone tower of the monastery today serves as a mausoleum for the remains of the rebels killed there during the fighting. The number of dead is traditionally placed at 1000.

⁵⁹ For the events leading to the Chiprovtsi Uprising, its brief course, and its bloody aftermath, see: Iv. Duichev, *Чипровец и въстанието през 1688 година* [Chiprovets and the Uprising in 1688] (Sofia, 1938); *Чипровци. 1688-1968*. [Chiprovtsi. 1688-1968] (Sofia, 1971), which contains an extensive bibliography; and P. Cholov, *Чипровското въстание 1688 г.* [The Chiprovtsi Uprising 1688] (Sofia, 1988).

Chapter 3. Monasticism and the Cultural Role of Mount Athos

[1] Iv. Duichev, «Манастирите — огнища на народния дух» [The Monasteries - - Hearths of the National Spirit], introduction to B. Nikolov and M. Manolov, *Огнища на българщината. Пътувания из манастирите* [Hearths of the Bulgarian National Spirit. Journeys Through the Monasteries] (Sofia, 1989 [2nd. ed.]), pp. 6-7.

[2] See D. Obolensky, *The Byzantine Commonwealth: Eastern Europe, 500-1453* (New York, 1971), pp. 296-97, 302-03.

[3] Detailed analyses of the Byzantine monastic movement can be found in G. Ostrogorsky, *History of the Byzantine State*, J.M. Hussey, trans., (New Brunswick, 1957), pp. 158f, 254f, 456f, and in H.W. Haussig, *A History of Byzantine Civilization*, J.M. Hussey, trans., (New York, 1971), pp. 76f, 210f, 320f. It is not the purpose of this work to examine in great detail the technical aspects of monasticism in its various forms: eremitic, *lavra*, cœnobitic, and idiorythmic. Suffice it to say that all of those forms of monasticism were found in both Byzantium and in Bulgaria at one time or another.

[4] More complete accounts of the origins and development of Athonite monasticism can be found in: J.J. Norwich, R. Sitwell and A. Costa, *Mount Athos* (London, 1966); F.W. Hasluck, *Athos and Its Monasteries* (London, 1924); P. Sherrard, *Athos, the Mountain of Silence* (London, 1960); and *Le Millenaire du Mont Athos, 963-1963. Études et Mélanges*, 2 vols., (Chevetogne, 1963-64).

[5] G. Neshev, "Les monastères bulgares du Mont Athos," *EH*, VI, (Sofia, 1973), pp. 97-98. During the fifteenth century the Athonite monasteries also appear to have been obliged to pay imposts on lands and crops that probably exceeded the total of the *maktu*. See Hasluck, *Athos and Its Monasteries*, pp. 31-33.

[6] Bulgarian pilgrims to Athos left behind them numerous examples of marginalia and other inscriptions as momentos of their visits. Many of these notes have been published. See, for example, I. Ivanov, *Бъл стар из Мак*, pp. 230f, and Stojanović I, #945, 946.

[7] The *Protos* was assisted by a steward (*oikonomos*), who regulated the general financial and commercial affairs of the community, and by an *ecclesiarches*, who superintended the central church and its services at Karyes. Prior to the Fourth Crusade (1204), the *Protos* was appointed by the Byzantine emperor rather than by the Patriarch. See Hasluck, *Athos and Its Monasteries*, pp. 22f.

[8] I. Ivanov, *Св. Иван Рилски и неговият манастир* [St. Ivan Rilski and His Monastery] (Sofia, 1917), pp. 153-54.

[9] D. Bolutov, *Български исторически паметници на Атон* [Bulgarian Historical Monuments on Athos] (Sofia, 1961), p. 34.

[10] The traditional founding date is given in M. Kovachev, *Български ктитори в Св. Гора. Исторически очерк, изследвания и документи* [Bulgarian Patrons on Mount Athos. Historical Article, Studies and Documents] (Sofia, 1943), p. 115. The more probable date is in Hasluck, *Athos and Its Monasteries*, p. 138.

[11] Ivanov, *Бъл стар из Мак*, pp. 587f, 605f; A. Ilyinskiy, *Грамоты болгарских царей* [Charters of Bulgarian Tsars] (London, 1970 [Orig. ed., Moscow, 1911]), doc. #3.

[12] Ivanov, *Ibid.*, pp. 540f.

¹³ Bolutov, p. 59; Kovachev, *Български ктитори*, pp. 119f; *id.*, *Българско монашество в Атон* [Bulgarian Monasticism on Athos] (Sofia, 1967), p. 29. For Bulgarian cultural influences in the Romanian Principalities, see V. Traikov and N. Zhechev, *Българската емиграция в Румъния XIV век-1878 година и участието й в стопанския, общественополитическия и културния живот на румънския народ* [Bulgarian Emigrants in Romania, 14th Century-1878, and Their Participation in the Commercial, Socio-Political and Cultural Life of the Romanian People] (Sofia, 1986).

¹⁴ Hasluck, *Athos and Its Monasteries,* p. 139.

¹⁵ M. Gechev, *Килийните училища в България* [Cell Schools in Bulgaria] (Sofia, 1967), p. 66.

¹⁶ N. Dragova, «Домашни извори на История славянобългарска» [Domestic Sources for the *Slaveno-Bulgarian History*], in *Паисий Хилендарски и неговата епоха (1762-1962)* [Paisii Hilendarski and His Era (1762-1962)] (Sofia, 1962), p. 313. The number of manuscripts in the monastery library during the seventeenth century is unknown.

¹⁷ S. Loch, *Athos: The Holy Mountain* (London, 1957), pp. 64-65. Loch claims to have seen the miraculous icon in the early 1950s and pronounced it a probable product of the fifteenth century.

¹⁸ Published in Ivanov, *Бъл стар из Мак*, pp. 489f.

¹⁹ Kovachev, *Български ктитори,* pp. 150, 152, gives the two lists of Bulgarian tsars. In his *Зограф. Изследвания и документи* [Zograf. Studies and Documents], I, (Sofia, 1942), pp. xix-xxi, Kovachev also published a 1639 Russian register that was written in Moscow and acquired by the monastery. This work was a copy of an older manuscript that also contained a list of certain Bulgarian and Russian tsars.

²⁰ Ivanov, *Бъл стар из Мак*, p. 264; Gechev, p. 24.

²¹ Ivanov, *Ibid.,* pp. 264-66, 590-94, 608f (a later copy, reissued by Stefan Uroš Dečanski [1321-1331], which contained additional property grants); Ilyinskiy, *Грамоты,* docs. #2, 4.

²² Ivanov, *Ibid.,* pp. 266-67, 338f, 440f, 475f; Iv. Duichev, "Chilandar et Zograf au Moyen Age," *Hilandarski zbornik* [Hilandar Collection], I (Belgrad, 1968), pp. 30-31.

²³ Iv. Duichev, *The Miniatures of the Chronicle of Manasses* (Sofia, 1963), pp. 25, 25n. The manuscript was one of the hundreds taken by Suhanov from Athos in 1654. Another Slavic copy of Manasses was made in Tulcha during the sixteenth-seventeenth centuries. See Tsonev, *Опис* II, #629.

²⁴ Ivanov, *Бъл стар из Мак*, pp. 267-68; Stojanović I, #1130; Stojanović IV, #6482.

Chapter 4. Slavic Education: The Foundation for Cultural Expression

¹ The chronology of Slavic education during the period of the medieval Bulgarian states can be found in Chakŭrov, pp. 28f.

² Gechev, pp. 8-9, 12, 66, 68; P.M. Noikov, «Поглед върху развитието на българското образование до Паисия» [A View on the Development of Bulgarian Education to Paisii], *ГСУифф*, XXI, 11 (1925), [offprint], p. 30.

³ Gechev, pp. 30-33; Chakŭrov, p. 89. Another monastery that established a school near the close of the fifteenth century was that of Kilifarevo, which in the late fourteenth century stood in the vanguard during the rise of the Tŭrnovo School. See I. Georgiev, «Село Килифарево и манастирът му Св. Богородица» [The Village of Kilifarevo and Its Monastery of the Blessed Virgin], ПСп, LXVII (1906), pp. 439f. Athonite *metohs* operated schools during the later fifteenth century in Samokov and Chelopechane. See H. Semerdzhiev, *Самоков и околността му* [Samokov and Its Vicinity] (Sofia, 1913), pp. 134-35, and Ivanov, *Бъл стар из Мак*, pp. 602f.

⁴ Noikov, p. 29.

⁵ *Ibid.*, pp. 31-32.

⁶ *Ibid.*, pp. 32-33; Chakŭrov, p. 105.

⁷ After the fall of Tŭrnovo to the Turks (1393) Konstantin fled Bulgaria for the court of the Serbian despot, Stefan Lazarević (1389-1427). Lazarević realized the cultural feather that Konstantin would lend to his cap by having a representative of the leading Balkan Slavic cultural center residing and working within the Serbian lands. He patronized Konstantin and permitted him to open a school in the Manasija (Resava) Monastery in 1407. Konstantin then commenced his pedagogical and philosophical activities, for which he had trained in Tŭrnovo, producing his *Saga* as a sort of standard Slavic grammar and pedagogical program. The text of that work eventually found its way to Athos, and from there to the Bulgarian lands. For a published text of the *Saga*, see B.S. Angelov, *Из старата българска, руска и сръбска литература* [On Old Bulgarian, Russian and Serbian Literature], II, (Sofia, 1967), pp. 211f.

⁸ Noikov, pp. 34-35. In 1640 the Bulgarian Catholic bishop, Petŭr Bogdan, made a tour of inspection throughout the Bulgarian lands and wrote a report of his observations to the Vatican. At one point, he opined that the Orthodox Bulgarian *daskals* copied liturgical books tirelessly but without inquiry and in great literary ignorance, thus resulting in the propagation of "thousands of mistakes" in the sacred literature and in the growth of heresy. «Описание,» p. 180. The extant works of those *daskals* do not verify Bogdan's critical evaluation.

⁹ Many of the student copyists left marginalia commemorating their feats in the manuscripts that they worked on. See: Tsonev, *Опис* I, #2, 168, 277; *id., Опис* II, #463; Stoyanov and Kodov, *Опис* III, #1052; Sprostranov, *Опис Св Синод*, #78; Iv. Goshev, «Врачанска епархия,» p. 4; Ivanov, *Бъл стар из Мак*, pp. 252, 254, 278. The above include only notations that were signed by students who identified themselves as such.

¹⁰ Gandev, *Проблеми*, p. 29.

¹¹ Another weakness of the cell school system lay in the fact that education was strictly male-oriented. Education for females only evolved during the nineteenth century after the influx of Western European ideas had made their impact. The typical Bulgarian of the fifteenth-eighteenth centuries would not have viewed the exclusion of females from the schools as a drawback.

¹² S. Gerlach, *Дневник*, pp. 268-69, described a cell school in the monastery of "St. Dimitŭr," near the Bulgarian village of Klisuritsa (Byala Palanka) in 1578. Gerlach noted that five monks taught at the monastery, and that the deacon from the village church, "St. Georgi," was one of the students.

[13] Gandev, *Проблеми*, p. 35; Chakŭrov, p. 104. One such *daskal* was Rashko, from Vratsa (1640).

[14] Gandev, *Ibid.*, p. 36; Chakŭrov, *Ibid.*

[15] Chakŭrov, p. 105.

[16] Noikov, p. 41. It would appear that the village school at Adzhar, which produced highly skilled writer-copyists, discussed in greater detail later in this work, was exceptional.

[17] Chakŭrov, p. 104. It is difficult to credit seventeenth century Bulgarian housewives with attending the cell schools. Perhaps, if Chakŭrov is correct (he furnishes no noted documentation for his contention), the *daskal* visited the women in their homes for informal lessons rather than instructing them in the classroom.

[18] There were also: *daskal* Peio of Vrachesh (1673), Pencho Gramatik, *daskal* Stoyan from Tryavna, *daskal* Todora Pirdopski, *daskal* Petŭr Lazar at Glozhene Monastery, *daskal* Gerasim at Rila Monastery, *daskal* Dimitŭr Koichev of Teteven, and *daskals* Petŭr and Nenko from Kalofer. These men identified themselves as teachers in the extant seventeenth century sources. A large number of men who bore the title of *gramatik* appear in the sources from the century and may have been active in teaching as well. Only those who left some concrete evidence for educational activity have been included in the above listing.

Chapter 5. The Forms of Orthodox Culture

[1] B. Raikov, «Етрополската калиграфско-художествена школа през XVI-XVII век» [The Etropole Calligraphical-Art School During the 16th-17th Centuries], *ИНБКМ*, XII [XVIII] (1971), p. 22. Islamic motifs were found in the fifteenth century manuscripts of Vladislav Gramatik. See the illustration in M. Stoyanov, *Украса на славянските ръкописи в България. Описание на украсата на славянските ръкописи от XI до началото на XIX в.* [The Decoration of the Slavic Manuscripts in Bulgaria. Inventory of the Decorations of the Slavic Manuscripts from the 11th to the Beginning of the 19th Centuries] (Sofia, 1973), p. 103.

[2] B. Tsonev, *История на българский език* [History of Bulgarian Language], I, (Sofia, 1919), pp. 258-59; Raikov, «Етрополската . . . школа,» p. 28; V. Vasilev, «Влахо-българската книжнина XVII век» [Wallacho-Bulgarian Writings 15th-17th Centuries], *Славяни* [Slavs], 7 (1973), pp. 44-46. For some Bulgarian Cyrillic manuscripts written in the Romanian Principalities and later found in the Bulgarian lands during the seventeenth century, see: Tsonev, *Опис* I, #48, 394; *id.*, *Опис* II, #767-69; *id.*, *Опис Пловдив*, #23; Stoyanov and Kodov, *Опис* III, #954p; Sprostranov, *Опис Св Синод*, #19; *id.*, *Опис Рил ман*, #1/11 (242); Goshev, «Стари записки» IV, #19; Ivanov, *Бъл стар из Мак*, pp. 249, 250-51.

[3] B. Tsonev made the earliest reference to a specific Etropole style of calligraphy in a description of a manuscript in *Опис* I, p. 126.

[4] See Raikov, «Етрополската . . . школа,» p. 28. For published illustrations of Etropole calligraphy, see: Stoyanov, *Украса*, pp. 197, 198, 201, 202, 209, 215; and V. Pandurski, *Паметници на изкуството в Църковния историко-археологически*

музей — София [Monuments of Art in the Church Historical-Archaeological Museum-Sofia] (Sofia, 1977), illus. #133-39, 192-94.

[5] B. Raikov, «Йеромонах Данийл и Етрополският книжовен център през първата половина на XVII в.» [*Ieromonah* Daniil and the Etropole Literary Center During the First Half of the 17th Cen.], in *Старобългарска литература. Изследвания и материали* [Old Bulgarian Literature. Studies and Materials], I, (Sofia, 1971), pp. 285-86; D. Petkanova [-Toteva], *Дамаскините в българската литература* [The *Damaskins* in Bulgarian Literature] (Sofia, 1965), pp. 44f.

[6] A. Muravyav, *Сношения России с Востоком по делам церковным* [Russian Relations with the East by Church Work], II (St. Petersburg, 1860), pp. 24-25, 44, 48, 57f, 62, 64, 95f; Iv. Snegarov, *Културни и политически връзки между България и Русия през XVI-XVIII в.* [Cultural and Political Contacts Between Bulgaria and Russia During the 16th-18th Cen.] (Sofia, 1953), pp. 9, 31f, 36f, 40.

[7] Tsonev, *Опис* I, #317; *id.*, *Опис* II, #634. For the literary interrelations between the Bulgarians and the Russians, see: Snegarov, *Културни и политически връзки*, pp. 98f; and B.S. Angelov, *Из историята на руско-българските литературни връзки* [On the History of Russian-Bulgarian Literary Contacts] (Sofia, 1972), *passim*. For Russian variant manuscripts and printed books found in the Bulgarian lands during the seventeenth century, many of which bore notations testifying to their use in the cell schools, see: Tsonev, *Опис* I, #103, 316, 320, 456, 499, 502; *id.*, *Опис* II, #634; *id.*, *Опис Пловдив*, #145, 146; Stoyanov and Kodov, *Опис* III, #879, 953, 1043; *id.*, *Опис* IV, #1340; Sprostranov, *Опис Св Синод*, #5, 8; Goshev, «Стари записки» I, #207; *id.*, «Стари записки» II, #245; *id.*, «Стари записки» IV, #9.

[8] S.M. Romanski, Българската книжнина в Румъния и едно нейно произведение» [Bulgarian Writing in Romania and One of Its Products], *ИССФУС*, I (1905), [offprint], pp. 1f. See also the definitive study by E. Turdeanu, *La literature bulgare du XIVe siècle et sa diffusion dans les pays roumaine* (Paris, 1947).

[9] For Pahomie, see Tsonev, *Опис* I, #164. For Bulgarian manuscripts written in the Romanian lands but circulating in the Bulgarian lands during the seventeenth century, see those noted in note 2, above, as well as: Tsonev, *Ibid*, #114, 124, 433; *id.*, *Опис* II, #461, 463, 571, 770; Sprostranov, *Опис Св Синод*, #76; *id.*, *Опис Рил ман*, #1/11 (242). For other seventeenth century Middle Bulgarian manuscripts, see: Stoyanov and Kodov, *Опис* III, #978; *id.*, *Опис* IV, #1153-55; Sprostranov, *Опис Св Синод*, #13, 66, 80-81, 118, 128; *id.*, *Опис Рил ман*, #1/6 (5); Kodov, *Опис БАН*, #55.

[10] Tsonev, *Опис* I, #225.

[11] See the seventeenth century notations in Rila manuscripts given in Sprostranov, *Опис Рил ман*, #1/11a, 3/13 (19), 1/2 (46), 1/11 (242).

[12] See Yu. Trifanov, «Сръбско-българска безюсова редакция в старата книжнина на южните славяни» [Serbo-Bulgarian "Yu"-less Phrasing in the Old Literature of the South Slavs], *Македонски Преглед*, XII, 2 (1940), pp. 27-55, for a detailed discussion of the differences between the Bulgarian and the Serbian literary languages during the period. Trifanov dealt specifically with the Resava variant on pp. 46-49, and his article argued that the so-called Serbian variant was actually a mixed Bulgaro-Serbian language.

¹³ The catalogs of manuscripts give at least 155 extant works produced within the Bulgarian lands during the seventeenth century in the Serbian variant. Such works constituted the predominant component in the corpus of every major Bulgarian literary center during the period.

¹⁴ Other known writer-copyists in the Serbian variant were: *pop* Bogdan from Slavovitsa (1641); *ieromonah* Makarii; *ieromonah* Kalinik at Kalugerovo Monastery (1646); Gerasim *ieromonah* at Cherepish Monastery (1682); *gramatik* Priniya (1635); Iov Shishatovats and *igumen* Varlaam at "The Holy Trinity" Monastery near Vratsa (1608); *daskal* Peio from Vrachesh (1673); Pimen Zografski at Seslavtsi Monastery (1618); *gramatik* Ban from Radomirtsi (1662); *daskal* Koyu at Etropole Monastery (1636); *monah* Evtimii at "Sedemte Prestola" Monastery (1643); *daskal* Petŭr (1698); *pop* Zhivko from Adzhar (1636); *pop* Nikifor (1602) and *pop* Viktor (1696) at Rila Monastery; Dŭshko *gramatik* from Lovech (1686); and *pop* Nikola (1601) at Kovachevtsi Monastery, near Samokov.

¹⁵ Evtimii's philological reforms included the creation of a more standardized alphabetical system for Slavic than had been used previously, the forging of a closer parallel between Slavic orthography and that of the Greek, and the attempt to bring the contemporary Slavic literary language closer to the older form of the ninth-tenth centuries. See E. Georgiev, Българската литература в общославянското и общоевропейско литературно развитие [Bulgarian Literature in General Slavic and General European Literary Development] (Sofia, 1973), pp. 102-04. The continuation of Evtimii's reforms by Tsamblak and Kostenechki are treated on pp. 108-13.

¹⁶ A fourteenth century copy of the *Life* is housed in the library of Zograf, and it actually may be an original work by Evtimii himself. For the published text, see Ivanov, *Бъл стар из Мак*, pp. 370f.

¹⁷ An annotated *Life* of Rilski in modern transcription can be found in Жития на българските светии [Lives of the Bulgarian Saints], I, (Sofia, 1974), pp. 156f. This version, edited by Bishop Partenii, also includes elements of the *Life* written by the twelfth century Greek, George Skylitzes. For the numerous recensions of Rilski's hagiography written by Evtimii, Skylitzes, and Dimitrios Kantakuzinos, among others, see: I. Ivanov, «Жития на св. Ивана Рилски. С уводни бележки» [The Life of St. Ivan Rilski. With Introductory Notes], ГСУифф, XXXII (1935-36), pp. 1-109; and B.S. Angelov, "Un canon de St. Jean de Rila de Georges Skylitzes," *Bb*, III, (Sofia, 1969), 171-85. In 1127 King István II of Hungary (1116-1131) carried the relics of Ivan Rilski off to his country, where they remained until 1137, when King Béla II (1131-1141) returned them to Sofia. In 1183 King Béla III (1172-1196) of Hungary captured Sofia from the Byzantines and transferred the relics of Rilski to his capital at Esztergom. Four years later (1187), Béla returned the relics to Sofia.

¹⁸ The earliest known copy of Evtimii's *Life* of Petka was found in the library of Zograf Monastery and published by I. Ivanov in *Бъл стар из Мак*, pp. 432-33. A modern transcription, including later expansions and annotations by other writer-copyists, can be found in Жития на българските светии, I, pp. 181-85. Following the debacle of the fall of Tŭrnovo (1393), Petka's relics were transferred to Vidin by the Bulgarian ruler of that region, Tsar Ivan Stratsimir. The tale of that episode was written by Grigorii

Tsamblak. A fifteenth century copy of Tsamblak's work was published in Ivanov, *Ibid.*, pp. 433-36. The story of Petka's relics did not end at Vidin. After that city's capture by the Turks (1396), her remains were carried to Serbia and reinterred at Belgrad. In 1521 that city fell to Sultan Süleyman I the Magnificent and Petka's relics were then sent to Istanbul, in care of the Greek Patriarchate. In 1641 the Patriarch gave them to the Moldavian prince, Vasile Lupu (1634-1653), in return for a large sum of money that was needed by the church for its tribute due the Turkish authorities. Lupu buried the relics in the city of Iași, where they remain to this day.

[19] Tsar Petŭr eventually renounced the throne for the monkly tonsure in a Preslav monastery. He was later canonized a saint by the Bulgarian Orthodox church. Both Kaloyan and Ivan Asen II were strong military leaders who fought off the threat to the infant Second Bulgarian Empire posed by the Latin Kingdom of Constantinople and the Greek Byzantine successor states in the Balkans, ensuring the continued survival and growth of their state. The victorious aspect of Asen's military prowess was stressed in the conclusion of Petka's *Life*.

[20] Evtimii wrote eulogies for: the Roman emperor, Constantine I the Great (324-337), and his mother, St. Helena; Mihail, a ninth century Bulgarian warrior from the village of Potuka, near the town of Kazanlŭk; and Nedelya, a third century victim of the Roman Emperor Diocletian's persecution of Christians and a native of Anatolia. The relics of both Mihail and Nedelya were brought to Tŭrnovo during the period of the Second Bulgarian Empire.

[21] Ivanov, *Бъл стар из Мак*, p. 369.

[22] Sprostranov, *Опис Рил ман*, #4/8 (61). The *povest* was published in both original and modern transcriptions by I. Ivanov in *Старобългарски разкази*, pp. 72f, 227f.

[23] The oldest copy of Peio's *Life* of Georgi was housed in Hilendar Monastery (late sixteenth century), #479, and was published in B.S. Angelov, *Из старата българска, руска и сръбска литература* [On Old Bulgarian, Russian and Serbian Literature], III, (Sofia, 1978), pp. 102f. A modern transcription can be found in *Жития на българските светии*, I, pp. 43f. For the *Service*, see Angelov, *Ibid.*, pp. 138f.

[24] Matei's *Life* was published in P. Syrku, *Очерки из историй литературных сношений Болгар и Сербов в XIV-XVII веках* [Investigations into the History of Bulgarian and Serbian Literary Relations in the 14th-17th Centuries] (St. Petersburg, 1901). The case for a sixteenth century Sofia School of literature was made by P. Dinekov in his two works: *Софийски книжовници през XVI век* [Sofia Writers During the 16th Century], I, *Поп Пейо* [Father Peio] (Sofia, 1939); and «Книжовният живот в София през XVI век» [Literary Life in Sofia During the 16th Century], *Родина*, III, 4 (1941), pp. 124-43.

[25] For Ioan's *Life*, see Stoyanov and Kodov, *Опис* III, #1044. It was first studied by B. Raikov in his «Неизвестно положно житие на Иван Рилски» [Unknown Eulogetic Life of Ivan Rilski], *Език и литература* [Language and Literature], 3 (1970), pp. 57-61. The 1636 manuscript is the single known extant copy of Ioan's *Life*. Pamfilii's *Life* of Pimen is housed in the library of Zograf Monastery. It was first published in D. Yanakiev, «Житие на преподобни монах отец Пимен Зографски, родом от София» [The Life of the Venerable Monk Friar Pimen Zografski, Native of Sofia], *Сердика*, III, 4 (1939),

pp. 5-10. A complete version in modern transcription was made by P. Dinekov, «Житието на Пимен Зографски» [The Life of Pimen Zografski], ИИБЛ, II (1954), pp. 233-48.

[26] For a biography of Damaskin Studit and information regarding editions of *The Treasury*, see Petkanova [-Toteva], Дамаскините, pp. 6-12.

[27] Sprostranov, Опис Рил ман, #4/10 (87), for the Rila *damaskin*. For seventeenth century Bulgarian *damaskins*, see Petkanova [-Toteva], *Ibid.*, pp. 106, 215f, 219f. In all, she attributed 27 *damaskins* to the century, listed on pp. 238-41, with published editions of each noted.

[28] D. Hristoskov and M. Mladenov, «Един новооткрит български ръкопис от XVII в.» [A Newly Discovered Manuscript From the 17th Cen.], Български език [Bulgarian Language], VII, 3 (1957), pp. 228-37; M. Moskov, «Един нов дамаскин» [A New *Damaskin*], Българска сбирка [Bulgarian Collection], XI, 10 (1904), pp. 628-34.

[29] L. Miletich, «Копривщенски дамаскин. Новобългарски паметник от XVII век» [Koprivshtitsa *Damaskin*. New Bulgarian Monument From the 17th Century], Български старини [Bulgarian Antiquities], II, (Sofia, 1908), p. 7. Eight *damaskins* contained Evtimii's *Life* of Petka: the Adzhar, Tihonravov, Koprivshtitsa, Troyan, Dryanovo A and B, Sliven, and Protopopintsi copies.

[30] The substitution was made in the Sliven, the two Dryanovo, and in the Tryavna *damaskins*. The latter copy was made by *daskal* Stoyan. See Tsonev, Опис II, #710.

[31] The Protopopintsi copy of Peio's *Life* has been published in B.S. Angelov, Из старата българска, руска и сръбска литература, II, pp. 276f. The "Drinov" copy was published in Tsonev, Опис I, #432. It was written in the late sixteenth century in a mixed Bulgaro-Serbian language. In 1614 the manuscript was in "Yastreb" Monastery, near Lovech.

[32] Sermons against drunkenness and evil women were included in the Koprivshtitsa *damaskin*. The tale of the murderous woman was part of a *sbornik*. See Tsonev, Опис II, #685. Tsonev, *Ibid.*, #712, gave a *damaskin*, which he dated to 1614, that included quotations from Solomon, Plutarch, Demokrates, and the Byzantine patriarch, Photios. "Scientific" lessons were included in the "Popstoikov" and "Drinov" *damaskins*.

[33] Sometimes the attempt to draw analogies resulted in ludicrous errors. In the Koprivshtitsa *damaskin*, for example, Alexander III the Great (356-323 BC) of Macedon, son of Philip II (382-336 BC), was identified as "Aleksandŭr from Plovdiv!" See Miletich, «Копривщенски дамаскин,» p. 126. Petkanova [-Toteva], Дамаскините, pp. 111-12, related the tale told in the Dryanovo B *damaskin* concerning the persecution of Christians under Roman Emperor Diocletian (284-305). Diocletian was termed, *tsar* (the contemporary term used by Bulgarians for the Ottoman sultan), and his military and administrative officers were called *paşas* and *kadıs*. Asia Minor was written as *Anadolu*. Diocletian proclaimed the persecutions in a *ferman*. Saint George was called a *sipahi* in the Roman army. Diocletian was described as the ruler of Anatolia (*i.e.*, Turkey). It required little wit on the part of the Bulgarian readership to make the analogy between the story of Saint George, as related in such terms, and the contemporary situation of the Christian Bulgarians. See Tsonev, Опис II, #708, for the use of the term, *dyavoli*.

[34] G. Neshev, Български довъзрожденски културно-народностни средища [Bulgarian Pre-Revival Cultural-National Centers] (Sofia, 1977), p. 71.

[35] See: Stojanović I, #1635, 1714, 1857; *id.*, II, #2087, 4274; and B. Angelov, *Старобългарско книжовно наследство* [Old Bulgarian Literary Heritage], I, (Sofia, 1983), p. 128.

[36] Gandev, *Проблеми*, pp. 67-68.

[37] For manuscripts by Bogdan, see: Tsonev, *Опис* I, #251; *id.*, *Опис* II, #621; Stoyanov and Kodov, *Опис* III, #971, 997. The printed book has not been cataloged but lies in the Sofia National Library, in the Series Books room, #R.ts. 494 1a, given in B. Angelov, *Старобългарско книжовно наследство*, pp. 121-22. Angelov, *Ibid.*, pp. 120-21, discussed the stylistic similarities between the Philotios and Kantakuzinos prayers. Other seventeenth century Bulgarians who produced manuscripts but are not treated on other pages of our study were: *pop* Iliya from Plovdiv (1605); *gramatik* Priniya; Samuiil Bakachich Rusin, a *damaskin* compiler (1691); Daniel Mama (1687); *pop* Peshov from Kostenets; *daskal* Peio from Vrachesh (1673); *gramatik* Ban from Radomirtsi (1662); *gramatik* Belcho from Staro Selo; *ieromonah* Evtimii from "Sedemte Prestola" Monastery; *daskal* Petŭr (1698); *monah* Tsvetonom at Zograf Monastery (1617); *pop* Manasie from Dryanovo (1644); and *pop* Metrofana (1680).

[38] Of course, no single manuscript possessed all of the possible notations as outlined in our text. Over 200 manuscripts examined in the research for our study bore some sort of Slavic notation. Those notations not written in Slavic (Bulgarian, Serbian or Russian) were written in Romanian using Cyrillic characters. Many of the marginalia contained in these manuscripts have been collected and published in modern transcription in *Писахме да се знае. Приписки и летописи* [We Wrote So That It Be Known. Marginalia and Chronicles], V. Nachev and N. Fermandzhiev, eds., V. Nachev, trans., (Sofia, 1984).

[39] For example: Tsonev, *Опис* I, #295; Ivanov, *Бъл стар из Мак*, pp. 254, 255, 268; Sprostranov, *Опис Св Синод*, #63; Stojanović IV, #6745.

[40] For Bulgarian artists in the Romanian Principalities and the interrelationships that existed between Romano-Bulgarian centers of artistic activity and those that eventually emerged in the Bulgarian lands, especially during the late sixteenth century, see A. Bozhkov, «Към въпроса за взаимните връзки между българското и румънското изкуство през XIV-XVII в.» [On the Problem of Reciprocal Contacts Between Bulgarian and Romanian Art During the 14th-17th Cen.], *ИИИИ*, VII (1964), pp. 41-99.

[41] For the purposes of our study, we will consider the following to be expressions of a Bulgarian nature: a.) the use of Slavic inscriptions, as opposed to Greek; b.) the treatment of Bulgarian subjects (*e.g.*, saints, secular figures); and c.) the inclusion of native Bulgarian ethnographic elements within traditional iconographic compositions.

[42] Among the churches decorated during the second half of the fifteenth century were: Dragalevtsi Monastery, "The Blessed Virgin of Vitosha" (1476); Boboshevo Monastery, "St. Dimitŭr (1488); the "Orlitsa" (She-eagle) *metoh* of Rila Monastery (1491); and Kremikovtsi Monastery, "St. Georgi" (1493). The church at Dragalevtsi was renovated and decorated under the patronage of a wealthy, well-educated Sofia notable, Radoslav Mavŭr, who may also have been the artist for the project. Kremikovtsi was renovated under the auspices of the Radivoi family from Sofia and the Greek Sofia metropolitan, Kalivet. For Dragalevtsi, see M. Kovachev, *Драгалевският манастир Св. Богородица Витоша и неговите старини* [The Dragalevtsi Monastery of the Blessed Virgin of

Vitosha and Its Antiquities] (Sofia, 1940), pp. 12f; for Kremikovtsi, see K. Paskaleva, *Църквата «Св. Георги» в Кремиковския манастир* [The Church of "St. Georgi" in Kremikovtsi Monastery] (Sofia, 1980), pp. 38-40.

[43] In urban areas possessing large Muslim populations, Christian churches were often built so that the level of the floors was below that of the ground to ensure that the height of the structures was lower than that of those dedicated to Islamic worship. The Christian faithful were forced to enter their churches by means of downward flights of steps cut into the ground. See A. Vasiliev, «Черковно строителство в София до Освобождението» [Church Construction in Sofia to the Liberation], *Юбилеен сборник на Софийското българско благотворително образователно дружество «Иван Н. Денкооглу»* [Jubilee Collection of the Sofia Bulgarian Charitable Educational Society "Ivan N. Denkooglu"] (Sofia, 1940), p. 65.

[44] For Athonite architectural influences in the Bulgarian lands during the late sixteenth and first half of the seventeenth centuries, see A. Protich, "Le Mont Athos et l'art bulgare," *La revue bulgare*, II, 3 (May-June 1930), p. 145. The tri-apsed architectural plan was a fourteenth century Athonite development that was reflected in churches constructed in Bulgaria and Serbia during that period. It is highly probable that the late sixteenth-early seventeenth century exemplars were affected by influences that sprang out of the Serbian lands, as well as by those directly from Athos.

[45] C. Diehl, "Byzantine Art," *Byzantium. An Introduction to East Roman Civilization*, N.H. Baynes and H.St.L.B. Moss, eds., (Oxford, 1962), p. 199, considered the sixteenth century development of the artist handbooks, and their attendant workshop form of artistic production, as the fossilization of Byzantine art. One such handbook, written in Greek, was published in A.N. Didron, *Manuel d'iconographie chrétienne* (Paris, 1845).

[46] See A. Protich, «Денационализиране и възраждане на българското изкуство от 1393-1878 г.» [Denationalization and Revival of Bulgarian Art from 1393-1878], in *България 1000 години (927-1927)* [Bulgaria 1000 Years (927-1927)] (Sofia, 1930), p. 384.

[47] Protich, "Le Mont Athos," pp. 146-47; A. Bozhkov, *Bulgarian Art* (Sofia, 1964), pp. 50-51; G. Millet, *Monuments de l'Athos* (Paris, 1927), pp. 219, 256, 262.

[48] For those readers interested in further pursuing the artistic styles used by seventeenth century, and earlier, Bulgarian artists in greater detail, the following works are recommended: A. Bozhkov, *La peinture bulgare des origines au XIXe siècle* (Recklinghausen, 1974); *id.*, *Българската историческа живопис* [Bulgarian Historical Painting], I, (Sofia, 1972); *id.*, *Българско изобразително изкуство* [Bulgarian Representational Art] (Sofia, 1988); *id.*, "Les monuments d'art en Bulgarie (XVe-XVIIIe s.)," *Actes du Premier congrès international des études balkaniques et Sud-est européennes*, II, *Archéologie* (Sofia, 1969), pp. 783-93; *id.*, «Творческият метод на българския художник от епоха на турското робство до Възраждането» [The Creative Method of the Bulgarian Artist from the Era of the Turkish Yoke Until the Revival], *ИИИИ*, X (1967), pp. 5-32; A. Grabar, *La peinture religieuse en Bulgarie* (Paris, 1928); N. Mavrodinov, *Старобългарската живопис* [Old Bulgarian Painting] (Sofia, 1946); and Ts. Tsernev, *Le style national dans le peinture bulgare ancienne (XI-XIX s.)* (Sofia, 1969).

⁴⁹ For the churches at Dragalevtsi, Vukovo and Dobŭrsko, see the following works by E. Floreva: Старата църква на Драгалевския манастир [The Old Church in Dragalevtsi Monastery] (Sofia, 1968); Средновековни стенописи. Вуково. 1598 г., and Старата църква в Добърско [The Old Church in Dobŭrsko] (Sofia, 1981). Rilski's image was painted in Zemen Monastery (mid-fourteenth century) and in the Tŭrnovo church of "SS. Petŭr and Pavel" (early fifteenth century). See: A. Grabar, Боянската църква / L'église de Boiana (Sofia, 1978 [2nd. ed.]), p. 73, plate LIV; Bozhkov, Българската историческа живопис, I, pp. 147f.

⁵⁰ V. Pandurski, Куриловският манастир (Архитектура и стенописи) [Kurilo Monastery (Architecture and Wall Paintings)] (Sofia, 1975), p. 12.

⁵¹ D. Marinov, «Описание на манастира Св. Николай, наречен още Сеславский в Софийската епархия» [Description of "St. Nikolai" Monastery, Also Called Seslavtsi, in the Sofia Bishopric], Религиозни разкази [Religious Stories], 2 (1896), p. 62.

⁵² Ibid., pp. 61-62.

⁵³ Two Greek inscriptions were written in Seslavtsi Monastery but they may have been elements in scenes painted at a later date. A small number of Greek inscriptions appeared in Karlukovo but, again, they were written within scenes painted later than 1602. One of the three artists who worked at Alino Monastery was a Greek. He worked on scenes for the east wall of the church and used Greek inscriptions; the rest of the the Alino compositions bore Slavic inscriptions. A number of scenes in Kuklen Monastery painted during the seventeenth century revival bore Greek inscriptions; the area south of Plovdiv, in which Kuklen was located, was heavily populated by Greeks. All Bulgarian figures represented in the Kuklen paintings were identified by Slavic inscriptions.

⁵⁴ Bilintsi has been studied extensively by E. Floreva, Манастирската църква Архангел Михаил в Билинци [The Monastery Church Archangel Mihail in Bilintsi] (Sofia, 1973). Also see P. Kŭrdzhanov, История и състояние на манастира «Св. Архангел Михайл» при с. Билинци [History and Condition of the Monastery "Holy Archangel Mihail" Near the Village of Bilintsi] (Trŭn, 1904).

⁵⁵ Snegarov, Културни и политически връзки, p. 45.

⁵⁶ Floreva, Билинци, pp. 8-10.

⁵⁷ Ibid., pp. 25-26, for a more detailed discussion of such elements in individual scenes.

⁵⁸ A. Vasiliev, Ктиторски портрети [Donor Portraits] (Sofia, 1960), p. 69, gives 18 donor portraits by mid century, but he includes those painted in essentially Greek monuments at Bachkovo Monastery and the village of Arbanasi, near Tŭrnovo, in his count. Our count does not include those portraits. Bilintsi portrayed its original donor; there were two monastic donors at Karlukovo; six donors at Dobŭrsko; five at Alino; a single donor at Balsha; and a single donor at Dragalevtsi. An extended discussion of the evolution of donor portraiture in Bulgarian art, and the strong Romanian influences exerted upon it during the Ottoman period, can be found in Bozhkov, Българската историческа живопис, I, pp. 178f.

⁵⁹ The donor inscription at Kurilo is now lost but it was published in Pandurski, Куриловският манастир, p. 5. For Kremikovtsi, see D. Marinov, «Описание на Кремиковския манастир Св. Георги» [Description of Kremikovtsi Monastery "St. Georgi"], Религиозни разкази, 9 (1896), pp. 376f.

⁶⁰ For the church in Vŭrbovo, see A. Vasiliev, «За изобразителните изкуства в Северозападна България» [For the Representational Arts in Northwest Bulgaria], *Комплексна научна експедиция в Северозападна България през 1956 г.* [Complex of Scientific Expeditions in Northwest Bulgaria During 1956] (Sofia, 1958), p. 203. For the Svishtov and Vidin churches, see Bozhkov, *Българската историческа живопис*, I, p. 178. Refer to *id.*, «Към въпроса за взаимните връзки между българското и румънското изкуство през XIV-XVII в.,» pp. 67f, 72f, for general artistic influences that reached out from the Romanian Principalities to the Bulgarian lands.

⁶¹ In the western lands: the village churches of Yana ("St. Anna"), Boboshevo ("St. Iliya"), Tsarevets ("St. Nikolai"), and Mala Tsŭrkva (Iskŭr); and the the monastery churches of Podgumer and Mishlovshtitsa. In the southcentral lands: Kilifarevo Monastery; and the village church of Golyamo Belovo ("St. Nikolai").

⁶² A good study of Bulgarian icons can be found in K. Paskaleva, *Икони от България* [Icons From Bulgaria] (Sofia, 1981), with text and 100 color plates.

⁶³ See N. Mavrodinov, «Църкви и манастири в Мелник и Рожен» [Churches and Monasteries in Melnik and Rozhen], *ГНАМ*, V (1926 [1931]), pp. 285-306.

⁶⁴ See A. Bozhkov, «Социалната и творческа природа на българския художник през XV-XVIII век» [The Social and Creative Nature of the Bulgarian Artist During the 15th-18th Centuries], *Векове*, 1 (1984), pp. 24-25.

⁶⁵ See Iv. Gergova, «Църковната архитектура в Чипровския край до въстанието от 1688 г.» [Church Architecture in the Chiprovtsi Region to the Uprising of 1688], in *300 години Чипровско въстание*, pp. 66-72.

⁶⁶ For the Chiprovtsi School of goldsmithing, see M. Iosifova, «За стопанското и културното развитие на Чипровския край през XVII в.» [For the Economic and Cultural Development of the Chiprovtsi Region During the 17th Cen.], in *300 години Чипровско въстание*, pp. 41-47.

⁶⁷ Bozhkov, «Социалната и творческа природа,» pp. 18-19.

⁶⁸ Two extant liturgical manuscripts were the work of Pimen. See Tsonev, *Опис* I, #197; *id.*, *Опис* II, #534.

⁶⁹ Yanakiev [ed.], «Житие,» p. 9.

⁷⁰ Details of Pimen's biography can be found in *Ibid.*; P. Dinekov [ed.], «Житието на Пимен Зографски»; I. Vasilieva, «Да разкрием и изучим художественото наследство на Пимен Зограф» [To Reveal and Study the Artistic Legacy of Pimen Zograf], *Музеите и паметници на културата* [The Museums and Monuments of Culture], I (1963), pp. 19-21; and in V. Pandurski, «Пимен Софийски» [Pimen Sofiiski], *Бележити българи* [Noted Bulgarians], III, (Sofia, 1969), pp. 90-97.

⁷¹ Floreva, *Билинци*, p. 26, refuted the idea that Pimen decorated Bilintsi.

⁷² Pandurski, *Куриловският манастир*, p. 23, gives the donor inscription from Suhodol, which noted that Pimen worked there only during the months of July and August 1606. If he undertook and completed the decoration of the church at Kurilo, it required only the months of March-May 1596.

Chapter 6. Major Centers of Orthodox Cultural Activity

¹ The story of Hrelyo's death was related in a gravestone inscription, given in K. Jireček, *Пътувания по България*, p. 701. A stone defense tower at Rila Monastery, known as "Hrelyo's Tower," is the only extant structure from the fourteenth century. It bears an inscription that dates it to 1335. Rila Monastery is the most widely studied monastery in Bulgaria. The following works have been used extensively in the historical survey presented by our study: I. Ivanov, *Св. Иван Рилски и неговият манастир*; Iv. Duichev, *Рилският светец и неговата обител* [The Saint of Rila and His Monastery] (Sofia, 1947); H. Hristov, G. Stoikov and K. Miyatev, *The Rila Monastery: History, Architecture, Frescoes, Wood-Carvings* (Sofia, 1959); and G. Neshev, *Български довъзрожденски културно-народностни средища.* pp. 82f.

² The text of the Shishman charter to Rila was published in Ilyinskiy, *Грамоты*, #5, and in Ivanov, *Бъл стар из Мак*, pp. 597-98. In the charter, Shishman suggested that he was merely reconfirming rights and privileges conferred on the monastery by his royal predecessors.

³ The *ferman* of Bayezid was published in D. Ihchiev, *Турски документи на Рилския манастир* [Turkish Documents on Rila Monastery] (Sofia, 1910), p. 4.

⁴ The refounding of Rila Monastery by the brothers was related in a *sbornik* (1479) produced at the monastery by Vladislav Gramatik. See Ivanov, *Старобългарски разкази*, pp. 72-73. In 1466 a contract was drawn up between Rila Monastery and Panteleimon (Rusik) Monastery on Mount Athos, indicating that Rila was refounded prior to that date. See Ivanov, *Св. Иван Рилски*, p. 153.

⁵ Vladislav's work was published in original transcription in Ivanov, *Старобългарски разкази*, pp. 227f (modern transcription, pp. 71f).

⁶ For the *fermans*, see Ihchiev, *Турски документи на Рилския манастир, fermans* #4-12. *Vakıf* status was granted the monastery lands in 1508 by Sultan Bayezid II (1481-1512) because they formed part of the possessions of his *vezir*, Kara Mustafa *paşa*. Kara Mustafa was granted the option of transforming his holdings into *vakıf*. See *ferman* #4, Ibid. Also see G. Neshev, "Quelques documents turcs sur l'histoire du monastère de Rila de la periode du XVe au XVIIe s.," *EH*, IV, (Sofia, 1968), p. 235.

⁷ See the following documents in Ihchiev, *Турски документи на Рилския манастир, hucets* #8, 10; *sipahi* act #1; *ferman* #13.

⁸ See *Ibid., fermans* #15, 16; *hucet* #12.

⁹ See *Ibid., sipahi* acts #1, 2; *tefter* excerpt, #3.

¹⁰ Sprostranov, *Опис Рил ман*, #3/2 (28); Duichev, *Рилският светец*, p. 319; Ivanov, *Св. Иван Рилски*, p. 58.

¹¹ Ivanov, *Ibid.*, pp. 155-56; Muravyav, *Сношения Россий*, II, pp. 57-60; N.M. Dylevskiy, «Просително послание на Рилското манастирско братство до руския цар Михайл Феодорович Романов от 1627 година» [Supplication Message of the Rila Monastery Monks to the Russian Tsar Mihail Feodorovich Romanov From 1627], *ИИБЕ*, XIX (1970), pp. 689f; Snegarov, *Културни и политически връзки*, pp. 37-39. The responses of both the tsar and the patriarch to the Rila petition have gone unrecorded.

[12] Snegarov, *Ibid.*, pp. 39, 39n. In a number of charters granted to monasteries located within the borders of the Ottoman Empire, Tsar Mihail specified that delegations from those establishments were permitted only to be despatched once every six or seven years. Perhaps the 1628 delegation negated Arsenii's attempt in 1632. This may serve as evidence that the 1628 petition had been successful.

[13] Dylevskiy, «Просително послание,» illustration accompanying the text; Paskaleva, *Икони,* pp. 166-67; Bozhkov, *Българската историческа живопис,* I, pp. 149-51.

[14] See: Sprostranov, *Опис Рил ман,* #1/22 (47); Stojanović III, #5636, 5788; Stoyanov and Kodov, *Опис* III, #986; B. Raikov, *Етрополският книжовен център през XVI-XVII век. Палеографско и литературно-историческо изследване* [The Etropole Literary Center During the 16th-17th Centuries. Paleographical and Literary-Historical Study] (Sofia [Dissertation, Sofia Univ.], 1972), p. 22n.

[15] See: Ivanov, *Бъл стар из Мак,* p. 252; *id., Св. Иван Рилски,* p. 88; Stojanović I, #1492; Sprostranov, *Опис Рил ман,* #3/2 (28).

[16] Sprostranov, *Ibid.,* #1/29 (8); Stojanović I, #1528.

[17] Sprostranov, *Ibid.,* #1/6 (5), 2/15 (41); *id., Опис Св Синод,* #78; Stojanović III, #5715, 5716, 5948.

[18] See Gechev, p. 30. The older manuscripts included: a psalter (fourteenth century) with annotations from 1648 and 1653; a gospels (1529) written in Slavic but produced in Suceava, Moldavia, annotated in 1656 by a *pop* Aleksi; a work entitled, *Za lyubovyata* (For Love), which contained copies of works by Evtimii Tŭrnovski on Ivan Rilski; the hagiography of the Serbian saint, Stefan, written by Abbot Grigorii, was bound and annotated in 1634 by the monk, Stefan, from Samokov, at the order of the abbot of Rila, Arsenii; and a book of services (1567) written by the illustrious sixteenth century Bulgarian writer-copyist, Ioan Kratovski. See Sprostranov, *Опис Рил ман,* #1/11a, 3/13 (19), 1/2 (46), 1/23 (48), 4/8 (61).

[19] *Ibid.,* #3/2 (28).

[20] Rila possessed *metohs* in Panagyurishte, Koprivshtitsa, Karlovo, Teteven, Kazanlŭk, Klisura, Gabrovo, Etropole, and elsewhere. See Arhimandrit Kliment Rilets, «Рилските духовници таксидиоти» [Rila Ecclesiastic *Taxidiots*], *Духовна култура,* XI (1935), pp. 15f. For the late-sixteenth century *damaskin,* see Sprostranov, *Опис Рил ман,* #4/10 (78). See Petkanova [-Toteva], *Дамаскините,* pp. 47-48, for a discussion of why *damaskin* literature arose early at Rila Monastery. Our study accepts her dating of the manuscript, as opposed to the commonly held later seventeenth century date.

[21] Snegarov, *Културни и политически връзки,* pp. 104-06; Duichev, *Рилският светец,* pp. 324-25; B.S. Angelov, "Un canon de St. Jean de Rila," pp. 172-73; N.M. Dylevskiy, *Рилскы манастир и Россия в XVI и XVII веках* [Rila Monastery and Russia in the 16th and 17th Centuries] (Sofia, 1974 [2nd. ed.]), pp. 85f; Neshev, *Български довъзрожденски културно-народностни средища,* pp. 124f.

[22] Duichev, *Ibid.,* p. 324, maintained that the Bulgarians, through the efforts of the Rila monks, were already looking toward the Russians for liberation from Ottoman rule in a way similar to that pursued by Petŭr Parchevich and the Bulgarian Catholics in looking toward the Habsburg Empire. No hard evidence supporting Duichev's supposition is readily available.

[23] Semerdzhiev, pp. 134-35; Gechev, p. 67; Sreznevskii and Pokrovskii, *Описание рукописного*, pp. 112-13. A notation in a 1639 *sbornik* mentioned that a certain Bogdanin from Samokov paid tuition for his son's education. See: Tsonev, *Опис* I, #274; Stojanović I, #1078.

[24] See: A. Chilingirov, *Църквата «Св. Никола» в село Марица* [The Church of "St. Nikola" in the Village of Maritsa] (Sofia, 1976), for the Maritsa church; S. Zahariev, «Стенописите в старата църква в с. Мала Църква, Самоковско» [The Wall Paintings in the Old Church in the Village of Mala Tsŭrkva, Samokov Region], *ИИИИ*, VII (1964), pp. 141-50, for Mala Tsŭrkva. A note in a sixteenth century manuscript penned by Petŭr Ranov of Belchin (1692) indicated that a school may have been operated by his village church. See Tsonev, *Опис* II, #600.

[25] See: Tsonev, *Опис* I, #64; Sprostranov, *Опис Св Синод*, #28; Goshev, «Стари записки» IV, #28; Stojanović IV, #6760.

[26] Sprostranov, *Ibid.*, #78; Gechev, p. 73.

[27] *Daskal* Mihail, originally from Vratsa, died in Razlog in 1666. See D. Iotsov, *Културно-политическа история на Браца* [Cultural-Political History of Vratsa], I, *От римската епоха до Освобождението* [From the Roman Epoch to the Liberation] (Sofia, 1937), doc #38.

[28] See Floreva, *Добърско, passim.*

[29] Some general studies of Sofia include: A. Ishirkov, *Град София през XVII век* [The City of Sofia During the 17th Century] (Sofia, 1912); I. Ivanov, «София през турско време» [Sofia During Turkish Times], in *Юбилейна книга на град Софиа (1878-1928)* [Jubilee Book of the City of Sofia (1878-1928)] (Sofia, 1928), pp. 38-45; A. Monedzhikova, *София през вековете* [Sofia Through the Centuries] (Sofia, 1946); N. Todorov, "The Socio-Economic Life of Sofia in the 17th and 18th Centuries," in *La ville balkanique*, pp. III, 1-20; and *id., The Balkan City, passim.*

[30] Gerlach, *Дневник*, p. 264. This author's explanatory notes are bracketed in the text.

[31] «Описание,» pp. 182-83. This author's explanatory notes are bracketed in the text.

[32] D.A. Ihchiev, «Материали за историята ни под турското робство» [Materials for Our History under the Turkish Yoke], *ИИДв*, I (1905), pp. 79, 101; Tsvetkova, *Хайдутството*, docs. #23, 25-30.

[33] To conclude that the Turks destroyed seven churches in Sofia between 1578 and 1640 would be pure conjecture. Bogdan noted only that two had met such a fate. As for the remaining five in question, a number of possibilities are open: a.) they had been intentionally destroyed by acts of Muslim fanaticism; b.) they had been confiscated by the Turks and converted into mosques; c.) a combination of both the foregoing possibilities; d.) they had fallen into decay and had been abandoned by their Orthodox congregations; or e.) the converse of the latter possibility.

[34] For Kurilo, see D.A. Ihchiev [ed.], «Турски документи за Софийската епархия» [Turkish Documents for the Sofia Bishopric], *Преглед* [Review], I, 6-7 (1908), pp. 322-23. For Mehmed's *ferman*, see *Ibid.*, I, 8 (1908), pp. 388f.

[35] See: P. Mutafchiev, *Избрани произведения*, II, pp. 259-60, 281-82, 285-86; Marinov, «Описание на Кремиковския манастир,» p. 305; Kovachev, *Драгалевският манастир*, pp. 18, 125; V. Pandurski, «Стенописите в Илиенцкия манастир край София» [Wall Paintings in Ilientsi Monastery Near Sofia], *ИИИИ*, XIII (1969), pp. 5-28.

IN THE SEVENTEENTH CENTURY

Examples of seventeenth century icons from Sofia can be found in the National Art Gallery of Old Bulgarian Art, Aleksandŭr Nevski Crypt, Sofia, and in the Church Museum in Sofia. See Pandurski, Паметници на изкуството, plates #121, 148, 180, 210.

[36] See: Stojanović I, #1130; Stojanović IV, #6571; Tsonev, Опис Пловдив, #5; id., Опис I, #2; id., Опис II, #684; Sprostranov, Опис Св Синод, #47.

[37] For the extant evidence, see: Tsonev, Опис I, #456; id., Опис II, #684; Stoyanov and Kodov, Опис IV, #1153; Sprostranov, Опис Св Синод, #5, 8, 21, 47; Goshev, «Стари записки» I, #158, 368; id., «Стари записки» IV, #20.

[38] See: Kovachev, Драгалевският манастир, pp. 20-21; Milev, pp. 51-52; Sprostranov, Опис Св Синод, #96.

[39] Sprostranov, Ibid., #34; Goshev, «Стари записки» IV, #34.

[40] Sprostranov, Ibid., #8; Goshev, Ibid., #9.

[41] Ivanov, Бъл стар из Мак, p. 278.

[42] Sprostranov, Опис Св Синод, #47, 109.

[43] The Slavic name for Sofia, Sredets, was borne by the city since its reconstruction by Slavic colonists in the early ninth century. Throughout the periods of the two medieval Bulgarian states and into the seventeenth century, Bulgarian authors commonly referred to the city by its Slavic name, or by its more ancient one, Serdica. The first known recorded use of the name, Sofia, appeared in a charter granted Dragalevtsi Monastery (1376) by Tsar Ivan Shishman. At present, that document rests in the library of Zograf Monastery. Sofia became the official name of the city only during the Ottoman period. For a discussion of this question, see: Ishirkov, Град София, pp. 10-12; and M. Drinov, Избрани съчинения, II, (Sofia, 1971), pp. 356f.

[44] The term, *Mala sveta gora* in Bulgarian, was first coined by Jireček in the original 1876 Czech and German editions of his История на българите. See the Sofia, 1978 Bulgarian edition, pp. 439 and 439n. Since his time, some historians have attempted to create the impression that the term was more than a descriptive one, that it, in fact, designated a highly organized, extensive monastic complex, analogous to that on Mount Athos. See, for example: V. Atanasov, Урвич и Бистрица. Кокалянски манацтир и Мала Света Гора. Археологическо-исторически бележки [Urvich and Bistritsa. Kokalyane Monastery and Little Mount Athos. Archaeological-Historical Notes] (Sofia, 1905); Iv. Bogdanov, Български твърдини. Книжовни огнища, крепости, манастири в София и Софийско [Bulgarian Strongholds. Literary Centers, Fortresses, Monasteries in Sofia and the Sofia Region] (Sofia, 1971); and *ieromonah* A. Topalov and A. Spilkov, Седемте престола. Кратка история на манастира «Рожденство Пресветыя Богородицы» [The Seven Altars. Short History of the Monastery "Birth of the Blessed Virgin"] (Sofia, 1947). Atanasov first advanced the theory, but with qualifications, noting that his source was local legend (pp. 27-29). Bogdanov, a somewhat nationalistic author of popular histories and not a professionally trained historian, accepted Atanasov's theory as established fact, and he proceeded to identify the *lavra* and the member communities of the supposed complex (pp. 17f, 23f, 39f, 79f) without noting his supporting evidence. Topalov and Spilkov identified certain member establishments that conflicted with those put forth by both Atanasov and Bogdanov, and, in fact, listed some that had no possibility of forming part of such a monastic complex, having been founded later, during the sixteenth and seventeenth centuries. Not a single solid piece of evidence is currently

known to substantiate the theory of a centrally organized monastic complex in the Sofia region at any time. The term, "Little Mount Athos," may well serve as a literarily descriptive one, as it was used by A. Vasiliev, «Софийската Света Гора» [The Sofia "Holy Mountain"], *Славяни*, 5 (1971), pp. 28-31, but its continued use otherwise would be to perpetuate an historical myth.

⁴⁵ A piece of marginalia (1627) left by one Paisii spoke of the lands owned by the monastery as being rich in forests, vines, and fruit trees. See: D. Marinov, «Описание на манастира Св. Богородица, наречен още Елешнишки в Софийската епархия» [Description of the "Holy Virgin" Monastery, Also Called Eleshnitsa, in the Sofia Bishopric], *Религиозни разкази*, 1 (1896), p. 31; Mutafchiev, *Избрани произведения*, II, p. 286.

⁴⁶ See Sprostranov, *Опис Св Синод*, #66, 93, 103.

⁴⁷ See: *Ibid.*, #81, 109; *id.*, *Опис Рил ман*, #1/6 (5); Goshev, «Стари записки» II, #243; Stojanović III, #5948.

⁴⁸ See: Tsonev, *Опис* II, #534; Goshev, «Стари записки» III, #315. The paintings at Seslavtsi have been stylistically linked to those on Mount Athos from the late sixteenth century. Those in Seslavtsi bear marked similarities to those in Eleshnitsa and Kurilo, speaking for Pimen as the master artist of all three. See Mutafchiev, *Избрани произведения*, II, p. 282.

⁴⁹ Goshev, *Ibid.*, #374.

⁵⁰ For these Kurilo manuscripts, see: Goshev, «Стари записки» IV, #24; Sprostranov, *Опис Рил ман*, #1/6 (5); Tsonev, *Опис* I, #45.

⁵¹ For the sixteenth century manuscript, see Goshev, «Стари записки» V, #41.

⁵² One such traveler was Hans Dernschwam, who in 1555 noted in his travel account that a monastery called, "Mother of God," existed on the lower slopes of Vitosha, and that it was staffed by a number of monks. See H. Dernschwam, «Дневник на . . . за едно пътуване до Константинопол и Мала Азия (1553-1555)» [Daybook of. . . for a Journey to Constantinople and Asia Minor (1553-1555)], *Чужди пътеписи за Балканите* [Foreign Travel Accounts of the Balkans], III, *Немски и австрийски пътеписи за Балканите, XV-XVI в.* [German and Austrian Travel Accounts of the Balkans, 15th-16th Cen.], M. Ionov, ed., (Sofia, 1979), p. 265.

⁵³ Kovachev, *Драгалевският манастир*, pp. 6, 10-11.

⁵⁴ *Ibid.*, pp. 12f.

⁵⁵ *Ibid.*, pp. 125f.

⁵⁶ Goshev, «Стари записки» IV, #21. The monastery library houses two works of interest for this period: a manuscript gospels (1534), covered by Velo the Goldsmith (1646); and a printed Russian gospels (1658) that bears two notes by the Kyustendil metropolitan, Mihail Kratovski (1645-1676). See Kovachev, *Драгалевският манастир*, pp. 52, 190f.

⁵⁷ Most left only their initials and dates. A few wrote their full names: Fra Antonio, Fra Daniel Theodorović from Zhelezna (1666), Maria, Ivan Nikolić (1662), and others. See Kovachev, *Ibid.*, p. 22. Daniel was a Catholic priest in Sofia during 1661. See Milev, p. 187. Exactly why Catholics patronized Dragalevtsi is unclear. One may posit that its fame as a spiritual center, its close proximity to Sofia, and its naturally beautiful mountain setting all played a part in cementing its general popularity.

⁵⁸ Kovachev, *Ibid.*, pp. 18-19, 155f, 217-18.

⁵⁹ *Ibid.*, pp. 19-20, gives two Ottoman *kadı* court documents in which Eremiya figures. The first was dated 9 February 1647, at which time Eremiya purchased a few water mills for the monastery from Petko, Todor and Velko, all from the village of Boyana. The second was dated 27 March 1663. In that year Stoyan Stoev and Stoyu Kalchov, both from Dragalevtsi village, appeared before the *kadı* to inform him that the monk, Eremiya, from the monastery had been in one of the monastery's houses located in Zoziosh *çiftlik*, which was in the locale of the village. Apparently, Eremiya had lit a fire during the night for warmth while he slept. Unfortunately, near midnight, sparks from the fire ignited the building, and as it lay close to the stable of the two Bulgarian plaintiffs, their property had also caught fire and was destroyed. Eremiya, a horse, and a cow had perished in the flames. The two men sought and received redress for their destroyed property.

⁶⁰ Whether or not the valuables that were at one time housed in Kokalyane were actually those of Shishman is unimportant in our context. The legend itself is what matters. That such objects did exist was given credence by the discovery of a silver cup, worked in the tradition of eleventh century Byzantine gold and silver smithing, found at the monastery during the late nineteenth century. It was commonly referred to as the "tsar cup" by the local population, and it was described for the first time by V.D. Stoyanov, «Пролетна разходка от София до Кокалянския мънастир през с. Бистрица, и завращание от поменътия мънастир до София през селата Кокаляне, Панчерево и Горубляне» [Springtime Walk From Sofia to Kokalyane Monastery Through the Village of Bistritsa, and Returning From Said Monastery to Sofia Through the Villages of Kokalyane, Pancherevo and Gorublyane], *ПСп*, XL (1892), pp. 689-91. Also see Atanasov, *Урвич и Бистрица*, pp. 7f.

⁶¹ Goshev, «Стари записки» III, #368.

⁶² For Alexios' charter, see Jireček, *Пътувания по България*, pp. 64, 64n.

⁶³ See: Neshev, *Български довъзрожденски културно-народностни средища*, p. 180; Tsonev, *Опис* I, #167; Goshev, «Стари записки» IV, #3.

⁶⁴ Ivanov, *Бъл стар из Мак*, pp. 606-07.

⁶⁵ Sprostranov, *Опис Св Синод*, #46; Goshev, «Стари записки» V, #46.

⁶⁶ Sprostranov, *Ibid.*, #8; Stojanović I, #1130, 1357; Ivanov, *Бъл стар из Мак*, pp. 251, 267; Gandev, *Проблеми*, p. 41.

⁶⁷ Etropole Monastery is commonly referred to in the sources by its popular name, *Varovitets* ("Of Lime"). Because of the abundance of limestone found in the locale, that material served as the primary building blocks used in constructing the monastery.

⁶⁸ Mutafchiev, *Избрани произведения*, II, pp. 306-07; Kiel, p. 132.

⁶⁹ I. Ivanov, *Северна Македония. Историческа издирвания* [Northern Macedonia. Historical Discoveries] (Sofia, 1906), p. 252. For the mining industry, especially iron ore mining, see: *Ibid.*, pp. 303-06; G.K. Georgiev, *Старата железодобивна индустрия в България*, pp. 156f; and Davies, "Ancient Mining," pp. 405f.

⁷⁰ Two Etropole parish priests are known to have been active writer-copyists, *pop* Stoyu (1618) and Ioan Gramatik (1639). Both are discussed later in our study. In 1613 a certain student, Todor, noted the existence of a school in the town of Etropole.

⁷¹ Mutafchiev, *Избрани произведения*, II, p. 321; A. Tatsov, «Етрополският манастир Варовитец» [Etropole Monastery *Varovitets*], *Българска сбирка*, XXI, 3

(1915), pp. 139; Pandurski, *Паметници на изкуството,* plate #52. The old church of the monastery has since been destroyed and the 1158 slab has disappeared.

⁷² The beadroll in which pilgrims to the monastery signed their names was published in Stoyanov and Kodov, *Опис* III, #1017. A silver cross produced in Vratsa by master Iovan Panov (1666) was donated to Etropole Monastery by *ierei* Stoyan from Oryahovo. Another such cross, undated, was worked by master silversmith Mavrudiya Dragulinov from Kameno Pole. In 1692 the inhabitants of Etropole donated a silver reliquary to the monastery church that had been created by order of *ieromonah* Simon. See: Mutafchiev, *Ibid.,* p. 321, 322, 323; B. Raikov, *Етрополският книжовен център,* p. 21.

⁷³ For the manuscripts, see: Mutafchiev, *Ibid.,* p. 327; Stoyanov and Kodov, *Ibid.,* #921, 932, 971, 978, 986, 997, 1042, 1044; Tsonev, *Опис* I, #10; Sprostranov, *Опис Св Синод,* #85, 86, 92, 97, 107; B. Raikov and A. Dzhurova [eds.], *Българска ръкописна книга, X-XVIII в. Каталог* [The Bulgarian Manuscript Book, 10th-18th Cen. Catalog] (Sofia, 1976), #499 (catalog #222), 573 (catalog #218); Goshev, «Стари записки» IV, #11. Of the printed books, two, dated 1494, were printed in Cetinje by Đorđ Crnojević. A third was a copy of the famous Ostrožka Bible, dated 1580-81. See Raikov, *Етрополският книжовен център,* p. 22n.

⁷⁴ Of 15 notable Slavic medieval ruling princes whose names head the monastery beadroll, only three — Asen, Mihail Shishman (1323-1330), and Ivan Shishman — are Bulgarian. The others are Serbs. Serbian names also commonly appear throughout the beadroll. A Serb priest, *pop* Uroš, is credited with illuminating a manuscript produced at the monastery. A 1642 note in another work mentioned the existence of a Serbian *mahalle* in the town of Etropole. See: Stoyanov and Kodov, *Ibid.,* #1050; Raikov, *Ibid.,* pp. 70-72; Mutafchiev, *Избрани произведения,* II, p. 320.

⁷⁵ Etropole's contacts with the Romanian lands are demonstrated by two pieces of seventeenth century marginalia. The Romanian, Naum Matei *gramatik,* left a note in the manuscript illuminated by *pop* Uroš. In 1616 *pop* Vlŭcho from Etropole mentioned that he bound a manuscript at the time that the Turks "enslaved Vlashka." See: Stoyanov and Kodov, *Ibid.;* Mutafchiev, *Ibid.,* pp. 328.

⁷⁶ For Rafail's works, see Sprostranov, *Опис Св Синод,* #85, 92, 96, 97, 99.

⁷⁷ For Ioan's works, see: Goshev, «Врачанска епархия,» #15 (1); Tsonev, *Опис* I, #76; Stoyanov and Kodov, *Опис* III, #1044; Raikov, *Етрополският книжовен център,* p. 97; and *id.,* «Неизвестно положно житие на Иван Рилски» [Unknown Eulogetic Life of Ivan Rilski], *Език и литература* [Language and Literature], 3 (1970), pp. 57-61.

⁷⁸ Sprostranov, *Опис Св Синод,* #86, 89, 102, 107.

⁷⁹ Stojanović I, #1357; Tsonev, *Опис* I, #10, 304; Stoyanov and Kodov, *Опис* III, #1017, 1050; Ivanov, *Бъл стар из Мак,* p. 251.

⁸⁰ Raikov, «Йеромонах Даниил,» p. 282.

⁸¹ See: Goshev, «Врачанска епархия,» #33; Tsonev, *Опис* I, #98. A manuscript produced in Sofia (1598) and subsequently donated to Iveron Monastery on Athos contained a note that mentioned a certain Daniil being tonsured in the Sofia church of "St. Nikola." See Stojanović I, #893. In all his works, Daniil followed the orthographical principles of the so-called "lamb's tail" school, which characterized the literary products

of the Sofia region during the second half of the sixteenth and the early seventeenth centuries.

⁸² Stoyanov and Kodov, Опис III, #1042.

⁸³ Goshev, «Врачанска епархия,» #4 (18); Raikov, Етрополският книжовен център, p. 56 (catalog of manuscripts); Tsonev, Опис I, #304.

⁸⁴ Stoyanov and Kodov, Опис III, #956; Stojanović I, #1191.

⁸⁵ Raikov, Етрополският книжовен център, pp. 70-72, 73-74 (catalog of manuscripts); Sprostranov, Опис Св Синод, #99; Stoyanov and Kodov, Ibid., #921; Goshev, «Врачанска епархия,» #5.

⁸⁶ See: Stojanović IV, #6744; Stoyanov and Kodov, Ibid., #1044; Tsonev, Опис I, #304.

⁸⁷ Stoyanov and Kodov, Ibid., #1050; Sprostranov, Опис Св Синод, #100.

⁸⁸ Mutafchiev, Избрани произведения, II, p. 328; Tsonev, Опис I, #10; Raikov, Етрополският книжовен център, p. 40.

⁸⁹ Raikov, Ibid., p. 201. Ioan and Koyu's 1636 prologue twice mentioned the defeat of the Byzantine Emperor Nikephoros I (802-811) in 811 by the Bulgarian Han Krum (802-814). See Stoyanov and Kodov, Опис III, #1044. For seventeenth century Etropole manuscripts with copies of pre-Ottoman Bulgarian writings, see: Tsonev, Ibid., #304; Stoyanov and Kodov, Ibid., #978, 1042, 1043, 1044, 1050; Sprostranov, Опис Св Синод, #89, 107; Goshev, «Врачанска епархия,» #4.

⁹⁰ Raikov, «Йеромонах Даниил,» pp. 285-86.

⁹¹ For the legend of Glozhene, see Nikolov and Manolov, Огнища на българщината, p. 27. For the cell schools at the two monasteries, see: Stoyanov and Kodov, Опис III, #1044; Sprostranov, Опис Рил ман, #2/10 (6); Gechev, pp. 39, 71; Chakŭrov, p. 106.

⁹² Sprostranov, Опис Св Синод, #54; Goshev, «Стари записки» V, #54; Tsonev, Опис I, #75; B. Angelov, Старобългарско книжовно наследство, pp. 123-24, 124-25.

⁹³ See: Tsonev, Опис I, #251, 304; id., Опис II, #621; Stoyanov and Kodov, Опис III, #956, 971, 997; Stojanović I, #1357; Ivanov, Бъл стар из Мак, p. 251; Goshev, «Врачанска епархия,» #4; Raikov, Етрополският книжовен център, p. 97.

⁹⁴ See: Iotsov, p. 34; I. Georgiev, «Град Враца. Принос към историята му» [The City of Vratsa. Contribution to Its History], СбНУ, XX (1904), pp. 1-75.

⁹⁵ For "St. Nikola" as the bolyar church, see: Tsonev, Опис I, #98; Sprostranov, Опис Св Синод, #18. The total number of Vratsa churches is mentioned in B. Angelov, Из истор на старо и въз лит, p. 116. For a school at "St. Nikola," see: Tsonev, Ibid., #124; Sprostranov, Ibid.; Stoyanov and Kodov, Опис IV, #1170. For the second Vratsa school, see: Gechev, p. 70; Chakŭrov, p. 106. For the four Vratsa daskals, see: Iotsov, pp. 291-92 (doc. #38); Gandev, Проблеми, p. 41.

⁹⁶ See: Tsonev, Опис I, #98, 124; Stoyanov and Kodov, Опис III, #932; id., Опис IV, #1170; Sprostranov, Опис Св Синод, #18; Ivanov, Бъл стар из Мак, pp. 253, 254; Goshev, «Врачанска епархия,» pp. 2-3.

⁹⁷ See S. Mihailov, «Разрушеният манастир Св. Тройца до Враца» [The Ruined Monastery of "The Holy Trinity" Near Vratsa], ИАИ, XVIII (1952), pp. 395-96, for the probable location and date of the monastery's founding.

⁹⁸ See Tsonev, Опис I, #141, 162, 168, 277.

⁹⁹ Shishatovats must have left the monastery soon after completing his 1608 manuscript. He signed the so-called *Boyana Beadroll* at Dragalevtsi Monastery in 1612, in which he noted that he had traveled to "foreign lands," and he specifically mentioned visiting the Transylvanian town of Timişoara. Varlaam wrote a note commemorating his pilgrimage to Jerusalem in a manuscript that is currently partially extant in a Leningrad library. See: S. Stanchev and M. Stancheva, Боянският поменик [The Boyana Beadroll] (Sofia, 1963), p. 86; B. Angelov, *Из истор на старо и въз лит*, pp. 118-19, 119n; B.S. Angelov, *Из старата българска, руска и сръбска литература*, II, pp. 247-48.

¹⁰⁰ See Nikolov and Manolov, p. 25, for the legend. A general history of Cherepish Monastery can be had in A. Vasiliev, Черепишки манастир «Успение пресветия Богородично» [Cherepish Monastery "The Assumption of the Most Blessed Virgin"] (Sofia, 1943).

¹⁰¹ Yanakiev, «Житие,» p. 9; Goshev, «Врачанска епархия,» #4, 33.

¹⁰² Tsonev, *Опис* I, #292.

¹⁰³ Ivanov, *Бъл стар из Мак*, p. 250; Stojanović IV, #6711.

¹⁰⁴ Tsonev, *Опис* I, #15, 295.

¹⁰⁵ Mutafchiev, *Избрани произведения*, II, p. 388.

¹⁰⁶ *Ibid.*, pp. 372-73.

¹⁰⁷ The oldest images of the two brothers rendered in mural paintings were created in the church of "The Holy Wisdom" (eleventh century), Ohrid, the cultural capital of the Macedonian lands, and in the church at Staro Nagoričane Monastery, "St. Georgi" (fourteenth century), also in the Macedonian lands. Some scholars credit Pimen Zografski with the paintings at Dolna Beshovitsa. G. Chavrŭkov, *Български манастири. Паметници на историята, културата и изкуството* [Bulgarian Monasteries. Monuments of History, Culture and Art] (Sofia, 1974), p. 44, accredits a certain Pavel from the village of Dolna Beshovitsa with the work.

¹⁰⁸ Goshev, «Стари записки» IV, pp. 4-5.

¹⁰⁹ Iotsov, pp. 291-92 (doc. #38), gives an inscription on a gravestone found in the cemetery near the church of "St. Nikolai" in Razlog. Mihail died in 1666.

¹¹⁰ Zhivko taught mostly from old Greek books in his possession. The only known evidence for his school is contained in an anonymous work known as the *Adzhar Copy*, which consists of 150 pages of apocryphal stories. See B. Angelov, «Старобългарски книжовини средища. Аджар (Свежен) — Карловско» [Old Bulgarian Literary Centers. Adzhar (Svezhen) — Karlovo Region], *ИНБКМ*, XII [XVIII] (1972), pp. 45, 45-46n.

¹¹¹ Stojanović IV, #6744, 6745; Tsonev, *Опис Пловдив*, #73, 74.

¹¹² Stojanović I, #1644; Ivanov, *Бъл стар из Мак*, p. 254; B. Angelov, *Из истор на старо и въз лит*, p. 136; Chakŭrov, p. 106; Gechev, p. 73; Iv. Undzhiev, *Карлово. История на града до Освобождението* [Karlovo. History of the City to the Liberation] (Sofia, 1968), p. 87.

¹¹³ See: Tsonev, *Опис Пловдив*, #5, 45, 74, 87, 115, 119; *id.*, *Опис* II, #601, 622, 623, 632, 633; *id.*, «Книжовни старини от Елена» [Literary Antiquities From Elena], *ГСУифф*, XIX, 7 (1923), p. 41; Stoyanov and Kodov, *Опис* III, #992; *id.*, *Опис БАН*, #88; B. Angelov, *Из истор на старо и въз лит*, pp. 140, 146-49.

[114] Stojanović I, #1644; Ivanov, *Бъл стар из Мак*, p. 254; Tsonev, *Опис Пловдив*, #45, 115; M. Stoyanov, «Един български културен център в Родопите през турската епоха» [A Bulgarian Cultural Center in the Rhodopes During the Turkish Era], *ГМ-По*, I (1954), p. 262.

[115] Stoyanov, *Ibid.*, p. 259; B. Angelov, *Из истор на старо и въз лит*, pp. 137f.

[116] Angelov, *Ibid.*, p. 137; S. Velkov, «Едно старинно евангелие» [An Antique Gospel], *Църковен вестник* [Church News], XXXI, 32 (1930), pp. 367-68.

[117] Angelov, *Ibid.*, p. 50, 107, 108-09, 110, 113; *id.*, «Старобългарски книжовини средища. Аджар,» pp. 50-51, 54; Tsonev, *Опис* I, #326; *id.*, *Опис Пловдив*, #145; Stoyanov and Kodov, *Опис* III, #966, 972; Stojanović I, #1840.

[118] See Stoyanov, «Един български културен център в Родопите,» pp. 255-56.

[119] See *Ibid.*, p. 256. There exists an inscription on the monastery fountain bearing the date and names of donors.

[120] See: *Ibid.*, p. 262; Gechev, pp. 43, 71; Sprostranov, *Опис Св Синод*, #8; Tsonev, *Опис Пловдив*, #45, 47, 48, 49, 50; Goshev, «Стари записки» IV, #9.

[121] Tsonev, *Ibid.*, #50.

[122] *Ibid.*, #47, 48, 49, 51.

[123] *Ibid.*, #50, mentioned contacts with the Serbian lands. Ivanov, *Бъл стар из Мак*, p. 492, gives Kuklen's listing in the Zograf beadroll.

Bibliography

The titles contained in the following bibliography are organized in two sections: Published Sources and Critical Source Studies; and Secondary Materials. Each section is divided into titles representing books or articles. Sources written in Cyrillic are listed alphabetically by author, editor or transliterated title. Although the listing is extensive, it does not represent every work consulted. Only published forms, including catalog listings, of manuscripts and official Ottoman documents have been listed. Articles cited in the notes to the text that have been published in a single- or multi-volume collection are not listed separately if more than one article from the collection has been consulted, in which case, the title of the collection has been listed.

1. Published Sources and Critical Source Studies

Books

Angelov, B.S., *Из старата българска, руска и сръбска литература* [On Old Bulgarian, Russian and Serbian Literature], II and III. Sofia, 1967-78.

Blount, H., *A Voyage into the Levant*. London, 1636.

Bolutov, L., *Български исторически паметници на Атон* [Bulgarian Historical Monuments on Athos]. Sofia, 1961.

Boppe, A. [ed.], *Journal et correspondence de Gedoyn "le Turc" consul de France à Aleppo (1623-1625)*. Paris, 1909.

Boscowich J., *Journal d'un voyage de Constantinople et Pologne, fait a la suite de son excellence Mr. Jaq. Porter ambassadeur d'Angleterre*. Lausanne, 1772.

Bozhinov, V., and L. Panaiotov [eds.], *Macedonia. Documents and Material*, Eng. lang. eds., M. Macdermott and G. Pavlov. Sofia, 1978.

Bozhkov, L., *Едно описание на Дунава и едно пътуване през България през 17-о столетие* [A Description of the Danube and a Journey Through Bulgaria During the 17th Century]. Sofia, 1930.

Brocquiere, Bertrandon de la, *The Travels of. . . to Palestine and his return overland to France. 1432 and 1433,* trans., T. Johnes. Hafod, 1807.

Browne, E., *Relation de plusieurs voyages faits en Hongrie, Servie, Bulgarie, Macedoine, Thesalie, Austriche . . .* Paris, 1674.

Burmov, A., and P.H. Petrov [eds.], Христоматия по история на България [Readings on Bulgarian History], I, От найстари времена до средата на XVIII в. [From Oldest Times to the Middle of the 18th Cen.]. Sofia, 1964.

D., C. [?], *Voyage de Levant fait par le commandement du roi en l'année 1621. par le Sr. . .* Paris, 1624.

Demina, E. I., Тихонравовский дамаскин Болгарский памятник XVII в. [Tihonravovo *Damaskin.* 17th Century Bulgarian Monument]. 2 v. Sofia, 1968-71.

Didron, A. N., *Manuel d'iconographie chrétienne.* Paris, 1845.

Dorev, P. [ed.], Документи за българската история [Documents for Bulgarian History], III, Документи из турските държавни архиви [Documents in the Turkish State Archives] *(1564-1908),* pt. 1, *(1564-1872).* Sofia, 1940.

Duda, H., and G. D. Gŭlŭbov [eds.], *Die Protokollbücher des Kadiamtes Sofia.* Munich, 1960.

Duichev, Iv., Софийската католишка архиепископия през XVII в. Изучване и документи [The Sofia Catholic Archbishopric During the 17th Cen. Studies and Documents]. Sofia, 1939.

Dŭrvingov, P. [ed.], Евлия Челеби и западните български земи. Евлия Челеби и книжовните му трудове. Турция и българите в XV, XVI, XVII в. [Evlia Celebi and the Western Bulgarian Lands. Evlia Celebi and His Literary Works. Turkey and the Bulgarians in the 15th, 16th, 17th Cen.]. Sofia, 1943.

Evlia Celebi, Пътепис [Travel Account], trans., S. Dimitrov. Sofia, 1972.

Fermendžin, E. [ed.], *Acta Bulgariæ ecclesiastica ab a. 1565 usque ad a. 1799. Collegit et digessit.* Zagreb, 1887.

Fischer-Galati, S. [ed.], *Man, State, and Society in East European History.* New York, 1970.

Gerlach, S., Дневник на едно пътуване до Османската порта в Цариград [Daybook of a Journey to the Ottoman Porte in Constantinople], trans., M. Kiselincheva. Sofia, 1976.

Grozdanova, E., Българската народност през XVII век. Демографско изследване [The Bulgarian Nationality During the 17th Century. Demographic Study]. Sofia, 1989.

_____, and S. Andreev, Българите през XVI век. По документи от наши и чужди архиви [The Bulgarians During the 16th Century. On Documents from Domestic and Foreign Archives]. Sofia, 1986.

Gŭlŭbov, G.D., *Турски извори за историята на правото в българските земи* [Turkish Sources for the History of Law in the Bulgarian Lands], I. Sofia, 1961.

Hristova, B., D. Karadzhova and A. Ikonomova [eds.], *Български ръкописи от XI до XVIII век запазени в България. Своден каталог* [Bulgarian Manuscripts from the 11th to the 18th Centuries Preserved in Bulgaria. Reference Catalog], I. Sofia, 1982.

Ihchiev, D.A. [ed.], *Турски документи на Рилския манастир* [Turkish Documents on Rila Monastery]. Sofia, 1910.

Ilyinskiy, G.A. [ed.], *Грамоты болгарских цареы* [Charters of Bulgarian Tsars]. London, 1970 [Orig. ed., Moscow, 1911].

Ishirkov, A., *Западните краища на българската земя. Бележки и материали* [The Western Regions of the Bulgarian Lands. Notes and Materials]. Sofia, 1915.

Ivanov, I., *Български старини из Македония* [Bulgarian Antiquities in Macedonia]. Sofia, 1931 [2nd. ed.].

———, *Старобългарски разкази. Текстове, новобългарски превод и бележки* [Old Bulgarian Tales. Texts, New Bulgarian Translation and Notes]. Sofia, 1935.

Извори за българската история [Sources for Bulgarian History], IV, XX, XXI and XXVI, *Турски извори за българската история* [Turkish Sources for Bulgarian History], I, V, VI and VII. Sofia, 1959, 1974, 1977 and 1986.

Kiselkov, V., *Владислав Граматик и неговата повест* [Vladislav Gramatik and His Novella]. Sofia, 1947.

Klisarov, G.S. [ed.], *Доосвобожденски пътеписи* [Pre-Liberation Travel Accounts]. Sofia, 1969.

Knolles, R., *The Turkish History.* 2 v. London, 1687.

Kodov, H. [ed.], *Опис на славянските ръкописи в библиотеката на Българската академия на науките* [Inventory of the Slavic Manuscripts in the Library of the Bulgarian Academy of Sciences]. Sofia, 1969.

Kovachev, M., *Зограф. Изследвания и документи* [Zograf. Studies and Documents], I. Sofia, 1942.

Kuluzniacki, E., *Werke des Patriarchen von Bulgarien Euthymus (1375-1393) nach de besten Handschriften herausgegeben.* Vienna, 1901.

Leo, M., *La Bulgarie et son peuple sous la domination ottomane. Tels que les ont vus les voyageurs anglo-saxons 1568-1878. Découverte d'une nationalité.* Sofia, 1949.

Leval, A., *Voyages en Levant pendant les XVI, XVII et XVIII siècles.* Budapest, 1897.

Matejić, M., and P. Matejić [eds.], *Hilandar Slavic Manuscripts.* Columbus, 1972.

Mihailović, K., *Memoirs of a Janissary.* trans., B. Stolz. Ann Arbor 1975.
Miyatev, P. [ed.], Чужди пътеписи за Балканите [Foreign Travel Accounts of the Balkans], II, Маджарски пътеписи за Балканите, XVI-XIX в. [Hungarian Travel Accounts of the Balkans, 16th-19th Cen.]. Sofia, 1976.
Muravyav, A., Сношения России с Востоком по делам церковным [Russian Relations with the East by Church Work], 2 v. St. Petersburg, 1860.
Mutafchieva, V., and S. Dimitrov, *Sur l'état du système des timars des XVIIe-XVIIIe ss.* Sofia, 1968.
Nachev, V., and N. Fermandzhiev [eds.], Писахме да се знае. Приписки и летописи [We Wrote So That It Be Known. Marginalia and Chronicles], trans., V. Nachev. Sofia, 1984.
Naima, M., *Annals of the Turkish Empire from 1591 to 1659 of the Christian Era,* trans., C. Fraser. New York, 1973 [Orig. pub., London, 1832].
Papadopoullos, T. H., *Studies and Documents Relating to the History of the Greek Church and People under Turkish Domination.* Brussels, 1952.
Pernot, H. [ed.], *Voyage en Turquie et en Grèce du R. P. Robert de Dreux aumonier de l'ambassadeur de France (1665-1669).* Paris, 1925.
Petrov, P.H. [ed.], По следите на насилието. Документи за помохамеданчвания и потурчвания [On the Traces of Violence. Documents for Islamization and Turcification], 2 v. Sofia, 1987-1988 [2nd. ed.].
Quiclet, M., *Les voyages de . . . a Constantinople par terre.* Paris, 1664.
Raikov, B. [ed.], Абагар на Филип Станиславов. Рим, 1651 [*Abagar* of Filip Stanislavov. Rome, 1651]. Sofia, 1979 [Reproduction ed.].
_____, and A. Dzhurova [eds.], Българска ръкописна книга, X-XVIII в. Каталог [The Bulgarian Manuscript Book, 10th-18th Cen. Catalog]. Sofia, 1976.
Rainov, N., Орнамент и буква в славянските ръкописи в Народната библиотека в Пловдив [Ornament and Lettering in the Slavic Manuscripts in the National Library in Plovdiv]. Sofia, 1925.
Rycaut, P., *The History of the Turkish Empire, From the Year 1623 to the Year 1677.* London, 1680. [Also, the London, 1687 ed.].
_____, *The History of the Turks. Beginning with the Year 1679 (until the End of the Year 1698 and 1699).* London, 1700.
_____, *The Present State of the Ottoman Empire.* London, 1687. 104 p. [Also, the London, 1668 ed.].
Schiltberger, J., Пътепис [Travel Account], trans., V. Mutafchieva. Sofia, 1971.
Sprostranov, E. [ed.], Опис на ръкописите в библиотека при Цв. Синод на Българската църква в София [Inventory of the Manuscripts in the Library under the Holy Synod of the Bulgarian Church in Sofia]. Sofia, 1900.
_____ [ed.], Опис на ръкописите на библиотека на Рилския манастир [Inventory of the Manuscripts in the Library of Rila Monastery]. Sofia, 1902.

Sreznevskii, V.I., and I. Pokrovskii [eds.], *Описание рукописного отделения Библиотеки Императорской Академий Наук* [Description of the Manuscript Sections of the Libraries of the Imperial Academy of Science], I, *Рукописи* [Manuscripts], I. St. Petersburg, 1910.

Stainova, M. [ed.], *Опис на турски документи за църковно-националната борба на българския народ и за християнските църкви в Османската империя (XV-XX в.)* [Inventory of Turkish Documents for the Church-National Struggle of the Bulgarian People and for the Christian Churches in the Ottoman Empire (15th-20th Cen.)]. Sofia, 1971.

Stanchev, S., and M. Stancheva, *Боянският поменик* [The Boyana Beadroll]. Sofia, 1963.

Stoyanov, M., *Украса на славянските ръкописи в България. Описание на украсата на славянските ръкописи от XI до началото на XIX в.* [The Decoration of the Slavic Manuscripts in Bulgaria. Inventory of the Decorations of the Slavic Manuscripts from the 11th to the Beginning of the 19th Cen.]. Sofia, 1973.

_____, and H. Kodov, *Опис на славянските ръкописи в Софийската народна библиотека* [Inventory of the Slavic Manuscripts in the Sofia National Library], III and IV. Sofia, 1964-71.

Syrku, P., *Очерки из историй литературных сношений Болгар и Сербов в XIV-XVII веках* [Investigations into the History of Bulgarian and Serbian Literary Relations in the 14th-17th Centuries]. St. Petersburg, 1901.

Thevenot, J. de, *The Travels of Monsieur . . . into the Levant,* trans., A. Lovell. Farnborough, 1971 [Orig. Fr. ed., Paris, 1664-84].

Todorov, N. [ed.], *Положението на българския народ под турско робство. Сборник с документи и материали* [The Position of the Bulgarian People under the Turkish Yoke. Collection of Documents and Materials]. Sofia, 1953.

_____, and A. Velkov, *Situation démographique de la Péninsule balkanique (fin du XVe s. début du XVIe s.).* Sofia, 1988.

Todorov-Hinalkov, V., *Възстания и народни движения в предосвободителна България според новооткритий турски официални документи* [Uprisings and National Movements in Pre-Liberation Bulgaria According to Newly Discovered Turkish Official Documents]. Sofia, 1929.

Tsonev, B., *История на българский език* [History of Bulgarian Language], I. Sofia, 1919.

_____ [ed.], *Опис на ръкописите и старопечатните книги на Народната библиотека в София* [Inventory of the Manuscripts and Old Printed Books in the National Library in Sofia], I. Sofia, 1910.

_____ [ed.], *Опис на славянските ръкописи в Софийската народна библиотека* [Inventory of the Slavic Manuscripts in the Sofia National Library], II. Sofia, 1923.

_____ [ed.], *Славянски ръкописи и старопечатните книги на Народната библиотека в Пловдив* [Slavic Manuscripts and Old Printed Books in the National Library in Plovdiv]. Sofia, 1920.

Tsvetkova, B. [ed.], *Чужди пътеписи за Балканите* [Foreign Travel Accounts of the Balkans], I, *Френски пътеписи за Балканите, XV-XVIII в.* [French Travel Accounts of the Balkans, 15th-18th Cen.]. Sofia, 1975.

_____ [ed.], *Хайдутството в българските земи през 15/18 век* [*Haidut* Activity in the Bulgarian Lands During the 15th/18th Centuries]. Sofia, 1971.

_____ [ed.], *Опис на тимарски регистри запазени в Ориенталския отдел на Народната библиотека «Кирил и Методий»* [Inventory of *Timar* Registers Housed in the Oriental Room of the National Library "Cyril and Methodius"]. Sofia, 1970.

Voynov, M., and L. Panayotov [eds.], *Documents and Materials on the History of the Bulgarian People*. Sofia, 1969.

Vŭzvŭzova-Karateodorova, K. [ed.], *Непресъхващи извори. Документална материали из историята на Пловдив и Пловдивско* [Unfailing Sources. Documentary Materials on the History of Plovdiv and Plovdiv Region]. Plovdiv, 1975.

Zahariev, S., *Географико-историко-статистическо описание на Татар-Пазарджишката кааза* [Geographical-Historical-Statistical Description of Tatar-Pazardzhik *kaza*]. Vienna, 1870 [photocopy ed., Pazardzhik, 1970].

Жития на българските светии [Lives of the Bulgarian Saints], I. Sofia, 1974.

Жития на светиите [Lives of the Saints]. Sofia, 1974.

Articles

Andreev, S., «Документи за данъчните и други принудителни задължения на населението на Смолянско и съседните области от XVII век» [Documents for the Taxes and Other Compulsory Obligations of the Population of Smolyan Region and Adjacent Regions in the 17th Century], *Родопски сборник* [Rhodopes Collection], III (1972), pp. 323-37.

Angelov, B.S., "Un canon de St. Jean de Rila de Georges Skylitzes," *Bb*, III (1969), pp. 171-85.

Argirov, S., «Един български ръкопис от XVII в.» [A Bulgarian Manuscript From the 17th Century], *Пражлия музей. Периодическо списание* [Prague Museum. Periodical Bulletin], XLIV (1894), pp. 169-200.

_____, «Люблянският български ръкопис от XVII век» [The Ljubljana Bulgarian Manuscript From the 17th Century], *СбНУ*, XII (1895), and XVI-XVII (1899), pp. 463-560, and 246-313.

Babinger, F., "Robert Bargrave in Bulgarien (1652)," *ИИДв*, XIV-XV (1937), pp. 145-50.

Dernschwam, H., «Дневник на ... за едно пътуване до Константинопол и Мала Азия (1553-1555)» [Daybook of... for a Journey to Constantinople and Asia Minor (1553-1555)], *Чужди пътеписи за Балканите* [Foreign Travel Accounts of the Balkans], III, *Немски и австрийски пътеписи за Балканите, XV-XVI в.* [German and Austrian Travel Accounts of the Balkans, 15th-16th Centuries], ed., M. Ionov. Sofia, 1979, pp. 224-76.

Dinekov, P. [ed.], «Житието на Пимен Зографски» [The Life of Pimen Zografski], *ИИБЛ*, II (1954), pp. 233-48.

Draganova, S., «Неизвестен турски документ за положението на рударското население в Самоковската каза през първата половина на XVII век» [An Unknown Turkish Document for the Position of the Ore-mining Population in Samokov *Kaza* During the First Half of the 17th Century], *ИДА*, XX (1970), pp. 189-95.

Duichev, Iv. [ed.], «Описание на България от 1640 г. на архиепископа Петър Богдан (По случай 300-годишнината)» [Description of Bulgaria From 1640 by Archbishop Petŭr Bogdan (On the Occasion of His 300th Anniversary)], *АрПП*, II, 2 (1939-40), pp. 174-210.

Dylevskiy, N.M., «Просително послание на Рилското манастирско братство до руския цар Михайл Феодорович Романов от 1627 година» [Supplication Message of the Rila Monastery Monks to the Russian Tsar Mihail Feodorovich Romanov From 1627], *ИИБЕ*, XIX (1970), pp. 689-99.

Filipov, A. [ed.], «Описание на Евлия Челеби из българските земи през средата на XVII век» [Description of Evlia Celebi on the Bulgarian Lands During the Mid 17th Century], *ПСп*, LXXI (1909), pp. 639-724.

Goshev, Iv. [ed.], «Стари записки и надписи» [Old Notes and Inscriptions], pts. I-V, *ГСУбф*, IV (1927); VI (1929); XII (1935); XIII (1936); XIV (1937), pp. 335-78; 1-36; 1-41; 1-57; 1-50.

_____ [ed.], «Църковни старини из Врачанска епархия» [Church Antiquities in the Vratsa Bishopric], *ГСУбф*, XI, (1933-1934), pp. 1-54.

Grozdanova, E., «Турски документи за данъка джизие през XVII-XVIII в. като извори за историята на балканските страни» [Turkish Documents for the Tax *Cizie* During the 17th-18th Cen. as Sources for the History of the Balkan Countries], *ИДА*, XVIII (1970), pp. 289-303.

Gŭlŭbov, G.D., «Два турски документа от XVII в. за стопанската и обществената дейност на българските занаятчии» [Two Turkish Documents from the 17th Cen. for the Economic and Social Work of Bulgarian Artisans], *ИИИ*, XVIII (1967), pp. 289-97.

_____ [ed.], «Османо-турски извори за българската история [Ottoman Turkish Sources for Bulgarian History], I, Няколко стари османо-турски държавни документи относно войниганите» [Some Old Ottoman Turkish State Documents Regarding the *Voynuks*], *ГСУифф*, XXXIV, (1937-38). [Offprint. 70 p.].

_____ [ed.], «Османо-турски извори за българската история [Ottoman Turkish Sources for Bulgarian History], II, Един закон и други държавни документи по събирането на момчета за еничерите» [A Law and Other State Documents on the Collection of Youths for the Jannisaries], *ГСУифф*, XXXV, 6 (1939). [Offprint. 36 p.]

_____ [ed.], «Османотурски извори за българската история [Ottoman Turkish Sources for Bulgarian History], III, Три стари закона и други османотурски документи относно войниганите» [Three Old Laws and Other Ottoman Turkish Documents Regarding the *Voynuks*], *ГСУифф*, XXXIX (1942-1943). [Offprint. 98 p.]

_____ [ed.], «Османотурски извори за историята на София» [Ottoman Turkish Sources for the History of Sofia], *Сердика* [Serdica], VI, 1-2; 3-4; 5-6 (1942), pp. 87-96; 87-97; 104-17.

Hristoskov, D., and M. Mladenov, «Един новооткрит български ръкопис от XVII в.» [A Newly Discovered Manuscript From the 17th Cen.], *Български език* [Bulgarian Language], VII, 3 (1957), pp. 228-37.

Ihchiev, D.A., «Материали за историята ни под турското робство» [Materials for Our History under the Turkish Yoke], *ИИДв*, I (1905), pp. 60-130.

_____ [ed.], «Турски документи за Софийската епархия» [Turkish Documents for the Sofia Bishopric], *Преглед* [Review], I, 6-7; 8 (1908); II, 1 (1909), pp. 318-25; 388-98; 28-30.

Ionov, M.P., «Българските земи преди 300 години, отразени в дневниците на Кинсперг (1672-1674 г.)» [The Bulgarian Lands 300 Years Ago, Reflected in the Daybooks of Kinsberg (1672-1674)], *ГСУфиф*, LXV, 3 (1973), pp. 303-84.

_____, «Един неизвестен пътепис за нашите земи от XVII в.» [An Unknown Travel Account for Our Lands From the 17th Cen.], *ИИДв*, XXV (1967), pp. 283-306.

_____, «Европейски пътеписи — извор за историята на българските земи през XVII век» [European Travel Accounts — Source for the History of the Bulgarian Lands During the 17th Century], *ГСУфиф*, LXII, 3 (1969), pp. 1-191.

Iorga, N., "La France dans le sud-est de l'Europe, III, La croisade à la fin du XVIe siècle. Voyageurs, mercenaires et aventuriers au commencement du XVIIIe siècle," *Revue historique du Sud-est européen*, XIII, 4-6 (1936), pp. 105-46.

Ivanov, I., «Паметници на български царе и царици» [Monuments of Bulgarian Tsars and Tsaritsas], *ИИДв*, IV (1915), pp. 219-29.

———, «Владислав Граматик. Пренасяне тялото на св. Ивана Рилски от Търново в Рила, 1469» [Vladislav Gramatik. The Transfer of the Relics of St. Ivan Rilski From Tŭrnovo to Rila, 1469], *Духовна култура* [Spiritual Culture], I, 3-4 (1920), pp. 211-16.

———, «Жития на св. Ивана Рилски. С уводни бележки» [The Life of St. Ivan Rilski. With Introductory Notes], *ГСУифф*, XXXII (1935-36), pp. 1-109.

Jerkov, J., "Un fragment inedit de l'histoire de la Bulgarie de Petar Bogdan Bakšič," *EB*, XIV, 1 (1978), pp. 98-109.

Jireček, K., «Стари пътешествия по България от XV-XVIII столетие» [Old Travels in Bulgaria From the 15th-18th Centuries], *ПСп*, III, IV, VI, VII (1882-84), pp. 60-83; 67-105; 1-44; 96-127.

Kabrda, J., "Les documents turcs relatifs aux impôts écclésiastiques prélèvés sur la population bulgare au XVIIe siècle," *Arhiv orientalni*, XXIII, 1-2 (1955), pp. 136-77.

Kaludova, I., «Документи за положението на населението в европейската част на Османската империя XVII-XIX в.» [Documents for the Position of the Population in the European Part of the Ottoman Empire, 17th-20th Cen.], *ИДА*, XXIV (1972), pp. 201-37.

Kesyakov, H., «Пътуване през българско в 1635 година» [Travel Through the Region of Bulgaria in 1635], *ПСп*, XIX-XX (1886), pp. 63-69.

Milchev, A., «Два документа от втората половина на XVII в., за политическите връзки на Русия с българи, сърби и румъни» [Two Documents From the Second Half of the 17th Cen., for the Political Contacts of Russia with the Bulgarians, Serbs and Romanians], *ИИИ*, XIV-XV (1964). pp. 469-74.

Miletich, L., «Копривщенски дамаскин. Новобългарски паметник от XVII век» [Koprivshtitsa *Damaskin*. New Bulgarian Monument From the 17th Century], *Български старини* [Bulgarian Antiquities], II. Sofia, 1908, pp. 1-204.

———, «Свищовски дамаскин» [Svishtov *Damaskin*], *Български старини*, VII. Sofia, 1923, pp. 1-308.

Moskov, M., «Един нов дамаскин» [A New *Damaskin*], *Българска сбирка* [Bulgarian Collection], XI, 10 (1904), pp. 628-34.

Mutafchieva, V., «Нови османски документи за вакъфите в България под турска власт» [New Ottoman Documents for the *Vakıfs* in Bulgaria under Turkish Rule], *ИДА*, VI (1962), pp. 269-74.

Nachov, N., «Аджарският ръкопис» [The Adzhar Manuscript], *СбНУ*, XVI-XVII (1900), pp. 483-91.

———, «Лист от хроника, намерен в с. Голямо белово» [Page From a Chronicle, Located in the Village of Golyamo Belovo], *Български преглед* [Bulgarian Review], V, 2 (1898), pp. 149-51.

Neshev, G., "Quelques documents turcs sur l'histoire du monastère de Rila de la periode du XVe au XVIIe s.," *EH,* IV. Sofia, 1968, pp. 233-42.

Plyakov, Z., «Документи за регламентацията на търговската дейност в българските земи през XV-XVII в.» [Documents for the Regulation of Commercial Activity in the Bulgarian Lands During the 15th-17th Cen.], *ИИИ,* XIX (1967), pp. 263-70.

Popov, N., and K. Vŭzvŭzova-Karateodorova, «Неизвестен опит за въстание през 1689 година на българите от североизточна България според неиздаден турски документ» [Unknown Attempt at an Uprising During 1689 by the Bulgarians From Northeast Bulgaria According to an Unpublished Turkish Document], *ИНБКМ,* XII [XVIII] (1971), pp. 81-87.

Pundev, V., «Сборникът Абагар от епископ Филип Станиславов» [The Collection *Abagar* by Bishop Filip Stanislavov], *ГНБП,* (1924). [Offprint, 1926, 49 p.].

Raikov, B., «Към въпроса за мястото на Абагар в старата българска литература» [Toward the Problem of the Place of *Abagar* in Old Bulgarian Literature], *ИИБЛ,* XVIII-XIX (1966), pp. 279-86.

———, «Неизвестно положно житие на Иван Рилски» [Unknown Eulogetic Life of Ivan Rilski], *Език и литература* [Language and Literature], 3 (1970), pp. 57-61.

Shishmanov, Iv.D., «Стари пътувания през България в посока на римския военен път от Белград до Цариград» [Old Travels Through Bulgaria in Line with the Roman Military Road From Belgrad to Istanbul], *СбНУ,* IV (1891), pp. 320-483.

Shopov, A., «Евлия Челеби. Пътуването му из Македония, Сърбия и България» [Evlia Celebi. His Journey Through Macedonia, Serbia and Bulgaria], *ПСп,* LXII (1902), pp. 161-94.

Sprostranov, E., «Материали по историята на Рилския манастир» [Materials on the History of Rila Monastery], *СбНУ,* XVIII (1901), pp. 171-206.

Stoikov, R., «Български селища с населението им в турски регистри за джизие от XVII в.» [Bulgarian Settlements with Their Inhabitants in Turkish Registers for *Cizie* From the 17th Cen.], *ИДА,* VIII (1964), pp. 147-64.

———, "La division administrative de l'eyalet de Roumelie pendant les années soixante du XVIIe s. Selon un registre turc-ottoman de 1668-1669," *Studia balcanica,* I, *Recherches de géographie historique.* Sofia, 1970, pp. 205-27.

Stoilov, A.P., «Хрисовол от цар Иван Шишман, даден на манастиря св. Богородица при с. Драгалевци в Витоша» [Royal Decree of Tsar Ivan Shishman, Given to the Monastery of the Holy Virgin Near the Village of Dragalevtsi on Vitosha], *Преглед*, I, 5 (1908), pp. 252-55.

Stojanović, L., «Стари записки и натписи» [Old Notes and Inscriptions], pts. I-V, *Зборник за историју, језик и књижевност српского народо* [Collection for the History, Language and Literature of the Serbian People], I, *Споменици на српском језику* [Memoirs of the Serbian Language], I-XI (1902-25).

Telbizov, K., "Liste des chartes de privilèges octroyées aux XVIIe-XIXe ss. aux compagnies commerciales des Bulgares de Ciprovec dans la Principauté de Roumanie, en Transylvanie et au Banat," *EB*, 4 (1976), pp . 64-78.

Tsonev, B., «Един важен дамаскин от XVII в.» [An Important *Damaskin* From the 17th Cen.], *ГСУифф*, I (1914), pp. 1-5.

_____, «Книжовни старини от Елена» [Literary Antiquities From Elena], *ГСУифф*, XIX, 7 (1923), pp. 1-61.

Tsvetkova, B., «Нови документи за историята на освободителните движения в българските земи през XVII в.» [New Documents for the History of the Liberation Movements in the Bulgarian Lands During the 17th Cen.], *ИИИ*, XIX (1967), pp. 243-62.

_____, «Турски документи за статута на селища във В. Търновски окръг през XVII в.» [Turkish Documents for the Settlements in Veliko Tŭrnovo Region During the 17th Cen.], *Известия на Окръжния музей във Велико Търново* [Journal of the Regional Museum in Veliko Tŭrnovo], III (1966), pp. 61-67.

Velkov, S., «Едно старинно евангелие» [An Antique Gospel], *Църковен вестник* [Church News], XXXI, 32 (1930), pp. 367-68.

Yanakiev, D. [ed.], «Житие на преподобни монах отец Пимен Зографски, родом от София» [The Life of the Venerable Monk Friar Pimen Zografski, Native of Sofia], *Сердика*, III, 4 (1939), pp. 5-10.

2. Secondary Sources

Books

Akrabova-Zhandova, Iv., *Икони в Софийския археологически музей* [Icons in the Sofia Archaeological Museum]. Sofia, 1965.

Angelov, B., *Из историята на старобългарската и възрожденската литература* [On the History of Old Bulgarian and Revivalist Literature]. Sofia, 1977.

———, *Старобългарско книжовно наследство* [Old Bulgarian Literary Heritage], I. Sofia, 1983.

Angelov, B.S., *Из историята на руско-българските литературни връзки* [On the History of Russian-Bulgarian Literary Contacts]. Sofia, 1972.

Angelov, D., *Богомилството в България* [Bogomilism in Bulgaria]. Sofia, 1969 [3rd. ed.].

Atanasov, N. *Социалният фактор в културно-литературния ни живот преди Освобождението* [The Social Factor in Our Cultural-Literary Life Before the Liberation]. Sofia, 1910.

Atanasov, V., *Урвич и Бистрица. Кокалянски манацтир и Мала Света Гора. Археологическо-исторически бележки* [Urvich and Bistritsa. Kokalyane Monastery and Little Mount Athos. Archaeological-Historical Notes]. Sofia, 1905.

Benz, E., *The Eastern Orthodox Church. Its Thought and Life,* trans., R. Winston and C. Winston. Chicago, 1963.

Bogdanov, Iv., *Български твърдини. Книжовни огнища, крепости, манастири в София и Софийско* [Bulgarian Strongholds. Literary Centers, Fortresses, Monasteries in Sofia and the Sofia Region]. Sofia, 1971.

Bousquet, G., *Histoire du peuple bulgare depuis les origines jusqu'à nos jours.* Paris, 1909.

Bozhkov, A., *Bulgarian Art.* Sofia, 1964.

———, *Българската историческа живопис* [Bulgarian Historical Painting], I. Sofia, 1972.

———, *Българско изобразително изкуство* [Bulgarian Representational Art]. Sofia, 1988.

———, *La peinture bulgare des origines au XIXe siècle.* Recklinghausen, 1974.

България 1000 години (927-1927) [Bulgaria 1000 Years (927-1927)]. Sofia, 1930.

България 1300. Институции и държавни традиции [Bulgaria 1300. Institutions and State Traditions], II and III. Sofia, 1982-83.

Butler, T. [ed,], *Bulgaria: Past and Present. Studies in History, Literature, Economics, Music, Sociology, Folklore and Linguistics,* I. Columbus, 1976.

Chakŭrov, N., *История на българското образование* [History of Bulgarian Education], I. Sofia, 1955.

Chavrŭkov, G., *Български манастири. Паметници на историята, културата и изкуството* [Bulgarian Monasteries. Monuments of History, Culture and Art] Sofia, 1974.

Chilingirov, A., *Църквата «Св. Никола» в село Марица* [The Church of "St. Nikola" in the Village of Maritsa]. Sofia, 1976.

Чипровци. 1688-1968. [Chiprovtsi. 1688-1968]. Sofia, 1971.

Cholov, P., *Чипровското въстание 1688 г.* [The Chiprovtsi Uprising 1688]. Sofia, 1988.

Danchev, G., *Владислав Граматик. Книжовник и писател* [Vladislav Gramatik. Man of Letters and Writer]. Sofia, 1969.

Danov, G.D., *Гложене и Гложенският манастир. (Исторически очерк с маршрути)* [Glozhene and Glozhene Monastery. (Historical Article with Itineraries)]. Sofia, 1970.

Dimitrov, G., *Княжество България в историческо, етнографическо отношения* [The Principality of Bulgaria in Historical, Ethnographical Perspectives]. 3 v. Sofia, 1894-1900 [Orig. pub., Plovdiv, 1895-99].

Dinekov, P., *et. al.* [eds.], *Търновска книжовна школа. 1371-1971* [The Tŭrnovo Literary School. 1371-1971], I. Sofia, 1974.

_____, *Софийски книжовници през XVI век* [Sofia Writers During the 16th Century], I, *Поп Пейо* [Father Peio]. Sofia, 1939.

Drinov, M., *Избрани съчинения* [Collected Works], ed., Iv. Duichev. 2 v. Sofia, 1971.

_____, *Съчинения* [Works], ed., V.N. Zlatarski, 3 v. Sofia, 1909-15.

Duichev, Iv., *Чипровец и въстанието през 1688 година* [Chiprovets and the Uprising in 1688]. Sofia, 1938.

_____, *Из старата българска книжнина* [On Old Bulgarian Literature]. 2 v. Sofia, 1940-44.

_____, *The Miniatures of the Chronicle of Manasses.* Sofia, 1963.

_____, *Рилският манастир. История, минало и паметници* [Rila Monastery. History, Past and Monuments]. Sofia, 1960.

_____, *Рилският светец и неговата обител* [The Saint of Rila and His Monastery]. Sofia, 1947.

250 години от Чипровското въстание. 1688-1938. Купровец — Кипровец — Чипровец. Котиловци. Челюстница. Жаравци. Кутловица [250 Years After the Chiprovtsi Uprising. 1688-1938. Kuprovets — Kiprovets — Chiprovtsi. Kotilovtsi. Chelyustnitsa. Zharavitsa. Kutlovitsa]. Sofia, 1939.

Dylevskiy, N.M., *Рилскы манастир и Россия в XVI и XVII веках* [Rila Monastery and Russia in the 16th and 17th Centuries]. Sofia, 1974 [2nd. ed.].

Filov, B.D., *L'art antique en Bulgarie.* Sofia, 1925.

Fine, J.V.A., Jr., *The Bosnian Church: A New Interpretation. A Study of the Bosnian Church and Its Place in State and Society from the 13th to the 15th Centuries.* New York, 1975.

Floreva, E., *Алинските стенописи* [The Alino Wall Paintings]. Sofia, 1983.

_____, *Манастирската църква Архангел Михаил в Билинци* [The Monastery Church Archangel Mihail in Bilintsi]. Sofia, 1973.

_____, *Средновековни стенописи. Вуково. 1598 г.* [Medieval Wall Paintings. Vukovo. 1598]. Sofia, 1987.

_____, *Старата църква на Драгалевския манастир* [The Old Church in Dragalevtsi Monastery]. Sofia, 1968.
_____, *Старата църква в Добърско* [The Old Church in Dobŭrsko]. Sofia, 1981.
Fortescue, A.K., *The Orthodox Eastern Church*. London, 1927.
Gandev, H., *Българската народност през 15и бек. Демографско и етнографско изследване* [The Bulgarian Nationality During the 15th Century. Demographic and Ethnographic Study]. Sofia, 1972.
_____, *Проблеми на българското възраждане* [Problems in the Bulgarian National Revival]. Sofia, 1976.
Garsoian, N.G., *The Paulician Heresy*. The Hague, 1967.
Gechev, M., *Килийните училища в България* [Cell Schools in Bulgaria]. Sofia, 1967.
Genchev, N., *Българската култура XV-XIX в. Лекции* [Bulgarian Culture 15th-19th Cen. Lectures]. Sofia, 1988.
Georgiev, E., *Българската литература в общославянското и общоевропейско литературно развитие* [Bulgarian Literature in General Slavic and General European Literary Development]. Sofia, 1973.
Georgiev, G.K., *Старата железодобивна индустрия в България* [The Old Metallurgical Industries in Bulgaria]. Sofia, 1978.
Georgieva, Ts.B., *Еничарите в българските земи* [The Janissaries in the Bulgarian Lands]. Sofia, 1988.
Gibb, H.A.R., and H. Bowen, *Islamic Society and the West*, I, *Islamic Society in the Eighteenth Century*. 2 pts. London, 1965-67 [2nd. ed.].
Grabar, A., *Боянската църквата / L'église de Boiana*. Sofia, 1978 [2nd. ed.].
_____, *La peinture religieuse en Bulgarie*. Paris, 1928.
Grozdanova, E., *Българската селска община през XV-XVIII век* [The Bulgarian Village Commune During the 15th-18th Centuries]. Sofia, 1979.
Hajek, A., *Bulgarien unter der Türkenherrschaft*. Stuttgart, 1925.
Hasluck, F.W., *Athos and its Monasteries*. London, 1924.
_____, *Christianity and Islam under the Sultans*. 2 v. Oxford, 1929.
Haussig, H.W., *A History of Byzantine Civilization*, trans., J.M. Hussey. New York, 1971.
Hristov, H., G. Stoikov and K. Miyatev, *The Rila Monastery: History, Architecture, Frescoes, Wood-Carvings*. Sofia, 1959.
Hristov, H. [ed.], *Страници от българската история. Очерк за ислямизираните българи и националновъзродителния процес* [Pages from Bulgarian History. Essay for Islamizised Bulgarians and the National Revival Process]. Sofia, 1989.
Inalcik, H. *The Ottoman Empire: The Classical Age, 1300-1600*, trans., N. Itzkowitz and C. Imber. London, 1973.

Iotsov, D., *Културно-политическа история на Враца* [Cultural-Political History of Vratsa], I, *От римската епоха до Освобождението* [From the Roman Epoch to the Liberation]. Sofia, 1937.
Ishirkov, A., *Град София през XVII век* [The City of Sofia During the 17th Century]. Sofia, 1912.
Ivanov, I., *Северна Македония. Исторически издирвания* [Northern Macedonia. Historical Discoveries]. Sofia, 1906.
―――――, *Св. Иван Рилски и неговият манастир* [St. Ivan Rilski and His Monastery]. Sofia, 1917.
Из миналото на българите мохамедани в Родопите [On the Past of the Bulgarian Muslims in the Rhodopes]. Sofia, 1958.
Jireček, K., *История на Българите* [History of the Bulgarians]. Sofia, 1978 [4th ed.].
―――――, *Пътувания по България* [Travels In Bulgaria], v. II of *Княжество България* [The Principality of Bulgaria]. Sofia, 1974 [Reprint of Plovdiv, 1899 ed.].
Kabrda, J., *Le système fiscal de l'église orthodoxe dans l'Empire ottoman*. Brno, 1969.
Kiel, M., *Art and Society of Bulgaria in the Turkish Period*. Maastricht, 1985.
Kiselkov, V., *Рилски манастир* [Rila Monastery]. Sofia, 1937.
Konstantinov, G., *Стара българска литература от св. св. Кирил и Методий до Паисий Хилендарски* [Old Bulgarian Literature from SS. Cyril and Methodius to Paisii Hilendarski]. Sofia, 1942.
Kosev, D. [ed.], *България в света от древността до наши дни* [Bulgaria in the World from Antiquity to Our Times]. 2 v. Sofia, 1979.
―――――, *et. al.* [eds.], *История на България* [History of Bulgaria], II-IV. Sofia, 1981-83.
―――――, *et. al.* [eds.], *Паисий Хилендарски и неговата епоха (1762-1962)* [Paisii Hilendarski and His Era (1762-1962)]. Sofia, 1962.
Kovachev, M., *Български ктитори в Св. Гора. Исторически очерк, изследвания и документи* [Bulgarian Patrons on Mount Athos. Historical Article, Studies and Documents]. Sofia, 1943.
―――――, *Българско монашество в Атон* [Bulgarian Monasticism on Athos]. Sofia, 1967.
―――――, *Драгалевският манастир Св. Богородица Витоша и неговите старини* [The Dragalevtsi Monastery of the Blessed Virgin of Vitosha and Its Antiquities]. Sofia, 1940.
Krŭstev, K., and V. Zahariev, *Old Bulgarian Painting*. Sofia, 1961.
Kŭrdzhanov, P., *История и състояние на манастир «Св. Архангел Михайл» при с. Билинци* [History and Condition of the Monastery "Holy Archangel Mihail" Near the Village of Bilintsi]. Trŭn, 1904.

Lewis, B., C. Pellat and J. Schacht [eds.], *The Encyclopedia of Islam*, II. London, 1965.
Loch, S., *Athos: The Holy Mountain*. London, 1957.
Lybyer, A.H., *The Government of the Ottoman Empire in the Time of Suleiman the Magnificent*. Cambridge, 1913.
Macdermott, M., *A History of Bulgaria, 1393-1885*. New York, 1962.
Manova, E., Предвъзрожденски стенописи от XVI-XVII век в с. Марица [Pre-Revival Wall Paintings from the 16th-17th Centuries in the Village of Maritsa]. Sofia, 1977.
Marenin, N., Манастир Хилендар [Hilendar Monastery]. Sofia, 1900.
Markova, Z., Българското църковно-национално движение до Кримската война [The Bulgarian Church-National Movement to the Crimean War]. Sofia, 1976.
Mavrodinov, N., Старобългарската живопис [Old Bulgarian Painting]. Sofia, 1946.
Milev, N., Католишката пропаганда в България през XVII в. [Catholic Propaganda in Bulgaria During the 17th Cen.]. Sofia, 1914.
Millenaire du Mont Athos. 963-1963, Etudes et Mélanges. 2 v. Chevetogne, 1963-64.
Millet, G., *Monuments de l'Athos*. Paris, 1927.
Mishev, D., *The Bulgarians in the Past. Pages from the Bulgarian Cultural History*. Lausanne, 1919.
Monedzhikova, A., София през вековете [Sofia Through the Centuries]. Sofia, 1946.
Mutafchiev, P., Избрани произведения [Collected Works], ed., D. Angelov. 2 v. Sofia, 1973.
Neshev, G., Български довъзрожденски културно-народностни средища [Bulgarian Pre-Revival Cultural-National Centers]. Sofia, 1977.
Nikolaev, V., Характерът на минните предприятия и режимът на рударския труд в нашите земи през XVI, XVII и XVIII в. [The Character of Mining Enterprises and the Regime of Ore Mining in Our Lands During the 16th, 17th and 18th Cen.]. Sofia, 1954.
Nikolov, B., and M. Manolov, Огнища на българщината. Пътувания из манастирите [Hearths of the Bulgarian National Spirit. Journeys Through the Monasteries]. Sofia, 1989 [2nd. ed.].
Nikolov, I., Католическата пропаганда в България [Catholic Propaganda in Bulgaria]. Sofia, 1964.
Norwich, J. J., R. Sitwell and A. Costa, *Mount Athos*. London, 1966.
Obolensky, D., *The Bogomils. A Study in Balkan Neo-Manichæism*. Cambridge, 1948.
_____, *The Byzantine Commonwealth: Eastern Europe, 500-1453*. New York, 1971.

Ostrogorsky, G., *History of the Byzantine State*, trans., J. M. Hussey. New Brunswick, 1957.
Pandurski, V., *Куриловският манастир (Архитектура и стенописи)* [Kurilo Monastery (Architecture and Wall Paintings)]. Sofia, 1975.
———, *Паметници на изкуството в Църковния историко-археологически музей — София* [Monuments of Art in the Church Historical-Archaeological Museum-Sofia]. Sofia, 1977.
Panova, S., *Българските търговци през XVII век* [Bulgarian Merchants During the 17th Century]. Sofia, 1980.
Pantazopoulos, N. J., *Church and Law in the Balkan Peninsula During the Ottoman Rule*. Thessaloniki, 1967.
Paskaleva, K., *Икони от България* [Icons From Bulgaria]. Sofia, 1981.
———, *Църквата «Св. Георги» в Кремиковския манастир* [The Church of "St. Georgi" in Kremikovtsi Monastery]. Sofia, 1980.
Penev, B., *История на новата българска литература* [History of Modern Bulgarian Literature], I, *Начало на Българското възраждане. Българската литература през XVII и XVIII век* [Beginning of the Bulgarian Revival. Bulgarian Literature During the 17th and 18th Centuries]. Sofia, 1976 [Orig. pub., Sofia, 1932].
Petkanova [-Toteva], D., *Дамаскините в българската литература* [The *Damaskins* in Bulgarian Literature]. Sofia, 1965.
Petrov, P.H., *Съдбоносни векове за българската народност. Края на XIV век-1912 година* [Fateful Centuries for the Bulgarian Nationality. The End of the 14th Century-1912]. Sofia, 1975.
Polivyanni, D.I., *Средновековният български град през XIII-XIV век. Очерци* [The Medieval Bulgarian City During the 13th-14th Centuries. Essays], trans., I. Ilieva. Sofia, 1989.
Popov, M., *Българските манастири* [The Bulgarian Monasteries]. Sofia, 1927.
Protich, A., *L'architecture religieuse bulgare*. Sofia, 1924.
Radoslavov, B., *Рудничарството в Етрополския балкан* [Ore Mining in the Etropole Mountains]. Sofia, 1930.
Raikov, B., *Етрополският книжовен център през XVI-XVII век. Палеографско и литературно-историческо изследване* [The Etropole Literary Center During the 16th-17th Centuries. Paleographical and Literary-Historical Study]. Sofia [Dissertation, Sofia Univ.], 1972.
Runciman, S., *The Medieval Manichee*. Cambridge, 1967.
Sakŭzov, Iv., *Данъчната система в средновековните манастири* [The Taxation System in Medieval Monasteries]. Sofia, 1924.
———, *Стопанските връзки между Дубровник и българските земи през 16 и 17 столетие* [Commercial Relations Between Dubrovnik and the Bulgarian Lands During the 16th and 17th Centuries]. Sofia, 1930.

Semerdzhiev, H., *Самоков и околността му* [Samokov and Its Vicinity]. Sofia, 1913.

Shaw, S. J., *History of the Ottoman Empire and Modern Turkey*, I, *Empire of the Gazis: The Rise and Decline of the Ottoman Empire, 1280-1808*. Cambridge, 1976.

Sherrard, P., *Athos, the Mountain of Silence*. London, 1960.

Shishkov, S.N., *Българо-мохамеданите (Помаци). Историко-земеписен и народоучен преглед с образи* [Bulgaro-Muslims *(Pomaks)*. Historical-Geographical and Popular Studies Review with Illustrations]. Plovdiv, 1936.

———, *Пловдив в своето минало и настояще. Историко-етнографски и политико-икономически преглед* [Plovdiv in the Past and Present. Historical-Ethnographic and Political-Economic Review]. Plovdiv, 1926.

———, *Помаците в трите български области: Тракия, Македония, и Мизия* [*Pomaks* in the Three Bulgarian Provinces: Thrace, Macedonia, and Mœsia], I. Plovdiv, 1914.

Snegarov, Iv., *История на Охрид архиепископия (от основаването й до завладяването на Балканския полуостров от турците)* [History of the Ohrid Archbishopric (From Its Founding to the Turkish Conquest of the Balkan Peninsula]. 2 v. Sofia, 1924-32.

———, *Кратка история на съвременните православни църкви (българска, руска и сръбска)* [Short History of the Contemporary Orthodox Churches (Bulgarian, Russian and Serbian)], II. Sofia, 1946.

———, *Културни и политически връзки между България и Русия през XVI-XVIII в.* [Cultural and Political Contacts Between Bulgaria and Russia During the 16th-18th Cen.]. Sofia, 1953.

Spiridonakis, B. G., *Essays on the Historical Geography of the Greek World in the Balkans During the Turkokratia*. Thessaloniki, 1977.

Stanimirov, S., *Политическата дейност на българите католици през 30-те — 70-те години на XVII век. Към историята на българската антиосманска съпротива* [The Political Activity of the Bulgarian Catholics During the 30s/70s of the 17th Century. Toward the History of the Bulgarian Anti-Ottoman Resistance]. Sofia, 1988.

Старобългарска литература. Изследвания и материали [Old Bulgarian Literature. Studies and Materials], I. Sofia, 1971.

Stavrianos, L. S., *The Balkans Since 1453*. New York, 1958.

Stoichev, S.P., *История на Клисурския манастир «Св. Кирил и Методий»* [History of Klisura Monastery "SS. Cyril and Methodius"]. Vratsa, 1922.

Стопанска история на България 681-1981 [Economic History of Bulgaria 681-1981]. Sofia, 1981.

Stoyanov, K.H., *Българските еснафи през турското робство (История, организация дейност)* [Bulgarian *Esnafs* During the Turkish Yoke (History, Organizational Effort)]. Varna, 1943.

Structure sociale et développement culturel des villes Sud-est européennes et adriatiques aux XVIIe-XVIIIe siècles. Bucharest, 1975.

Sŭbev, T., *Самостойна народностна църква в средновековна България* [The Independent National Church in Medieval Bulgaria]. Sofia, 1987.

Sugar, P. F., *Southeastern Europe under Ottoman Rule, 1354-1804.* Seattle, 1977.

Tatsov, A., *Етрополски манастир «Св. Тройца»* [Etropole Monastery of "The Holy Trinity"]. Etropole, 1915.

Tishkov, P., *История на нашето занаятчийство до Освобождението ни* [History of Our Craftsmanship to Our Liberation]. Sofia, 1922.

Todorov, N., *The Balkan City, 1400-1900*, trans. P.F. Sugar. Seattle, 1983.

————, *La ville balkanique sous les Ottomans (XV-XIXe s.).* London, 1977.

Tongas, G., *L'ambassadeur Louis Deshayes de Courmenin (1600-1632).* Paris, 1937.

Topalov, A., and A. Spilkov, *Седемте престола. Кратка история на манастира «Рожденство Пресветыя Богородицы»* [The Seven Altars. Short History of the Monastery "Birth of the Blessed Virgin"]. Sofia, 1947.

Traikov, V., and N. Zhechev, *Българската емиграция в Румъния XIV век-1878 година и участието й в стопанския, общественополитическия и културния живот на румънския народ* [Bulgarian Emigrants in Romania, 14th Century-1878, and Their Participation in the Commercial, Socio-Political and Cultural Life of the Romanian People]. Sofia, 1986.

300 години Чипровско въстание (Принос към историята на българите през XVII в.) [300 Years Chiprovtsi Uprising (Contribution to the History of the Bulgarians During the 17th Century)]. Sofia, 1988.

Tsernev, Ts., *Le style national dans la peinture bulgare ancienne (XI-XIX s.),* trans., S. Tsonov and M. Puliev. Sofia, 1969.

Tsvetkova, B., *Извънредни данъци и държавни повинности в българските земи под турска власт* [Extraordinary Taxes and State Services in the Bulgarian Lands under Turkish Rule]. Sofia, 1958.

————, *Народ непреклонен* [People Unbending]. Sofia, 1968.

————, *Проучвания на градското стопанство през XV-XVI век* [Studies of Urban Economy During the 15th-16th Centuries]. Sofia, 1972.

————, *Турският феодален ред и българският народ* [The Turkish Feudal Order and the Bulgarian People]. Sofia, 1962.

Turdeanu, E., *La litterature bulgare du XIVe siècle et sa diffusion dans les pays roumains.* Paris, 1947.

Undzhiev, Iv., *Карлово. История на града до Освобождението* [Karlovo. History of the City to the Liberation]. Sofia, 1968.

Vaporis, N. M., *Some Aspects of the History of the Ecumenical Patriarchate of Constantinople in the Seventeenth and Eighteenth Centuries*. [Published by the author, Boston], 1969.

Vasiliev, A., Черепишки манастир «Успение пресветия Богородично» [Cherepish Monastery "The Assumption of the Most Holy Virgin"]. Sofia, 1943.

_____ [ed.], *Комплексна научна експедиция в Северозападна България. Доклади и материали* [Complex of Scientific Expeditions in Northwest Bulgaria. Papers and Materials]. Sofia, 1958.

_____, *Ктиторски портрети* [Donor Portraits]. Sofia, 1960.

_____, *Образи на Кирил и Методий в България* [Images of Cyril and Methodius in Bulgaria]. Sofia, 1970.

_____, *Социални и патриотични теми в старото българско изкуство* [Social and Patriotic Themes in Old Bulgarian Art]. Sofia, 1973.

_____, *Тетевенските църкви* [The Churches in Teteven]. Sofia, 1948.

Ye'or, Bat, *The Dhimmi: Jews and Christians under Islam,* trans., D. Maisel, P. Fenton and D. Littman. Rutherford, 1985.

Юбилейна книга на град София (1878-1928) [Jubilee Book of the City of Sofia (1878-1928)]. Sofia, 1928.

Yurdanov, Yu., *История на българската търговия до Освобождението: Кратък очерк* [History of Bulgarian Commerce to the Liberation: Short Article]. Sofia, 1938.

Zahariev, I., *Чипровци* [Chiprovtsi]. Sofia, 1983.

Zhekov, A., *Възникване на манастирите в България и културно националното им значение. Кратък исторически очерк* [The Rise of Monasteries in Bulgaria and Their Cultural Nationalistic Significance. Short Historical Sketch]. Veliko Tŭrnovo, 1926.

Zlatarski, V., *Нова политическа и социална история на България и Балканския полуостров* [Modern Political and Social History of Bulgaria and the Balkan Peninsula]. Sofia, 1921.

Articles

Angelov, V., «Старобългарски книжовни средища. Аджар (Свежен) — Карловско» [Old Bulgarian Literary Centers. Adzhar (Svezhen)—Karlovo Region], *ИНБКМ*, XII [XVIII] (1972), pp. 43-58.

Arnakis, G. G., "The Greek Church of Constantinople and the Ottoman Empire," *Journal of Modern History*, XXIV (Sept., 1952), pp. 235-50.

Balaschev, G., «Храмът Св. Теодор Стратилат в Недобърско» [The Church of St. Teodor Stratilat in Nedobŭrsko], *ИБАД*, III (1912-1913), p. 327.

————, «Новозаветният манастир Св. Врач (бележки)» [The New Testament Monastery of "The Sacred Healer" (Notes)], *Родопски напредък* [Rhodope Progress], IV (1906), pp. 261-65.
Bobchev, S. S., "Notes comparées sur les corbacis chez les peuples balkaniques et en particulier les Bulgares," *Revue international des études balkaniques,* (1938), pp. 428-45.
Bosev, V., «Още за ролята на православието през османското робство» [More on the Role of Orthodoxy During the Ottoman Yoke], *Философска мисъл* [Philosophical Thought], IV (1969), pp. 86-91.
Bozhkov, A., «Делото на Йоан от Кратово» [The Work of Ioan from Kratovo], *Изкуство* [Art], XVIII, 10 (1968), pp. 23-25.
————, «Два ценни паметника на българската монументална живопис от XVI и XVII в.» [Two Important Monuments of Bulgarian Monumental Art from the 16th and 17th Cen.], *Изкуство*, XV, 9 (1965), pp. 9-12.
————, «Към въпроса за взаимните връзки между българското и румънското изкуство през XIV-XVII в.» [On the Problem of Reciprocal Contacts Between Bulgarian and Romanian Art During the 14th-17th Cen.], *ИИИИ*, VII (1964), pp. 41-99.
————, "Les monuments d'art en Bulgarie (XVe-XVIIIe s.)," *Actes du Premier congrés international des études balkaniques et Sud-est européennes,* II, *Archéologie.* Sofia, 1969, pp. 783-93.
————, «Социалната и творческа природа на българския художник през XV-XVIII век» [The Social and Creative Nature of the Bulgarian Artist During the 15th-18th Centuries], *Векове* [Centuries], 1 (1984), pp. 12-25.
————, «Стенописите в Добърско и Алинския манастир от XVII век» [The Wall Paintings in Dobŭrsko and Alino Monastery from the 17th Century], *Изкуство*, XVI, 5 (1967), pp. 18-29.
————, «Творческият метод на българския художник от епохата на турското робство до Възраждането» [The Creative Method of the Bulgarian Artist from the Era of the Turkish Yoke Until the Revival], *ИИИИ*, X (1967), pp. 5-32.
Chaplikov, V., «Българо-католически книжовници» [Bulgaro-Catholic Writers], *Парчевич (1674-1924)* [Parchevich (1674-1924)]. Sofia, 1924, pp. 74-81.
Davies, O., "Ancient Mining in the Central Balkan," *Revue internationale des études balkaniques,* III (1953), pp. 405-18.
Diehl, C., "Byzantine Art," *Byzantium. An Introduction to East Roman Civilization,* eds., N.H. Baynes and H.St.L.B. Moss. Oxford, 1962, pp. 166-99.
Dimitrov, S., «Демографски отношения и проникване на исляма в Западните Родопи и долината на Места през XV-XVII в.» [Demo-

graphic Relationships and Penetration of Islam in the Western Rhodopes and the Valley of the Mesta During the 15th-17th Cen.], *Родопски сборник*, I (1965), pp. 63-114.

————, «Проникване на мохамеданството сред българите в Западните Родопи през XVII век» [Penetration of Islamization Among the Bulgarians in the Western Rhodopes During the 15th-17th Centuries], *Родопи* [Rhodopes], 6 and 7 (1972), pp. 12-14; 15-17.

————, "Some Aspects of Ethnic Development, Islamisation and Assimilation in Bulgarian Lands in the 15th-17th Centuries," *Aspects of the Development of the Bulgarian Nation*. Sofia, 1989, pp. 36-59.

Dinekov, P., «Българската литература през XVII в.» [Bulgarian Literature During the 17th Cen.], *Литературна история* [Literary History], I (1977), pp. 5-15.

————, «Книжовният живот в София през XVI век» [Literary Life in Sofia During the 16th Century], *Родина* [Motherland], III, 4 (1941), pp. 124-43.

Duichev, Iv., «Архиепископ Петър Парчевич. Политическото значение на българското католичество през XVII в.» [Archbishop Petŭr Parchevich. The Political Significance of Bulgarian Catholicism During the 17th Cen.], *Родина*, I, 4 (1939), pp. 5-19.

————, «България и Западния свет през XVII в.» [Bulgaria and the Western World During the 17th Cen.], *Родина*, I, 1 (1938), pp. 113-33.

————, "Byzance après Byzance et les slaves (XVe-XVIIIe s.)," *Ivan Dujcev. Medioevo byzantino-slavo*, II. Rome, 1968, pp. 287-311.

————, "Chilandar et Zograf au Moyen Age", *Hilandarski zbornik* [Hilandar Collection], I. Belgrad, 1968, pp. 21-32.

————, «Политическата дейност на Петър Парчевич за освобождение от турско владичество» [The Political Efforts of Petŭr Parchevich for Liberation from Turkish Domination], *Българо-румънски връзки и отношения през вековете* [Bulgaro-Romanian Contacts and Relations Through the Centuries], I. Sofia, 1965, pp. 157-93.

————, «Прояви на народностно съзнание у нас през XVII в.» [Manifestations of National Consciousness Among the Bulgarians During the 17th Cen.], *Македонски преглед* [Macedonian Review], XIII, 2 (1942), pp. 26-52.

Enchev-Vidyu, Iv., «Из Гложенския манастир» [On Glozhene Monastery], *ИБАИ*, VI (1930-1931), pp. 294-96.

————, «Из църквите около Рилския манастир» [On the Churches Around Rila Monastery], *ИБАИ*, VI (1930-1931), pp. 286-94.

————, «Алинския манастир» [Alino Monastery], *ИБАИ*, IV (1926-1927), pp. 288-91.

Fischer-Galati, S., "Reverberation of the Austro-Turkish War in the Balkan Peninsula (1593-1606)," *Essays in Memory of Basil Laourdas*. Thessaloniki, 1975, pp. 349-60.

Gandev, H., «Българската граматност и книжовно предание през XVII и XVIII век» [Bulgarian Literacy and Literary Traditions During the 17th and 18th Centuries], *Родина*, III, 4 (1941), pp. 116-23.

———, «Демократизация на българската църква (XV-XVII в.)» [Democratization of the Bulgarian Church (15th-17th Cen.)], *Векове*, 1 (1984), pp. 5-12.

Genov, G.P., «Положението на Християните в Турция според Мюсюлманското право» [The Position of the Christians in Turkey According to the Muslim Law], *ГСУюф*, XXIV, 5 (1929), pp. 9-22.

Georgiev, I., «Град Враца. Принос към историята му» [The City of Vratsa. Contribution to Its History], *СбНУ*, XX (1904), pp. 1-75.

———, «Село Килифарево и манастирът му Св. Богородица» [The Village of Kilifarevo and Its Monastery of the Holy Virgin], *ПСп*, LXVII (1906), pp. 427-47.

Georgieva, Ts.V., «Етнонимът българи в системата на българския исторически спомен през XV-XVII век» [The Ethnic Name "Bulgarian" in the System of the Bulgarian Historical Memory During the 15th-17th Centuries], *Изследвания в чест на Х. Гандев* [Studies in Honor of H. Gandev], ed., B. Tsvetkova. Sofia, 1983, pp. 155-71.

———, "Organisation et fonctions du corps des janissaires dans les terres bulgares du XVIe jusqu'au milieu du XVIIIe siècles," *EH*, V. Sofia, 1970, pp. 319-36.

———, «Развитие и характер на кръвния данък в българските земи» [Development and Character of the Blood Tax in the Bulgarian Lands], *ГСУфиф*, LXI, 3 (1968), pp. 35-72.

———, "Le rôle des janissaires dans la politique ottomane et les terres bulgares (XVIe-milieu du XVIIe s.)," *EH*, VIII. Sofia, 1975, pp. 179-90.

Goshev, Iv., «Към историята на Черепишкия манастир» [Toward the History of Cherepish Monastery], *ГСУбф*, XXII (1944-45), pp. 1-34.

Grozdanova, E., "Les fondements économiques de la commune rurale dans les regions bulgares (XVe-XVIIIe s.)," *EB*, 1 (1974), pp. 30-45.

———, «Ролята на традиционната селска община за опазване на българската народност и народностното самосъзнание» [The Role of the Traditional Village Commune for Protecting the Bulgarian Nationality and National Self-Consciousness], *Българската нация през Възраждането. Сборник от изследвания* [The Bulgarian Nation During the Revival. Collection of Studies], ed., H. Hristov. Sofia, 1980, pp. 139-77.

Holban, M., "Autour de Parcevich," *RESEE*, 4 (1969), pp. 613-46.
Hupchick, D.P., "Seventeenth-Century Bulgarian *Pomaks:* Forced or Voluntary Converts to Islam?," *Society in Change Studies in Honor of Béla K. Király*, eds., S.B. Várdy and A.H. Várdy. New York, 1983, pp. 305-14.
Inalcik, H., "L'empire ottoman," *Actes du Premier congrès international des études balkaniques et Sud-est européenes*, III. Sofia, 1969. pp. 75-103.
———, "The Foundations of the Ottoman Economic-Social System in Cities," *Studia balcanica*, III, *Le ville balkanique, XV-XIX ss.* Sofia, 1970, pp. 17-24.
———, "The Ottoman Decline and Its Effects upon the *Reaya*," *Actes du IIe Congrès international des études du Sud-est européen*, III, *Histoire*. Athens, 1978, pp. 73-90.
Ivanov, I., «Старини и църкви в Югозападна България» [Antiquities and Churches in Southwest Bulgaria], *ИБАД*, III (1912-1913), pp. 53-72.
Ivanova, V., «Ореховският манастир и неговите грамоти» [Orehovo Monastery and Its Charters], *ИИДв*, XI-XII (1931-1932), pp. 84-118.
Kapitanov, H., «Българското присъствие в Европа. Основатели на първите манастири във Влахия» [The Bulgarian Presence in Europe. Founders of the First Monasteries in Wallachia], *Духовна култура*, 8-9 (1971), pp. 22-39.
Kliment [Rilets], «Рилските духовници таксидиоти» [Rila Ecclesiastic *Taxidiots*], *Духовна култура*, XI (1935), pp. 15-23.
Koev, P., «Гр. Ловеч, исторически бележки до освобождението му» [The City of Lovech, Historical Notes to Its Liberation], *Гр. Ловеч, бележки и спомени* [The City of Lovech, Notes and Recollections]. Lovech, 1927, pp. 3-31.
Kŭnchov, V., «Бележки за Курилския манастир» [Notes for Kurilo Monastery], *ПСп*, LXII (1900-1901), pp. 769-98.
Marinov, D., «Описание на Кремиковския манастир Св. Георги» [Description of Kremikovtsi Monastery "St. Georgi"], *Религиозни разкази* [Religious Stories], 9 (1896), pp. 376-84.
———, «Описание на манастира Св. Богородица, наречен още Елешнишки в Софийската епархия» [Description of the "Holy Virgin" Monastery, Also Called Eleshnitsa, in the Sofia Bishopric], *Религиозни разкази*, 1 (1896), pp. 28-33.
———, «Описание на манастира Св. Николай, наречен още Сеславци в Софийската епархия» [Description of "St. Nikolai" Monastery, Also Called Seslavtsi, in the Sofia Bishopric], *Религиозни разкази*, 2 (1896), pp. 58-62.
Mavrodinov, N., «Църкви и манастири в Мелник и Рожен» [Churches and Monasteries in Melnik and Rozhen], *ГНАМ*, V (1926 [1931]), pp. 285-306.

Mihailov, S., «Разрушеният манастир Св. Тройца до Враца» [The Ruined Monastery of "The Holy Trinity" Near Vratsa], *ИАИ*, XVIII (1952), pp. 395-96.

_____, «Църквата Св. Теодор Тирон и Теодор Стратилат в с. Добърско» [The Church of "SS. Teodor Tiron and Teodor Stratilat" in the Village of Dobŭrsko], *ИАИ*, XXIX (1966), pp. 5-40.

Mikov, V., «Българите мохамедани в Тетевенско, Луковитско и Белослатинско» [The Bulgarian Muslims in the Regions of Teteven, Lukovit and Belo Slatino], *Родина*, III, 3 (1941), pp. 51-68.

Miletich, L., «Из историята на българската католишка пропаганда в XVII в.» [On the History of Bulgarian Catholic Propaganda in the 17th Cen.], *Български преглед*, I, 10; 11 (1894), pp. 62-82; 146-89.

_____, «Нашите павликяни» [Our *Pavlikyani*], *СбНУ*, XIX (1903), pp. 1-364.

_____, «Поземлената собственост и войнишките общини в турско време» [Land Ownership and *Voynuk* Communes in Turkish Times], *ПСп*, LXVI (1905), pp. 307-35.

_____, «Заселение на католишките българи в Седмиградско и Банат» [Settlement of Catholic Bulgarians in Transylvania and the Banat], *СбНУ*, XIV (1897), pp. 284-544.

Milev, N., «Факторите на българското възраждане» [The Factors in the Bulgarian Revival], *Юбилеен сборник в чест на Ив. Д. Шишманов* [Jubilee Collection in Honor of Iv.D. Shishmanov]. Sofia, 1920, pp. 129-57.

Miyatev, K., «Карлуковският манастир Св. Богородица» [Karlukovo Monastery of "The Blessed Virgin"], *ГНАМ*, VI (1932-1934), pp. 274-86.

_____, «Старини по горното течение на Марица» [Antiquities from the Upper Course of the Maritsa], *ИБАИ*, V (1928-1929), pp. 336-41.

_____, «Старинни църкви в Западна България» [Old Churches in Western Bulgaria], *ИБАИ*, XIII (1939), pp. 228-45.

_____, «Съкровищата на Рилския манастир» [The Treasury of Rila Monastery], *ГНАМ*, IV (1926), pp. 314-61.

Mutafchiev, P., «Репорт върху състоянието на старопланинските манастири от Искър до Троян» [Report Regarding the Condition of the Balkan Mountain Monasteries from the Iskŭr to Troyan], *ГНАМ*, I (1920), pp. 76-84.

Mutafchieva, V., "De l'exploitation féodale dans les terres de population bulgare sous la domination turque aux XVe et XVIe siècles," *EH*, I. Sofia, 1960, pp. 145-70.

_____, «Към въпроса за статута на българското население в Чепинско под османска власт» [Toward the Problem of the Status of the Bulgarian Population in the Chepino Region under Ottoman Rule], *Родопски сборник*, I (1965), pp. 115-27.

Nedev, S., «Дубровник в нашето минало (XIII-XVII в.) [Dubrovnik in Our Past (13th-17th Cen.)], *ИВНД*, VIII (1969), pp. 137-49.

Neshev, G., «Българските манастири и тяхната роля за съхраняването на народността в първите векове на османското владичество» [Bulgarian Monasteries and Their Role in the Formation of Nationality in the First Centuries of Ottoman Domination], *Първи конгрес на Българското историческо дружество* [First Congress of the Bulgarian Historical Society], I. Sofia, 1972, pp. 453-57.

─────────, "Les monastères bulgares du Mont Athos," *EH*, VI. Sofia, 1973, pp. 97-115.

─────────, «Православните институции през XV-XVIII в.» [Orthodox Institutions During the 15th-18th Cen.], *Православието в България* [Orthodoxy in Bulgaria]. Sofia, 1974, pp. 125-51.

Noikov, P.M., «Поглед върху развитието на българското образование до Паисия» [A View on the Development of Bulgarian Education to Paisii], *ГСУифф*, XXI, 11 (1925). [Offprint, 60 p.].

Panaiotova, D., «Църквата Св. Петка при Вуково» [The Church of "St. Petka" Near Vukovo], *ИИИИ*, VIII (1965), pp. 221-54.

Pandurski, V., «Пимен Софийски» [Pimen Sofiiski], *Бележити българи* [Noted Bulgarians], III. Sofia, 1969, pp. 90-97.

─────────, «Стенописите в Илиенцкия манастир край София» [Wall Paintings in Ilientsi Monastery Near Sofia], *ИИИИ*, XIII (1969), pp. 5-28.

─────────, «Църковни старини из Трънско и Брезнишко» [Church Antiquities in the Regions of Trŭn and Breznik], *Църковен вестник*, LXI, 36 (1961), pp. 5-7.

Paskaleva, V., «За началния етап в образуването на българската нация» [For the First Step in the Education of the Bulgarian Nation], *ИПр*, 6 (1962), pp. 29-52.

Plyakov, Z.S., «Градското занаятчийско производство в българските земи през XV-XVII в.» [Urban Artisan Production in the Bulgarian Lands During the 15th-17th Cen.], *ИПр*, 6 (1973), pp. 68-87.

─────────, «За регламентацията на градското занаятчийско производство в българските земи през XV-средата на XVII в.» [For the Regulation of Urban Artisan Production in the Bulgarian Lands During the 15th-mid 17th Cen.], *ИИИ*, XXI (1970), pp. 87-148.

Popov, K., Кюстендил под турско робство и участието на кюстендилци в националноосвободителните борби. Кюстендил през XV-XVIII в.» [Kyustendil under the Turkish Yoke and the Participation of the Inhabitants of Kyustendil in the National Liberation Struggles. Kyustendil in the 15th-18th Cen.], *Кюстендил и Кюстендилско* [Kyustendil and the Region of Kyustendil]. Sofia, 1973, pp. 85-111.

Protich, A.,"Le Mont Athos et l'art bulgare," *La Revue bulgare,* II, 3 (1930), pp. 143-55.

Raikov, B., «Етрополската калиграфско-художествена школа през XVI-XVII век» [The Etropole Calligraphical-Art School During the 16th-17th Centuries], *ИНБКМ,* XII [XVIII] (1971), pp. 19-39.

⎯⎯⎯⎯, «Към въпроса за мястото на Абагар в старата българска литература» [Toward the Place of *Abagar* in Old Bulgarian Literature], *ИИБЛ,* XVIII-XIX (1966), pp. 279-86.

Rizaj, S., "Counterfeit of Money on the Balkan Peninsula from the XV to the XVII Century," trans., Z . Zigić. *Balcanica,* I. Belgrad, 1970, pp . 71-9.

Romanski, S.M., «Българската книжнина в Румъния и едно нейно произведение» [Bulgarian Writing in Romania and One of Its Products], *ИССФУС,* I (1905). [Offprint, 100 p.].

Sakŭzov, Iv., «Манастирското стопанство през турско време» [The Monastic Economy During Turkish Times], *Духовна култура,* XXVI and XXVII (1925). [Offprint, 35 p.].

Shishmanov, Iv., «Паисий и неговата епоха. Мисли върху генезиса на новобългарското възраждане» [Paisii and His Era. Thoughts on the Genesis of the Modern Bulgarian Revival], *СпБАН,* VIII (1914), pp. 1-18.

Snegarov, Iv., «Търновски митрополити в турско време» [Tŭrnovo Metropolitans in Turkish Times], *СпБАН,* LII (1925), pp. 207-54.

Stancheva, M., «Към изучаването на градската материална култура и бит в София през епохата на турското владичество» [Toward the Study of Urban Material Culture and Standard of Living in Sofia During Turkish Domination], *ИЕИМ,* IX (1966), pp. 271-79.

Stoianovich, T., "The Conquering Balkan Orthodox Merchant," *Journal of Economic History,* XX (Summer, 1960), pp. 234-313.

⎯⎯⎯⎯, "Land Tenure and Related Sectors of the Balkan Economy 1600-1800," *Journal of Economic History,* XIII (Fall, 1953), pp. 398-411.

Stoyanov, M., «Един български културен център в Родопите през турската епоха» [A Bulgarian Cultural Center in the Rhodopes During the Turkish Era], *ГМ-По,* I (1954), pp. 255-63.

Stoyanov, V., «Пролетна разходка от София до Кокалянския мънастир през с. Бистрица, и завращание от поменътия мънастир до София през селата Кокаляне, Панчерево и Горубляне» [Springtime Walk From Sofia to Kokalyane Monastery Through the Village of Bistritsa, and Returning From Said Monastery to Sofia Through the Villages of Kokalyane, Pancherevo and Gorublyane], *ПСп,* XL (1892), pp. 686-96.

Tatsov, A., «Етрополският манастир Варовитец» [Etropole Monastery *Varovitets*], *Български сбирка,* XXI, 3 (1915), pp. 138-41.

Todorov, N., «По някой въпроси на балканския град през XV-XVIII в.» [On Some Problems of the Balkan City During the 15th-18th Cen.], *ИПр*, XVIII (1962), pp. 32-58.

_____, "The Socio-Economic Life of Sofia in the 16th and 17th Centuries," *La ville balkanique sous les Ottomans (XV-XIXe s.)*. London, 1977. p. III, 1-20.

_____, «Турската колонизация и демографските промени в българските земи» [Turkish Colonization and Demographic Changes in the Bulgarian Lands], *Етногенезис и културно наследство на българската народност* [Ethnogenesis and Cultural Legacy of the Bulgarian Nationality]. Sofia, 1971, pp. 69-74.

Trifanov, Yu., «Сръбско-българска безюсова редакция в старата книжнина на южните славяни» [Serbo-Bulgarian "Yu"-less Phrasing in the Old Literature of the South Slavs], *Македонски преглед*, XII, 2 (1940), pp. 27-55.

Tsvetkova, B., "Les *celep* et leur role dans la vie économique des Balkans a l'époque ottomane," *Studies in the Economic History of the Middle East*. London, 1970, pp. 172-92.

_____, "Changements intervenus dans les conditions de la population des terres bulgares (depuis la fin de XVIe jusqu'au milieu de XVIIIe s.)," *EH*, V. Sofia, 1970, pp. 291-318.

_____, "L'évolution du régime féodal turc de la fin du XVIe jusqu'au milieu du XVIIIe siècle," *EH*, I. Sofia, 1960, pp. 171-206.

_____, «Към въпроса за класовите различия в българското общество през епохата на турското владичество» [Toward the Problem of Class Distinctions in Bulgarian Society During the Era of the Turkish Domination], *ИПр*, VIII, 2 (1952), pp. 166-74.

_____, «Откупната система (илтизам) в Османската империя през XVI-XVIII в. с оглед на българските земи» [The Tax Farming System *(iltizam)* in the Ottoman Empire During the 16th-18th Cen. with a View of the Bulgarian Lands], *Известия на Институт за правни науки* [Journal of the Institute for Legal Sciences], XI, 2 (1960), pp. 195-223.

_____, «Поземлените отношения в българските земи под османско владичество до средата на XVII век» [Land Relationships in the Bulgarian Lands under Ottoman Domination to the Mid 17th Century], *ИПр*, VII, 2 (1951), pp. 158-92.

_____, "Problems of the Bulgarian Nationality and the National Consciousness in the XV-XVIII c.," *EH*, VI. Sofia, 1973, pp. 57-90.

_____, "Le service des *celep* et le ravitaillement en bétail dans l'Empire ottoman (XVe-XVIIIe s.)," *EH*, III. Sofia, 1966, pp. 145-72.

_____, "La situation internationale et le peuple bulgare à la fin du XVIe et début du XVIIe siècle," *East European Quarterly,* VI, 3 (1972), pp. 321-36.

_____, "Sur le sort de Tarnova, capitale bulgare au Moyen age après sa prise par les osmanlis," *Bb,* II (1966), pp. 181-98.

_____, "To the History of the Resistance Against the Ottoman Feudal Domination in the Danube Region of Bulgaria during the 15th-18th Centuries," *EH,* IV. Sofia, 1968, pp. 213-31.

_____, "Typical features of the Ottoman social and economic structure in South-Eastern Europe during the 14th to the 16th centuries," *EH,* IX. Sofia, 1979, pp. 129-49.

_____, «За стопанския облик и за феодалните задължения на някой селища в Родопите и прилежащите райони през XV-XVII в.» [For the Economic Aspect and For the Feudal Obligations of Various Settlements in the Rhodopes and Adjoining Regions During the 15th-17th Cen.], *Родопски сборник,* I (1965), pp. 41-60.

Vasiliev, A., «Черковно строителство в София до Освобождението» [Church Construction in Sofia to the Liberation], *Юбилеен сборник на Софийското българско благотворително образователно дружество «Иван Н. Денкооглу»* [Jubilee Collection of the Sofia Bulgarian Charitable Educational Society "Ivan N. Denkooglu"]. Sofia, 1940, pp. 52-74.

_____, «Една старинна църква при с. Студена» [An Old Church Near the Village of Studena], *ГНАМ,* VII (1942), pp. 165-84.

_____, «Проучвания на изобразителните изкуства из някой селища по долината на Струма» [Studies on the Representational Arts in Various Settlements in the Valley of the Struma], *ИИИИ,* VII (1964), pp. 151-92.

_____, «Софийската Света гора» [The Sofia "Holy Mountain"], *Славяни* [Slavs], 5 (1971), pp. 28-31.

_____, «Църкви и манастири из Западна България» [Churches and Monasteries in Western Bulgaria], *ГНАМ,* IV (1949), pp. 49-114.

_____, «За изобразителните изкуства в Северозападна България [For the Representational Arts in Northwest Bulgaria], *Комплексна научна експедиция в Северозападна България през 1956 г.* [Complex of Scientific Expeditions in Northwest Bulgaria During 1956]. Sofia, 1958, pp. 173-258.

Vasilieva, I., «Да разкрием и изучим художественото наследство на Пимен Зограф» [To Reveal and Study the Artistic Legacy of Pimen Zograf], *Музеите и паметници на културата* [The Museums and Monuments of Culture], I (1963), pp. 19-21.

Vasilev, V., «Влахо-българската книжнина XV-XVII век» [Wallacho-Bulgarian Writings 15th-17th Centuries], *Славяни,* 7 (1973), pp. 44-46.

Vecheva, E., "Les associations commerciales des habitants de Dubrovnik dans les terres bulgares durant les XVIe-XVIIe s.," *EH*, IX. Sofia, 1979, pp. 173-86.

Velchev, V., «Търновската книжовна школа и предренесанството движение на Балканите» [The Tŭrnovo Literary School and the Pre-Renaissance Movement in the Balkans], *Език и литература,* 3 (1972), pp. 13-25.

Velcheva, B., «Показателни местоимения и наречия в новобългарските паметници от XVII и XVIII в.» [Demonstrative Pronouns and Dialects in New Bulgarian Monuments From the 17th and 18th Cen.], *ИИБЕ*, X (1964), pp. 159-233.

Zahariev, S., «Стенописите в старата църква в с. Мала Църква, Самоковско» [The Wall Paintings in the Old Church in the Village of Mala Tsŭrkva, Samokov Region], *ИИИИ*, VII (1964), pp. 141-50.

Index

aba, 43
Abagar, 80–81, 82
Abbasids, 22
Abgar, 80
Abu Bekir, 60
acts of the apostles, 160, 170, 172, 176
Adolphus, Gustavus II, 1
Adriatic Sea, 39
Adzhar, 107, 108, 111, 115, 124, 170, 173, 178–179, 180–181, 182, 189, 194, 198
Adzhar, church, 178–179
Adzhar *damaskin*, 180
Africa, 183
Agapii, Karlukovo abbot, 135, 177
agrarian laws, 29–30, 36, 49–50
Ahmed I, 71, 145
akıncıs, 23, 61–62
akçe, 5, 31–32, 35–36, 48, 49, 69, 152, 169
Albania, 128
Albanians, 13, 39
Ali, caliph, 60
Alino Monastery, 53, 130, 132, 134, 135, 150, 163
Ananiya, 72
Anatolia, 3, 13, 62
Andronii, Etropole abbot, 167, 169
Angelos, Alexios III, 97
Arbanasi, 67, 68
Arbanasi, "Nativity" church, 68
architecture, 129–130, 140
Armenia, 77
Armenians, 8, 18, 39, 42, 199
Arsenii, Rila monk, 146, 147, 148

art, 54, 56, 87, 89–90, 91, 92, 94, 95–96, 98, 99, 102, 103, 105, 108, 109, 127–138, 147, 150, 151, 154–155, 159, 164–165, 171, 176–177, 178, 186, 189, 193, 195, 197, 198
artisans, 34, 37, 40, 41, 42–43, 43–44, 47–48, 49–50, 53–54, 67, 68, 104, 106, 120, 137–138, 152, 162, 170, 174, 178, 193
artist handbook, 103, 131, 137, 138, 197
artists, 68, 72, 95, 96, 101, 127–128, 129, 130, 131, 132, 133–134, 136–137, 138–140, 150, 151, 154, 159, 161, 165, 166, 171, 177, 189
Asen, Ivan I, 117
Asen, Ivan II, 73, 94, 118, 123
Asen, Koloman I, 94
Asia, 1, 4, 13, 31, 183
Atanas of Boboshevo, 147
Atanasii, Rila abbot, 147
Athonite styles of art, 131
Athos Peninsula, 90, 92
avaris, 20, 21–22, 26, 35, 49, 55
Avram, Dragalevtsi abbot, 162

Bachkovo Monastery, 68, 72, 181
Balkan calligraphic letters, 110
Balkan Mountains, 18, 23, 75, 78, 107, 111, 113, 122, 136, 157, 158, 159, 160, 165, 173, 175
Balkan Peninsula, 1–4, 6, 8, 16, 44, 45–46, 50, 74, 76, 77, 80, 88, 91, 92, 93–94, 95, 97, 99, 103, 104, 110, 115, 116, 122, 125, 127–128, 131, 136, 138, 144, 183, 185, 190
Balsha, church, 133

299

INDEX

Baltic Basin, 45
ban, 28
Banat, 83
banditry, 36, 57–58, 116, 144, 145
Basarab, Matei, 125
bashtina, 19, 29, 35, 37
Basil II Bulgaroktonos, 89
Bayezid I, 144
bazaar, 44, 56
beadroll, 96–97, 162–163, 166, 198
Bedreddin, *şeyh*, 60
Bedreddins, 60
Bektaş Veli, *haci*, 60
Bektaşi, 60–61
Belchin, church, 150
Belgrad, 4, 45, 83, 154, 161
berat, 5, 68, 69, 70
Berende, church, 133
Berkovitsa, 39, 43, 185
Bernini, Gianlorenzo, 1
bey, 4, 5, 75
beylerbey, 4, 34, 48, 63
Bible, 156, 182
Bilintsi, 134
Bilintsi Monastery, 113, 130, 134, 139
Birimirtsi, 159
Black Sea, 18, 37, 39, 186, 191, 192
Boboshevo, 147, 151
Boboshevo, church, 151
Boboshevo Monastery, 100, 107
Bogdan (Bakshich), Petŭr, 59, 70, 72–73, 76, 79, 153, 154, 156
Bogdan of Dobŭrsko, 135
Bogdan of Slavovitsa, 125
Bogomils, 77, 80, 116
bolyar, 37, 51, 54, 61, 62, 87, 88, 89, 115, 123, 129, 159, 161, 174, 191, 193
book of hours, 102, 170, 172, 179
bookbinding, 125, 162, 171–172, 177
books, 105, 113, 119, 126–127, 156, 163, 167, 187
Boris I, 73, 78, 87, 88–89, 115, 123
Bosnia, 4, 25, 75, 79, 80, 128
Boyana, church, 132
Boyana Monastery, 157

Bresnitsa, 173
Breznik, 71
Budapest, 25
Buhovo, 159
Buhovo Monastery, 157, 158–159
Bulgaria, medieval, 22, 28, 37, 73–74, 77–78, 80, 87–90, 90–91, 94–95, 97, 98, 99, 100, 103, 107, 109–110, 112, 113, 115–116, 116–117, 118, 119, 123, 127, 132, 133, 139, 143–144, 147, 148, 149, 150, 151, 160, 162, 163, 164, 165, 167, 170, 171, 173, 174, 180, 181, 188, 191, 195, 196
Bulgarian (Middle) Church Slavonic, 112, 113–114, 119, 120, 122, 125
Bulgarian Archbishopric-Patriarchate of Ohrid, 66–67, 99, 117
Bulgarian Catholics, 25, 59, 75–77, 78, 82–83, 137, 197
Bulgarian Exarchate, 64
Bulgarian lands, 96–97
Bulgarian national revival, 68, 76, 99, 139, 140, 159, 194, 197
Bulgarian Orthodox church, 37, 66–67, 73, 78, 87–88, 90, 99, 109, 118, 123, 127, 140, 191
Bulgarian Patriarchate of Tŭrnovo, 66–67, 73, 99, 115, 118, 122–123
Bulgarian saints, 52, 53, 59, 62, 89, 115–118, 120, 132–133, 137, 140, 144, 148, 149, 151, 157, 159, 163, 165, 168, 169, 170, 172, 176, 179, 188, 196, 198
Bulgaro-Saxons, 25, 75–76, 79
Burgas, 18, 23, 33, 39, 184, 185
Byala, 168
Byzantine Empire, 2, 4, 7, 22, 73, 77–78, 80, 82, 87–88, 89, 90–91, 98, 99, 110, 117, 118, 121, 125, 128, 131, 139, 143, 163, 171, 181, 197
Bzovnik, 114

calligraphy, 101, 102, 103, 108, 109–112, 125, 131, 137, 167, 168–169, 170, 178, 179, 180, 182

INDEX

Candia, 63, 64
canons, 147
çarşi, 42, 43
çavuş, 41
celepkeşan, 25
celeps, 24, 25, 30, 45, 50, 53, 135, 178, 186, 194
cell schools, 101, 103–104, 105, 109, 113, 114, 139, 145, 147, 148, 150, 152, 153, 155, 156–157, 158, 161, 163, 168, 173, 174, 177, 178–179, 180, 181–182, 193, 195–196
çeltukçıs, 24
Cervantes, Miguel de, 1
Cetinje, 125, 163, 167, 171
Chalcedonian Peninsula, 90
Chelopechane, 107, 158–159
Chelopechane, church, 168
Chepino, 63–65
Cherepish Monastery, 100, 107, 113, 139, 173, 175–176, 178
Chernorizets Hrabŭr, 89, 112
Cherven, 139
Chiprovtsi, 16, 24–25, 42–43, 47, 48, 75–76, 79–80, 82–83, 137–138
Chiprovtsi Council, 79–80
Chiprovtsi Monastery, 59, 83
Chiprovtsi School of goldsmithing, 138
Chiprovtsi uprising, 16, 47, 58, 75, 83, 176, 197
chronicles, 98, 126–127, 188
Church Slavonic, 101, 102, 107, 108, 112–115, 122, 125, 138, 148, 152, 165, 172, 173, 180, 182, 188
churches, 30, 38, 39–40, 51–54, 58, 59, 64, 65, 68, 69–70, 72, 74, 92, 96, 103, 105, 110, 113, 125–126, 127, 128, 129–131, 132–133, 134, 136, 137, 138, 139–140, 147, 150–151, 152–153, 154–155, 160, 161–162, 166, 174, 176–177, 181, 193, 197, 198
çift, 19, 21, 27, 35
çift resmi, 20, 35
çiftlik, 33–34, 185–186
Çirmen, 13, 183
Çirmen, battle, 115
cizye, 3, 14, 19–20, 21–22, 22–23, 26, 27, 35–36, 40, 49, 54, 55, 194
Clement VIII, 75
Clementine College, 75
commerce, 37, 39, 43, 44–46, 154
Constantine and Helena, 119, 123
Constantine I, 123
Constantinople, 8, 89, 117, 128, 131, 181, 192; *See also* Istanbul
conversions, 17, 27, 57, 59, 60–65, 82, 183, 198
conversions, forced, 62–65
corvées, 20, 21, 22, 23, 27, 37, 62
craft industries, 37, 39–40, 42–43, 44, 49, 75, 120, 138, 162
Crete, 63, 136
Crimean Tatars, 16–17, 65–66, 167
Crnojević, Đord, 163
Croatia, 4, 8, 75
Croats, 13, 39
Cromwell, Oliver, 1
cultural patrons, 52–54, 55, 56, 68, 72, 91, 92, 94–95, 96–97, 125–126, 127, 129, 134, 135, 138, 139, 146, 149, 150, 155, 156, 160, 161, 162, 166–167, 169, 170, 172, 174, 176, 177, 179, 181, 188, 189–190, 193, 194, 196
curriculum, 101–103, 104, 106–107, 156, 195–196
Cyril and Methodius, 78, 87–88, 99, 132–133, 177
Cyrillic, 79, 80, 99, 101, 102, 110, 132, 133, 156

Dalmatia, 8, 80
damaskin, 81, 121–124, 148, 172, 179, 180, 182, 188, 196–197
Damaskin Studit, 121, 122
Danail, Stoyan and Vladko of Sofia, 156
Daniil Etropolski (Mazach), 67–68, 107–108, 111, 114–115, 124, 164, 168–170, 171, 172, 173, 175, 176

301

Danube River, 8, 15, 16, 37, 39, 65–66, 78, 83, 95, 110, 111, 123, 174, 176, 185
Danubian Plain, 66, 123, 136, 165, 167, 186, 191, 195, 198
Danubian Principalities, 82, 95, 128, 154; *See also* Romanian Principalities
daskal, 101–102, 103, 105–106, 109, 112, 126, 152, 155, 168, 170, 171, 173, 174, 180
David, Ioasif, and Teofan, 144
death rates, 14–15
demography, 13–17, 23, 24, 26, 27, 35, 37, 39, 40, 47–48, 62, 66, 73, 78, 152, 174, 183–184, 190–191, 198
dervencis, 23–24, 30, 53, 165
derviş orders, 59–61, 191
Descartes, René, 1
devşirme, 3–4, 23, 26, 34, 59, 61, 183
dime, 29
Dimitrashko, Raicho, 149
Dimitriev of Karlovo, 179
Dimitrievich, Avram, 108, 114, 124, 178, 179–180, 180–181, 182
Doblishko, Nesho, 158
Dobroslavtsi, 135
Dobrudzha, 60, 195, 198
Dobŭrsko, 151
Dobŭrsko, church, 53, 130, 132, 134, 135, 151
Dolna Beshovitsa Monastery, 133, 177, 178
Dolni Kamenartsi, 158
Dolni Lozen, 163
Dolni Lozen Monastery, 107, 157, 163
donor portraits, 134, 135, 136, 177
Dorostol Monastery, 139
Dovrena of Birimirtsi, 164
doxology, 168, 171
Dragalevtsi Monastery, 107, 129, 132, 135, 155, 156, 157, 160, 161–162
Dragan, *daskal*, 108, 114, 164
Dragan of Novoseltsi, 155
Draganov, Iovan, 179
Draginov, Metodii, 63, 64–65
Dragoman, 83

Dragul, *dyak*, 115, 175
Drinov *damaskin*, 123
Dubrovnik, 18, 39, 45–46, 74, 75, 79, 80, 100, 137, 154, 162
Dubrovnik merchants, 18, 45–47, 74, 75, 79, 100, 138, 154, 162
ducat, 68, 69
Dupnitsa, 42, 96, 113, 115, 145, 150, 151
Dupnitsa, "Holy Arhangel Mihail" church, 150
Dupnitsa, "St. Nikola" church, 150
dyak, 101, 102–103, 156

Edirne, 88
education, 51, 52, 54, 56, 65, 75, 77, 79–80, 82, 83, 87, 88, 89–90, 91, 95–96, 98, 99–107, 109, 111, 113, 120, 121, 123, 124, 125, 126, 127, 133–134, 138, 139, 145, 147, 148–149, 150–151, 153, 155–157, 164–165, 166, 169, 170–171, 173–174, 177, 178, 179, 180, 181–182, 187, 188, 195–196
Egypt, 90
elders, 28, 40, 52, 53, 64, 106
Elena, 18, 179
Elena *damaskin*, 179
Eleshnitsa, 158
Eleshnitsa Monastery, 107, 139, 155, 156, 157, 158, 168, 177
emvatikon, 69, 70
England, 18, 45
eparchy, 51, 67
epidemics, 14–15, 183
Epiros, 73
Epivatos, 117, 118
Eremiya, Dragalevtsi abbot, 162
ermeniya, 103
esnaf, 40–42, 44, 48, 53–54, 56, 104, 135, 138–139, 152, 161, 193; *See also* guilds
Etropole, 24, 42, 48, 53, 96, 111, 114, 165–166, 168, 169, 170, 172, 176, 193, 194

Index

Etropole calligraphic style, 111–112, 125, 131, 167, 169, 170, 172, 173, 179, 182
Etropole, "Holy Arhangel Mihail" church, 166
Etropole Monastery, 53, 107, 108, 110, 111, 115, 120, 124, 125, 147, 149, 156, 164, 165, 166–168, 169, 170–172, 173, 175, 178, 179, 182, 189
Etropole Pass, 165
Etropole *sbornik*, 171
Etropole School, 125, 131, 167, 168–169, 170–171, 172, 173, 178, 180, 182
Etropole, "St. Georgi" church, 166
Etropole, "St. Paraskeva" church, 166
eulogies, 118, 119, 125
Europe, 1–2, 13, 31, 34, 46, 76, 82, 128, 167
Europe, Central, 14, 183
Europe, Eastern, 1–2, 13, 18, 73, 77, 87
Europe, Western, 1–2, 18, 22, 31, 37, 40, 45–46, 74, 76–77, 110, 123, 128, 131, 137–138, 154, 162, 167, 197
Evliya Celebi, 40, 42
Evtimii Tŭrnovski, 67, 89, 99–100, 102, 103, 110, 112, 114, 115, 117, 118–120, 122–123, 127, 133, 148, 150, 153, 164, 169, 172, 180, 196
eyalet, 4, 17, 34
Eygen, *paşa*, 83

Far East, 45
Feodor I Ivanovich, 146
ferman, 9, 55, 144, 145, 146, 155
fiefs, 5–7, 19, 20–21, 22, 26, 27, 28, 29, 32–33, 35, 36, 50, 57–58, 185, 191–192; See also sipahilık
Filip of Adzhar, 108, 115, 124, 180–181, 182
Filipa, Razlog priest, 178
Filoteya Temnishka, 117
Florence Council, 74
Fourth Crusade, 73
France, 45, 73
Franciscans, 74–75, 80

Gabrovo, 16, 23
Gavriil, Tŭrnovo metropolitan, 169
Gavril, archbishop, 63
Gavril, Glozhene abbot, 173
Gavril Lesnovski, 116, 132, 159, 168, 172
Georgi Novi Sofiiski, 62, 120, 123, 132–133, 148, 159
Georgov, Spas, 170
Gerasim, Cherepish monk, 176
Gerlach, Stefan, 152–153
German Monastery, 157, 163
Germans, 46
Gino, Etropole butcher, 169
Giray, Selim, 16, 65–66
Glavanovtsi, 176
Glozh, Kievan prince, 173
Glozhene Monastery, 107, 111, 169, 172–173
Golcha Voivoda, 176
goldsmithing art, 137–138
Golyamo Belovo, 63, 64–65
Goranovtsi, church, 151
Gorna Dzhumaya, 17, 184, 186
Gorni Lom, church, 136
Gorni Lozen, 155, 163
Gorni Voden, 72
Gorni Voden Monastery, 72, 181
Gorova Monastery, 113, 125
gospels, 98, 120, 147, 150, 160, 161, 162, 168, 169, 172, 173, 176, 188
Gradeshnitsa Monastery, 107, 176, 178
gramatik, 101, 102, 103, 109, 112, 114, 168
Granitsa, 144
Great Schism, 77
Greek Orthodox church, 48, 51, 57, 58–59, 66, 67–68, 69, 70, 73, 78, 87, 99, 109, 131, 152, 153, 169
Greek Patriarchate, 9, 51, 65, 66–67, 68–70, 71, 73, 91, 92, 93, 125, 161, 192
Greeks, 7–8, 9–10, 13, 18, 39, 45, 46, 47, 51, 66, 71, 72–73, 90, 91, 92, 93, 99, 100, 121, 129, 152, 153, 157, 190, 192, 196, 197–198, 199
groş, 31–32

guilds, 37, 40–42, 48, 53–54, 68, 193, 195; See also esnaf
Gushavo Monastery, 137

Habsburg Empire, 15–16, 65–66, 74, 76, 82–83, 136, 154, 174, 176
hagiography, 115, 117, 118–120, 121, 122–123, 147, 148, 149, 153, 155, 163, 165, 168, 169, 170, 172, 176, 188, 196; See also Lives
haiduts, 16–17, 65, 82, 126, 154, 176
han, 65, 88
Hanafid School of law, 52, 62, 128
hane, 14, 17–18, 21–22, 23, 35, 40, 49, 170
hane, "free", 26
Hanseatic League, 45
haraç, 20, 54, 194
Haritoniya, Dolna Beshovitsa monk, 177
has, 5, 26, 27, 32, 48–49, 185–186, 191
Hasan, hoca, 64
Hasiya of Dobŭrsko, 135
hellenization, 72–73, 185, 186
Heraclea, 117
Herzegovina, 4
Hesychist movement, 110
High Divan, 155
Hilendar Monastery, 94, 97–98, 100, 113, 114, 134, 150, 155, 164
hisba, 40–41, 44
Holland, 45
Holy Land, 92, 117, 123, 135
Holy See, 74
"Holy Trinity" Monastery, Vratsa, 107, 115, 169, 174–175, 175–176, 178
hospodar, 91
Hrelyo, 143, 144
Hrisant, Etropole abbot, 166
Hungary, 47, 74, 82, 110, 128
hymnal, 170, 171, 173

Iannina, 120
Ibrahim, sultan, 145–146, 170

Iconoclasm, 90
iconography, 129, 130–131, 132, 133, 134, 135, 140, 150, 159, 165, 177, 197
iconostasis, 94, 137, 151
icons, 90, 92, 94, 95–96, 105, 136–137, 147, 149, 152, 155, 162, 166, 176
Ilarion Müglenski, 117, 119, 125, 133, 163, 169, 172, 176
Ilientsi Monastery, 139, 155, 157, 160
illumination, 102, 111, 137, 168–169, 170, 171, 179, 182
Illyrian, 80, 81
iltizam, 32, 49
imam, 64
inflation, 7, 31–32, 34, 35–36, 37, 49, 57–58
Innocent III, 73
inscriptions, 133, 135, 137, 138, 147, 156, 159, 160, 161–162, 165, 166, 177, 189
Ioakim Osogovski, 116, 132, 147, 148, 151, 159, 163, 168, 172
Ioan Ekzarh, 112
Ioan, Eleshnitsa "reader", 158
Ioan, Etropole priest, 171
Ioan Gramatik, 114, 120, 168, 170, 171
Ioan, Karlukovo monk, 177
Ioan Kratovski, 156
Ioanikii, Rila abbot, 146
Ioasif, Rila abbot, 147
Iosif, Kurilo abbot, 160
Iosif, Sopot abbot, 179
[I]Ovan of Sofia, 155, 156, 158
Iovko of Etropole, 179, 180
Ipek, 67
Iran, 14
Iskŭr Gorge, 160, 175
Iskŭr River, 43, 160, 162, 175
islamization, 17, 33–34, 50, 186, 191
Istanbul, 3, 4, 6, 7, 8, 13, 19, 23, 25, 26, 45, 46, 63, 69, 71, 91, 122, 154, 155, 161, 191; See also Constantinople
Italy, 79, 81, 131, 137
Ivan Aleksandŭr, 95, 98, 143, 159, 161
Ivan IV Groznyi, 146

INDEX

Ivan of Sofia, 156
Ivan Rilski, 89, 115–117, 119, 120, 125, 132, 137, 143, 144, 145, 146, 147, 148–149, 151, 153, 155, 157, 159, 160, 161, 163, 166, 168, 169, 172, 176, 179, 188
Ivanika of Niš, 155

Jagiełło, Władysław, 128
Janissaries, 3–4, 6–7, 23, 34–35, 36, 37, 57–58, 60, 61, 64, 70, 71–72, 191
Jerusalem, 92, 168, 175
Jews, 8, 18, 42, 45, 46–47, 199
Jordanian Desert, 117

kadı, 30, 32, 40, 58, 60, 71–72, 145, 154
Kalevit, Sofia metropolitan, 159
Kalinik, daskal, 108
Kalinik, Etropole monk and daskal, 171
Kalinik, Kalugerovo monk, 176
Kalist, Eleshnitsa abbot, 158
Kalist of Dragalevtsi, 155, 161
Kaloyan, 73, 94–95, 117
Kalugerovo (Chikotino) Monastery, 176, 178
Kameno Pole, 175
Kantakuzenos, John VI, 143
Kantakuzinos, Dimitrios, 119, 125
Karlovo, 96, 108, 111, 124, 173, 178, 179, 181, 182, 189
Karlukovo, 177
Karlukovo Monastery, 133, 135, 176–177, 178
Karyes, 92
Karyes Assembly, 92–93, 95
Kastoria, 45
kaza, 4, 17
kethüda, 41; See also ustabaşı
Kiev, 119, 149
Kievan metropolitanate, 112
Kiril Filosof, 161
Kiril, Zograf monk, 96

Kliment Ohridski, 112, 132, 172
Klokotnitsa, battle, 73
kmet, 28
knez, 28, 40
kocabaşı, 28
Koiko Gramatik, 173
koine, 121
Kokalyane Monastery, 54, 157, 162–163
Komnenos, Alexios I, 163
Konstantin, Christian sipahi, 144
Konstantin Kostenechki Filosof, 89, 99, 102, 103, 114, 115, 119, 150
Konstantin Presbyter, 112
Koprivshtitsa damaskin, 122
Köprülü, Ahmed, 63, 68
Korovo, 63
Kosovo Pole, battle, 144
Kostadin, Sofia priest, 156
Kostandovo, 64
Kostenets, 113, 180
Kostenets damaskin, 180
Kotel, 18, 24
Kotel Pass, 18
Koyu Tetevenski, 108, 120, 168, 170, 171, 173
Koziya Monastery, 113
Kozma Presbyter, 112
Kralcho, Eleshnitsa monk, 158
Kratovo, 120
Kremikovtsi, 158–159
Kremikovtsi Gospel, 160
Kremikovtsi Monastery, 135, 155, 157, 159–160
Krŭstyu Gramatik, 108, 114, 124, 178, 182
Krum, 88
Krupnik, 144
Kŭrdzhali, 23
Kuklen, 96, 181, 198
Kuklen Monastery, 72, 108, 111, 124, 156, 164, 165, 173, 178, 179, 181–182, 189
Kumanovo, 66
Kumaritsa, 135
Kurilo, 154, 160
Kurilo Monastery, 54, 130, 132, 133, 135, 139–140, 154, 155, 157, 160

Kutlovitsa, 16, 17, 23, 24, 25, 26, 43, 83, 184, 186, 189
Kutsovlahs, 67
Kyustendil, 13, 16, 17–18, 23, 24, 26, 42, 43, 53, 66, 67, 96, 129, 144, 150, 151, 183, 184, 189, 194

lamb's-tailed letters, 111–112
Latin, 77, 79, 161
Lazar, Etropole furrier, 172
Lazarović, Stefan, 114, 119
Lenten offices, 114, 159, 170, 173
Lesnovo Monastery, 114
Levant, 31, 45
Lilov, Ivan, 79–80
literary activity, 54, 56, 65, 77, 80–81, 82, 87, 88, 89–90, 91, 95–96, 98, 99, 100, 102–103, 109–125, 138, 147, 151, 152, 158–159, 165, 166, 169, 170, 173, 174, 175, 176, 177, 178, 180, 182, 186, 187–189, 193, 195, 196–197, 198
literati, 67–68, 91, 95, 96, 110, 112, 113, 122, 127, 145, 164, 167, 169, 170, 172, 173, 182
Little Mount Athos, 157
Lives, 115, 117, 119, 120, 123, 124, 125, 168, 172, 180; *See also* hagiography
Locke, John, 1
lonca, 41
Long War, 15, 154, 174
Lorretto, 77, 80
Louis XIV, 1
Lovech, 16, 17, 23, 96, 100, 166, 184, 186, 187, 189
Lozen Mountains, 157, 162, 163
Luka, 116
Lukovit *damaskin*, 123
Lyulin (Gorna Banya) Monastery, 157
Lyulin Hills, 157

Macedonia, 95

Macedonian lands, 65, 67, 96, 114, 116, 119, 120, 122, 166
madancıs, 24–25, 53; *See also* miners
mahalle, 38–39, 39–40, 43, 53, 54, 56, 106, 138, 162
Makarie, Cherepish monk, 175–176
Makarii, *ieromonah*, 125
Makarios, Tŭrnovo metropolitan, 169
maktu, 91
Mala Tsŭrkva, church, 150
Malamir, 88
Mali, Mladen, 163
Malo Malovo Monastery, 130
Manasija (Resava) Monastery, 114
Manasses, Konstantin, 98
manastir resmi, 70
Manichæism, 78
Manov, Tsona, 156
manuscripts, 89, 91, 92, 94, 95, 96, 98, 102–103, 105, 107, 108, 109–110, 110–111, 111–112, 113–114, 119, 120, 122, 125–127, 148, 149, 151, 155–156, 156–157, 158–159, 160, 161, 163–164, 166–168, 169–170, 170–171, 172, 175–176, 177, 179–180, 187–188, 195–196
marginalia, 14, 58, 63, 64–65, 95, 107, 124, 125–127, 148, 155–156, 156–157, 158–159, 160, 168, 169, 170–171, 174, 176, 177, 179, 187, 188–189, 195–196
Marinov, Iliya, 75–76, 79
Marinovs, 75
Maritsa, 150
Maritsa, church, 130, 133, 134, 150
Maritsa River, 115
Markanovs, 75
Marmara Sea, 117
Marotin, 36
martoloses, 23, 24, 48
Martsianopol, 76
Matei Lambadarii Gramatik, 119, 120, 152, 164
"Matejče" Monastery, 114, 119
Mavŭr, Radoslav, 161

INDEX

Mediterranean Sea, 45
Mehmed I, 60, 144
Mehmed II the Conqueror, 8, 9
Mehmed IV, 58, 63, 146, 155
Melentii Makedonski, 125
Melnik, 42, 47, 137
menologion, 139, 147, 150, 158, 159, 163, 168, 170, 171, 175, 179, 180, 182, 188
merchants, 8, 37, 38, 39, 43–47, 47–48, 49, 50, 67, 68, 69, 74, 75, 83, 100, 104, 106, 129, 138, 152, 174, 179, 193; *See also tüccar*
metoh, 56, 93–94, 98, 100, 102, 104, 105, 106, 122, 138, 146, 148, 149, 150, 151, 163, 176, 193
metropolitanate, 51, 63–64, 66, 67–68, 69–71, 71–72, 93, 104, 120, 137, 152–153, 155, 161, 166, 198
Middle East, 13, 78, 190
migrations, 15–16, 33, 36, 37, 49–50, 183
Mihai Viteazul the Brave, 174, 175
Mihail, Athonite monk, 169
Mihail, *daskal*, 108, 174, 178
Milente of Rila, 147
Miliya of Eleshnitsa, 158
Miljutin, Stefan Uroš II, 152, 153
millet, 8–10, 50, 51, 66, 192, 198; *See also* Orthodox *millet*
miners, 24–25, 42–43, 53, 71–72, 74, 75, 106, 166, 167, 176, 194; *See also madancıs*
mining industries, 24–25, 37, 42–43, 49, 75, 114, 137–138, 165–166
miri, 5, 19, 20, 26, 27, 32, 55, 185–186
Mirkovo, 58
Misaila, Etropole abbot, 166
missal, 120, 172, 173, 176, 188
Mladen, Stotse, 158
Mœsia, 190
Mohammed, 60
Moisei, Aron and Ioan, 94
Moldavia, 76, 110, 125, 127, 149, 160
Moldavians, 92
Molière, Jean-Baptiste, 1

monasteries, 30, 51, 54–56, 64, 68, 69–70, 70–71, 72, 88–90, 98, 99, 100–101, 103–105, 107, 108, 110, 112–113, 119, 121, 122, 125–126, 127, 128, 129, 137, 138–139, 139–140, 143, 145, 147, 149, 150, 152, 153, 155–156, 157–162, 165, 166, 174–176, 181, 186, 187, 193, 195, 196, 198
Monastery of the Caves, Kiev, 149
Monastery Ravine, 174
monasticism, 87–90, 100, 116, 143, 145, 157, 195
Montenegro, 125
Monteverdi, Claudio, 1
Moravia, 87
Morea, 63
Moscow, 119, 146
Mount Athos, 71, 89, 90–94, 96, 97, 98, 100, 103, 110, 114, 119, 120, 122, 125, 127, 128, 131, 134, 139, 143, 145, 147, 151, 165, 179, 181, 195
Mount Murgash, 158
Mount Ostrech, 173
Mount Poluvrak, 163
Mount Vitosha, 116, 150, 157, 161, 162
Müglen, 117
mukataa, 49
mülk, 5, 7, 26, 29–30, 32–33, 185
mültezim, 32
Murad IV, 71
murals, 90, 92, 96, 129, 130–134, 137, 150, 151, 152, 155, 158, 159, 160, 161, 176–177, 181
Muscovite Patriarchate, 146
müsellems, 23, 61–62
Muslim reaction, 57–59, 65, 106, 120, 126, 132, 136, 151, 154, 155, 164, 183, 188, 191, 196, 197, 198
Mustafa, *bey*, 35

Naiden, Karlukovo priest, 177
nationalism, 76–77, 83, 99, 123, 172, 194, 197, 198

307

natural disasters, 14–15, 64, 126, 146, 176, 183, 188
Naum, 132, 159
Naum Matei, 168
Neamți Monastery, 113
Nedelko, Karlukovo *daskal*, 177
Nedelya, 119, 133
Nedyalko of Adzhar, 108, 115, 124, 180–181, 182
Nedyalko of Etropole, 171
Nedyalko Zograf, 166
Nemanja, Stefan, 97
Nevrokop, 42, 96
New Bulgarian, 81, 106–107, 108, 121, 122, 148, 151, 172, 180, 181, 188, 196–197
Newton, Isaac, 1
Niš, 65, 83, 155
Nicæa, 73
Nicholas I, 73
Nikifor, Eleshnitsa monk, 158
Nikifor, Rila monk, 147
Nikodim, Kuklen abbot, 181
Nikodima, Zograf monk, 156
Nikola Gramatik, 155, 163
Nikola Gramatik of Etropole, 171
Nikola Gramatik of Sofia, 161
Nikola, *maistor*, 72
Nikola of Dragalevtsi, 161
Nikola of Samokov, 150
Nikola of Vratsa, 108, 174
Nikola, Vratsa goldsmith, 137
Nikolai Novi Sofiiski, 59, 120, 132, 159
Nikopol, 13, 17, 18, 23, 38, 39, 40, 43, 45, 47–48, 78, 80, 81, 94, 183, 185
nomokanon, 176
North Africa, 13, 14, 190
Novoseltsi, 155

Obreshkov, Nesho, 158
ocak, 62
Ohrid, 66–67, 87, 88, 94, 99
Omurtag, 88
Onufrii, Etropole monk, 171

Orehovo Monastery, 98
Oreshte, 80
Orthodox church, 8, 9, 10, 28, 51, 54, 56, 59, 64, 66, 68, 77, 80, 81–82, 90, 93, 131, 190, 192
Orthodox *millet*, 8, 9–10, 28, 50–51, 66, 67, 68–70, 90, 99, 104, 129, 190, 192, 193, 198, 199; *See also* millet
Osogovo Monastery, 114
Osogovo Mountains, 116
otechnik, 147
Ottoman central government, 3–4, 5–6, 7, 8, 9, 16, 17, 19, 20–21, 22, 24, 25, 27, 28–29, 30–31, 31–33, 34, 35, 36, 39, 40–41, 43, 45–46, 47, 49, 50, 51, 52, 54, 55, 58, 59, 60, 62, 67, 68–69, 70, 71–72, 74, 90, 99, 104, 145–146, 166, 170, 188, 191, 195; *See also* Porte
Ottoman decline, 6–7, 31–35, 36, 57–58, 68–69, 73, 126, 136, 138, 145, 146, 154, 183, 191, 195
Ottoman provincial government, 4–5, 17–18, 18–19, 24, 29, 30, 31, 33, 34, 36, 38–39, 40–41, 49, 52, 54, 58, 59, 71–72, 75, 82, 106, 128, 139, 145–146, 152, 154–155, 188, 193

Paşa, *sancak*, 13, 183
Pahomie, K., 113, 150
Paisii Hilendarski, 76, 95, 98, 139, 190, 199
Pakurina, Aspazios, 181
Pakurina, Gregorios, 181
Palestine, 90
Pamfilii, Zograf monk, 120, 124, 139
panegyric, 169, 176
Papacy, 73–74, 77, 79; *See also* Vatican
Parchevich, Petŭr, 76–77, 82
Parchevs, 75
Pasho of Dolni Dŭbnik, 169
Pastuh, church, 151
Patleina Monastery, 88–89
patristic writings, 121
Paulicians, 75, 77–78, 88; *See also pavlikyani*

INDEX

Pavel, Dragalevtsi abbot, 161
Pavel of Dolna Beshovitsa, 133
Pavel, *pop*, 170
Pavla, Vratsa goldsmith, 137
pavlikyani, 75, 77–80, 81–82, 83
Pavlova, Petka, 177
Pazardzhik, 23, 42, 49, 63, 64–65, 96
Peć, 67
peşkeş, 68, 69
Peflagoniya, 96
Pehlivan Mehmed, *paşa*, 63–64
Peika, Sopot monk, 179
Peio of Sofia, 119–120, 123, 152, 164
Peiyachevich, Georgi, 82–83
Peiyachevs, 75
Pernik, 17, 23, 24, 116, 129, 184, 189
Peshov of Kostenets, 113
Petka and Podruzie of Vŭrbovo, 136
Petka Tŭrnovska, 117–118, 119, 122–123, 125, 133, 153, 160, 163, 168, 169, 172, 176, 179, 180, 188
Petko of Sofia, 156
Petra, Stoina and Vulcha of Vrazhdebna, 158
Petrich, 186
Petŭr I, 116–117, 118, 147, 149, 157, 160, 163
Petŭr of Dupnitsa, 150
Petŭr of Mirkovo, 58, 65, 126
Peyu and Petko, Dragalevtsi monks, 160
Phanariots, 69
philotimon, 70
Philotios, Greek patriarch, 125
Photios, Greek patriarch, 73
piastre, 31
pilgrimage, 92, 93, 96–97, 100, 135, 144, 166, 168, 175, 179
Pimen Zografski, 96, 108, 120, 124, 139–140, 150, 154–155, 159, 160, 163, 165, 175, 176, 178
Pirin Mountains, 191
Pirot, 71, 83, 96
Plana Hills, 150, 157, 162
Pleven, 16, 43, 45, 100, 125, 173
Pliska-Aboba, 87, 88–89

Plovdiv, 17, 33, 38, 39, 40, 43, 48, 49, 63–64, 67, 72–73, 78, 96, 98, 111, 156, 164, 181, 184, 187, 192
Pohomie, 71
Poland, 47, 58, 128, 136
pomak, 63
Popov, Dimitre, Dupnitsa furrier, 150
Popstoikov *damaskin*, 122, 123
Porte, 16, 26, 32, 34, 36, 46, 49, 57, 59, 63, 65, 68, 69, 91, 144, 183; *See also* Ottoman central government
Preslav, 76, 87, 88–89, 99, 116
Prisiyan, 88
Prisyan, 114
Prohor Pshinski, 116, 132, 151, 159
prologue, 168, 169, 171, 172
pronoia, 22
Protopopintsi *damaskin*, 124
Protos, 92, 93
Provadiya, 39, 185
psalms, 176
psalter, 102, 125, 155, 156, 158, 163, 171, 172, 176, 177, 179
Purcell, Henry, 1

Radivilovskiy, Antoniy, 149
Radivoi of Sofia, 159–160
Rafail, Etropole abbot, 114, 167, 168, 170
Raikovo, 65
rakiya, 55
Rashko, *daskal*, 108, 174
Razgrad, 184, 185
Razlog, 64, 96, 108, 150, 151, 178
reader, 169
reaya, 5–6, 7, 19, 24, 25, 26, 27, 33–34, 35, 36, 43, 54, 184, 196, 197
reaya, common, 14, 20, 22, 27, 30, 51, 184
reaya, privileged, 14, 20, 22–26, 27, 30, 45, 48, 51, 53, 68, 104, 166, 184, 186, 193–194, 195
Rembrandt van Rijn, 1
Resava (Serbian) Church Slavonic, 81, 112, 114–115, 122, 167
Resava River, 114

309

Rhodope Mountains, 17, 23, 27, 63–64, 65, 72, 107, 108, 111, 181, 191, 198
Rila *damaskin*, 122
Rila Monastery, 26, 55, 70, 72, 89, 93, 96, 100, 102, 104, 105, 107, 110, 111, 113, 114, 119, 122, 125, 129, 143–149, 150, 151, 167, 181, 189, 194, 195
Rila Mountains, 55, 107, 116–117, 143, 144, 150, 157, 160
Rila River, 116
Rilski *povest*, 119, 120, 145
Roman Catholic church, 57, 73–74, 75, 77, 79, 81–82
Roman Catholic mission, 25, 74–77, 79–80, 81–82, 161, 197; *See also* Bulgarian Catholics
Roman Zagorets, 163
Romanian lands, 70, 95, 110, 113, 128, 138
Romanian Orthodox church, 109
Romanian Principalities, 70, 91, 110, 113, 127, 136, 145, 171; *See also* Danubian Principalities
Romanians, 95, 110, 113
Romanov, Mihail Feodorovich, 146, 147, 149
Rome, 75, 76, 77, 80, 154
royal charters, 92, 94–95, 98, 143–144, 146, 151, 161, 163
Rozhen Monastery, 137
Rumeli, 4, 13, 48, 63, 152
Ruse, 33, 36, 38, 42, 43, 46
Russia, 16, 18, 70–71, 74, 76, 89, 91, 112–113, 119, 128, 134, 136, 138, 145, 146, 149, 150, 156, 167
Russian (Church Slavic) Church Slavonic, 112–113, 115, 125
Russian Orthodox church, 109, 112
Russians, 91, 92, 93, 113, 149

Sacred Congregation, 76
Saga of the Alphabet, 102, 114
Saga of the Holy Mountain of Athos, 125
"St. Anna," Athonite *skete*, 125

"St. Dimitrii" Monastery, 116
"St. Georgi" Monastery, Pleven, 100
"St. Panteleimon" Monastery, Athos, 93, 100
"St. Petŭr" Monastery, Pazardzhik, 63
Salinat, Petr, 75
Samokov, 24, 42, 53, 71–72, 96, 107, 150, 194
sancak, 4, 13, 14, 17, 18, 22, 34, 35, 183, 184
sancakbey, 4
Sarajevo, 45
Sardica Council, 153
Saski, 42–43
Sava, 97
Saxons, 24–25, 42–43, 46, 74, 75, 166
sbornik, 120–121, 122, 147, 148, 155, 162, 169, 176, 179, 188, 196–197
Scholarios, Gennadios, 9
Selcüks, 22
Selim I the Grim, 62, 190
Selymbria, 117
Serbia, medieval, 95, 97, 110, 119, 128, 143, 152, 167, 171, 172
Serbian lands, 25, 65, 96, 97, 113, 120, 128, 138, 145
Serbian Orthodox church, 9, 109
Serbian Patriarchate of Peć (Ipek), 67
Serbs, 7–8, 9, 13, 24–25, 71, 91, 92, 93, 97, 114, 144, 163, 166, 167, 190, 199
Şeriat, 3, 8, 27, 30–31, 40, 58, 191
sermons, 120, 121, 122, 123, 124
services, 168, 169, 172, 179, 188
Seslav, 159
Seslavtsi, 159
Seslavtsi Monastery, 132, 139–140, 155, 157, 159
Sevlad Gramatik, 168, 171
Shakespeare, William, 1
Shishatovats, Iov, 175
Shishman, Ivan, 115, 117, 125, 143–144, 151, 161, 162, 175
Shumen, 23, 33, 46, 184, 185
Sidor, 108
Sidor, *daskal-gramatik*, 182

INDEX

Silistra, 13, 17, 18, 39, 43, 46, 185
Simeon I, 87, 88–89, 99, 115–116
Simeon, Kuklen monk, 182
Singel (?), Stefan, 155
sipahi, 5, 6–7, 29, 32–33, 34, 35, 37, 55, 57, 61, 71–72, 144, 145, 192
sipahilık, 5–7, 19, 22, 23, 26, 32, 34, 36; *See also* fiefs
skete, 94, 125
Skopje, 45, 65
Skrino, 115, 160
Skylitzes, George, 120, 147
Slaveno-Bulgarian History, 76, 190
Slavovitsa, 125
Slavs, 87, 88, 91, 177
Sliven, 23–24, 43
Smolyan, 65
Sofia, 4, 13, 16, 17–18, 23, 24, 30, 35, 38, 39, 42, 43, 45, 46, 47, 48, 53–54, 62, 66, 67, 71–72, 75, 83, 94–95, 96, 98, 104, 107–108, 110, 111, 114, 116–117, 119–120, 129, 132, 135, 137, 138–139, 143, 149, 152–162, 167, 168, 169, 173, 175, 177, 178, 181, 182, 183, 184, 186, 187, 189, 193, 194, 198; *See also* Sredets
Sofia, "Holy Savior" church, 153
Sofia, "Holy Wisdom" church, 120
Sofia Plain, 157, 159, 160, 162, 164, 193
Sofia, "St. Archangel" church, 153, 163
Sofia, "St. Georgi" church, 139, 152
Sofia, "St. Ivan Rilski" church, 153
Sofia, "St. Luka" church, 153
Sofia, "St. Marina" church, 119, 152, 153
Sofia, "St. Nedelya" (Kiriaki) church, 153
Sofia, "St. Nikola" church, 153, 156–157
Sofia, "St. Petka" church, 153
Sofia, "St. Petka of the Saddlemakers" church, 53–54, 139, 153
Sofia, "Vseh svetih" church, 153
sokolars, 24
Solni bazaar, Sofia, 156
Sopot, 179
Sopot Monastery, 179
Spain, 45

Sredets, 96, 157
Sredna Gora *damaskin,* 172
Sredna Gora letters, 111–112
Sredna Gora Mountains, 23, 108, 111, 122, 148, 172, 178, 180, 181, 194
Stahna of Sofia, 161
Stainov, Nedko, 170
Stancho of Sofia, 156
Stanimaka, 67
Stanislavov, Filip, 58, 80–81
Stano, Mati, 158
Staru of Glozhene, 170
Stefan, Bilintsi monk, 134
Stefan Dušan, 95, 143
Stefan Ohridski, 125
Stefan, Rila abbot, 146
Stefan, Sofia priest, 156
Stefan Svetagorets, 124
Stoiov, Raiko, 170
Stoyan and Stoyan, Sofia bakers, 160
Stoyan, Etropole miner, 176
Stoyu of Etropole, 168
Struma River, 95, 116, 150
Strupets Monastery, 176
sŭbor, 52
sufi, 59, 60
Suhanov, Arsenii, 96, 98
Suhodol Monastery, 139–140
Süleyman I the Magnificent, 13, 74, 190, 191
sultan, 3, 4, 5, 6, 7, 19, 23, 26, 27, 32, 36, 45, 48, 60, 65, 68, 69, 71–72, 144, 145, 170, 185, 188, 191
Sungular, Sofia *mahalle,* 162
sunni, 59, 60
Suseava Monastery, 113
Svishtov, 39, 45, 47, 136, 185
Svishtov, "SS. Petŭr and Pavel" church, 136

Tabahana, Sofia *mahalle,* 162
tales, 121, 122, 123, 197
tapu, 19, 20–21, 28, 29, 36
Tatars, 173

311

Index

Tavalichevo, church, 151
tax registers, 14, 17, 20, 22, 23, 26, 33, 48, 54, 184
taxes, 18–19, 19–20, 21–22, 26–27, 28, 29, 32, 35–36, 40, 41, 44, 47, 49, 50, 54, 55, 57, 59, 62, 64, 68, 69–70, 81–82, 91, 144, 185, 191, 192, 194
taxes, ecclesiastical, 8, 54, 63, 68, 69–71, 71–72, 73, 192, 198
taxidiot, 56, 93–94, 97, 98, 100, 105, 106, 122, 146, 148, 149, 163, 175, 195
Teodor Teodosii Tŭrnovski, 89
Teodosii, Kurilo abbot, 160
Teodosii of Etropole, 168
Teofan, Kuklen abbot, 182
Teofilakt, bishop of Ohrid, 160
Terter, Georgi II, 98
Teteven, 120, 168, 173
Teteven Monastery, 107, 108, 111, 170, 172–173, 176
thaler, 68
Thessaloniki, 25, 42, 45, 64, 87, 91, 121
Thrace, 96, 117, 186, 190, 198
Thracian Plain, 107, 165, 191, 195
Tih, Konstantin Asen, 98
timar, 5, 144
tithes, 19, 21, 35, 49, 145–146
"To the Virgin," prayer, 125
Todor, *daskal*, 124
Todor of Sofia, 156, 164, 182
Todor of Vratsa, 108, 174
Todor Pirdopski, 113
Toma of Sofia, 139
towns, 14, 15, 17–18, 21, 34, 36, 37–39, 43, 44–45, 46, 47–48, 48–50, 53–54, 55–56, 72–73, 94, 104, 105, 106, 107, 108, 118, 126, 127, 129, 134, 138–139, 143, 146, 159, 165, 173, 184, 185, 186, 187, 191, 192, 193, 195
Transylvania, 25, 46–47, 48, 58, 83, 136, 138, 154, 175
travel accounts, 14, 58, 152–153, 161
Treasury, 121–122
Trent Council, 74
Triaditsa, 153

Troyan *damaskins*, 179
Troyan Monastery, 179
Trŭn, 82, 96
Tsamblak, Grigorii, 99, 112, 115, 119, 125, 172
Tsarevets, church, 177
Tŭrgovishte, 184, 185
Tŭrnovo, 16, 17–18, 23, 33, 38, 39, 43, 45, 47, 66, 67–68, 72–73, 89, 91, 95, 96, 99–100, 102, 103, 110, 112, 113, 114, 115, 117, 118, 119, 122–123, 127, 144, 145, 149, 162, 166, 169, 173, 176, 184
Tŭrnovo School, 99–100, 102, 103, 108, 110, 112, 113, 115, 120, 122, 127, 164, 172, 180
Tŭrnovo, "St. Georgi" church, 72
Tŭrnovo uprising, 16
Tŭrnovo uprising (first), 154
Tŭrvarishta, 151
tüccar, 43–44; *See also* merchants
Turks, 2–4, 6, 7–8, 13, 17, 18, 22, 28, 31, 38, 40, 42, 45, 58, 59, 62, 65, 66, 74, 82, 83, 90, 91, 97, 100, 115, 118, 123, 124, 132, 136, 144, 145, 152, 153, 154, 157, 162, 163, 167, 175, 178, 190, 192, 196
tuzcıs, 24
Tuzla, 75
Tvrtko I, 79

Uglješa, Jovan, 115
Ukraine, 173
Umayyads, 22
Uroš, Etropole priest, 171
Urvich fortress, 162
Urvich Monastery, 162
Urvich *sbornik*, 162–163
ustabaşı, 41, 42

vakıf, 26–27, 33, 48–49, 55, 91, 93, 145, 185–186, 195

INDEX

vali, 34
Vardim, 82
Varlaam, Etropole abbot, 168, 170
Varlaam, "Holy Trinity" near Vratsa abbot, 169, 175
Varna, 23, 33, 38, 185
Varna, battle, 128
varosh, 38–39
Vasilii Sofiyanets, 164, 168, 170, 171
Vasilii, Teteven monk, 173, 176
Vatican, 73–74, 74–76, 80, 81, 153; *See also* Papacy
Vatopedi Monastery, 97
Velásquez, Diego, 1
Velo, Sofia goldsmith, 137, 162
Venice, 63, 73, 74, 80, 121, 136, 137
vezir, 34
Vidin, 13, 16, 17–18, 26, 32, 38, 42, 43, 45, 49, 67, 96, 119, 136, 183, 184, 186
Vidin, "St. Panteleimon" church, 136
Vidin, "St. Petka" church, 136
Vienna, 25, 74, 82, 154
Viktor of Rila, 147
vilayet, 17, 184
village commune, 28–31, 35–36, 40, 51–53
villages, 17–18, 21, 23–24, 25, 28–31, 36, 38, 49–50, 51–53, 54, 55–56, 58–59, 64, 65, 66, 67, 72, 83, 94, 100, 104, 105–106, 107, 108, 118, 125, 127, 128, 129, 134, 138, 144, 146, 150–151, 153, 159, 163, 164, 173, 176, 178, 181, 184, 186, 187, 193, 195, 196
Virpino Monastery, 98
Visarion, bishop, 65
Visarion, metropolitan, 134
Visarion, Rila abbot, 147
Visok, 96
Vit River, 172
Viza, 13, 183
Vladislav Gramatik, 119, 120, 145
Vlahs, 13
Vlaio, Etropole priest, 172
Vlŭcho, Etropole bookbinder, 171
voevoda, 125, 136

voynuks, 23, 25, 26, 30, 45, 50, 53, 186, 194
voynuks, "reserve", 26
Vranko, Nikola, 156
Vratsa, 17, 24, 96, 107, 108, 111, 115, 137, 138, 139, 149, 165, 167, 169, 173, 174, 175, 176, 177, 178, 184, 186, 187, 189, 193, 194
Vratsa, "St. Nikola" church, 174
Vrazhdebna, 158
Vŭrbovo, church, 136
Vukovo, churches, 53, 130, 132, 133, 151

Wallachia, 71, 110, 166, 167, 172, 173, 175
Wallachians, 92
warfare, 15–17, 31, 45, 58, 62–63, 65–66, 74, 82–83, 91, 97, 115, 123, 126, 128, 136, 144, 154, 167, 174, 175, 176, 183, 188, 191
woodcarving, 137, 151
Wren, Christopher, 1
writer-copyists, 109, 110, 111, 113, 114–115, 121, 123, 124–125, 125–126, 152, 155, 158, 164, 167–168, 170, 171, 172, 173, 175, 178–179, 180, 188, 189

Yakim, *daskal*, 108, 155
Yakoruda, 18
Yakov, bishop, 144
Yakov, Zograf monk, 176
yamaks, 23
Yambol, 23, 26
Yancho of Pirdop, 168
Yankul Gramatik, 168, 171
"Yastreb" Monastery, Lovech, 100
yayas, 61–62
yiğitbaşı, 41, 42
yürüks, 7, 23, 62

Zagorie, 96
Zaharii, Etropole abbot, 115, 167, 168, 170, 171

INDEX

Zaharii Zograf, 139
zeamet, 5, 48
Zemen Monastery, 133
Zhelyava, 159
Zhelyava Monastery, 157, 158–159
Zhitůne, 35
Zhivko of Adzhar, 108, 170–171, 178–179
zimma, 3
zimmis, 3–4, 5, 7–9, 10, 20, 21, 50, 54, 57

Zlatitsa, 165
Znepole, 96
Zograf Monastery, 94–97, 98, 100, 102, 104, 113, 119, 120, 139, 147, 150, 156, 163, 164, 168, 176, 178, 179, 182
Zoroastrianism, 59
župan, 97

www.ingramcontent.com/pod-product-compliance
Lightning Source LLC
Chambersburg PA
CBHW070746020526
44116CB00032B/1983